COCKEYED
HAPPY

COCKEYED HAPPY

Ernest Hemingway's Wyoming Summers with Pauline

Darla Worden

Library of Congress Control Number: 2021936736

The Letters of Ernest Hemingway (in the USA) © The Ernest Hemingway
Foundation and Society 2021
The Letters of Ernest Hemingway (outside the USA) © The Hemingway
Foreign Rights Trust 2021
Editorial matter © The Hemingway Letters Project, The Pennsylvania
State University 2021
The Cambridge edition of *The Letters of Ernest Hemingway, Volume 3 & 4*
(2015, 2017) by Ernest Hemingway. Copyright © Hemingway Foreign Rights Trust

Interior design: Nord Compo
Map design: Chris Erichsen

Printed in the United States of America
5 4 3 2 1

For Anna

CONTENTS

Part II: 1930

Part III: 1932

Part IV: 1936

Part V: 1938–1939

Epilogue: 1940

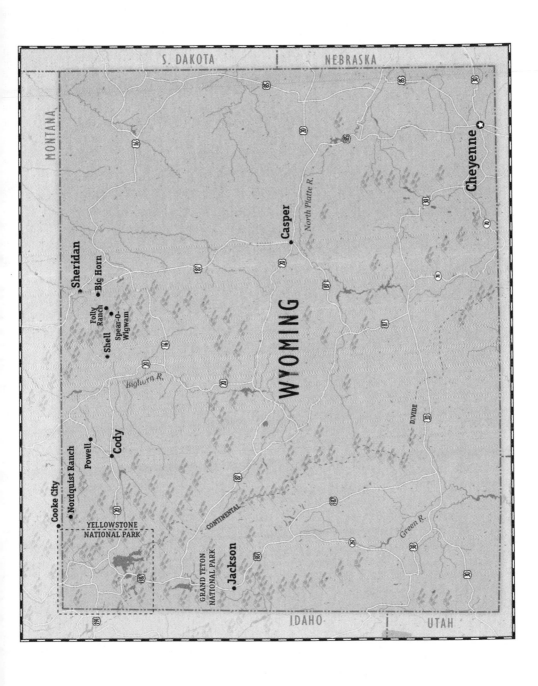

Part I

1928

What Ernest Loved About Pauline

Keen editorial eye
Her family became his family: Jinny, Mother Pfeiffer
Uncle Gus's support
Strong again
"Someone to feel swell with" after a day's work
The "feeling of us against the others"
Willing to join him on adventures
Believed in the "promotion of masculine society"
Vowed to always let him have his way
She could give him "little Pilar" in three years
Her throat never got sore like his
~~Spontaneous lovemaking~~*

---

* List compiled by the author from comments made by Ernest Hemingway
(EH) and Pauline Pfeiffer.

EXPLORERS COME WEST

HE'D NEVER BEEN OUT WEST BEFORE, but he'd heard it had some of the best fly-fishing in the world. As Ernest steered the yellow Model A toward the Bighorn Mountains, they reminded him of the Sierra de Guadarrama in Spain—the same color and shape but bigger. He missed Spain already. Because of Patrick's birth, he'd had to skip the San Fermin Festival in Pamplona this summer, and he swore he'd return next year. But for now, he and Bill Horne had driven three days from Kansas City to reach a dude ranch in Wyoming, where Ernest hoped to go fishing and finish his book.

Ernest recorded mileage each day—340, 380, 320. He liked to keep lists and record things, like how many fish he caught and game he shot. They had crossed a corner of Nebraska and come up the North Platte River into Wyoming—a changing landscape with hills like sand dunes, rocky outcroppings, buttes topped with scrubby ponderosa pine, and miles of sagebrush-speckled plains.

The entire country was baking in a heat wave, and forget about finding a cool drink to quench your thirst because of Prohibition—something that Ernest was having a hard time adjusting to after the Roaring Twenties in Paris, where liquor flowed freely. Finding liquor in America was like tracking game: you had to be stealthy. In Kansas City, though, he had connections, and he had brought four quarts of bootleg scotch for the trip.

Ernest had been planning to go out to Idaho, where you had to pack in on horseback, but Bill invited him to Folly Ranch and Ernest had accepted in spite of his feelings about dude ranches. If he could catch an enormous amount of trout without working too hard for them, he'd be happy. He also needed a respite from the awful heat and a quiet place to work.

It was July 30 when they turned onto a steep shale road that snaked up the mountainside, the coupe leaving a trail of red dust as it climbed. Ernest maneuvered the roadster around potholes, bumping over rocks and ruts, trying to stay away from the edge as Bill peered over the sheer drop-off where boulders the size of cars had tumbled thousands of feet to the valley floor.

"Look out, Ernie!" Bill yelled when Ernest came too near. The view was seductive—they could see the little towns of Sheridan and Big Horn in the valley below.

"Ernie, look out!" Bill shouted again.

"Do me a favor, Horney," Ernest said. "When you get out, just close the door." Bill didn't make a peep after that.

Ernest met Bill when they were in the *autoambulanzia** for the Red Cross in the Great War, on the Italian front, where they'd had to avoid more than potholes. He'd been nineteen, Bill, twenty-seven, and they'd traveled from New York to Paris, then to Milan and eventually Schio, Italy, where they were assigned to their posts. Bill had been there for him when Ernest was injured—227 shrapnel wounds in his leg—and they had been friends ever since.

The air became cooler as they gained altitude, and the breeze felt good. Kansas City had been too bloody hot, over ninety degrees each day. He hadn't been able to work in that heat, especially while worrying about Pauline, dangerously ill in the hospital. After the caesarean, she had to stay in the hospital for ten days due to gas distention, and at times Ernest had worried that it was the end for her. When she was finally out of the woods, he had taken her and their new son, Patrick Miller Hemingway, to stay with her family in Piggott, Arkansas, to recover while Ernest went fishing with Bill.

At a plateau, Ernest spotted a spring and pulled off the side of the road to fill up the car with water. The Ford was a wedding gift from Pauline's

---

* ambulance drivers.

rich uncle, Gus, who shipped it to them when they arrived in Key West, Florida, last April.* The company had only made fifty thousand of the model, and Uncle Gus wanted Pauline and Ernest to be one of the first to own one. Ernest had already logged seventy-six hundred miles in the car, beginning in Key West with his new father-in-law, Paul Pfeiffer, and driving together to the Pfeiffer home in Piggott. Pauline, who was then eight months pregnant, took the train. Riding for five days with someone you have only just met, in dreadful heat, on gravel roads, stopping at night to sleep in "tourist cabins," was a sure way to get to know a person.

And now driving with "Horney," someone he had not seen in seven years, was an opportunity to catch up—so much had happened. After Ernest married Hadley Richardson in 1921, they had moved to Paris. He had lived there until this spring, when he and Pauline had returned to the United States so their baby could be born here. He'd seen Bill just a few times on brief visits from Paris to the Hemingway family home in Oak Park, outside Chicago, where Bill lived. Now that Ernest was back, maybe he would see Bill more often. This trip gave them a chance to reminisce about their time in the war together; perhaps some of those stories would make their way into his new novel.

His first novel, *The Sun Also Rises*, had been published two years earlier while he was in Paris. He'd written about men who returned to Paris after the Great War—Gertrude Stein had called them "The Lost Generation"—drifters without purpose after what they had seen in the war. His new book took place in Italy, where Ernest had spent months recuperating in a Milan hospital after his injuries and had fallen in love with his nurse, Agnes von Kurowsky. His leg eventually healed, but his heart had been broken on receiving a letter from Agnes after he returned home, saying she was dumping him to marry a duke.

That was ten years ago, but he could still conjure those feelings—feelings he was putting into the story of a soldier falling in love with his nurse in Italy. He was on page 486, with a third still left to write, and he hoped to finish the "bloody book" in the solitude of Wyoming before Pauline joined him in a few weeks.

---

* They were married May 10, 1927.

At the spring, the men stretched their legs. Ernest was six feet tall, and Bill was even taller. The alpine meadows around them exploded with Indian paintbrush, lupine, and black-eyed Susans, and in the distance, they spotted a mountain range with a tall, snowcapped peak despite the summer heat. Bill said he felt "just as much explorers as Columbus was in the *Santa Maria*." Ernest welcomed the chance to discover this new place with the "Horned article" or "Article" for short—Ernest affectionately gave friends, family, even himself nicknames. Wyoming was the blank page just waiting for him to put his mark on it. To write, he needed something new: new lands, new experiences, and new people.

That's how *The Sun Also Rises* had come to him. After attending the bullfights in Pamplona with his friends, he'd been on fire. He had sat down at his typewriter, and ten weeks later had written a bestselling novel that was based on his experience. Critics called it a new style that combined journalistic reporting and real people with fiction techniques. It was thrilling to have written a book like that at age twenty-six, a book that rocked the literary world, even if many of those friends no longer spoke to him.

Back in the car, the road was so narrow in places that any cars headed downhill needed to yield to cars going uphill by allowing them to pass. Luckily, there weren't many cars coming down—mostly just cattle grazing in the mountain meadows and crossing the road when they felt like it.

Ernest steered onto a road that looked like a cattle trail and stopped at the ranch gate, where Eleanor Donnelley, their hostess, stood waiting to greet them, along with a surprise: fifteen of her friends from Bryn Mawr.

Shit, Ernest thought, so much for working.

STRENGTH
IN THE AFTERNOON

PAULINE WAS RESTING on the sofa of her parents' home in Piggott, writing Ernest a letter. Her mother would not allow her to use the typewriter upstairs, so she was forced to write the letter by hand. "Mother is a dragon about the steps," she wrote. The doctor had been clear after Patrick's birth: no stairs, no lifting, and no more children for three years unless she wanted to be an invalid or a corpse. Even though Ernest had hoped for a daughter they would name Pilar, he had seemed content with another son: Patrick Miller Hemingway, born June 28, 1928.

John Hadley Nicanor Hemingway, or "Bumby," was nearly five years old and lived with his mother, Hadley, in Paris. Now the father of two boys, Ernest might joke to his friends that fatherhood was overrated, and he couldn't understand why anyone would want to be a father. He warned them that babies bellow, and they can drive you crazy. But truth was, Ernest was a proud papa, bragging about Patrick's size and health and how he would teach Patrick to hunt quail one day.

Pauline had known Ernest would get restless while she recovered in Piggott with its unbearable heat, and he couldn't concentrate when a baby was crying, so she supported the idea of his Wyoming fishing trip with Bill. She recognized Ernest's need for male companionship—the "promotion of masculine society," she called it. They had barely unpacked their bags in Key West last spring when John Dos Passos, Waldo Peirce, and Henry "Mike" Strater arrived and stayed for nearly a month. She didn't object—despite being seven months pregnant—knowing how Ernest loved to discover new places and to share them with friends.

He hadn't been the first in his group to discover Key West; "Dos" was. They met in Paris and realized that their paths might have crossed during the Italian ambulance service. Dos—a well-known traveler and journalist—told Ernest about a trip he'd taken through Florida and about the magic of Key West. Ernest had wanted to see it for himself, so that's where he and Pauline stayed upon arriving from Paris. As much as they both fell in love with Key West, there was no way Pauline wanted to deliver her first child there. Instead, she looked for good obstetrical hospitals and chose one in Kansas City.

The Pfeiffer home in Piggott, Arkansas, had ample room for Pauline and Patrick to stay while mother and baby recovered. After all, her father had purchased it from the town's master builder, who had created it for his own family that included twenty-three children. The Pfeiffers had moved there from St. Louis, Missouri, after Pauline's high school graduation; her parents had wanted her to be able to graduate with her friends before relocating to their new home.

The two-story white Colonial Revival farmhouse in Piggott had five bedrooms, a music room, pressed tin ceilings, and glass-paneled doors. Situated on the edge of town, it was still just eight blocks from the town square across the street from the school. Paul Pfeiffer had deemed the home perfect for his family, which included Pauline, then seventeen and heading to college, and her younger siblings—Karl, entering seventh grade; sister Virginia, "Jinny," beginning fifth grade; and Max, starting kindergarten. Paul had made a generous offer to the builder, and the Pfeiffers moved in.

Because the closest Catholic church was thirty miles away and Mary Pfeiffer was a devout Catholic, Paul converted the music room into a chapel for her. Two years before Pauline returned to the house with infant Patrick, she had spent many hours in that chapel praying to Saint Joseph during the one-hundred-day ultimatum Hadley had given Ernest and Pauline when she discovered their affair.

Pauline had been living with Jinny in Paris in the spring of 1925 when they'd met Ernest and Hadley at Kitty Cannell's apartment near the Eiffel Tower. Kitty, the fashion editor for the *New York Times*, had invited the Pfeiffer sisters to an afternoon tea for Hadley. Kitty thought Pauline and Hadley would be fast friends because they had so much in common—they'd grown up in St. Louis and shared a friend, Katy Smith.

Hadley had met Katy at parochial school in St. Louis, and Pauline knew Katy from the University of Missouri Journalism School. She and Katy were in the first graduating class of journalists at a school that was the first of its kind in the country.

In another coincidence, Ernest knew Katy and her two brothers, Bill and Y. K., from childhood summers in Michigan—the Hemingway and Smith families both had retreats there. The Smith siblings were some of Ernest's closest friends, and he'd once had a crush on Katy.

At the tea, the ladies had been getting acquainted as Pauline told stories about her job in Paris at *Vogue*, where she was an editor. She described her boss, Main Bocher, as "ambrosial"—a popular superlative of the era. She and Jinny enjoyed the fast-paced, witty repartee of the times, using slang with ease.

When Ernest came in sweaty and disheveled from boxing with Kitty's lover Harold Loeb at a local gym, Pauline thought he seemed like a boring oaf. Jinny was the one who found Ernest fascinating. The two of them ended up sitting alone in the kitchen, chatting away about bicycle racing or some other sport. Seven years older than Jinny, Pauline had the role of looking out for her little sister, and she later lectured Jinny on the impropriety of it all. They were there to support Hadley, who didn't have many friends in Paris, not to talk with her husband alone in the kitchen. Pauline could not have imagined at that afternoon tea what the future would have in store for her.

Ernest and Jinny had become close friends after that day at Kitty's, sometimes meeting each other for dinner or drinks at a Left Bank café, and they still were. Not that Pauline minded. She was happy her sister and husband got along so well—Jinny had helped smooth a path with the Pfeiffer family when Pauline had worried about introducing Ernest to her parents, afraid what they would think when they learned he was a married man. Jinny emphasized to her parents how much Pauline loved

Ernest, and they had accepted him into the family despite the circumstances, partly due to her support and approval.

In the fall of 1925, Jinny was undecided about her future plans and returned to Piggott. Alone in Paris, Pauline had begun stopping by the Hemingways' apartment above a sawmill on her way home from the *Vogue* office to visit Hadley, who had become her friend. Hadley was often exhausted after taking care of Bumby all day, so she went to bed early, leaving Pauline and Ernest alone to discuss something he'd written. At age thirty, Pauline was between Ernest, twenty-six, and Hadley, thirty-four, in age, and she found herself in the middle of this friendship, feeling equally comfortable with Ernest and Hadley.

By then, her feelings for Ernest had changed. She no longer thought of him as that boring oaf she'd met at Kitty's apartment. He was so handsome, with dark hair and dark eyes that studied you as you spoke, really listening. Other than her brief engagement to her cousin Matthew Herold, which had ended after she moved to Paris, she was inexperienced around men and unprepared to resist Ernest's charms even if he was married to her friend.

———

After Hadley had confronted Ernest about his affair with Pauline and saw that he wasn't willing to end it, she gave Ernest and Pauline an ultimatum: stay apart for one hundred days. If they still wanted to be together after that time, Hadley would give Ernest a divorce. Hadley had bet that when the two spent time apart, the flame between them would die.

While Ernest stayed in Paris at Gerald Murphy's studio, Pauline went home to Piggott to serve out the sentence. She had plenty of time to think about their actions and admitted they had overlooked Hadley's feelings. Pauline told Ernest that she feared while they were crazy in love with each other, Hadley "had been locked out."

Pauline had written Hadley to apologize and say that she didn't want Hadley to move forward with the divorce until she was certain that was what she wanted. Pauline cared for Hadley and didn't blame Hadley if she didn't trust her.

One day Ernest stopped by Hadley's Paris apartment to talk to her about their situation, and when she saw Ernest so emotionally distraught, she took pity on him and decided to call off her hundred-day separation. Ernest could have his divorce. Pauline had been "cockeyed happy" when she received the news in Piggott; her prayers to Saint Joseph had been answered.

Now that some time had passed, some of their relationship with Hadley had been repaired through Pauline's affection for Bumby. She'd been in his life since he was a toddler, loving him like her own child. Hadley had once written to Ernest, "Pauline has sent splendid letters about everything a mother and ex-wife wants to know. I am most grateful."

The doctor had ordered Pauline to rest, so it was no wonder her mother was forcing her to strictly follow the rules as she focused on regaining her strength on the sofa in Piggott. "I'm not allowed to do anything," she complained to Ernest. "But I'm getting very strong, and soon there will be a big fight, and then I can do all the things I want." What she wanted was to be with him in Wyoming. "With you away, it seems as though I am just a mother, which is certainly not very gripping," she wrote. "But in three weeks I'll begin to get ready to go to Wyoming, where I shall be just a wife."

Patrick was faring well, surrounded by a household of women who doted on him—Pauline's mother, Mary; sister Jinny; and beloved housekeeper, Lillie—so Pauline was confident that he would be perfectly fine when she was away. In the hospital she'd quickly weaned him to a bottle, preparing the way for others to help with feedings. She had discovered that to keep Patrick pacified, increasing his formula did the trick. "We have a little slogan to keep Patrick a good boy," she wrote to Ernest. "It is Raise The Formula."

Being Mrs. Ernest Hemingway was Pauline's great joy; she believed that she and Ernest were two halves of the same person, and they were meant to be together. Even their birthdays—Ernest's on July 21 and

Pauline's on July 22, one day apart—were a meaningful coincidence. She willingly gave up her career at *Vogue* and her Paris world for him, exchanging cocktails at the Ritz and couture dresses for bootleg whiskey and maternity clothes and a life that revolved around Ernest's hobbies and needs. Giving birth to Patrick connected Pauline to Ernest in the same way that Hadley was—as mother to Ernest's child, Pauline would always have a special role in Ernest's life.

She knew how he could be, though; women seemed to gravitate to him, and he didn't like to be alone. But he was fishing in the Wyoming wilderness, so no need to worry about him finding company there.

FIFTEEN GIRLS

It wasn't that Ernest didn't like girls, he did—but that's what had gotten him in a jam with Hadley. After they'd met Pauline at Kitty's tea and she'd started stopping by their apartment, he realized she was a damned good editor and she admired him. Then one night when he was walking her to the corner, he realized he'd fallen in love and his troubles began.*

It was a curse, loving two women, and for a while he felt "shot all to hell inside." At first he'd thought it could just go on with Hadley as his wife and Pauline as his girl, but neither would settle for that arrangement. Pauline was a strict Catholic who insisted on being his wife, not his mistress, and he'd been forced to choose. There was no way he could give up the new, exciting love with Pauline, although he'd felt terrible about Hadley. He had written a letter telling her, "—and I think perhaps the luckiest thing Bumby will ever have is to have you for a mother . . . and I pray God always that he will make up to you the very great hurt that I have done you—who are the best and truest and loveliest person that I have ever known."

In the divorce he'd given Hadley every penny that he would ever make from *The Sun Also Rises*—he wanted to be certain she and Bumby

---

* In an unpublished sketch written by Hemingway in the 1920s (Item 648a, Ernest Hemingway Collection, John F. Kennedy Presidential Library and Museum, published in the *Hemingway Review*, Spring 1990), he wrote: "He had been married for five years and he'd never gone with another woman and suddenly he found himself in love with her."

would be taken care of—and it had worked out wonderfully. The book had sold well and was still selling; two Broadway producers had even contacted him about possibly adapting it for the stage, which would mean more money for Hadley and Bumby.

It hadn't taken long for Hadley to forgive him. She invited Ernest to come and see Bumby as much as he wished, and she'd forgiven Pauline to a degree since she would be in Bumby's life. When Hadley received Ernest's cable about Patrick's difficult birth, she wrote, "Give Pauline my love and Bumby's and heartiest congratulations on the size & sex & I imagine the attractiveness of her son and her own recovering from what I am sure must have been a hideous time." Hadley even enclosed a check to help with expenses.

In Paris, when Bumby was an infant, Ernest had walked down the street to the Closerie des Lilas to escape the "squalation" stage, as he called it, and sit in a booth with the light streaming over his shoulder as he wrote a story called "Big Two-Hearted River" about a young man named Nick Adams and a trout stream. This time, instead of a French café, he'd find solace in a remote Wyoming ranch and an actual trout stream.

Bill had told Ernest that Folly Ranch was a dude operation, and Ernest had still wanted to come despite his feelings about them. Popular among wealthy East Coast families, dude ranches sprang up in the 1920s as a way for ranchers to supplement income from cattle operations. Although he agreed to the visit, Ernest preferred spending time with the ranch hands and wranglers, the real people who lived and worked on the land, rather than dudes who came from the pages of the Social Register. This area in Wyoming was an incubator of dude ranch operations. Along Red Grade Road alone there were three—Teepee, Spear-O-Wigwam, and Folly—with several more in the valley below.

Eleanor Donnelley, of Chicago's R. R. Donnelley publishing family, had been a guest at Teepee Ranch when she fell in love with the Bighorn Mountains and borrowed money to buy land along Teepee's southern border. Her father paid off her debt, which she had said was "pure folly," and her Folly Ranch got its name. She invited many of her cousins, who attended Yale and Bryn Mawr (where Hadley had briefly attended university before dropping out due to health issues), to help her on the ranch each summer during their college breaks.

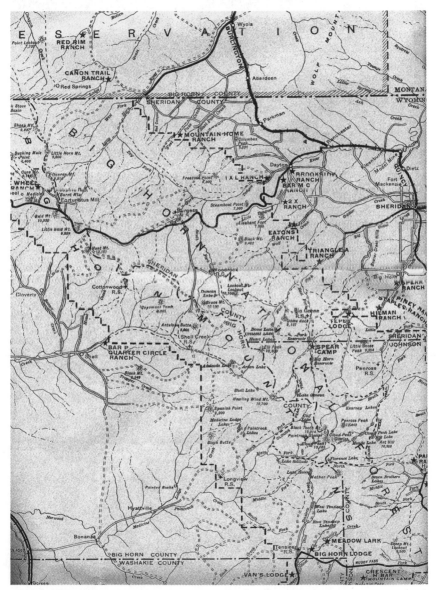

The Sheridan area was a popular location for dude ranches with an East coast clientele. *The Wyoming Room, Sheridan County Public Library System*

Folly Ranch was a small dude ranch operation, and most of its guests were friends and family of Eleanor Donnelley. *The Wyoming Room, Sheridan County Public Library System*

Folly Ranch was a typical "dude" setup, with guests staying in rustic log cabins, taking meals together family style in a main lodge, and participating in group activities like fishing, hiking, horseback riding, swimming in cold mountain lakes, and pack trips. Despite Ernest's misgivings about dude ranch life, Bill thought it was heaven, maybe in part because of the women, who were still mostly single, a few divorced, and "all very attractive."

Evenings were spent with the other guests, playing bridge and charades and singing around the piano. Ernest entertained the group with stories about Dorothy Parker and F. Scott Fitzgerald, and then digressed into a story about a bullfight, with his hands doing much of the talking as he acted out "both the matador and the bull."

With his sights on future fishing, Ernest had been studying a map of Wyoming and Montana on the wall, and he pointed out a little stream along Yellowstone Park's eastern border in northern Wyoming to Bill. It dropped down south through wilderness, then turned north to the Yellowstone River, hundreds of miles and several mountain ranges away from Folly.

Ernest and Bill Horne (back row, second from right, Ernest Hemingway; right, Bill Horne) sit with the Folly girls after swimming, 1928. *The Wyoming Room, Sheridan County Public Library System*

"Horney," Ernest said, "that's the place. Someday you and I'll go there and slaughter em!"

On his first morning on the ranch, Ernest rose early and worked, writing four pages before joining Bill to explore the wilderness. Folly, nestled into a private valley on four hundred acres with its own lake and a stream passing through, miles from the nearest town, seemed fine enough as Ernest and Bill tromped through the lightly timbered pine forests and open grassy meadows, fishing gear in tow.

Ernest's father, Clarence, an obstetrician, had taught Ernest and his five siblings to appreciate nature and the natural world. They had spent summers at their family retreat on Walloon Lake near Petoskey, Michigan, where Clarence taught them life skills like making a fire, identifying plants and animals, and shooting a gun. He told them to respect nature, including never killing anything unless you were going to eat it—a lesson that stuck with Ernest, who released fish that he didn't plan to consume. His first day at Folly, he caught twelve fish and recorded it in his fishing log.

Ernest with his rod and fishing creel in the Bighorns, 1928. *Ernest Hemingway Collection, John F. Kennedy Presidential Library and Museum, Boston*

On the second day, one of the Bryn Mawr girls took Ernest and Bill fishing on the east fork of Big Goose Creek, and the men discovered a nice stream called Cross Creek, but Ernest only caught two fish. On the third day, he set out alone, fished by himself, and caught thirty fish, the limit: twenty-six were eastern brook trout, and four were rainbows.

When he returned from his solo fishing day, the ranch was buzzing with preparations for Eleanor's annual party. Each August, she hosted two hundred couples who braved the mountain road, some by car, some by horse, to attend the social event of the season. Her famous dance and supper party was followed by a massive bonfire with wood stacked in the shape of a large teepee. The Bryn Mawr girls and Eleanor's wranglers and ranch hands were baking cakes, making punch, arranging flowers, building the dance floor, and stacking wood for the bonfire.

Guests began arriving at 7:00 PM, and couples soon crowded the floor, Ernest and Bill and the Bryn Mawr girls among them, dancing to

Wood stacked in the shape of a teepee for a bonfire at Eleanor Donnelley's annual party, 1928. *The Wyoming Room, Sheridan County Public Library System*

Lyle Corey's orchestra—square dances, waltzes, and two-steps—until a brief rainstorm paused the music. The dance floor was promptly dried and the party continued.

At midnight, a supper of sandwiches, cake, ice cream, and coffee was served, followed by the giant bonfire—its striking and somewhat frightening silhouette against the dark night a spectacle that left some guests speechless and produced so much heat, guests had to step back from the roaring flames. Eventually, the fire died and couples returned to dancing under the stars. Eleanor and friends enjoyed a 4:00 AM breakfast, then finally went to bed.

The late-night revelry was too much for Ernest. At 6:00 AM he packed his car and left without saying goodbye, desperate to find a quiet writing space. Bill would understand; he'd always supported Ernest and his writing—and besides, he'd have the Folly Ranch girls to entertain him.

The bonfire created a frightening silhouette and produced so much heat that guests had to stand back, 1928. *The Wyoming Room, Sheridan County Public Library System*

WYOMING WINE

SHERIDAN, LOCATED TWENTY MILES FROM FOLLY, was a charming town built by railroad and coal money. Stately Victorian homes sat upon wide, tree-lined boulevards, and it boasted two movie theaters and a Carnegie library for local literature lovers. The Sheridan Inn, a fine old hotel where Buffalo Bill Cody once auditioned acts for his Wild West Show, with its many-gabled roof and wide veranda, was conveniently located across the street from the train depot and walking distance to the downtown commercial district. Ernest signed the guest register the morning of August 3.

During the next week, Ernest produced nearly forty pages in his six-foot-by-nine-foot room, taking breaks by playing poker at the Mint Bar on Main Street. There, he met Howard Vickery, a local newspaper editor who offered to introduce Ernest to the local bootleggers, a nice French couple who sold wine and beer from their home on the edge of town. It wasn't always easy to find good booze during Prohibition, especially with the scar on his forehead that some people viewed with suspicion. Having a local connection made a difference.

He had gotten the scar in Paris the previous March after he and Pauline had been out to dinner with their friends Archibald and Ada MacLeish. "Archie" was a Yale-educated poet and his wife Ada, a concert singer living in Paris. In the night, Ernest had gone into the bathroom and, in the dark, yanked down a pull to a skylight instead of the toilet chain, sending the skylight crashing down on his head, slicing his face. Pauline called Archie for help, and they transported Ernest to the hospital for stitches that resulted in the large scar. He was getting used to it, but it gave him a rakish appearance, and

The Sheridan Inn in 1928, where Ernest worked on *A Farewell to Arms*.
The Wyoming Room, Sheridan County Public Library System

nobody in Key West believed he was a writer. His publisher, Charles Scribner's Sons, had removed the scar from a recently taken publicity photo for his upcoming novel.

———————

The valley was baking as Ernest drove down a dusty road north of town, to a row of small wooden houses away from the grand homes that lined Loucks Street. Sheridan didn't benefit from the cool mountain breezes felt at Folly Ranch. It was flatland, surrounded by yellow grain fields, green alfalfa, and sugar beet crops—and August was often the hottest month of the year.

Ernest pulled up in front of a modest home and knocked on the door.* A plump old woman with white hair answered and led him to

———————

* This chapter is based on EH correspondence and details found in "Wine of Wyoming," the short story about the French bootleggers in Sheridan he published in 1930.

a table on the back porch, bringing him a cold beer. A car pulled up and stopped, and two men walked toward the house. Ernest hid the beer under the table, not wanting to cause any trouble in case these men were agents. When the woman told them she didn't have any beer, they left.

The French bootlegger and his neighbor worked at the coal mine but relied on the extra money from their bootlegging operation to make a living. Ernest paid four dollars a gallon for wine and one dollar a gallon for beer, and he sat on the vine-shaded porch drinking the cold brew that tasted as good as the beer he had drunk at Brasserie Lipp in Paris.

He admired the snow-covered peak in the distance, and talked with the woman when she came back to the porch. When she learned Ernest was eating his meals at the hotel restaurant, she didn't approve—the food was no good there; he should eat with them. That evening, Ernest returned for dinner, talking with the couple in a combination of French and English.* They were a nice family just trying to make a living in this strange, dry country. Ernest learned the husband and their neighbor had been arrested twice on liquor charges, earlier in the year, paying a considerable amount in fines.

The wife was a good cook, serving chicken, fried potatoes, salad, corn, and cucumbers—and the husband brought out some of his new wine, "light and tasting of grapes." After dinner the discussion turned to religion; they were Catholics, and Ernest told them that he and his wife were, too. Ernest said that Pauline would love to meet them when she visited, and he promised to stop by.

Ernest didn't share with the French couple the story about when he felt he had really become a Catholic. It was after he and Pauline were married. He'd never had problems making love before and he didn't know why it was happening, so he made the rounds to doctors and even to a mystic who suggested he drink calf's blood every day. Finally,

---

* In a newspaper article appearing in the *Billings Gazette*, October 18, 1970, the French bootlegger couple was identified as the Moncinis. Their family challenged the article saying that the Moncini couple was misidentified, and that the neighbors named Pichot were probably the bootleggers Hemingway wrote about.

Pauline suggested that he go to a cathedral and pray. When he returned he found Pauline in bed, and they "never had any trouble again." Ernest missed Pauline terribly and was looking forward to the day she would arrive.

THEY GOT IT WRONG

THE *SHERIDAN JOURNAL* WROTE about Eleanor's annual party: "Among Miss Donnelley's guests is Ernest Hemingway, well known author who among recent years, has spent much of his time abroad. Mr. Hemingway who is an ardent and efficient fisherman, has written many well-received novels, his latest success, *Men Without Women*, now meeting with tremendous approval throughout the east."

Since the success of his novel *The Sun Also Rises*, Ernest had become fairly "well known" in the US press, as the article stated, which was sometimes good (he always enjoyed positive reviews of his work, and it helped sell books) and sometimes extremely annoying (when they got things wrong or pried into his personal business). When Ernest and Hadley were breaking up, he hadn't told his conservative Oak Park parents out of shame and fear of what they would say, but the newspapers had done the job for him.

His father wrote to him, asking if the rumors of his breakup were true, and asked him to "please write to me so I can deny the awful rumors." It took him several months after receiving the letter to fess up that indeed he and Hadley had separated, but still he denied his involvement with Pauline. He tried to minimize his parents' concerns, saying Bumby and Hadley were doing well and they were the best of friends—and Ernest urged his parents to show him a little loyalty and not believe everything they hear.

Here in the *Sheridan Journal* was another instance of the paper having it all wrong: he'd only written *two* novels, *The Torrents of Spring* and *The Sun Also Rises*—not "many" as the paper stated. The novel had been successful, and his experience had been almost as one *New York Times* critic described: Ernest "wrote a book and woke up to find himself famous." The critic, Percy Hutchison, wrote, "Seldom has a book received such instantaneous recognition or been greeted with greater enthusiasm," despite the grumblings from some readers that it was disgusting. Even Ernest's own mother had called it "one of the filthiest books of the year." His dad, who had also been disappointed, was a little more tactful when he said he wished his son would use his wonderful ability in the future on a different subject.

His most recent book, *Men Without Women,* was not a novel as the *Sheridan Journal* had reported, but a collection of short stories published on October 14, 1927, while he was still in Paris. The jury was still out on whether it was indeed a success. His editor, Maxwell Perkins, said it was selling well, but some critics were not impressed, finding Ernest's subjects "lacking." The *New York Times Book Review*, however, called him a "master in a new manner of the short story form. . . . His style is his own."

Ernest loved the praise but couldn't stand criticism: What did critics know? He was proud of the stories in *Men Without Women*, especially one called "Fifty Grand," a damn good story about Jack Brennan, an aging boxing champ, during his last fight with Jim Walcott. The *Atlantic Monthly* had published "Fifty Grand" the previous year—the first national magazine to publish his short fiction after years of Ernest sending out stories and receiving rejections. More proof that these stories were good: "The Killers" appeared in Edward J. O'Brien's *The Best Short Stories of 1927*.

It irked him that he hadn't seen much recent advertising by Scribner's for *Men Without Women.* When Ernest asked Mr. Perkins about it, he responded that Scribner's had "eased off" advertising because business at Scribner's had been slow and it was a presidential year. Still, Ernest had seen a lot of advertising for Thornton Wilder's *The Bridge of San Luis Rey*, and it seemed like Scribner's had promoted *Men Without Women* at the first of the year, then dropped all marketing. Ernest was frustrated that it appeared other writers were "getting rich while he was making less than a newspaper correspondent."

He was supporting two families—Hadley and Bumby in Paris, and now Pauline and Patrick—and money was always on his mind despite Pauline's family wealth. He wasn't killing pigeons in Luxembourg Gardens for dinner anymore,* but there never seemed to be enough money. He hadn't sold a single story this year because he needed all his creative juice to go into his new book and he was nearly broke.

In January he had been working on a father-and-son novel when a new idea about the war, which had started out like a short story, continued to grow. In March, the skylight accident—the blood and stitches—brought back memories of the trenches and the fighting. Ernest had set aside the father-and-son story, twenty-two chapters, to pour his energy into the short story that had turned into a novel. He once told F. Scott Fitzgerald that in fiction, "war was the best subject of all, offering maximum material combined with maximum action." And now as he approached the story's ending, he needed a quiet space to finish the book—and the Sheridan Inn had not been the tranquil place he'd thought it would be. Guests visited each other in their rooms at all hours, talking in the halls, making a racket. Across the street, trains rattled through day and night, blowing their whistles. After four days in town he checked out, this time moving to an empty ranch at the base of the Bighorn Mountains also owned by Eleanor Donnelley, called Lower Folly.

---

* There are stories that he was so poor in Paris he once killed a pigeon in the Luxembourg Gardens for dinner.

A CLEAN,
WELL-LIGHTED RANCH

ON AUGUST 8, just outside the little town of Big Horn at the foot of Red Grade Road, Ernest pulled into an empty ranch without a dude in sight. The U-shaped house surrounded a swimming pool, built in a style that could have been found in a Chicago suburb, except it was built with logs.

Built by Chicago architect Stanley Anderson, the ranch house called Lower Folly was built with logs in a suburban architectural style.
The Wyoming Room, Sheridan County Public Library System

He quickly settled into his peaceful new surroundings and wrote—finishing seventeen and one-half pages his first day—a total of 2,550 words. Ernest often calculated his word production with ciphering in the margin of his notebooks or manuscripts, giving him satisfaction that he was moving toward the finish.

In celebration of a good day's work, he ate and drank too much with the ranch guys that night. The next morning, Ernest suffered from "gastric remorse,"* so he wrote letters instead of working on his novel. Though he loved to receive letters, he didn't write many when he was working on a book—he needed all his writing energy to go into his work. When the pain of a hangover impeded his creativity, however, he liked to write letters so he could feel like he had still accomplished something.

He wrote to Waldo Peirce, his painter friend from Paris** now living in Maine, describing Wyoming and how it reminded him of Spain. Waldo had joined him in Pamplona the previous year, instead of Pauline, because the Spanish people were against divorce and Ernest felt it was too soon to introduce his new wife since Hadley had been with him during prior years.

Ernest told Waldo he longed for the bullfights, especially on Sunday around 5:00 PM—it was the first time he had missed the festival since 1923. How he wished he could be there instead of in Wyoming writing his book, and he vowed to see more toros again.

In 1925 he'd gone to the bullfights with Paris friends Harold Loeb, Lady Duff Twysden, and her fiancé Pat Guthrie. When he returned to the apartment above the sawmill where he lived with Hadley and Bumby, he sat down just before his twenty-sixth birthday to write the story of Lady Brett Ashley and the unconsummated love affair with Jake Barnes, finishing the first draft on September 21.

He modeled some of the characters in the book, originally called *Fiesta*, on his friends, and they had felt betrayed. Harold Loeb, Kitty's boyfriend, had been terribly hurt, wondering what he'd ever done to Ernest to deserve this treatment. Kitty never spoke to Ernest again, which

---

* hangover, a condition Ernest frequently suffered.
** Waldo Peirce became known as the American Renoir.

was fine with him because he didn't like her. Duff appeared to take it in stride, but then Ernest mostly stopped seeing her and that crowd altogether. It was during that time he'd met Pauline and a new group of friends: Waldo Peirce, Scott and Zelda Fitzgerald, John Dos Passos, Sara and Gerald Murphy, and Ada and Archie MacLeish.

His new book about the war also had characters based on real people. The nurse, Catherine Barkley, shared characteristics of Agnes von Kurowsky, his first true love and heartbreak. As in *The Sun Also Rises*, he was writing fiction and, as such, was free to borrow details from real life but could make up as much as he wanted. That's something his friends who saw themselves in *The Sun Also Rises* hadn't understood: the characters may have resembled them, and some of the stories he told may have been based on what happened in Pamplona—but it was still fiction. It was important to get the setting right using facts to do so, to make the story believable.

He finished his letter to Waldo, telling his friend that he was lonely without Pauline and that he planned to finish the book before she arrived to join him later that month.

During the day on the ranch when he was working, he was fine, but it was the evenings that got to him. Ernest wanted Pauline to be with him after a day's work, "someone to feel swell with," instead of feeling "just horribly cock-eyed lonesome." He described it as a feeling that rose up "like fog coming up from a river bottom." He didn't do well being alone; the last time he was separated from Pauline for this long he didn't do well at all.

———————

Back in October 1926, Ernest should have been celebrating the success of *The Sun Also Rises*, yet he wasn't feeling celebratory; he felt like his life was falling apart. Pauline was in Piggott, serving out Hadley's hundred-day separation ultimatum, and he was alone in Paris. At first, he and Pauline had written ardent, loved-filled letters to each other, and those had helped him get through the long days. But when Hadley found out about their correspondence, she told them there was to be *no* communication between them for the hundred days; that was the deal. So they had to resort to sneaking messages through Jinny and in telegrams written in code with words like "bears," "Jesuits," and "cubists." "Started" meant Hadley was starting divorce proceedings, and "hurry" from Ernest or "coming" from Pauline meant they were to reunite immediately.

Over time, though, Ernest noticed that the tone of Pauline's letters had changed. He used to be "cockeyed happy" when a letter came, but then she started sounding like the Piggott Chamber of Commerce newsletter, sharing news of domestic events that he didn't care about. He needed her to reassure him that she loved him, and he feared that she was changing her mind. He was so despondent that maybe he had lost Hadley *and* Pauline that he wrote, "Last fall I said perfectly calmly and not bluffingly [a]nd during one of the good times that if this wasn't cleared up by christmas [*sic*] I [w]ould kill myself."

He'd told Pauline during that time, "I love you so Pfife . . . and what I miss worse is not having intimacy with you—nor any feeling of us against the others." He had needed her there with him so he wouldn't have to be alone. What a relief it had been when Hadley called off the hundred-day ultimatum, saying she'd move forward with the divorce and Ernest and Pauline were free to be together.

Soon Pauline would arrive in Wyoming and it would be them against the others again. He just wished she'd hurry.

WEDDING PANTS

PAULINE RECEIVED A CALL from the Piggott operator with a telegram: Ernest had ordered her some "wedding pants" for her upcoming trip to Wyoming. Wedding pants? What could they be? For her wedding in Paris she'd worn an off-white chemise—not pants—with a string of pearls. Her hair was cropped in the popular Paris fashion, the way she still wore it today. And Ernest had looked so handsome in his three-piece tweed suit.

What an intoxicating time it had been, once Ernest's divorce from Hadley was final and they were free to start planning their own wedding. As a Catholic who took her beliefs seriously, living with a devout family in Paris, attending Mass without fail, and avoiding meat on Fridays, Pauline insisted on a wedding sanctioned by the Roman Catholic Church. Her requirement meant that Ernest, who had been raised a Protestant, needed to produce a baptism certificate from the Roman Catholic Church. Ernest explained he had received last rites from a Catholic priest, entering into communion with the Catholic church when he was hospitalized in Milan. He would need to travel to Italy with his friend Guy Hickok, a writer for the *Brooklyn Daily Eagle* based in Paris, to find that priest, hoping he would provide the proof that Ernest needed.

Pauline hadn't wanted him to go; surely there must have been another way to secure the necessary proof. As much as she admired what Ernest was willing to do for her, she had only just reunited with her true love after their separation, when he announced he was leaving for Italy. Was he punishing her for taking too long to return? She knew he had been hurt that she'd taken a month to return to Paris after receiving word that

Hadley had agreed to a divorce, spending Christmas with her extended family in New York City first. He'd told her he understood, but she knew he had hoped she would get on the very next ship from the United States, as they had planned the minute she heard that Hadley had called off the separation. Was his trip to Italy a payback to see how it felt to be left behind?

While Ernest was in Italy, Pauline stayed busy. Her first order of business was to find a place for them to live. She found a gorgeous flat on Rue Ferou, a quiet street near the Luxembourg Gardens. Uncle Gus offered to help finance the lease for the apartment (which she and Ernest continued to lease while they were back in the States, keeping it available for future visits). Jinny had also returned to Paris, and the two of them had shopped for furnishings and decorated it with lovely antiques and rugs.

They also cleaned Ernest's bachelor pad—a.k.a. Gerald Murphy's studio—while Ernest was gone, returning it to pristine shape. Pauline sorted Ernest's clothes for washing and mending, organized his papers and letters—and realized that they would need to hire a maid to help with their new life together.

Sara and Gerald Murphy had been supportive of the relationship between Ernest and Pauline, despite its complications. They liked Hadley well enough, but felt Ernest needed a more sophisticated wife when he took his place in the world as the best writer of his time, and thought Pauline was his perfect match.

Pauline missed Ernest terribly while he was in Italy, writing, "If you will just come back to me you can have your own way all the time. I shall cross you in nothing." He had returned early—ostensibly because he and Guy got into an argument on the trip—and Pauline had kept her promise to this day, continuing to let him have his way and shaping her life around his needs.

Once Ernest was back in Paris, there had been more work to do to appease the Roman Catholic Church: his marriage to Hadley had to be annulled. Since he and Hadley had not been married in the Catholic church, an annulment was granted, though it made Bumby a bastard in the eyes of the church since it meant he had been born out of wedlock.

Pauline was sorry about Bumby, but knew she had sinned by having an affair with Ernest and would need to make amends with God. She had no intention of committing the sin of marrying outside the church.

On May 10, 1927, nearly two years after that fateful tea at Kitty's, Pauline and Ernest were married in a Catholic ceremony in the side chapel of Saint Honoré on the Place Victor Hugo with Jinny and Ernest's banker, Mike Ward, as attendants.

Now back in the United States, Pauline had traded the Paris days of working for *Vogue*, drinking at the Ritz, and dancing to Cole Porter for her new role as Mrs. Hemingway, a job that although exciting, could be very demanding, and required her to do things that she'd never done before, like heading to the wild west of Wyoming.

When the "wedding pants" package arrived in Piggott she learned that the operator had actually said "wading pants," not wedding pants. They were fishing waders for spending time in Wyoming's rivers. She wrote to Ernest, telling him that she could not wait to wear her wedding pants day and night, even if they made her look like "a duffel bag with feet." Her days of couture in Paris were behind her, at least for now

TAXI SERVICE

When Bill Horne had asked Ernest to join him at Folly Ranch, he didn't know what to expect, but he was delighted by what they found. He thought it was heaven, or a close facsimile. "With a swell cook, Folly the collie, active trout ponds"—not to mention the girls—it had everything a guy could want.

Bill counted Ernest as one of his best friends. After the war, when Ernest was recovering from a broken heart and living with his parents in Oak Park, Bill had offered "to grubstake* him" in Chicago so he could work on being a writer. Bill had been working in advertising, making a fabulous salary of $200 a month, and had saved $900. He was practically rich; the two of them could easily live on that kind of money. At the time, Bill recognized that Ernest had talent, but had no idea how much.

After Ernest married Hadley and moved to Paris, Bill hadn't seen much of his friend for seven years. In a small world, Bill knew some of Ernest's Paris circle. He had attended Princeton with Harold Loeb, who had become friends with Ernest, playing tennis and drinking wine together, and Harold had helped to get Ernest's first book, *In Our Time*, published by his own publisher, Boni & Liveright. When Ernest had gone to the bullfights in Spain, Harold went too, but Bill knew he'd been hurt when Ernest cast him as the heavy character, Robert Cohn, in *The Sun Also Rises*.

---

* Grubstake: to provide supplies or funds to mining prospectors in exchange for a share in their profits.

Bill thought Ernest was a guy who was dominant "because he was smarter, talked better, and looked better than anyone else." Bill watched the cute Folly Ranch girls fawning over Ernest and understood Ernest's need to get away, to be alone to finish his novel.

Maybe they would have more adventures together now that Ernest was back in the United States. Next time, perhaps, they'd explore the Clarks Fork of the Yellowstone that Ernest had pointed out on the map. But it was time for Bill to return to his advertising job in Chicago.

On his last day on the ranch, Eleanor asked a favor. She and some of the Folly Ranch guests were getting ready to depart on a ten-day pack trip deep into the backcountry of the Bighorns, from the Medicine Wheel Ranch, some twenty miles away. She asked Ernest to help shuttle the group to the departure location at Medicine Wheel, and Bill gladly offered to ride with him, giving them time to catch up since he hadn't seen much of Ernie once he'd moved into Sheridan to write.

Eleanor and seventeen Folly campers rode horses seven miles down the mountain to Lower Folly, where Ernest and three additional cars waited for taxi duty. The four-car convoy made a quick stop at Brown Drug in Sheridan for supplies, then headed up "the highest mountain," as Eleanor described it, stopping midway on the steep climb during a brief rainstorm for lunch. The drive to Medicine Wheel Ranch, which they had been told was twenty miles, turned out to be forty miles, because someone had miscalculated the distance. The campers and their drivers got lost before finally bumping across a pasture to arrive at their destination in the late afternoon.

As soon as they reached the ranch, Ernest and Bill had to turn around and head back down the mountain. As Bill said farewell to his new Folly friends, he vowed to stay in touch, particularly with Eleanor's first cousin Bunny Thorne.

Ernest sits with Frances "Bunny" Thorne on his Model A in the Bighorns, 1928.
The Wyoming Room, Sheridan County Public Library System

A VISIT TO OAK PARK

THE NEXT MORNING, after breakfast at Lower Folly, Ernest drove Bill to the depot and they said their goodbyes. Perhaps he would see Horney again this fall—Ernest hadn't been home in years, and he wanted to take Pauline and Patrick to Oak Park to visit his parents and show off his new son, maybe meeting up with Bill then.

Ernest had seen his parents recently, however, if only briefly, during a chance encounter the previous spring in Key West. Before leaving Paris, Ernest had written to his parents to let them know that he and Pauline were heading to Key West for a few months, then traveling to Piggott to visit Pauline's family, and, finally, continuing to Kansas City for the baby's birth. His parents, however, had already left Oak Park on a trip of their own, and didn't receive Ernest's letter. They were traveling to Florida with Clarence's brother, Will, who had convinced Clarence to invest a large portion of the family's savings in Florida real estate. Clarence was alarmed that their investment had lost much of its original value and he wanted to check it out for himself.

One morning, Ernest had been fishing off the P&O pier when he looked down the boardwalk and could not believe his eyes. There, his parents and Uncle Will were walking toward him—turned out they had decided to spend a day sightseeing in Key West. Ernest couldn't believe his good luck to run into them. He called Pauline at the hotel and told her about his surprise, and that they'd be picking her up to spend the day together. It would be Pauline's first time meeting his parents.

41

The introduction was awkward at first. After all, Clarence had once called Pauline "a love pirate" who had broken up Ernest's family. By day's end, though, feelings had been soothed and his parents softened toward Pauline, who was going to be the mother of their grandchild. Grace Hemingway, in the typical self-absorbed fashion that annoyed Ernest, spent much of the day talking about herself and her newest passion: painting. She was determined to get her work into a Paris show and asked Ernest for his help. In contrast to his mother's exuberance, Ernest thought his father seemed distracted and appeared rather frail, which concerned Ernest.

Ernest had a soft spot for his father, the man who had taught him to love nature and who gently encouraged him to use his talent to write stories that were unlike *The Sun Also Rises*. But Ernest felt his mother was always ready to believe the worst about him and was not loyal. As much as he didn't relish spending time with her, he would like to see his father again soon. He'd need to talk to Pauline to see if they could fit in a visit to Oak Park, since they were planning to travel to Paris in the fall.

MAXIMUM INSURANCE

AFTER DEPOSITING BILL at the Sheridan train depot, Ernest stopped at the post office in Big Horn. The little town, with its false front general store and post office, had once been a bustling outpost on a popular stagecoach route to Montana's gold mines. These days it was nearly a ghost town, the sort of place one might half expect to see tumbleweeds blowing through, with hardly a soul in sight.

The historic Big Horn Post Office building was built with a false front.
The Wyoming Room, Sheridan County Public Library System

When he picked up his mail he found an insured package from Piggott, Arkansas, waiting for him. His manuscript. He'd left it in Piggott, afraid to travel with it after the terrible loss he had experienced years ago when his manuscripts had been stolen at a train station in Paris. He'd asked Pauline to send it to him after he was settled, and she had insured it for $1,000, the maximum value available. She enclosed a letter, joking, "It cost me $2.38, almost what a baby costs." She wanted him to know that she realized its great worth.

———————

In December 1922 Ernest, then married to Hadley, was working as a stringer for the *Toronto Sun* in Paris when he received an assignment to cover the Lausanne Peace Conference in Switzerland. He and Hadley had fought about it; she didn't want him going off on assignment and leaving her alone in a strange city again. Why did he need to go when they had her trust fund to live on? She didn't understand why he needed to take these jobs. To make up with her, Ernest asked her to meet him at Chamby-sur-Montreux, Switzerland, where they could take a winter vacation after he'd finished.

As she packed, Hadley had an idea. She knew how Ernest loved to work in the morning—how happy it made him—so she decided to surprise him by bringing all his manuscripts, everything he'd written before and during Paris, including carbon copies. Why she had felt the need to bring the carbon copies too was still a mystery to Ernest, but she had. At the Gare de Lyon, she went inside the train station to get a drink of water and when she returned to her train compartment, the suitcase was gone. At first she had thought that she must be in the wrong compartment, but after getting a porter to help her search, reality sunk in. The case had been stolen.

When Hadley's train arrived in Switzerland, Ernest tried to concentrate on her words, to make sense of what was she telling him, but she was crying so hard he couldn't understand her. When he finally realized she was saying they were gone, all gone, he took the next train back to Paris to check for himself and found the manuscript drawer empty.

———————

Gertrude Stein told him, "Start over and concentrate," and that's what he'd done. He had suffered a great loss and it was painful, but in the end he thought some of the stories were even better when he'd rewritten them. Still, as much as he'd tried to forgive Hadley, it had changed his relationship with her. And since that day, he'd become very careful about his manuscripts and keeping them safe.

Back at the ranch house, Ernest read over the manuscript, 575 pages in all, and he was so pleased that he drank nearly a gallon of wine and a half-gallon of beer and forgot to eat supper. The next morning he awoke with gastric remorse, so he wrote letters.

First he wrote to his childhood friend and neighbor Isabelle Simmons Godolphin that Pauline would be coming out in a week, and that he was thankful because he feared he was beginning to get "sheepherder's madness," that fabled affliction caused by lack of female companionship, where the sheep start to look attractive. Ernest knew they would need to follow the doctor's advice and be very careful and scheduled so Pauline didn't get pregnant again for three years. Gone was the spontaneity they had enjoyed before Patrick's conception, but he would just be happy to have Pauline by his side again.

He wrote to Maxwell Perkins, reporting that he'd only fished three times since he arrived because he was "driven by the writing"—on page 575, and it seemed good. He told his editor he would be "awfully happy" when he'd finished the book and could have some family life again, and asked Mr. Perkins to send copies of *Men Without Women* and *The Sun Also Rises* to Howard L. Vickery at the *Sheridan Post Enterprise*. Always concerned about money, he asked about sales of *Men Without Women* before closing.

ANGEL CHILD

PAULINE'S STOMACH WAS FLAT AGAIN. She had worked hard to lose the weight because she'd seen what had happened when Hadley didn't lose her pregnancy weight after Bumby. She was getting her strength back, too, by climbing the stairs. There was nothing she could do about the gigantic scar across her abdomen from the caesarean, but Ernest thought she was brave. She had earned her war wound after eighteen hours of labor.

Now she was doing everything her mother and the doctor ordered to prepare for the trip. "Hurry up and send for your wife, I'll even pay for my own passage," she joked in a letter to Ernest.

To pass the time until she could leave, Pauline entertained herself by writing to Ernest, packing clothes for the trip, and planning Patrick's baptism. Ernest had given his permission for the baptism to take place even though he couldn't be there—he understood Pauline couldn't depart for Wyoming until she'd reserved Patrick's place in heaven.

On August 14, Patrick Miller Hemingway was baptized in the Pfeiffers' home chapel. Pauline wrote to Ernest, "He didn't make a noise until the priest said 'Patrick, do you renounce the Devil with all his works and prophets,' and he gave a little groan and a little whine of protest. Ernest, he is an *angel* child. He never had the colic once, and he hardly ever cries. . . . I think we may like him very much."

Some mothers might have had reservations about leaving their two-month-old baby with family for a whole month, but Pauline didn't. Jinny was doing a fine job of raising Patrick. In fact, it sometimes seemed like Jinny had more maternal instincts than Pauline did. The doctor said Patrick was gaining weight too fast, so Jinny had stopped Patrick's two o'clock formula feedings and started him on orange juice.

Ernest believed nurses and grandparents could raise a baby just as well as he and Pauline could, and Pauline had never been a mother before, so what did she know? First and foremost, Pauline was Ernest's wife, and he'd made it clear that he needed her with him.

FATHERHOOD

BUMBY HAD BEEN BORN when Ernest was only twenty-four years old, and he had felt unprepared to be a father. Now, at age twenty nine, he had another son to care for. Ernest didn't believe that a child should interfere in the relationship of the couple—the couple should come first. Sometimes, when he and Hadley had gone out alone in Paris, they had left Bumby in the care of their trustworthy cat, F. Puss, a very good babysitter.* Patrick would be in good hands, too, with Pauline's family back in Piggott while Pauline and Ernest enjoyed some time alone together in Wyoming.

He didn't understand people like his friend Waldo Peirce, who was so keen on having children. Ernest had tried to alert Waldo to the perils of fatherhood—Patrick had nearly killed Pauline because he was so large, and then there was the noise to contend with from a bellowing baby. Not to mention, he warned, there was no guarantee children won't grow up to be "shits."

---

* This comes from page 195 in *A Moveable Feast*: "Here were no baby-sitters then and Bumby would stay happy in his tall cage bed with his big, loving cat named F. Puss. There were people who said that it was dangerous to leave a cat with a baby. The most ignorant and prejudiced said the cat would suck a baby's breath and kill him. Others said that a cat would lie on a baby and the cat's weight would smother him. F. Puss lay beside Bumby in the tall cage bed and watched the door with his big yellow eyes, and would let no one come near him while we were out. . . . There was no need for baby-sitters. F. Puss was the baby-sitter."

Ernest planned to be there for the important things, raising his sons as his father had done for him—teaching them to shoot and fish, to love being in the outdoors. But he only half-joked when he said parenting was a part-time job, with nannies, nurses, grandparents, and aunts to help out.

Ernest's relationship with his own father was good enough, but he'd been disappointed that he hadn't been invited to the family's Michigan retreat this summer. When Ernest had written to inquire about visiting before the baby was born, his father had not seemed open to the idea. He advised that Pauline give birth in St. Louis or Kansas City.

As Ernest worked now to finish his manuscript, he thought perhaps this book would be a story his father would enjoy. While his father had tried to be kind in his assessment of *The Sun Also Rises*, his mother was more concerned about what the Oak Park people would think about the book.

When he finished his writing for the day, he looked for entertainment in the afternoon. He'd made friends with Eleanor's cousin Gaylord Donnelley, and the two of them spent time talking, fishing, and visiting Sheridan's bootleggers.

IMPROVISING

GAYLORD DONNELLEY HAD BEEN SPENDING his past three summer breaks from Yale working at Folly Ranch. Although his cousin Eleanor was ten years older, she was his dear friend, always looking out for him. When she bought the ranch, she invited him to visit, promising room and board in exchange for his service as handyman, chore boy, chauffeur, assistant wrangler, assistant guide, stove tender, and whatever other jobs needed to be done.

On his way back to the ranch after doing errands in Sheridan, Gaylord often stopped by Lower Folly, where Ernie was "batching it." Gaylord knew Ernest's typical schedule was to work from 6:00 AM until noon, and that he welcomed male company in the afternoon. Gaylord found Ernest kind, friendly, and extremely likable despite their age difference. When Gaylord shared his aspirations, Ernest had been optimistic about Gaylord's future prospects in academia or business.

On their afternoon jaunts, the two men patronized several local brewers in Sheridan. One was Sheridan's street cleaner, who patrolled the street with a can on wheels. A request would be made, a rendezvous point established, and the street cleaner would retrieve moonshine in brown bags from inside the manure can. Gaylord thought the pints were "not much worse for the association."

Another secret spot in town was a wonderful cool bar in the basement of Brown's Drugstore, reached through a trapdoor at the rear of the building. Gaylord found the establishment's gin fizz to be especially delicious on a day when the thermometer outside was over a hundred degrees.

On a fishing trip with Ernest to a fly camp at Cross Creek in the
Bighorns, located just below the snowcapped Cloud Peak, Gaylord learned
a lot about fly-fishing—and also about improvising. Ernest taught him
that when in need of a flask, a baby's bottle could be filled with whiskey,
and it didn't break when it was dropped on a rock in the river.

Ernie was always a lot of fun to be around, and one Sunday afternoon
a group from Folly got together: Gaylord, his friend Bill Poole, a lovely
friend of Eleanor's named Josie Wall Merck (who was divorced), and
Ernest. Over a jug of beer, Ernest entertained the group as the three men
vied for Josie's attention. Gaylord had known Josie for several years and
had even visited her in New York, thinking he might have the inside track
to her affections. But he could see that even Josie was not immune to
Ernest's charms. Gaylord couldn't be mad; he liked Ernest and considered
him a new friend. Gaylord hoped that one day when Ernest was in the
East, he might even visit him at Yale.

WAITING FOR PAULINE

ON AUGUST 18, as Ernest pulled out of the driveway at Lower Folly, his characters Frederic and Catherine were in a hospital delivery room with Catherine's labor pains. Ernest was on page 600, about two days from the end, and although he had tried to finish it before Pauline arrived, he was stuck, trying to get the words right.

On the veranda of the Sheridan Inn, waiting for Pauline's train, which was almost two hours late, he wrote letters as the anticipation was killing him. It had been three weeks since he'd seen his wife, too many nights sleeping alone. He looked forward to showing her the Wyoming he'd discovered—the Bighorn Mountains and locals like the French bootleggers. Pauline would enjoy sitting on the couple's porch, drinking wine and speaking French with them.

When Pauline finally stepped off the train—her dark hair cropped, figure in shape, no outward signs of the time she'd been through—Ernest was thrilled. He took her to a party at the Hortons' HF Bar dude ranch with a number of Folly friends, who later reported that "Mrs. Ernie," as the Folly crowd called her, was "a smooth number who danced the Charleston."

The next day they drove up Red Grade Road ten miles past Folly Ranch, where Ernest turned the roadster down a gravel road and stopped outside a lodge built in the shape of a spear, with a point and shaft. Located at 8,300 feet, Spear-O-Wigwam was another dude ranch, this one owned by Senator Willis Spear; he'd hired a New York architect to design the complicated structure shaped like the Spear cattle brand. The

An aerial view of Spear-O-Wigwam, the lodge was built in the shape of an arrow. *The Wyoming Room, Sheridan County Public Library System*

Welcome to the Spear-O-Wigwam. *Courtesy Travis Cebula*

The massive fireplace at the Spear-O-Wigwam anchors the room. *Courtesy Travis Cebula*

lodge housed the kitchen, dining hall, and a communal area large enough to accommodate two hundred people, with a massive stone fireplace in the center. On the walls, mounted heads, hides, antlers, Indian relics, and muzzle-loading guns were hung for décor.

Ernest and Pauline were escorted to the Rosebud Cabin—a rustic pole-log cabin with two bedrooms and a bathroom, their home for the next week. Although it didn't have a fireplace, it had a cozy stove and a view of a bubbling stream from the bedroom; they could open the windows and hear the water rushing past. The furniture was made from logs, and Ernest could write at a desk tucked beneath the window. The cabin had a front deck with chairs positioned to take in the view of the distant peaks.

On their arrival, Ernest took a day off from writing to explore the ranch with Pauline. But the next day he needed to get back to work on the book's ending, so he sent Pauline fishing with a guide and sat down at the desk in the Rosebud Cabin to write.

The rustic Rosebud Cabin at Spear-O-Wigwam circa 1930. Its name was later changed to the Hemingway Cabin. *The Wyoming Room, Sheridan County Public Library System*

Ernest wrote beneath the cabin window, writing some thirty-nine endings for *A Farewell to Arms. Courtesy Travis Cebula*

FRESH MOUNTAIN AIR

PAULINE DIDN'T MIND being on her own, acquainting herself with the land. The fresh air was therapeutic, and the freedom she felt was intoxicating after being confined for so long. In Wyoming, she felt strong again, and she was determined to keep up with Ernest as they hunted and fished their way across the state.

Pauline was delighted to receive a letter from Jinny shortly after her arrival, reporting on Patrick's progress. Jinny was trying to get Patrick "raised" by the time they returned from Wyoming. Patrick ruled the household, everyone doted on his needs. He let them know his displeasure if he wasn't put out on the swing at 4:00 PM, crying until he got his way.

Jinny described his many attributes, saying, he had "handsome eyes, a mouth like Bumby's, and beautiful skin that browned in the sun." She said she'd found a Dutch product called KLEEN that kept his knees clean.

Jinny and her friend Ayleene Spence liked to push Patrick in his carriage to Piggott Square and show him off to merchants and friends. They stopped at the soda fountains in Reve's Drug Store and Porters's Drug Store, so the ladies who gathered there in the afternoon for cherry Cokes could admire baby Patrick.

Pauline knew Patrick was surrounded by love and being perfectly cared for, making it easier for her to be away. Ernest expected this of her; he'd been the same with Hadley too, demanding that they leave Bumby with his nurse, sometimes for months. This was only the first time she would need to choose between her husband and her child. She knew there would be more times to come. And she would choose Ernest.

On the way to Wyoming, Pauline had stopped in St. Louis to visit her dentist. She overheard women gossiping about the writer Ernest Hemingway—that he had married his second wife, also from St. Louis like his first. The women speculated that the character Lady Brett Ashley in his scandalous novel *The Sun Also Rises* must have been based on his new wife. Pauline was amused, but she didn't correct them to say that the character was actually based on Lady Duff Twysden.

Just as Ernest's crush on Duff had been the inspiration behind *The Sun Also Rises*, his previous love for Agnes von Kurowsky had inspired his new book, but this didn't bother Pauline. She understood that writers and artists needed inspiration, and she didn't care where it came from as along as Ernest was hers.

While at Spear-O-Wigwam, Pauline met the Spears' daughter Elsa, who had just returned from a pack trip. The people at the ranch couldn't have been nicer to Pauline. In the mornings she rode with them into the pristine wilderness around the ranch, along trails to crystal-clear lakes and streams. After her adventures, Pauline always came back in time to bring Ernest lunch or to do anything he asked. She looked forward to the time when he would finish the book so she would have him to herself.

THE END

So close. As Ernest sat in the little log cabin and tried on different endings, weighing different options, he was ready to finish the bloody book. He wrote in a frenzy for three days, beginning the day with breakfast at the lodge—steak, eggs, red onion, and wine— not speaking to other guests, intent on eating and getting to work. Then he headed back to the cabin to write until Pauline brought him lunch.

On August 23, five days after picking Pauline up from the depot, after multiple attempts, he finally knew what the ending would be. It was inspired by Patrick's birth as Ernest had sat helplessly by, fearing that both Patrick and Pauline would die. Ernest finished the first draft.

The feeling was exhilarating. Ernest would put the book aside and let it cool off for a while before he started the revision, something that was pretty important and would take between six weeks and two months—at least that's how long it had taken him to edit *The Sun Also Rises*. He was now free to fish and drink and have fun with Pauline. She wore her "wedding pants," and they caught thirty trout apiece every day.

A rustic but comfortable writing place at Spear-O-Wigwam. *The Wyoming Room,*
Sheridan County Public Library System

SEEING D'AMERICA

ON AUGUST 24, the *Sheridan Journal* reported: "Ernest Hemingway, writer of prominence and author of the new novel 'Men Without Women' that is meeting with such demand in the east, is a guest at the Wigwam lodge. Mr. Hemingway is accompanied by Mrs. Hemingway and for the past three years they have made their home in Paris."

Ernest and Pauline were leaving Spear-O-Wigwam, however, now that his book was finished, to see more of the Cowboy State. They drove over the top of the Bighorns, past the turnoff to Medicine Wheel Ranch, where Ernest and Bill had deposited the Folly packers, through pastures of late-blooming wildflowers. They swerved around hairpin curves in Shell Canyon, a deep chasm carved out of sedimentary stone and granite, and heard the roar of the waterfall before they came upon it as it plunged one hundred twenty feet to the canyon floor. The magnificent walls in the canyon eventually opened to the small town of Shell, population fifty, their first stop.

Owen Wister, author of *The Virginian*, considered by many to be the first true Western novel, was staying near Shell. He was a guest at Trapper Creek Lodge, built in 1927 by the Wyeth family of Wyeth Pharmaceuticals on a dude ranch they'd purchased the previous year. Maxwell Perkins had recommended that Ernest visit Wister, saying that Wister would be delighted to meet Ernest, and indeed Ernest found him a "sweet old guy." They made plans to connect when they were both in Paris, possibly even later that fall when the Hemingways were anticipating being there.

From Shell, Ernest and Pauline drove through a ranching valley near Greybull in the white-hot light of August, passing through wild mustang country near Cody. The area, called the Bighorn Basin, had been discovered by explorer John Colter in 1807. The ancient land was unlike any place else on earth, mostly uninhabited and otherworldly, with massive red rock formations where fossils and dinosaur bones had been found.

Some of the houses they passed were no more than shacks. Wyoming had been going through an economic slump, with much of the state's revenue coming from tourism driven by the popularity of car travel. Ernest liked to tell his friends he was "Seeing D'America," a spoof on the national advertising campaign "See America First," encouraging Americans to take car trips and see the country in all its glory. The newfound popularity of dude ranches, along with the attraction of Yellowstone National Park, helped draw guests to the state to support the economy. Even so, many residents, like the Sheridan bootleggers and other working-class people, struggled to make a living.

Ernest and Pauline fished in the Sunlight River and the Clarks Fork, that lonely little river near the Montana state line, between the Absaroka and Beartooth Mountains, that Ernest and Bill had spotted on the map at Folly Ranch. Jackson Hole, their next stop, was over two hundred miles away through Yellowstone National Park. They were headed to the Bar BC Ranch, owned by another Scribner's author, Maxwell Struthers Burt, who wrote *Diary of a Dude Wrangler* and *The Delectable Mountains*. The ranch was popular with an East Coast literary crowd, including the prominent publisher Alfred Knopf. As a Princeton alumnus, Struthers also hosted many affluent Eastern city dwellers.

An advocate for the unspoiled American West, Struthers had owned and operated the Bar BC Ranch since 1912. He was a "furious foe of Prohibition" and had written about it in an essay, "The Dry West," that appeared in the February 1928 issue of *Scribner's Magazine*.

As Ernest and Pauline neared Jackson Hole, they entered a valley surrounded by the Gros Ventre and Teton Ranges—giving the area its name "hole." The Snake River curved through the valley floor with ancient cottonwoods lining its banks. Ernest and Pauline drove east through sagebrush flats, toward the river, the jagged Tetons towering above them. They passed a charming chapel built miles from civilization on the valley floor, the Chapel of the Transfiguration, with a window that framed the view of the stunning peaks.

When they reached a bench of land, they dropped down to a terrace where the Bar BC stretched along the Snake River. Nestled against the hill, invisible from above, the compound included cabins, a lodge, a dining hall, a laundry/utility building, corrals, man-made pools, and an assortment of barns, sheds, and log structures with red or green roofs.

Struthers gave the Hemingways a cabin with a porch that faced the magnificent Snake River, where Pauline and Ernest fished, catching "three big ones"—two-, two-and-a-half-, and three-pound cutthroat trout. But they arrived too early in the season; the water was running high and they couldn't wade. Ernest heard fishing was grand at the end of September when they shut off the dam.

Ernest was "cockeyed" about shooting, never traveling without three guns. He'd brought his .22-caliber Colt automatic pistol, a .410-gauge shotgun, and a .12-gauge Winchester pump to Wyoming. On the drive back to Sheridan, Ernest entertained himself by shooting prairie dogs from the car.

The cabin where Ernest and Pauline stayed at the Bar BC as it looks today, restored by Grand Teton National Park. *Courtesy Katherine Wonson, 2012*

MONEY IN THE BANK

It was early September when Ernest and Pauline returned to Sheridan, checking into the Sheridan Inn to wait for prairie chicken season to open on September 15. Senator Spear had invited them to join his camp in the Wolf Mountains on the Crow Indian Reservation for the shoot. Ernest found a letter from Maxwell Perkins waiting for him at the post office with a check for $3,718.66—royalties from *Men Without Women*. He was happy to have the money, his earnings were down to ninety dollars per month, and life was expensive.

He wrote to Mr. Perkins to thank him for the letter and the check, and to inform him that the first draft of the book was finished. He shared his Wyoming adventures, describing how much the country reminded him of Spain. The only thing he didn't like, he told his editor, were dude ranches: dreadful places—he could write a story about them. Finally, he noted that he and Pauline would be returning to Piggott the following week, then heading to Key West for the winter to revise the new novel.

Without a book to work on, Ernest caught up on his correspondence. He wrote on Sheridan Inn stationery to Waldo Peirce, Guy Hickok, and Archibald MacLeish with updates about Patrick (he weighed sixteen pounds), wonderful fishing (they caught thirty trout apiece each day for nearly a week), and Pauline (she was feeling strong again) and signed his letters respectively, "Yours in haste HEM," "Yours always Ernest," and "Pappy."

He wrote to his sister Madelaine ("Sunny"), telling her he and Pauline had decided to postpone their trip to Paris until the spring; instead, they would be staying in Key West so Ernest could finalize his book there. They didn't have a home—living in hotels, with relatives, on ranches— and felt they needed to stay in one place this winter. Key West was a fine place to work, and Sunny was invited to come down and stay once they found a house to rent. She could come with them to Paris when they decided to go. He signed off, "Your always Bro Ernie."

He sent his friend Sylvia Beach in Paris, founder of Shakespeare and Company bookstore, a postcard with a drawing of a sheepherder on the front, telling her that he and Pauline had a son named Patrick and that the new book was done.

Before leaving for the prairie chicken hunt in Montana, Ernest and Pauline visited their Sheridan bootlegger friends and told them they were heading to the Crow Reservation. The French couple asked them to be sure to come back after hunting, when the wine would be ready.

A LADY IN THE CAR

PAULINE AND ERNEST awoke early on September 14 and dressed, both wearing white button-down shirts and belted dungarees with the legs cuffed, and little black berets, then drove an hour to the Wolf Mountains to meet Willis Spear and his crew. They piled in Spear's car to ride with

Ernest and Pauline at hunting camp on the Crow Indian Reservation, 1928.
The Wyoming Room, Sheridan County Public Library System

Pauline with her pistol in a holster. She was determined to hunt and fish and keep up with Ernest, 1928. *Ernest Hemingway Collection, John F. Kennedy Presidential Library and Museum, Boston*

him, and he stopped to speak to a sheepherder. Sheepherders often lived by themselves on the range without seeing another soul for months, so they weren't accustomed to company. This sheepherder was using some colorful language.

"Now, now, there's a lady in the car," Spear reprimanded.

The herder peered into the car, looking into the back seat, and defended himself, saying, "I don't see no lady!"

With her cropped hair and boyish figure, wearing dungarees and a beret, Pauline probably did look like a boy, and she laughed off the sheepherder's comment.

At camp, Pauline was delighted to see her friend Elsa Spear and Elsa's mother, who had traveled to the camp to enjoy a prairie chicken dinner

Ernest sitting on the wheel well as Senator Willis Spear and his party prepare to hunt prairie chickens, 1928. *The Wyoming Room, Sheridan County Public Library System*

that night. While at Spear-O-Wigwam, Elsa had not appreciated Ernest's cussing or what she considered his lack of manners when he pointed at the food he wanted and sometimes grabbed things from Pauline's hands. But she, like most everyone, was converted to Ernest's charms—she came to understand that was just Ernest; it was hard to get mad at him. It was lucky the hunting party had shot nine prairie chickens that day, enough to feed the large group.

A FAREWELL TO WYOMING

DESPITE THEIR LUCK on the first day of hunting, on the second day they hadn't seen a single prairie chicken. Ernest and Pauline returned to Sheridan hot and tired—they'd been up since 5:00 AM—and they were thirsty when they finally reached town that afternoon. Ernest turned down the dusty road and stopped at the bootleggers' house. The wife gave them her last two bottles of beer and told them to come back that night—her husband would have the wine.

With their time in Wyoming over, they planned to start the drive back to Piggott the next morning. But there was still much to do: Ernest needed to send his father a telegram and get the car looked over by a mechanic. After dropping the car at the garage, he walked back to the hotel in the heat. When the time came for dinner, he was too tired to see the bootleggers and speak in a foreign language, but there was no way to reach the couple and tell them they wouldn't be coming.

The next morning, Ernest and Pauline both felt guilty about not showing up for dinner, so they decided to stop to say goodbye on the way out of town. Ernest could tell the French couple was disappointed. The husband had been eager to show off the wine he had made. When Ernest and Pauline hadn't shown up for dinner, he'd drunk three bottles himself.

After saying goodbye, Pauline and Ernest drove through the hills outside Sheridan, leaving the Bighorns behind. Ernest's life spread out before him like the road ahead. His new novel seemed good; maybe the critics would even like it. He was itching to revise the book now, but wanted to make sure he waited long enough. Even though he'd finished writing *The Sun Also Rises* in September, he'd waited until December to start the revisions, and he felt that schedule should be repeated.

While he waited, he would use the time to visit his family in Oak Park, Illinois, and he could go to the East Coast to see Scott and Zelda, and Archie and Ada MacLeish—who were back in the States now too—and maybe take in a football game or two. He could even stop by to visit Gaylord Donnelley at Yale.

When he saw his father, he'd tell him about Wyoming and the fish Ernest and Pauline had caught—despite the fact that his father didn't seem as interested in hunting and fishing as he once was. Would his father like his new book? Ernest hated that he had disappointed him with *The Sun Also Rises* and hoped maybe this time he'd like what Ernest wrote.

Just as in his own childhood, when his family escaped Oak Park's heat by spending time at Windemere Cottage on Walloon Lake, Wyoming could be the place where Ernest brought his own family for a retreat, teaching his sons to shoot and fish as his father had done for him.

In the golden September light, as the shadows became longer and the days shorter, Pauline and Ernest drank whiskey and ate apples in a fine cold wind as they drove. Ernest's lips were chapped from the sun and alkali—even worse than in Key West. He had never felt stronger, he was in fine shape, and he hadn't been sick or had an accident since being back in America. When he had told this to Maxwell Perkins, he would need to say "knocking on wood."

He was superstitious and he believed in luck; it was why he carried a worn rabbit's foot in his pocket. Once, long ago in Paris, when he had been married to Hadley, living in the apartment above the dance hall, there had been a moment when he had felt lucky. He should have knocked on wood then. He should always remember to knock on wood.*

---

* When Hemingway penned his fictional memoir, *A Moveable Feast*, at the end of his life, he looked back on his early years in Paris, writing on page 34: "'My,' she said. We're lucky that you found the place.' 'We're always lucky,' I said and like a fool I did not knock on wood. There was wood everywhere in that apartment to knock on too."

Part II

1930

What Ernest Loved About Pauline

Keen editorial eye
Her family became his family: Jinny, Mother Pfeiffer
Uncle Gus's support
Strong again
"Someone to feel swell with" after a day's work
The "feeling of us against the others"
Willing to join him on adventures
Believed in the "promotion of masculine society"
Never worried like other wives
Vowed to always let him have his way
She could give him "little Pilar"
~~Her throat never got sore like his~~
~~Spontaneous lovemaking~~

THE L BAR T

IN MAY 1930, the heat arrived in Key West, then hurricane weather, making it impossible to think. Ernest wrote to Waldo, "Have been drinking too since the damned heat came—Had to drink on acct. the heat—Then when the rain set in found a damn good excuse [to] drink on acct. of the rain."

It was time to move to a cooler climate, and Wyoming was a good place to work. He'd written seventy-four pages of a new nonfiction book about bullfighting, but he'd suffered a few delays. First, he'd sliced his index finger clean to the bone on Charlie Thompson's punching bag, requiring six stitches. He couldn't type or hold a pen.

Then he was laid low by the grippe while visiting Pauline's family in Arkansas. He had to stay in bed and dose with quinine, postponing any work on the book and the trip West with Pauline and Bumby, now age six, who was visiting for the summer from Paris. Ernest had met Bumby's ship in New York and started feeling ill on the drive to Arkansas.

While in Piggott, they had celebrated Patrick's second birthday with the Pfeiffers on June 28, in heat just as stifling as in the Keys. Ernest hadn't slept well in forty consecutive hot nights and he would welcome the refreshing mountain air. Ernest, Pauline, and Bumby set out on July 2 for Wyoming. Patrick was too young to come along, so he stayed behind with the Pfeiffers and his French nurse, Henriette, hired last year while they were in Paris.

Their new Model A Ford coupe, with its rumble seat and running boards, was a comfortable touring car, the second from Uncle Gus after Ernest's sister Sunny wrecked the first one while staying with them in

Key West. Ernest had driven this new car to the bullfights in Paris last year with Jinny and Guy Hickok and then shipped it to the States when they returned. Uncle Gus had even offered to buy them a third car—a newer model for the trip West—and although Ernest enjoyed a fine new car, he had demurred. He told Gus this car was still performing fine; why not use the money on more important things? Uncle Gus told Ernest that he understood the wisdom of taking his current car west as long as it was still driving well.

Uncle Gus and his wife Louise didn't have children of their own, so they gave their attention—and money—to their nieces and nephews, wanting to share their wealth, made in pharmaceuticals, with the entire family. Gus and Ernest had struck up a friendship, and Ernest had dedicated *A Farewell to Arms* to him in appreciation of his many kindnesses and support.

The Hemingways stopped in Kansas City at Ernest's relatives, the Lowrys, who had hosted them during Patrick's birth. Then they drove through Nebraska, where it was 108 degrees in the shade as the Midwest and southern Great Plains continued to suffer through a heat wave and drought, contributing to dust storms that further devastated the parched land.*

In addition to the land being dried up, the country's economy had dried up. The Great Depression had begun: banks had been closed, stockbrokers were jumping out windows to their death, families had lost their jobs and their savings and were living in the streets. Ernest stopped along the road to give some of these weary travelers a ride, and they shared their sad tales of loss.

When they reached Sheridan, Ernest determined that the area was too settled—he wanted a place where no one would know him. Since the publication of *A Farewell to Arms* the past fall, people wrote fan letters and were starting to recognize him in public, so he wanted to find a remote location deep in the mountains. Horney had given him a tip about an isolated ranch where he'd heard the "fishing is simply godwonderful." It was near the border between Wyoming and Montana, located on the

* The Dust Bowl started in 1930 from poor agricultural practices, sweeping across Western prairies through 1936.

Clarks Fork River, which Ernest and Pauline had fished on their previous trip. It might be the perfect place.

Located in the northwest corner of Wyoming near Yellowstone National Park, the ranch Horney had told them about was a day's drive from Sheridan. Ernest steered the coupe around the boulders and ruts on Red Grade Road as they made their way from Sheridan over the Bighorns while Bumby peered out the window at the precipice, not making a sound. They drove through Shell Canyon and the prehistoric-looking Bighorn Basin, finally reaching Yellowstone National Park's east entrance, only to sit for hours while crews worked to repair the road. When they were finally allowed to enter the park, they headed north, exiting in Montana near the western mining town of Cooke City, and from there took a dirt road ribbed like corduroy back down into Wyoming to land that bordered the park's east side.

The Nordquist Ranch cabins still stand today. *Darla Worden*

Nordquist Ranch was surrounded by rugged land. *Darla Worden*

The view south from Nordquist Ranch. *Darla Worden*

In 1872, when Yellowstone National Park's boundaries had been drawn, it had been impossible to contain all the geological wonders inside; nature colored outside the lines. Rugged volcanic mountains, deep canyon chasms, soaring peaks, and roaring rivers spilled out onto neighboring lands to the east. This was serious country, not for novice outdoorsmen; the secluded and rough land included miles of inaccessible terrain. The area* was famous for wildlife—elk, bighorn sheep, deer, moose, black bears, and grizzlies, the largest predators in the United States—wildlife that Ernest intended to hunt before leaving in October. And it had a reputation for world-class trout fishing. Ernest had said on their 1928 visit that it had been the best he'd experienced.

On July 14 the coupe turned down a dirt road with grass growing between the tracks, through a stand of quaking aspens, then crossed a rickety log bridge that led to a wide open meadow. L Bar T Ranch wrangler Ivan Wallace later told the story that he couldn't believe his eyes—his job was to bring dudes to the ranch by wagon or horseback because the roads were boulder-strewn and impossible. About four miles from the ranch, Ivan would need to tie a log to the back of the wagon so the weight would keep them from tumbling down a steep hill with a deep swamp at the bottom. Yet here was the first car to ford the Clarks Fork River, with a driver looking relaxed as he sped with his wife and young son toward the ranch entrance.

Ernest introduced himself but didn't mention the rocks or the swamp. "I'm a writer looking for a place to work," he said. "My name is Ernest Hemingway."

The wrangler had never heard of him, and that was the way Ernest liked it. Ivan took them to meet Olive Nordquist, who owned the L Bar T with her husband, Lawrence. (The ranch was named by using the first and last letters of his name.) She showed them to a new double cabin she felt would be just right for the family.

---

* In 1964 the area was designated as the North Absaroka Wilderness Area.

JACK'S ROOM

As THEY DROVE across a wide clover meadow near a little grouping of log cabins, Bumby—or "Jack" as he preferred to be called now by everyone except "Papa"—was happy to reach the ranch after being cooped up inside the coupe.

He had started his voyage nearly a month earlier in France with Aunt Jinny after his summer break from school began. Aunt Jinny had been visiting in Paris and had offered to bring him back on the *Lafayette* to New York City, where Papa met the ship. From there they drove to Pauline's family home in Piggott to pick up Pauline, but Papa got sick and they had to stay in town for a while, which was fine with Jack.

Jack couldn't recall a time when Pauline had not been in his life; he felt sorry for other children who only had one mother when he had two marvelous mothers. He gave her the nickname "Paulinoes" when he was small; he would ask his dad a question and Papa would reply, "Ask Pauline, Pauline knows," so Jack thought her name was Paulinoes, and the nickname stuck.

On the way to Wyoming, when they stayed with Pauline's family in Arkansas, the Pfeiffers treated him like one of their own. Jack enjoyed exploring Piggott and experiencing the privileges associated with being the bank president's step-grandson. At the local drugstore he was allowed to charge sodas, and he sampled sweets that weren't available in Paris.

After his dad recovered, they drove from Arkansas through wide open plains, on scary mountain roads near Sheridan, and through Yellowstone National Park. Jack had never seen land like this before except in movies*—cliffs, canyons, buttes, waterfalls. At the L Bar T Ranch, he looked up at two giant peaks towering above the valley floor, like fingers pointing at the sky.

One of the first real cowboys Jack had ever met, Ivan, showed them to a brown log cabin where Jack would have his very own room. Jack went to the corral, the place horses were saddled for rides and brushed after a day on the trails. Ivan sized up Jack and matched him with "Pinky," a white horse with liver-colored speckles. Jack knew he and Pinky would become the best of friends.

---

* Aunt Jinny took Jack to see movies at the cinema in Paris.

PAULINE'S RESPITE

PAULINE BREATHED IN THE SAGE-SCENTED air and felt herself relax. Situated in a valley with a river running through the meadow and a majestic mountain range in view, the ranch was lovely. She'd finally have some time alone with her husband. She had hardly seen him in Key West except for when he came home to get clean clothes. Although she never objected to Ernest's time with his friends, since renting a house in Key West the previous January they'd had an endless stream of visitors, including Maxwell Perkins, Archie MacLeish, Mike Strater, John Hermann, and Burge Saunders. Ernest enjoyed showing them his haunts and taking them deep-sea fishing, but Pauline was prone to seasickness, so sometimes opted out, preferring to stay home and meet the group on the dock at cocktail hour.

At the ranch, no friends would be dropping by, and she'd get a break from caring for a busy toddler. Pauline's family relished the opportunity to host Patrick and Henriette while Pauline and Ernest enjoyed some time alone together in Wyoming, or "Wyo-tana," as Patrick called it. He was a precocious two-year-old who spoke French because he had lived in Paris from the time he was nine months to eighteen months old. When they returned to Key West, he could say only a few English words and phrases, like "hobo" and "I don't know." Pauline's family promised to help him learn more English while his parents were away.

Pauline didn't mind that Jack was with them at the ranch; he'd have his own activities with other children and could run freely while Pauline and Ernest explored the area on their own. When Jack was with them, Pauline kept Hadley up to date on his activities, having

83

Pauline in front of one of the Nordquist cabins. *Ernest Hemingway Collection, John F. Kennedy Presidential Library and Museum, Boston*

managed to partially mend their fractured relationship through her devotion to Jack.

Pauline felt Jack was old enough to have a few responsibilities, so she assigned him two important chores. In the morning, it would be his job to start a fire in the little Franklin stove so the cabin would be warm when she and Ernest got up. He was also given the job of foraging for wild strawberries that grew in the area, filling two tumblers for Pauline's "ranch cocktails" that she made by adding gin. It was still Prohibition, so she and Ernest traveled with their own supply of booze, plus the ranch had connections to local bootleggers if they ran low.

In Paris last year, Pauline had become extremely ill, taking months to recover. She knew she needed to be strong. Ernest admired women who were strong, and she was determined to hunt and fish and ride hard all summer, to show him just how strong she could be. While Ernest worked on his bullfighting book, she donned dungarees and boots and headed to the corral to get outfitted with a horse of her own for a trail ride with the guides under blue Wyoming skies.

THE WORLD CHANGED

ERNEST STOOD ON THE FRONT PORCH of the cabin, squinting up at the mountain peaks as he wiped off his glasses on his shirt. His desk was positioned in a corner of the porch to take in the magnificent views of Index (11,699 feet) and Pilot (11,708 feet) Peaks, the highest in the Absaroka Range. He listened as the Clarks Fork of the Yellowstone River rushed by, literally flowing through his front yard. Ernest had once told F. Scott Fitzgerald that heaven would be his own trout stream that no one else could fish in; at the remote L Bar T Ranch, maybe he had found heaven.

The world had changed since Ernest's previous visit to Wyoming. On December 6, 1928, his father, Clarence Hemingway, had closed the door to his office, put a Civil War pistol to his head, and shot himself, shattering Ernest's family. Ernest hadn't learned it was suicide until he arrived in Oak Park for the funeral. He knew his father had appeared weak when he'd last seen him, but hadn't known that he'd been suffering from angina and diabetes. Clarence had been worrying himself sick about the precarious financial situation he'd created from investing in Florida swampland, a situation he had not shared with his family. He had asked his wealthy brother Will for help, but Will had turned him down. So, out of despair, Clarence had pulled the trigger.

Ernest had been with Bumby on December 6, 1928, when he received word that his father was dead. They were traveling from New York City to Key West, where Bumby would spend the winter with them, away from the damp Paris air. When Ernest received the telegram, he had to act swiftly, making arrangements for Bumby, then only five years old, to continue on the train to Key West by himself in the care of a porter while Ernest traveled to Oak Park for the funeral.

Pauline picked up Bumby from the train station and went into action, sending Ernest and Hadley telegrams that he had arrived. Next, she did her best to comfort Ernest's sister Sunny, who had come to live with them that fall to help with Patrick. Poor Sunny wouldn't be able to make it to Oak Park in time for the funeral, and she took her father's death so hard that Pauline had to call a doctor to give her a sedative.

Ernest had received heartfelt condolences from the Pfeiffer family and a letter from Hadley, who had wanted him to know she was thinking of him. Her own father, James Richardson, had killed himself twenty-five years earlier, so she understood what Ernest was going through. "Taty, I felt so sorry for you, the mixture of emotions! I remember how affectionately you talked of him to me in New York."*

Hadley was his dear friend, despite all they had been through. Ernest knew he had disappointed his parents with the divorce and by leaving Hadley and Bumby, and he'd continued to embarrass them with the rough language used in some of his stories. He wished his father could have seen the wonderful reviews of *A Farewell to Arms*—maybe he would have been proud of him. But Ernest would never know.

At least he had seen his father one last time before his death. Ernest had made the trip to Oak Park in the fall of 1928 alone, as it had seemed overwhelming to bring a baby to visit, and Pauline needed to spend time with Patrick after being away from him for a month during their Wyoming vacation. It had been a good visit despite the visible change in his father's health, but when Ernest departed, he hadn't realized how bad his father must have been feeling.

As the oldest son, Ernest became the man of the family, left to deal with the finances, the mortgage, and college funds for his siblings. His mother had been clueless about the state of the family's finances and was shocked to find out the dreadful state they were in. Ernest had started sending one hundred dollars a month to help out, which she didn't feel was enough. After the success of *A Farewell to Arms*, he'd been able to

---

* "Taty" was one of Hadley's pet names for him.

set up a $50,000 trust for her with the help of Pauline and generous Uncle Gus.

Ernest was feeling pressure with the loss of his father and the need to contribute to his mother's finances, not to mention concern over his own finances. Ernest and Pauline had been back in Paris when *A Farewell to Arms* was published on September 27, 1929, to glowing reviews. James Aswell, critic for the *Richmond Times-Dispatch*, wrote, "I have finished *A Farewell to Arms*, and am still a little breathless as people often are after a major event in their lives."

His friend John Dos Passos had written a review for the *New Masses:*

> Hemingway's *A Farewell to Arms* is the best written book that has seen the light in America for many a long day. I don't mean the tasty college composition course sort of thing that our critics seem to consider good writing. I mean writing that is terse and economical, in which each sentence and each phrase bears it maximum load of meaning, sense impressions, emotions. The book is a firstrate [sic] piece of craftsmanship by a man who knows his job. It gives you the sort of pleasure line by line that you get from handling a piece of wellfinished [sic] carpenter's work.

The book was even being dramatized in a play opening in New York. Ernest wasn't part of that venture, though, because of his focus on writing his bullfighting book. His agent did get him a small fee plus a cut of the profits if it succeeded. To make money on *A Farewell to Arms*, Ernest would have to sell sixty thousand copies before he earned out his advance and started receiving royalties—money he needed to support Hadley and Bumby, Pauline and Patrick, and his mother and siblings.

On October 29, 1929, financial matters had become even worse with Black Tuesday, the ensuing stock market crash, and the beginning of the

Great Depression. People couldn't afford to feed their families, so how could they buy books?

The Piggott State Bank, where Paul Pfeiffer served as president, permanently closed its doors after a run on the bank in February 1930. However, within days of the bank's closing, a group of businessmen created a new bank called Arkansas State Bank, with Pauline's parents, Paul and Mary, acting jointly as president to get it running before turning it over to a younger group of managers. Paul's real estate holdings had suffered too; profits were dwindling from his large tracts of land dependent upon tenant farmers, so he sold much of his land to the federal government. Still, despite some setbacks, the Pfeiffers' finances were in much better shape than those of many Americans.

As these events unfolded, publisher Nelson Doubleday made it even harder to make a living as a writer by announcing he would cut the price of Doubleday books from two dollars to one dollar, and other publishers followed to stay competitive. Ernest thought the publishing business was just about "belly up," and he joked that maybe he'd have to change careers and open a retail and wholesale fish business.

Ernest had sold only one story in 1930: "Wine of Wyoming," to *Scribner's Magazine*, about the French bootleggers he'd met in Sheridan. When he was writing a book, he couldn't stop to write articles and stories for magazines—he needed to focus on the book. Pauline had typed up the story—a whopping six thousand words. Ernest knew it was long and that Max (he no longer called him Mr. Perkins) would object to the French dialogue he included.

Ernest convinced Max by saying everyone that read *Scribner's* knew a little French and that the French was necessary to the story. Ernest had enlisted the help of Lewis Galentiere, a friend from his Paris days and now a noted American translator, to correct the French, paying him with a small Spanish knife with a blade of Toledo steel for his help. "Wine of Wyoming" would be published in the August issue of *Scribner's Magazine*.

Even with a dry spell between checks, life was different from Ernest's poor days living in Paris on Hadley's puny trust fund, borrowing money from friends for train fare and bullfighting tickets. He didn't talk about it, but the truth was that he liked traveling in a certain style, driving new cars from Uncle Gus and ordering a custom Springfield rifle that he'd brought on this trip. Pauline had been raised in a family of good taste. She knew where to get the best of everything, and Uncle Gus was only too happy to help finance the lifestyle of his beloved niece and her husband. Gus had even enlisted the help of his pharmaceutical company in Spain to do research for Ernest's new nonfiction book about bullfighting: putting ads in newspapers to encourage their readers to share books, newspaper clippings, and mementos from bullfights.

The lifestyle Ernest appreciated—traveling to Paris, the bullfights in Pamplona, deep-sea fishing in Key West, and the Wyoming retreats—was expensive. Despite help from Pauline's wealthy family and robust sales from *A Farewell to Arms*, it was important to keep money flowing. But he couldn't accept magazine assignments when the new book demanded all his energy. The result was long periods where no money was coming in between his advance and actual sales of the book.

He planned to finish his bullfighting manuscript before leaving the ranch and return to Spain in the spring to gather more photos for the book. He imagined it to be a treatise on bullfighting and hoped to publish it the following year.

Ernest had left instructions to ship his trunk of bullfighting materials to his new address at the L Bar T Ranch. The only outside communication to the ranch was through cables sent to Cody, Wyoming, that were phoned to the Crandall Ranger Station fifteen miles away, and mail that came from Cooke City once a week.

THEN THERE WERE
THE DISTRACTIONS

ERNEST ATE HIS BREAKFAST at the lodge, keeping to himself. He felt he "couldn't learn anything from the dudes so there was no use talking to them." He always preferred talking with the wranglers.

Sometimes on his way back to the cabin, he'd stop at the corral, watching Ivan and another wrangler, Chub Weaver, saddle horses while Ernest sucked on a piece of hay. As he leaned on the fence, he took in the sounds—the jingling of tackle, the slap of a saddle, horses' snorting—and the scent of the barn—animal, hay, dust, and manure.

One day after breakfast, Ivan made the mistake of telling Ernest that the "fishing is going to be great."

"I've just got to work," Ernest replied. Lately the river had been churned up from cloudbursts, which helped him ignore the water's temptation. He kicked the dirt and then stormed to his cabin.

A few minutes later he returned to the corral. "Damn you, Ivan," he yelled. "You've ruined my whole day now . . . so let's go fishing."

Ernest used Hardy tackle, and his leaders, the length of line attached to the main line where flies are tied, were already made with three flies. His favorites were a McGinty for the top, Coch-y-Bondhu for the middle, and a woodcock green-and-yellow for the tail fly. Most of the time Ernest liked to fish across the river and cast downstream, as his flies skittered across the current. The Clarks Fork was still muddy, but Ernest caught ten cutthroats with a spinner on a fly.

FLAYING DEAD HORSES

AFTER THE DEATH of Ernest's father, Max Perkins had become a good friend, even visiting Ernest in Key West. When a package arrived from Max at the L Bar T on July 24—sent to Piggott after Ernest had already left for Wyoming—Ernest opened it and found a letter and a set of proofs for *In Our Time*.

Ernest responded to Max the same day, reminding him where to send the mail—delivered to the ranch once a week from Cooke City with telegrams sent to Lawrence Nordquist, Painter, Wyoming, where there was a ranger phone in that direction. He wanted Max to understand that sending him the *In Our Time* proofs was a great inconvenience and that Max was asking him to "stop and flay dead horses" instead of focusing on his new bullfighting book.

Max knew that Ernest needed all his creative juices to go into the bullfighting book and could barely write letters when he was concentrating on new work. Ernest had once told his parents that he was "as pleasant to be around as a bear with carbuncles" until a book was finished.

The book's title had been *in our time*—lowercase, following the modernist fashion in Paris to experiment with punctuation and capitalization—when it was published in 1924 by Three Mountains Press. And it had been well received after publication by its first American publisher Boni & Liveright in 1925. Ernest wrote the book in a style called "cablese," with vignettes inserted between chapters—little stories that sprang from the cables he had sent to the *Toronto Star* when he was a stringer in Paris, covering Europe. The cables required brief, succinct stories to save on per-word transmission costs. They were like snapshots, capturing a moment in time, that packed a punch.

Scribner's wanted to bring the book out again, adding an introduction by a critic, an author's note, and new material—and rearrange chapters. Ernest told Max he would work on *In Our Time* when work on the bullfighting book stalled, but until then he didn't want to switch gears.

It made him nervous. He worried there could be libel issues from some of the characters, especially from the story "Up in Michigan," because the reason the book seemed so true was because most of it was true. Ernest felt he hadn't had the skills back then, and perhaps still didn't, to change names and circumstances.

Ernest was against adding new material or changing the order of the chapters. "I want it to be the book as I wrote it and as it was intended to be published—That is its only value—I will not doctor it up for any other purpose." Ernest implored, "Max please believe me that those chapters are where they belong."

Ernest told Max he planned to stay on the ranch until the bullfighting book was done. He had already interrupted his work too much by traveling and he'd regained his focus, writing seven hundred to twelve hundred words a day, every day, since he arrived except one. "—This is a good place and not getting mail is a hell of a fine thing and very good for working," he wrote, signing the letter, "Yours always—Ernest—"

LETTERS FROM PIGGOTT

PAULINE RECEIVED A LETTER from her mother reporting on Patrick's good health and spirits; her family adored Patrick and enjoyed watching him grow. Her parents tried to be understanding of the nomadic life that she and Ernest led, with their transcontinental travel, Paris apartment, and leaving Patrick for months at a time in the care of others. Although Arkansas was a long way from the bright lights of a big city, her parents were well-read, sophisticated people who accepted that the travel fueled their writer son-in-law's work. But when they heard the news that the Hemingways had returned to Key West in February and their grandson was not an ocean away, they were overjoyed. They hoped Pauline and Ernest would now stay in one place. Mary had told them, "Get a good strong anchor and sink it deep and stay put for a while."

They had put down an anchor in Key West, renting a charming home on Pearl Street that their friends Charles and Lorine Thompson had found for them and setting up their household. How wonderful to put their clothes in drawers instead of living out of a suitcase! Looking back on their European trip, from April 1929 to February of the current year, Pauline had realized the importance of taking time to recharge. It was easy for her to overexert herself, trying to keep up with Ernest.

Her health had deteriorated over time following their previous trip to Wyoming in 1928. Pauline had given birth to Patrick by caesarean section in June, come to Wyoming for hunting and fishing with Ernest in August, returned briefly to Piggott in September, and then headed on a tour of the East Coast in October, a whirlwind of parties and football games and visiting friends. She and Ernest had visited Ada and Archie MacLeish, Scott and Zelda Fitzgerald, and Gaylord Donnelley from Folly Ranch. Ernest had been in a celebratory mode after finishing the draft of *A Farewell to Arms* at Spear-O-Wigwam—who was she to hold him back?

The party ended on December 6 with news that Ernest's father had died. Pauline had gone into a protective mode of Ernest, taking charge of their household. The holiday month turned into a month of mourning as Ernest helped his mother, and Pauline made certain a comfortable home awaited him when he returned to Key West.

Ernest had poured himself into *A Farewell to Arms* revisions with Sunny, who had come to live with them in the fall, taking shifts with Pauline to type the manuscript. After completing the book on January 22, 1929, Ernest invited Max to come to Key West to pick it up and enjoy some deep-sea fishing. Other friends who visited were Waldo Peirce, Katy Smith, and John Dos Passos—a continuous party.

Their household had expanded from just the two of them to five people to feed and care for. Despite Sunny's help with Patrick and the manuscript, Pauline was stretched with needs from a demanding husband, an infant, an active five-year-old stepson, her sister-in-law, and an endless stream of guests. When their family entourage left Havana Harbor aboard the *Yorck*, bound for Boulogne, on April 5, 1929, Pauline had become extremely ill. The frenetic pace from the past year had finally caught up with her.

On the ship, Sunny stayed in a cabin with Patrick and Bumby to take care of them while Pauline slept all day, rallying only at night to accompany Ernest to dinner and drinks with new friends he had met. She knew better than to leave him alone, with so many women on the ship who would happily keep him company. Upon arrival in Paris, the doctor diagnosed her with exhaustion and a sinus infection so severe that she had to have her sinuses drained at the hospital twice.

Things got worse in Paris when she and Patrick both got the grippe and she couldn't get out of bed. She knew Ernest was not good around sick people, that he couldn't care for them. He had left them alone at the apartment, traveling south to Hendaye, Spain, to work on the revisions to *A Farewell to Arms* requested by Scribner's, leaving them on their own to recover.

When Pauline was a child, she would become delirious with just a slight fever, and her parents still worried about her. Her mother had recommended turning the children and household over to Virginia (Jinny) and going away to get some rest, because if Pauline lost her health, her life would be miserable.

It took months to get her strength back, and she still hadn't felt up to attending the bullfights in Pamplona in July with Ernest, so he went instead with Jinny and Guy Hickok. Pauline agreed to meet him after the festival, when she was feeling stronger. She made arrangements to send Patrick to Bordeaux with his new French nurse, Henriette, for two months, but before leaving Paris, Pauline took care to catch up on the chores she'd neglected while she was ill—mending Ernest's clothes, paying bills, and purchasing items that Ernest had requested.

The weather in Spain was glorious—sunny and warm—and she wrote to Jinny that they were having a fine time "swimming and loafing." With the revisions to *A Farewell to Arms* finished, Ernest was between books—and, as he often was before starting another project, he was moody. Pauline knew it had nothing to do with her; she took it in stride.

After being away from the United States for nearly a year, Ernest, Pauline, and Patrick returned to Key West with Henriette in February 1930. (Sunny had returned to Oak Park earlier, after touring Europe with a friend.) Pauline had her health back, and they were happy in Florida until the heat came and Ernest wanted to return to Wyoming's cooler climates.

Being at the ranch provided a reprieve from Pauline's duties as a toddler's mother, plus she got a break from cooking, cleaning, and managing a household. Pulling on her jeans and boots and adding a fishing vest and her black cap, she headed out on an adventure with the other guests and guides. When Ernest was ready for a break, she'd have a picnic waiting and horses saddled to explore fishing holes several miles downstream, just the two of them. Pure heaven.

Pauline wearing her "wedding pants" in a stream. *Ernest Hemingway Collection,*
John F. Kennedy Presidential Library and Museum, Boston

JACK AT THE RANCH

JACK HAD FINISHED HIS CHORES—starting the fire with soaked sawdust and a few small logs—so he was free to meet his new best friend, Billy Sidley, at the corral. Billy's family was from Chicago, and they'd been coming to the ranch for several summers—they even built their own log cabin at the ranch, and Billy's grandpa's ashes were scattered on a mountaintop here. Ivan made sure all the children had properly fitting saddles, and he had taught them to saddle up by themselves. Jack and Billy, decked out in chaps and cowboy hats, imagined themselves as real horse wranglers.

Jack's horse, Pinky, was an extremely clever animal. When Jack cinched the saddle tight, the way Ivan had shown him, Pinky would bloat up his stomach with air. After Jack was on the saddle, Pinky would release the air and the saddle would loosen and slip, causing Jack many accidents. Jack learned to tap Pinky on the ribs right before cinching, startling him into releasing the air, and Jack quickly tightened the cinch like a professional.

While adults went off on their own rides, the wranglers took the children to lakes and streams or up the Squaw Trail into Hurricane Mesa country. Some days, the kids would play horseback tag in the pasture, and at the end of the game, the horses were tired, ready to get to the barn, where their saddles would be removed and they'd get a good brushing. One day Jack forgot something at the cabin, so he decided to ride Pinky over to the cabin before taking him back to the barn, but Pinky didn't like that idea. Wanting to go with the other horses, he didn't budge. Jack resorted to giving Pinky the leather quirt and Pinky bolted, running full speed ahead through the cabins, where Olive Nordquist had stretched wire laundry lines through pine trees. Jack dodged the first wire, but the next one caught him across the chest and knocked him out of the saddle. Luckily, he wasn't seriously injured. After that, Jack was more cautious about using the leather quirt.

On days that Pauline went out with her own guides, Jack would hang back, waiting for the opportunity to go fishing with his dad. He desperately wanted to learn, and he hoped one day his father would take him along. When an invitation didn't come, and he saw Ernest take off alone with his fishing gear, Jack took matters into his own hands and followed him. He found Ernest chest-deep in the water and hid in the shadows to watch his dad fish, unnoticed.

Apparently Jack wasn't as stealthy as he'd imagined, because Ernest walked over to the bank. "You know, Schatz, trout spook awfully easily—" (Ernest's other nickname for Bumby was "Schatz.")

"I'm sorry, Papa, I only wanted—"

"If you really want to watch just stay back a little from the bank. You mustn't move around until I go further down. Then move very slowly and stay low," Ernest instructed.

"Yes Papa!" Jack was delighted that he hadn't been sent back to the ranch.

"That way the trout won't spook."

Jack sat quietly by the stream, watching his father fish and nearly dying with impatience. In France, Jack had caught his first fish in a gentle little river with a hook made from a safety pin, a line from strong black thread, and a willow shoot for a rod. Bait was rolled-up balls of dough that the cook had given him. He watched minnows in the crystal-clear water and dangled the bait until he felt a tug and pulled out a shiny minnow. It was thrilling as the minnow flopped on the dock. He caught minnow after minnow, using his pockets as a creel and bringing them back to the cook, who fried them for his supper. But the trout that Papa caught "were so beautiful," Jack became obsessed with catching one himself.

BIOGRAPHICAL CRAP

THE WEEKLY MAIL ARRIVED, and in it, a copy of a new Grosset & Dunlap edition of *The Sun Also Rises*. When Ernest turned it over and read the book jacket copy, he nearly blew a gasket. Soon after, he wrote to Max asking him to tell G. and D. "to at once remove that biographical crap [underlined three times] i.e. SHIT about me on the back wrapper explaining to G. and D. what my position is about personal publicity."

Early in their relationship, Ernest had told Max he was very sensitive about personal publicity and said any biographical material that Scribner's put out about him ought to be true. He had even written his mother after publication of *A Farewell to Arms*, asking her to tell reporters she had promised not to answer questions about him because Ernest wanted to keep his private life out of the press.

So how had this happened? He'd never approved this jacket copy. He didn't know who'd given the publisher the information, but if Grosset & Dunlap didn't remove all personal information about his war service, his marriage, and his private life, he would never publish another book with them. "So HeLp Me GoD," he wrote. "I tell you *[EH insertion: (this sort of thing)]* it takes any possible pleasure out of writing."

It was a reminder of the lesson Ernest had learned early in his career, when someone had circulated false information about his service in Italy: people thought *he* was the one telling the lies about his record. That's when he learned that he needed to control his publicity. In fact, going forward he would create the public persona that he wanted; he would decide what the world would be allowed to see. When Max's cable arrived a few days later, telling him that all the book jackets would be destroyed and no copies had yet been sold, or would be sold, with the offending cover, Ernest was still sore but had calmed down slightly. He sent Max a cable to thank him for his help.

VIVE LA MARRIAGE

AT FOLLY RANCH TWO YEARS EARLIER, one of the girls had captured longtime bachelor Bill Horne's interest. Bill and Frances "Bunny" Thorne were married on August 21, 1929, at Folly Ranch, and they sent Ernest and Pauline a telegram in Santiago, Spain, telling them the news. Ernest couldn't have been happier. Their friends John Dos Passos and Katy Smith had also recently married.

Ernest had witnessed Cupid's arrow striking both couples—Bill and Bunny in Wyoming and Dos and Katy in Key West. When Dos and Katy had visited at the same time last spring, Dos was smitten, later saying "from the first moment I couldn't think of anything but her green eyes."

Ernest believed in marriage. A man needed a woman by his side and in his bed. After a day's work, it was wonderful to be with your wife— even though things had become complicated since Patrick's birth and the doctor's warning that Pauline could not give birth again for three years without literally risking her life. Her Catholic beliefs prohibited birth control, so they followed a strict sexual regimen of careful scheduling and coitus interruptus.

Physical activity was something that helped distract Ernest, and Pauline wasn't like other wives, instead accepting his need for male company and adventure. When Ernest had been stranded for twelve days with Mike Strater, Archie MacLeish, John Hermann, and Captain Burge Saunders in the Dry Tortugas in the spring of 1929, and were finally rescued by an American yacht, Pauline hadn't worried. Ernest felt that was a good trait in a woman.

Ernest had invited the Hornes to join them at the L Bar T this sum-mer, sharing half their cabin, and Bill had responded, "Sure we are going with you if that's jake with you—gosh!" Ernest knew that Bunny was an intrepid adventurer; at Folly she'd slept on the ground in tents and had ridden on the ten-day pack trip in the Wyoming backcountry. The newlyweds planned to arrive August 8 and stay for two weeks.

Ernest wrote to "Orny" telling him not to worry about leaders— Ernest had plenty—and he also had a couple of rods they were welcome to borrow. But in case Bill wanted to buy a rod, Ernest enclosed a page torn from a catalog with a couple recommendations circled, saying it all depended on whether Bill wanted to spend the jack.

He also asked if Bill would be bringing whiskey. If not, they could buy it at the ranch, which had bootlegger connections in Red Lodge. And wouldn't it be great to be sitting on the porch drinking a cocktail after a fine day in the forest or the river? Ernest closed by giving the old "Article" his best, and sent love to Bunny from Pauline and him, sign-ing the letter "Steen," short for one of his nicknames, "Hemingsteen."

LIBEL ACTION

ERNEST TOOK TIME OUT of his writing schedule, something he was loath to do, to review the proofs for *In Our Time*, and he still found problems with Scribner's plan to reissue the book. Ernest wrote to Max, telling him his concerns. He had tried rewriting "Up in Michigan" to keep it from being libelous, but it took all the story's character away. Yet to publish it as it currently was could lead to a lawsuit from the real people depicted as characters in the story. The book would need to include a disclaimer that this story was not based on any living person.

The next matter was the book's introduction, which the publisher insisted on adding. Ernest suggested that the critic Edmund "Bunny" Wilson write it. Although Ernest despised most critics, he had appreciated Wilson's review of *The Sun Also Rises* and thought Wilson seemed decent enough. Ernest felt that *In Our Time* was a hell of a good book—it had been his first book and had a limited distribution in Paris, and he liked the idea of making it available to people who had read his other work. With a good introduction and a disclaimer, it should be ready.

Before ending his letter to Max, he reported that he'd worked six days every week on his new bullfighting book and had written sixty thousand words. Also, he had six cases of beer—enough to finish six more chapters. Ernest told Max he was sorry for sounding rude and that Max should not take it personally. It was just that when he was working hard and received a letter about a problem, it interrupted his concentration.

THE MAN WHO INVENTED MONTANA

BUNNY AND BILL took the train from Chicago, then boarded a bus and rode across the east half of Yellowstone National Park to Cooke City, Montana, arriving on August 8. A group of riders met them with mounts, and Ernest rode up on a big steed, "straight legged, Indian-fashion because of his gimpy knee" from his war injuries. According to Bill, "He looked like the man who invented Montana."

The group rode nine miles south down a valley, past Index and Pilot Peaks, to where the land rose above Clarks Fork into steep hills with narrow stretches of forest. In the distance, they saw ridges of Beartooth Buttes, fifteen miles to the east. It was just before dusk when the group got to the ranch.

The Hornes had arrived during a rainy spell; it had been raining for days, with cloudbursts putting the river "on the bum," for a week—the trout hid behind the rocks. Pauline entertained the couple with other activities until the streams cleared, while Ernest continued to work on his book and correspond with Max about *In Our Time*.

When the rain finally stopped, the fishing was glorious; Bill had never met such trout fishing. The fish were so hungry that many times the fishing party hooked two on at once, and occasionally three. The group caught more than a hundred fish. Most were returned to the stream, but some were eaten at dinner at the ranch house, or for breakfast in the cabin, with Ernest cooking them with salt, pepper, and lemon on the little stove.

Bill admired Ernest's dedication to writing the new bullfighting book. One day they had been at a spot where "the river was about to dive down into a canyon and become inaccessible. It was fast, beautiful water full of trout, the kind of thing an avid fisherman would sell his soul for." Yet while the group fished, "Ernest sat in the sun in an old rocker reading about Corridas." Ernest's trunk of Spanish bullfighting periodicals and books from Uncle Gus, along with materials Ernest had collected on his trips to Spain, had arrived.

One day, when fishing hadn't been good, Ernest had taken Bill on an adventure to check on bear bait that he and Ivan Wallace had set to catch a bear in the valley. Ranchers had complained that a bear had been coming down from the mountains and eating their cattle.

Ernest told Bill that he and Ivan had ridden up Index Peak to search for the perfect spot for the bait. They found a clearing along a fast-moving stream that would take a grizzly more than a few seconds to cross. Rocks and trees created a natural blind and offered hiding places for the men as they waited for the bear. For bait, they had shot a horse and set fire to it, creating a terrible stench. When the horse was cooked about halfway, they put out the fire and rode back to the ranch. It would take about a week for grizzlies to discover the carcass and watch it, making sure there weren't hunters nearby, before they feasted on it.

Bill rode up with Ernest to check on it, but the bait was still intact.

THE COW-EATING BEAR

AUGUST WAS AN UNUSUAL TIME of year for a bear to come down from the mountains and kill cattle—twenty head had been lost. The ranchers wanted it stopped, and recognized it was a job for a professional; that's why they'd hired Ivan Wallace. In addition to being the L Bar T wrangler, Ivan was a well-respected hunter and trapper, so they enlisted him to set the bait for the bear on Index Peak.

The day after Bill and Bunny returned home to Chicago, Ernest gladly paused work on his bullfighting book to ride with Ivan up Index Peak to check on the bait again. His horse Goofy was loaded down with food, raincoats, binoculars, and Ernest's precious new Springfield rifle, strapped in a scabbard.

One lucky day the previous year he'd been in the elevator of Abercrombie & Fitch in New York City when he ran into Milford Baker, a buddy from his Italian Red Cross ambulance driver days. They reconnected over their love of guns, and Milford turned out to be extremely knowledgeable—he offered to help Ernest order a custom-made Springfield rifle. They had written nine letters back and forth about the gun, with many personal details and measurements going into making it the perfect gun for Ernest, and in June, six months later, Ernest received it, calling it an absolutely splendid rifle. It was love at first sight.

Ernest bragged to friends that it was the most beautiful gun he'd ever seen and that it didn't have a kick. He sounded like a Springfield advertisement, saying he'd never seen a classier gun in his life and it could be used for "everything but shooting elephants." He would need to order another gun to take with him on safari in Africa for those conditions.

The only thing was its weight. At nine pounds it was too heavy to lug up a mountain. Ernest had spotted bighorn sheep on the mountainside with a scope from the ranch as he awaited the season opening on September 15 and wrote to Milford about ordering another lighter gun, perhaps a 6.5-mm Mannlicher, to use when he climbed. Would it be possible to get it in time for bighorn sheep season? In the meantime, he'd bring the Springfield on his saddle to hunt bears.

As Ivan and Ernest made their way up the mountain, something spooked Goofy; the horse bolted into the dense forest with Ernest holding on for dear life, afraid to bail off the horse in "fear of busting or losing" his gun. He stayed on the mare too long, and a sharp tree branch sliced his chin below the lip. Luckily the gun survived without damage, but Ernest didn't fare as well, with a gash that wouldn't stop bleeding. The men headed down the mountain to get Ernest to the doctor.

They rode to the Crandall Ranger Station, where the forest ranger agreed to have his daughter Velma Williams drive them to a doctor in Cody. The road was more of a mule trail than a passage for cars—narrow, steep, and winding as it traversed Sunlight Basin and Dead Indian Pass. It took them three hours to reach town, and they arrived at midnight.

Cody, Wyoming, was a Wild West outpost, the creation of Buffalo Bill Cody in 1896. Recognizing the money to be made, Cody had sat on a hill and seen the perfect spot for a new town that the railroad could go through, taking passengers to Yellowstone. When Ernest and Ivan rolled into town, the only doctor they could locate, Dr. Trueblood, was a veterinarian turned physician. He wanted to knock Ernest out with anesthesia before suturing the wound, but Ernest wouldn't have that; he insisted on using whiskey for an anesthetic.

Rejecting the doctor's offer of bootleg whiskey, Ernest convinced him to write a prescription for two bottles of Old Oscar Pepper, a Kentucky bourbon that during Prohibition was available only for medicinal purposes. After Ernest was stitched back up, the ranger's daughter drove, while the two men drank Ernest's medicine. She had to regularly stop to open and pass through cattle gates, and at each of these stops Ernest and Ivan would take another pull from the Old Oscar Pepper, feeling no pain by the time they arrived back at the ranch.

The *Cody Enterprise* ran a story about his visit:

> Ernest Hemingway was brought to Cody on Tuesday evening to receive surgical attention caused by an accident that afternoon when a horse bolted with him, carrying him through some heavy brush and tearing his face in such a manner as to require several stitches to patch up the wounds. Mr. Hemingway is a prominent author and writer of Chicago and Paris. He was driven to town by Miss Velma Williams.

The men slept off their bender, arising late the next morning and heading back up to the bear bait, hiding in the nearby blind. Ernest told Ivan stories as they waited—about Italy and driving an ambulance in the Great War, about the bombs exploding and the mud splashing him in the face, and about the nurse he met after he was wounded and how they fell in love—stories that he'd included in his book *A Farewell to Arms*.

"I haven't read any of your books," Ivan told Ernest.

"We get along pretty good—and by not reading anything I wrote, we can keep it that way," Ernest replied.

Their conversations would be followed by long periods of silence when Ernest would scratch notes into the tablet he'd brought along to capture the sights and sounds of the land.

Just after sunset, as Ernest watched the bait, a brown-colored black bear ambled out of the woods to feed on the carcass. Ernest's heart was pounding when he shot the old male from eighty-five yards. It was so dark he could hardly see. He killed the bear with two shots: the first shot, through the ribs, knocked it down and the second, through the shoulder, killed it instantly. It was Ernest's first bear.

The next day, upon returning to the L Bar T, Ernest approached Lawrence Nordquist about buying Goofy.

"If you want a good saddle horse, I can supply a much better one," Lawrence said.

"I don't want to ride him," Ernest said. "I want to shoot him for bear bait."

Sparing Goofy, at least for a time, Ernest shot a second bear on August 30 from one hundred yards, killing it instantly with a bullet through the neck.

Ernest's chin hadn't healed properly, so he had to return to Cody to have it restitched. Before leaving, he stopped at the corral and ripped two long strings of hair from Goofy's hide. When he arrived at the doctor's office, he told him he'd like his chin sewn up with the horse hair.

BIG GAME HUNTER

IN EARLY SEPTEMBER there was snow on the hills when Ernest implored his friends Mike Strater and Archie MacLeish to come to the L Bar T and hunt with him. Pauline and Jack would be leaving on September 13 for Jack's return to Paris at the start of the school year; Ernest would be alone on the ranch through October. His letters sounded like missives from the Wyoming Tourism Board, guaranteeing they'd get shots at elk, deer, and bighorn sheep, in addition to the world-class rainbow trout fishing. Lawrence Nordquist charged twenty-five dollars a day to guide two people into the backcountry, and a sixty-dollar license allowed for one elk, one deer, bear, game birds, and loads of trout. A license for bighorn sheep cost fifteen dollars extra.

Ernest planned to go to Africa in the spring, financed by Uncle Gus, who'd offered to stake Ernest and three friends. The two men had hatched the idea when they'd traveled together to Berlin last year. Ernest had invited Charles Thompson, Mike Strater, and Archie MacLeish to join him on safari.

As he lauded Wyoming's beautiful country, he also told his friends that it was home to the only dangerous animal in North America—the grizzly—and shooting it would be great training for Africa.

Ernest was also still arguing with Max, who didn't seem to understand how to get mail to him, over the publication of *In Our Time*. On September 3 he received a letter from Max dated August 18. It had been delayed because it had been sent to Painter instead of Cooke City, despite

Ernest's instruction about where to send his mail. Max was still stuck on the subject of additional material for the new printing.

Ernest replied that he felt he had accommodated Max's wish by including a revised version of "Mr. and Mrs. Elliot," originally titled "Mr. and Mrs. Smith,"* which Pauline was currently typing, and he promised to send Max the manuscript the next day if possible. But he didn't see how he could put in additional material. Plus, he was still worried about libel.

He set the letter aside that morning and came back to it later, writing in black ink. He hadn't had trouble with libel when the book was previously published, but its press run had been limited. In his view, it just wasn't worth the risk; if Scribner's must bring it out again, they do so at their own risk. This book was interrupting his focus on his bullfighting book, and it was all "skinning dead horses" to him.

Another concern about the "additional material" Scribner's was asking for: Ernest did not want to trick readers into thinking they were buying a book with new material by the author when they were not. And he had recommended Bunny Wilson to write the introduction if there really needed to be an introduction, and Max still hadn't told him if Wilson had agreed.

That night, before sending the letter, Ernest added more thoughts in pencil around the left, top, and right margins, like little animal tracks around a watering hole. He admitted to Max that he was "smashed up" from an accident, with a six-inch gash in his jaw. Still, Ernest wrote, he'd never been healthier or in better shape in his life.

---

* "Mr. and Mrs. Elliot" was restored to its original form as it appeared in the Autumn–Winter 1924–1925 Little Review. *Letters, Vol. 4,* 357n2.

GIRL FRIDAY

PAULINE WAS WRAPPING UP her last two weeks at the ranch as she typed up Ernest's short story "Mr. and Mrs. Elliot." It had been a wonderful summer, with time for herself when she wasn't acting as Ernest's editor and secretary. However, Jack needed to get back home to Paris for school, so they would soon need to return to Piggott to pick up Henriette and then continue to New York, where Henriette and Jack would board the ship.

Pauline would see Patrick only briefly while in Piggott, but after she dropped off Jack and Henriette, she'd return and become reacquainted with her son while they waited for Ernest to pick them up on the first of November. She looked forward to going back to Key West for some happy home life this winter.

Pauline had signed up for a marriage where Ernest's needs came first, and he expected her to be with him. There were times she had to choose between being a mother or a wife, something her family didn't understand.

But as much as Ernest sometimes acted like a disinterested father, Pauline had observed a touching scene one night while they sat at the lodge with a group of friends at Jack's bedtime. It was dark outside, and their cabin was the farthest from the lodge. Everyone knew Jack was afraid to cross the ranch alone at night, but they didn't want to embarrass him. All of a sudden Ernest jumped up.

"Damn," he said. "I forgot something at the cabin. I'll have to walk back with you, Bumby."

At the ranch, as Pauline made preparations to leave, she felt it was time for her and Ernest to update their wills. They had become friends with the Sidleys—Jack's friend Billy's parents—and William Pratt Sidley happened to be a Chicago lawyer. The will was witnessed by his wife, Elaine Dupee Sidley, and Lawrence Nordquist on September 13, 1930, naming William P. Sidley as Pauline's successor if she was unable to act as executrix. Before she left the ranch, they signed their new wills, leaving everything to each other, and then to the two boys.

Surely the need she had felt to update their wills was nothing more than being responsible parents. But the women in her family had been known to have "the gift," possessing clairvoyant powers, and once, in Paris, Pauline had demonstrated hers. She and Ernest had been sitting at a café and when a man walked up to their table, she had blurted out, "You're dead!" startling the man. Later that same day while crossing the street, he was hit by a car and died. Was the need she felt to write their wills a premonition?

She would be saying goodbye to Ernest for over a month while he stayed at the ranch to hunt. At least while she was away, she wouldn't worry about him getting in trouble at the secluded ranch miles away from civilization.

HIS TURN

JACK HAD WATCHED his father all summer from the sidelines, learning about casting and playing fish—not rushing a fish but not playing it too long either. He'd learned how to clean fish, and to place fish in a creel on fresh leaves, keeping them damp and cool. He'd even learned how to cook a fish; his father suggested leaving the lungs inside for better flavor and cooking it with salt, pepper, and lemon. But he still hadn't actually gone fishing. Jack could hardly wait for his turn to throw a line in the water. He was determined to catch a real fish.

On one of their last days on the ranch, Pauline invited Jack to go fishing with her outfit. He was given a rod with a six-foot leader and a grasshopper for bait. He had cast the wriggling grasshopper in the swirling back eddies and was waiting to see what happened when the line was suddenly pulled underwater. He felt a tug and gave a strong yank—his rod bent, and he felt a fish fighting to get away. Using the skills he'd observed while watching his father, Jack miraculously landed an eleven-inch rainbow cutthroat. It looked enormous compared to the minnows he'd caught in France, a reward for his patience all summer.

He ate every bit of his fish for supper at the ranch house that night amid much fuss. It was the perfect way to end his summer at the L Bar T, and it planted the seed for his obsession to become a fly-fisherman.

SNOW LIKE CHRISTMAS MORNING

ERNEST AND LAWRENCE NORDQUIST headed into the high mountains during a snowstorm, a two-day ride ahead of them to reach their hunting territory. High above the timber, on their first day of hunting, Ernest spied a group of sheep above timberline through the binoculars—standing out as four white spots due to the coloring on their rumps. The country was rough and rocky, the wind blew in hellacious gales, and there was nowhere to take cover.

To reach the herd, Ernest hiked around the mountain peak, then crawled on his belly to get a closer look. The group included an old ram with a beautiful head, and when Ernest was close enough for a good shot, he fired, dropping the ram to the ground.

The other sheep seemed puzzled, not understanding what had happened, and came over to see why the old ram wasn't running. They stayed there near him, not sure what to do, since their boss wasn't moving. Ernest could have shot all three.

From the size of the ram's horns, Ernest and Lawrence estimated it to be thirteen years old, very old for a sheep. They butchered him and appreciated his fine trophy head.

With the sheep bagged, the men headed lower on the mountain to hunt elk in thick timber. The elk weren't bugling yet, so it was hard to find them, but finally one afternoon they came across a bull and twelve cows hiding in the dense forest. When the herd emerged from the trees,

Ernest shot the bull with six points on each of its antlers, another fine trophy mount. He planned to send some of the elk meat to Bunny and Bill Horne if the weather stayed cold enough to ship it.

Ernest had ordered the 6.5-mm Mannlicher rifle with Milford Baker's help, but it didn't arrive before he left for camp. One day, one of the ranch hands made the two-day ride up to the camp to deliver Ernest's new gun to him along with his mail. Although Ernest had already taken his ram, he was delighted to get the new gun and do some practice shooting at a blue jay and a camp robber high in the top of a spruce.* The gun was very handsome, and it shot beautifully with both iron sights and scope.

It had been a successful hunt, and Ernest thought this country was wonderful. Game hunting was some of the best fun he had ever had. By the time he and Lawrence rode back to the ranch on September 28, they had spotted two grizzlies, a gray wolf, and two eagles.

---

* Camp robbers are several species of jays known for their fearlessness around humans to steal food from camps.

MAIL CALL

WHEN ERNEST RETURNED to the L Bar T, a stack of mail was waiting for him, including several letters and a wire from Max. It seemed that Max had sent the wire—and the mail—to the wrong address again. It must seem impossible for someone in New York City to understand that mail was only delivered once a week, shuttled from a town fourteen miles away. Although Ernest enjoyed the solitary life on the ranch without much communication to the outside world, it did add an extra layer of complications when there were weeklong lags between letters, and Max was trying to get Ernest's book ready to go to the printer on October 24.

Ernest was happy to learn from Max, at last, that Bunny Wilson had agreed to write the introduction for *In Our Time*. In his response to Max, Ernest inquired about the dramatization of *A Farewell to Arms*. After selling the rights, Ernest hadn't heard a word about the play. Had it been successful on Broadway? He told Max to let him know what had happened to the play.

He was on page 200 of the bullfighting book, he wrote, but he needed to go to Spain for the illustrations; unless he stopped in Spain en route to Africa next spring, the book might not be ready to bring out in 1931. Ernest hoped to have the first draft written by Christmas, and he thought it would be a damned fine book. He signed off, "Best to you always—Ernest."

ON STAGE AND SCREEN

ERNEST HADN'T HEARD from Pauline since she left Piggott for New York with Jack and Henriette on September 27. He wrote to Archie on October 6, and again on October 12, wondering if Archie might have seen her when she was in New York taking Jack to the ship.

At last, news about the play arrived, but it hadn't come from Max—it came from Milford Baker, who told him he had seen the play, and it had been "an awful mess." Ernest thanked Milford for being so frank and explained that he hadn't been involved in the production; his agent had sold the rights and he hadn't even read the script.

Despite the bad news about the play, good news arrived that Paramount was offering $80,000 to purchase the film rights for *A Farewell to Arms*. Matthew Herold, Pauline's cousin (and former fiancé) and also the Hemingways' attorney, was working on the legal details and sent Ernest a contract to sign and have notarized. Ernest explained there was not a notary anywhere near the ranch, and due to two weeks of rain the road was now impassable. He strongly urged that Paramount would need to accept his power of attorney signature.

After commissions to his agent and the producers, Ernest would get a cut of about $26,000—money he planned to start saving for his *own* family. His mother seemed to think he was made of money—she mistakenly thought he was getting rich from the Broadway play—and that he should be sending her more to help out. But he made clear it was time for him to start thinking of his family's future.

Ernest caught up on correspondence and worked on his book as he waited for the next hunting trip, this time with John Dos Passos. Ernest had written to Dos shortly after arriving at the ranch, extolling the virtues of the wild Wyoming country he'd discovered. When he made a new discovery about a new sport or a new place, he became evangelical, spreading the word. And, after all, Dos originally introduced Ernest to Key West.

Good ol' Dos had agreed to take the train out West and go hunting with Ernest in the high country. Although he couldn't see worth a damn and was not in good physical shape, Dos was always willing for an adventure. Dos would arrive in mid-October and meet Ernest for the end of hunting season.

DOS PASSOS
IN THE HIGH COUNTRY

WHILE HIS WIFE, Katy, stayed with relatives, Dos traveled to Billings, Montana, on October 21, 1930, where Ernest met him at the train. Dos wasn't surprised to see a new scar on Ernest's face in addition to the horseshoe-shaped scar on his forehead. He knew that as much as Ernest was a tough guy, he was also accident prone.

Although Dos was not a natural athlete like Ernest, or a hunter, he was happy to accompany his friend in a land he'd never seen before. They left the ranch on pack mules, flanking the edge of Yellowstone National Park. The elk, with their keen sense of smell, kept getting wind of the men and bolting into the park, where they were safe.

Unable to shoot well because of his nearsightedness, Dos occupied himself by taking in the scenery—bears, beavers in a pond—while "watching Hem as a hunter." Ernest could almost smell an elk before the elk smelled him. And he understood the topography like a great military tactician, knowing what land in the next valley would be like before his horse made his way to the top of the rim rock.

The hills were dotted with illegal stills, and mules were used to lug the illicit hooch from Montana into Wyoming, so the men did not lack for booze. They feasted on venison and elk steaks washed down with bootleg wine and whiskey hauled from Red Lodge through the Beartooth Gap.

On October 28 they rode forty miles back to the ranch to start packing for the trip back home. Their route would take them to Billings,

125

where Ernest would drop Dos at the train, before continuing to Sheridan, Kansas City, and Piggott. A wrangler at the ranch, Floyd Allington, was going to join them, heading back to Florida with Ernest to do some fishing.

LEAVE-TAKING

ERNEST TACKLED HIS PILE of mail before leaving the ranch, writing letters to Max, fellow writer Ford Madox Ford, translator Samuel Putnam, *Cosmopolitan* magazine editor Ray Long, and Caresse Crosby, who with her husband Harry had published some of Ernest's early works in Paris through their Black Sun Press.

Although the country was beautiful in the fall, winter would be coming soon and it was time to leave. He had logged ninety-two trout and shot two bears, a bull elk, and the old ram. He was on page 280, nearly done with his book, with plans to finish the last two chapters and the four appendices by Christmas.

On October 31 he packed up the Ford with fishing gear, rifles, sleeping bags, and a bottle of bootleg bourbon and headed out. Ernest was the driver, with Dos in the front seat and Floyd in the rumble seat. They spent the first night camping at Mammoth Hot Springs in Yellowstone, got up, shook the frost off their sleeping bags, and then set off for Billings.

It was just after sundown near Billings, and Ernest was driving when suddenly an oncoming car pulled out of its lane to pass without enough room. Ernest swerved to avoid a collision, rolling the roadster in a ditch. Floyd and Dos managed to climb out of the wreckage and extracted Ernest, who was pinned behind the wheel, his right arm badly injured. The men flagged down a passing motorist, who gave them a ride to Saint Vincent Hospital in Billings.

ADMITTANCE CLERK

WHEN THREE SCRUFFY-LOOKING MEN in dirty dungarees came into Saint Vincent's emergency room, the admittance nurse sized them up as cowboys.

"Occupation?" she asked as she filled out paperwork.

Ernest, in pain, clenched his shirt cuff in his teeth in an attempt to support his injured arm, mumbling when he spoke. "Writer," Ernest said.

She wrote "rider," as in bronc or bull rider.

Dos was uninjured, but Floyd had suffered a dislocated shoulder and Ernest's right arm was badly broken, an oblique spiral fracture above his elbow. He was admitted into the hospital for surgery, but it wasn't until the next day that the doctor came in to check on the patient and recognized Ernest Hemingway the *writer*, not rider.

It may have been headlights blinding Ernest that caused the accident, or it may have been the sun setting and the light hitting him right in the eyes—or, as Dos mentioned, it may have been the bootleg bourbon they'd been drinking. (Since they didn't want trouble over the illegal bourbon, they had quickly disposed of the evidence.) Dos telegraphed Pauline in Arkansas about the accident, and she boarded the next train to Billings.

SOS MAX

PLEASE FORWARD ALL MAIL FOR TEN DAYS SAINTVINCENTS HOSPITAL BIL-
LINGS MONTANA GETTING ALONG ALL RIGHT MAY BE HERE THREE WEEKS =
ERNEST.

PAULINE TAKES DICTATION

PAULINE HAD BARELY returned from New York to Piggott when Dos's telegram came. She went into action, arranging for Patrick to continue to stay with her family while she caught the next train to Billings. Dos met her at the depot in the repaired Ford—it had received only minor damage when it flipped, with two sprung doors and some scratches. When she arrived at Ernest's room, she found him heavily sedated with morphine and in great pain. But he would live, thank God. There was no need right now for the wills they had drawn up at the Nordquist Ranch.

After four days of unsuccessful attempts to maneuver the bones back into place, Ernest's physician, Dr. Louis Allard, determined that Ernest needed surgery. Ernest's luck prevailed when he got Dr. Allard for his doctor—Allard was a nationally known expert on orthopedic surgery.

On November 6, Dr. Allard operated on Ernest for two hours, setting his arm three times. Allard notched the bone, boring a hole through one side, then tied it together with kangaroo tendons. When Ernest heard about the kangaroo tendons, he made many jokes to his friends about his boxing ability improving.

He was required to keep his arm immobilized for the next couple weeks, and Pauline stayed by his side, attending to his needs, trying to make him comfortable. It was hard on her to see him in such pain.

When Ernest started feeling better, he wanted to catch up on correspondence, so Pauline rented a three-dollar-a-month noiseless typewriter and took dictation—something Ernest wasn't used to and didn't enjoy, preferring to write his own letters. For now it was the only option he had. Jacked up on morphine, he dictated a letter to Mike Strater.

He explained to Mike about his current condition, and that Pauline was doing fine and was typing the letter. She was finding the correspondence somewhat interesting until he got on the subject of guns. Pauline typed pages as Ernest expounded on the type of guns they would need for their African safari. Apparently, Charles Thompson had received a gun he'd also ordered from Milford Baker, but his gun wasn't sighted properly, and Ernest warned Mike not to judge a gun until it has been properly sighted. He reminded Mike that a man shoots best after practicing; it was like hours in the air, or the number of tarpon caught, or anything like that. Confidence at close range only comes with lots of shooting. Ernest recommended the merits of the old .30-30 Winchester for quick running shots and the lighter 6.5-mm Mannlicher for long-range shots. He continued by sharing a recap of his own shooting experience at the ranch with the Springfield and the Mannlicher, which had no kick. He'd shot the heads off numerous grouse. Ernest hoped the accident and his busted arm wouldn't postpone their safari another year, but if it did, they'd have more time to practice shooting.

On November 17, Pauline typed a letter from Ernest to Max, providing the details of the accident. Then Ernest offered an idea: "Why don't you have Scribner's insure me against accident and disease? I believe there would be big money in it. It might pay better than publishing my books. Since I have been under contract to you, I have had anthrax, cut my right eyeball, congestion of the kidney, cut index finger, forehead gashed, cheek torn open, branch ran through leg, and now this arm. However, on the other hand, during this whole period I have never been constipated."

Before the accident, Ernest had been on page 285 and confident of finishing it before Christmas. Now, he did not know when he'd have the use of his arm back, but he vowed to Max that even if he had to learn to write with his left hand or his big toe he could outwrite any writer who had hoped to see him put out of business. In the meantime, he would rely on Pauline to take dictation. He told Max, "It is fine to have Pauline here, but outside of that life is pretty dull."

For Pauline, though, it was hard to see Ernest suffering like this. She prayed his arm would heal well and soon they could return to Key West for his recovery.

NO MORE GUNS

After typing Ernest's last morphine-fueled diatribe about guns to Mike, Pauline had put her foot down: no more guns. So instead, in his next letter to Mike, Ernest rambled about the snuff racket (Mike's family had an interest in Burley's Tobacco), fishing for tuna, and a new fourteen-foot salmon rod he'd ordered.

Ernest's arm had been hurting like hell, and he complained about Max, whom Mike also had become friendly with. Even though Ernest wired Max on November 14, asking him to send *The Adventures of Ephraim Tutt* by Arthur Train and *Two Years* by Liam O'Flaherty, he hadn't received them.

Ernest said Max's office had a way of sending his mail to "any former address" he'd had instead of the current one. And he had yet to see the new edition of *In Our Time* published last month. Ernest wondered if Max was worried that he wouldn't like what Bunny Wilson had written. Ernest sarcastically complained that he might need to switch publishers if he could find one that could manage to send his mail to the correct address. He was upset about the whole business.

When Ernest finally received the copy of *In Our Time*, with the introduction by Wilson, he was not happy. Could this have been why Max delayed to send him a copy of the published book? Max had known that the only reason Ernest had wanted an introduction in the first place was for clarity—he wanted readers to understand that they were buying a previously published book, not a new creation. And Wilson was the only critic whom Ernest respected, so he had trusted him to write the introduction. Ernest had not even requested to see it before it went into print.

After receiving the copy of *In Our Time*, Ernest saw that Bunny had taken it upon himself to write a piece of criticism that included negative comments about the genesis of poetry by Ezra Pound and Dorothy Parker, both friends of Ernest's, not to mention criticizing "the romantic" ending of *A Farewell to Arms*.

Ernest had come to believe Max had double-crossed him with Bunny on the *In Our Time* introduction, that Max had erroneously thought that Ernest would be okay with someone in his own book making Ernest out as a "faking romanticist."

Maybe it was the result of the morphine, but he lay awake at night thinking about it.

A ROTTEN TIME

PAULINE ADMIRED ERNEST'S BRAVERY; she knew he was in pain and that dictating letters was a good way to occupy his time. But sometimes when Pauline was typing Ernest's letters, she would add a note of her own. On Ernest's letter to Max, she added a note to Max in pen, telling him that it was sad to see Ernest in such bad shape, in pain all the time for a month, and not sleeping at night. She encouraged Max to write Ernest letters; mail helped break up the hospital monotony.

Pauline had grown bored of typing, so when Ernest began a crazy letter to their poet friend Archie about their postponed trip to Africa, as well as other trips to Antibes and Cannes and Bordighera, she took creative liberties with the format as she typed:

> The lines
> of motors were as tightly
> packed as Fifth Avenue.
> You couldn't have thrown
> a stone in any direction
> without knocking out a . . .

She entertained herself by typing Ernest's words so they looked like poetry on the page. The letter to Archie concluded with:

> Well. Mac, I feel I've abused Pauline enough
> at pounding this mill, although she has been

trying to amuse herself by typing it very fancy,
and I hope you will show it to Mrs. M. as an

example of what a good wife can do in case you
should ever become an ex-writer like Papa.

Write to Piggott and see if you get Dotty to
write to Piggott, too. Give my best to Benchley
       and my love to
       Mrs. MacLeish and Mimi

When Ernest looked at the final letter, he objected to her fancy typing, so Pauline added a note asking Archie to imagine that it was just ordinary typing, and she promised not to do it again.

MONTANA
IN THE REARVIEW MIRROR

ON DECEMBER 18, 1930, Ernest sent Max a cable asking him to forward mail to Piggott. He hoped they would be leaving Montana in a few days.

Part III

1932

What Ernest Loved About Pauline

Keen editorial eye
Her family became his family: Jinny, Mother Pfeiffer
Uncle Gus's support
Strong again
Lovely figure again after Gregory's birth
"Someone to feel swell with" after a day's work
The "feeling of us against the others"
Willing to join him on adventures
Believed in the "promotion of masculine society"
Never worried like other wives
Vowed to always let him have his way
~~She could give him "little Pilar"~~
~~Her throat never got sore like his~~
~~Spontaneous lovemaking~~

RECOVERY

IT WAS HARD for Pauline to relax when she worried that she was pregnant again. The Sidley cabin was lovely, with its large living room and river rock fireplace, and space for Ernest to set up an office. But she was preoccupied with the fact that she had missed her cycle. The doctor had told her after Gregory was born on November 5, 1931, if she got pregnant again she would be putting her life in danger. She and Ernest had followed the calendar, being very careful, but perhaps their methods weren't foolproof. Ernest was worried too.

Perched on a hilltop at the L Bar T Ranch, the Sidley cabin was more spacious than the little double cabin they'd rented two years earlier with Jack, and it had a wide front porch providing a perfect vantage point for enjoying the distant peaks and river below. The Sidleys had offered their own cabin to the Hemingways out of gratitude for Pauline saving Elaine Sidley's life.

It had happened in a freak accident when the Sidleys had come to Key West for a visit. Ernest and William Sidley had been offshore fishing while Pauline and Elaine stayed on land, enjoying the Bayview Park pool. Pauline looked up to find Elaine floating facedown in the pool, quickly pulling her from the water and rushing her by ambulance to the hospital where Elaine was revived—then bringing her to the Hemingway home to recover. The Key West newspaper had even written about it: CHICAGO WOMAN DRAGGED UNCONSCIOUS FROM WATER BY MRS. ERNEST HEMINGWAY. The Sidleys insisted that from now on, whenever Ernest and Pauline came to the L Bar T, they would stay in the Sidley cabin.

The Sidley cabin where the Hemingways stayed at the Nordquist Ranch. *Courtesy Bob Richard*

In Key West, in addition to the Sidleys, Pauline and Ernest had entertained many Wyoming acquaintances while Ernest recovered from the car accident. Unable to write, or hold a fishing rod, or shoot a gun, Ernest had craved distractions. Lawrence and Olive Nordquist came for a visit, as did Chub Weaver, who took a break from wrangling on the ranch and had driven their repaired Ford from Billings and stayed to fish.

Ernest's sister Carol, Jinny, Max Perkins, Burge Saunders, and Paris friends John Herrmann, Josie Herbst, and Pat and Maud Morgan had arrived. Even Ernest's mother, Grace, showed up for a brief visit to check on her son and finally meet her grandson Patrick, who was nearly three at the time. Pauline had met Grace only once before, the day on the dock when she'd been pregnant with Patrick. She and Ernest's mother had settled into a comfortable relationship, with Pauline calling her "Mother Grace."

When Ernest could finally write again, six months after the accident, he didn't waste any time before diving into work on the bullfighting book he had titled *Death in the Afternoon*. He needed to go to Spain to gather materials for the book, and a plan had been made for Pauline and Patrick to meet him in Paris a few weeks later. Pauline had been wrapping up details on the purchase of a home they'd bought on Whitehead Street, and she also wanted to talk to Dr. Guffey about her pregnancy before leaving. She was then four months pregnant, had gained seven pounds, and planned to return from Paris to go to Kansas City again for the birth in the fall.

Little Pilar, that's what they'd planned to name their daughter. She had hoped she could give him the girl he wanted. But when their son Gregory Hancock Hemingway was born, Ernest hadn't seemed disappointed, instead proudly bragging about his size and strength.

Gregory had been delivered by caesarean like Patrick, and that's when Dr. Guffey had also delivered the grim news and the reason their current situation was so concerning. Ernest had called Guffey for advice and Pauline had taken the ergoapiol tablets the doctor prescribed to bring on her period; they'd worked in the past, but this time to no avail.

Fresh Wyoming air would be good for Pauline, with a break from her two sons, who were a handful. Thankfully they were staying with their grandparents and Aunt Jinny in Piggott. Ernest had been restless as he finished revising *Death in the Afternoon*. At least he'd be free from the distractions that he'd found in Key West: his new love of "marlin fishing in Havana" and the company of a twenty-three-year-old blonde named Jane Mason.

THE VIEW AHEAD

THE SENTRIES WERE WAITING, Pilot and Index Peaks standing guard over the valley as Ernest steered their new Ford V8 onto the L Bar T Ranch. He breathed it all in—the cool air, the scent of pine trees, the perfect tonic for his health as he continued to recover from bronchial pneumonia. He'd been in Havana in June when the marlin were running, and after fighting a strong one, he'd overheated and then got caught in a freezing squall. The sudden drop in his body's temperature was a recipe for bronchial trouble, and sure enough, it had laid him flat in bed for a week. Even now, nearly three weeks later, he still wasn't feeling like himself.

Worrying about Pauline wasn't helping his mood. Ernest had been extra careful but despite his precautions, she hadn't had her period. He told Dr. Guffey that he worried that "a certain amount of semen gets splattered around," and that his was "very virulent." They wouldn't be in this predicament if they had been allowed to practice birth control, but she wouldn't budge on her Catholic beliefs.

After Gregory's birth, Pauline had stayed in the hospital four weeks, and when she came home the doctor had insisted that she take it easy. They had been moving into their new home on Whitehead Street, with a new nurse from France who had come down with a mysterious ailment and was also in bed. Ernest had to set his own work aside and take care of their entire family plus the nurse while she recovered, just another in the series of setbacks on the book. A busted arm, traveling to Spain for photos, Gregory's birth, moving into a new home, and here he was,

149

eighteen months later, ready to get to work just as soon as Max sent the *Death in the Afternoon* proofs to Wyoming.

The book hadn't turned out to be what he'd originally hoped for—an exhaustive treatise on the sport of bullfighting. Instead it was less far-reaching. Scribner's had reduced the number of photos he could include from two hundred to seventy—but he still felt it could be sold as a classic book on bullfighting. Max read the manuscript in February and told Ernest that he thought it was a grand book, immensely important.

While he'd been in Key West this spring, waiting for Max to send him packages of proofs to edit, he'd started writing stories—they had been pouring out of him. He'd felt like he was in the best shape and he'd never written better. He'd had ten stories ready to go in a book before pneumonia had laid him flat, stories that perhaps were fueled by his new friend Jane Mason.

Ernest needed "new" to write: new experiences like marlin fishing, and new people, like Jane and her husband, Grant. On a lucky day, he'd met them on the *Ile de France* as he and Pauline sailed home from France for Gregory's birth. Jane and Grant lived in Havana, and, more luck, Grant was an executive at Pan Am, traveling the world for his job and leaving Jane home alone at their estate. Jane, with legs that went all the way to her neck, wasn't just damn beautiful; she was an accomplished sportswoman who loved hunting and fishing and was a lot of fun to be around. Pauline got seasick and didn't enjoy deep-sea fishing, plus she now had two boys at home to care for—but Jane had been available. Pauline also enjoyed Jane's company, and the two couples, Jane and Grant, Ernest and Pauline, had even double dated for a night on the town in Havana when Pauline visited.

On the drive to the ranch, Ernest had written to Jane from Scottsbluff, Nebraska, looking for someone to travel back to the States with Bumby in the fall. He knew Jane might be in London then; would she be willing to bring Bumby back with her? He closed by writing, "Take good care of yourself daughter because you are very valuable, Pauline is writing too. Much love and have a grand summer Ernest."

As he waited for the proofs in Wyoming, Ernest intended to fish and enjoy himself as much as possible. A new highway between Red Lodge and Cooke City threatened to destroy this land, his private paradise, as it brought busloads of tourists to the area and drove all the game into the safety of Yellowstone's boundaries. The construction crew had already destroyed one of his favorite fishing holes while digging for gravel and creating a dam that dried up a fork of the river above One Mile Creek.

One morning Ernest stopped at the corral to watch Ivan and Chub saddle horses for a trail ride. Both men had become his good friends. A man of many talents, Chub often accompanied Ernest and Pauline into the backcountry as their camp cook—although Pauline didn't care for him because he called her "Pauline" instead of "Mrs. Hemingway." Ivan finished saddling up Ernest's favorite horse, Old Bess, and handed the reigns to Ernest so he could ride downstream to a fishing hole.

The land surrounding the ranch was the wildest of wild, a geologist's dream, with the same magnificent rock formations found in Yellowstone—canyons, waterfalls, and jagged cliffs. One of the reasons it had remained so primitive, and without development, was because it was so rugged and remote. Now the new road would endanger that.

Ernest looked forward to Africa and the primitive country there, safe from tour buses and dude ranches. The safari had been postponed after his accident, at first rescheduled for this fall. But in the spring, when Ernest had felt the juice again, when the short stories flowed and he felt like he was working too well to leave the country, he postponed it again. Maybe next year instead of coming to Wyoming he'd go to Africa to shoot trophies.

Max had been relieved, wanting him to focus on finishing this book and starting on another one, but Ernest knew his hunting party would be disappointed. He had told Archie the news and he seemed okay with it, but he hadn't told Mike and Charles about it yet.

Since this might be his last summer at the ranch for a while, Ernest intended to enjoy it. He set out fishing with a fervor in the Clarks Fork River and high mountain lakes, sometimes with Pauline, sometimes with the guides, and sometimes alone. By the end of July he had caught one hundred fifty trout.

MOTHERHOOD

PERHAPS IT HAD BEEN CAUSED by stress or maybe the change in altitude, but Pauline's late period finally arrived, bringing a huge relief. She and Ernest would need to be even more careful than they had been in the past.

Motherhood was a merry-go-round of hiring nurses, planning travel schedules, and monitoring the children's activities—you couldn't leave them for one second without them getting into mischief. After Gregory's birth, three-year-old Patrick had tried to kill his brother in his bassinet with ant spray, and then a week later Patrick had eaten rodent poison and thrown up for two days. The house had been in total pandemonium while Pauline was supposed to be recovering in bed.

Dr. Guffey had warned her to stay off her feet for two months after Gregory's birth, but that had proved impossible—they were moving into a new home that Uncle Gus had helped them purchase. When she'd first seen it, she'd called it the haunted house because it was in such disrepair. It had needed extensive work, and when they'd returned home with their new baby, plumbers, electricians, and construction workers needed her supervision as they worked. She was the mother of an infant and a toddler; she managed a staff including a nurse, and then a construction crew, too. It was no surprise that she overexerted herself and landed back in bed at the mercy of Ernest's care.

Caring for others was not Ernest's strength, as she had learned early in their marriage when he'd left Pauline and Patrick alone in Paris, and she'd seen it again in Key West, when he'd been trying to finish the draft of *Death in the Afternoon*. With a baby's cries, a mischievous toddler demanding attention, and workmen hammering away in the background, he'd fled to a hotel room in Havana, ostensibly to chase the marlin, but Pauline wondered if he was chasing something else.

Ernest didn't allow fatherhood to alter his lifestyle at all; he still hunted and fished and traveled with his friends. And he expected Pauline to keep up. She'd seen what happened when Hadley had allowed Ernest to entertain himself: Ernest had met Pauline. Pauline didn't intend for that to happen again. Ernest had to come first.

She was trying to love motherhood, she really was, but domesticity didn't give her the same pleasure that being with her husband did. When he was away—which had been a lot lately—she missed him all the time. When he went to Spain to work on the bullfighting book, she wrote to him, "You are the punctuation and the grammar as well as the exciting story."

At least Pauline had resources to hire a new nurse, Ada, who seemed up to the task. Even Pauline's mother had complimented the way she handled Patrick, who was at an impressionable age; Mary Pfeiffer felt Patrick needed someone who understood him, because he was intelligent beyond his years and he strongly resented wrong treatment. Still, despite Ada's skill with Patrick and Gregory, Pauline's parents didn't understand all the time Ernest and Pauline spent away from the boys when they were so young and needed their parents.

Ernest had been this way with Hadley when Jack was a baby too, demanding that she leave Jack with a nurse so they could travel together alone. Shortly after first meeting Ernest and Hadley, Pauline had joined them for the bullfights in Pamplona, and she recalled Hadley had been sick with longing for her Bumby while he stayed with his nurse.

The time away from his parents hadn't affected Jack; he was a wonderful boy. On their last visit to the ranch, Jack had joined them and had fallen in love with the West, but this summer he was in France with Hadley and Paul Mowrer. Hadley and Paul had been seeing each other since shortly after Ernest's divorce—even though Paul had been married. Ironically, Hadley had found herself in a situation similar to the one Pauline had been in; however, Paul and his wife had been living separate lives for years. Their split was amicable, clearing the way for

Paul and Hadley to be together. Ernest approved of Paul, a journalist he'd known in Paris.

As she watched children playing horse tag and enjoying themselves at the ranch, Pauline thought one day, when Patrick and Gregory were older, they could come to the L Bar T Ranch too. But for now, it was her respite from domesticity, and she intended to enjoy herself.

"HEMINGWAY'S DEATH"

On July 27, when the mail came with a package from Max, Ernest was ready to get to work. However, when he opened it and read the galleys, he nearly fell out of his chair.

There at the top of each proof page, he read the slug line,* "Hemingway's Death." What was Max thinking?

He'd already told him to change it last month in Key West when he'd opened a package from Max and his eyes nearly popped out of his head. Max knew he was superstitious. Ernest could have had a stroke after seeing that—was that what they wanted?

Max had apologized by saying he understood omens, but he hadn't noticed the slug line or he would have changed it. He reminded Ernest that it wasn't personal; they had just followed "the regular rule" for the slug line: the author's name, and then the first important word of the title.

And yet, when the mail truck arrived on July 27, after Max had assured him that he understood Ernest's concern—it was still there! HEMINGWAY'S DEATH.

Irritating Ernest further, Max's letter inside did not answer Ernest's question about "the words." The words, often of the four-letter variety, had caused a fight in both *The Sun Also Rises* and *A Farewell to Arms*. Scribner's had insisted that he remove certain words that might draw the

---

* A slug line is the label at the top of every page, made from the author's last name and the first word of the title of the manuscript.

157

attention of the puritanical tyranny of the Obscenity Act. They were still living in prudish times in the United States, and some writers had seen their books confiscated due to obscenity charges. Scribner's wanted to change some perfectly useful words in *Death in the Afternoon* because the censors were still alive and well, just waiting to swoop down and make problems whenever they found "the words."

Didn't people understand these words were one of Ernest's writing tools that appeared in the dialogue of real people? That was how real people talked. Once, he'd counseled his sister Carol on the effectiveness of swearing, insisting swear words were so much better than slang words; they had staying power in the language, never go out of style, and were extremely useful. People needed to understand that he used certain words because there wasn't a way to avoid them and still convey the same feeling he was trying to give the reader.

Ernest had already toned down the language for *Death in the Afternoon*. If he had included real dialogue from the bullring, the book would never get published. He never used the words gratuitously; he used them sparingly, only when no other word would do. Ernest told Max that if he couldn't print the entire word, he could at least leave the first and last letter of the word. Ernest was exhausted by the fight; he just wanted to get the damn book to the printer.

It had been a wrestling match with Scribner's since he had first sent them the manuscript. They had cut the number of photos from the two hundred he'd wanted—photos that he had traveled through Europe on his own nickel to gather—to sixteen, a ridiculous number. He'd argued that the book needed to be properly illustrated and needed more photos than that, even if he had to use his own money to pay for them. In the end, they had compromised, agreeing to include seventy photos in the book.

Last spring, he'd sent the manuscript to Dos, a writer he trusted and respected, to read. Dos thought it was a good book but told him to cut the shit—where there was too much of Ernest philosophizing—and Ernest was appreciative of his comments, taking out the material Dos objected to. Ernest hoped this book would give him the win that he needed with readers and critics. It had been three years since *A Farewell to Arms* was published, and the public was waiting for more.

Ernest quickly read the proofs and dashed off a reply to Max, asking when he would be sending the rest of the page proofs. Ernest had not yet seen a frontispiece or jacket, and why hadn't Max asked him what title would go on the frontispiece? Ernest finished his letter and put it on the mail truck to Gardiner the next day.

THE FIVE-YEAR ITCH

BLUE WYOMING SKIES without a cloud in sight stretched overhead as Pauline headed out with the guides to a fishing hole, decked out in jeans, boots, a vest, and a bandana. Despite having two children, Pauline was still the same size as when she and Ernest had first met.

Pauline and Ernest had marked their fifth anniversary on May 10. It almost went unnoticed except for a telegram she'd received from their friend Jane Mason congratulating them, and announcing that she was giving them two live pink flamingos for their Key West home as an anniversary gift.

Ernest had started getting restless after five years of marriage to Hadley—the man was always searching for new, and the "new" had been Pauline and their subsequent affair. Now five years later, could he be susceptible to the five-year itch again when he'd left for Havana on a six-day fishing trip in April . . . but stayed two months? Pauline had once been the other woman in Ernest's life; she knew the signs. She planned to keep her husband's interest, quickly getting her shape back again after Gregory's birth, and experimenting with her hairstyle, growing it into a bob and recently dying it blonde like Jane's.

While Ernest was in Havana, Pauline had made several trips to visit him under the guise of bringing things he needed, but it was really to keep an eye on him. Of course, he was charmed by Jane. What man could be immune to her charms? Drop-dead gorgeous, Jane was featured in Pond's Cold Cream advertisements; she was an international debutante who had come out in New York and London, and she was also a tomboy who enjoyed fishing and shooting. Most of all, she flattered Ernest and fed his ego.

Pauline liked Jane well enough, and she didn't have any real proof of an affair. Ernest had written "I love Jane" in the boat's log, but that was probably him just being playful. She chose to believe Jane was just one of Ernest's passing infatuations—she knew that his motives were sometimes those of a writer, studying people, their mannerisms, and their language that he might one day use in his writing.

She would not give him an ultimatum as Hadley had once done; she'd simply wait it out, hoping that this thing, whatever it was, would fizzle out. Maybe Ernest was simply bored. But the opposite was true for Pauline; she loved him more all the time. When she'd been in the hospital recovering from Gregory's birth she'd written, "Lovelier than anyone, and you have made me very happy, and I was never lonely with you and I love you more now than I ever did and always will."

The ranch would be good for them. Here, she had him all to herself— sharing him only with the trout and the elk. Life on the ranch was nearly perfect, but the one thing she truly missed was going to Mass; the nearest Catholic church was two hundred miles away in Powell, Wyoming. She asked Ernest if he'd drive her, and being the dear husband that he was, he agreed to take her to the First Friday service in August.

A PILGRIMAGE TO POWELL

HE'D BEEN IN A FOUL MOOD, with his chest still bothering him from the pneumonia he'd had for more than a month. Scribner's and their modifications to his book weren't helping his temperament, either. But he agreed to drive Pauline four hours to Powell so she could attend Mass; perhaps the change of scenery would do him good. Ernest was a Catholic, just not as observant as Pauline, and he didn't like to have the church in his bed—the church's stance against birth control was seriously affecting their sex life. After the latest pregnancy scare he would need to be extra careful when they made love. It was a lot of pressure on a man who loved his wife and wanted her in his bed. He could kill her if he impregnated her—yet he still wasn't allowed to use birth control.

They drove from the ranch through a changing landscape, at first through mountain country of tightly packed forests opening up to wide panoramic views. When they reached the base of Dead Indian Pass, the land outside Cody changed to sagebrush flats with red colored dirt, buttes in the distance, and plains where wild horses still ran free.

He had packed his rifles to shoot grouse along the way, and although Pauline might not have loved hunting and fishing the way he did, she was a good sport accommodating him. While he was waiting for his arm to heal, he could cast and set the hook, but someone else had to reel in the fish—and Pauline had landed a record sailfish, seven feet, one inch—the Key West newspaper ran the headline MRS. HEMINGWAY IS NEWEST HOLDER OF FISH RECORD HERE.

She was becoming a good rider and a good shot too—maybe not as good as Jane, who had won trophies, but Pauline was getting better all the time. She was even going to join Ernest and Charles Thompson to hunt bighorn sheep on the ranch this fall.

After Mass, on the rough road back to the L Bar T, they experienced a minor problem when they hit a rock and broke the oil pan, requiring them to coast into Cooke City. After four days of hunting, when they returned to the ranch on August 8, they brought back a carload of sage grouse for Olive Nordquist. Ernest thought that it had been some of the best shooting of his life.

FINAL PROOFS

THE FINAL PAGE PROOFS were waiting for him from Max. He sat down and read the whole book, starting at 6:45 AM and finishing at 4:50 PM.

They were wrapping up the last book details. Max had sent the book jacket, and Ernest thought it looked fine, but he hadn't yet received the frontispiece. He told Max the book's dedication would read "To Pauline."

Ernest was ready to get this book to the printer, as he needed the money. Max's prediction that Ernest would be able to triumph over lagging book sales caused by the Great Depression wasn't true—the Depression still held the country in its vice two years after it had begun, and it was affecting sales. Thankfully, he'd received $24,000 from the sale of *A Farewell to Arms* movie rights to Paramount, but that was the last big money he'd made. He still received royalty checks from *A Farewell to Arms*, but it had been three years since it was published, so sales were slower as readers awaited his next book.

Before he caught pneumonia in June, he had been feeling wonderful, like a kid again, writing easily. He told Max that he had three excellent stories to sell him—"Homage to Switzerland," "The Light of the World," and "The Mother of a Queen"—and he'd sell the set for $2,100, which was $9,000 less than what Ernest thought they were worth.

He signed the letter "Yours always Ernest—," and got it ready to put on the mail truck the next day.

NO WORD

ERNEST HADN'T HEARD BACK from Jane whether Bumby could travel back to the States with her, so he wrote to Jane and Grant again at the end of August. He shared details of ranch life, and told them, "Poor Old Papa has a beard you cold hunt a pack of beagles through if there were only rabbits in it. Pauline is in Grand shape, we've had the best summer ever. Haven't heard from Hadley yet about Bumby back. Have a good time and write us, love Ernest." Bumby had called Ernest "Papa" since he was a young boy, and the name had stuck.

Ernest and Hadley had managed to work out an amicable schedule sharing the boy—and when Ernest had been in Paris the previous year, Hadley had even asked Ernest's advice about Paul Mowrer possibly becoming Jack's stepfather. Paul had been a friend of Ernest's when Ernest wrote for the *Toronto Star*, and now Hadley and Paul were talking about marriage. Hadley wanted to first make sure she had Ernest's blessing, since Paul would be an influence in their son's life. Ernest wholeheartedly gave his approval.

At a young age, Jack had become an international traveler, voyaging between France and the United States to be with his mother and father. The Paris winters, however, were hard on him. The damp cold caused bronchitis, and he was susceptible the way Ernest was to sore throats and the grippe. Hadley asked if perhaps Jack could spent the next winter in balmy Key West with Ernest and Pauline, and they gladly agreed.

Ernest had hired his friend Evan Shipman to come to Key West to work as Jack's tutor, so arrangements were falling into place—but the last detail was to find someone to sail from France to New York City with the boy in October. If only he would hear back from Jane.

THE MURPHYS

ERNEST HAD FIRST met Sara and Gerald Murphy in 1925 while living in Paris with Hadley. They were a cosmopolitan couple who loved embarking upon new adventures and meeting new people. Their lives were a nonstop schedule of parties and picnics, painting sets for the ballet in Paris, and hosting guests at "Villa America," their home in the south of France, where they lived *la belle vie*. They traveled with their three wonderful children, Honoria, Baoth, and Patrick; the world was their classroom. Everyone wanted to be the Murphys.

Gerald was a Yale graduate, an accomplished painter, and heir to the Mark Cross company. Tall and slender, he was an Irishman with neatly combed red hair, and somewhat of a dandy, enjoying dressing in clothes ranging from beautiful suits to dramatic capes. When Ernest took him to Pamplona, Gerald wore a pearl gray gabardine suit to the bullfights and was nicknamed "the man in the silver suit." Sara, a natural beauty, attracted the attention of men wherever she went. Ernest was one of her many fans, adoring her personality and direct manner.

The Murphys had introduced Ernest to their interesting friends, including Archie and Ada MacLeish, and Scott and Zelda Fitzgerald. Thanks to them, Ernest and Hadley had found themselves in a privileged circle of expats.

But then in 1929, the Murphys' son Patrick had been diagnosed with tuberculosis, forever changing their lives. Gerald gave up painting on the day they received the diagnosis, never touching a paintbrush again. Despite his fear of germs and hospitals, Ernest had joined Pauline, Jinny, and Dorothy Parker in Patrick's Swiss sanatorium for Christmas that year to try to cheer the poor boy with a merry party. Ernest and Pauline even named their own Patrick in honor of Patrick Murphy.

As Ernest was rounding up friends to join Pauline and him at the L Bar T, the Murphys were on the top of the list. Always game to try new things, they welcomed bringing their children to an unfamiliar land, providing them with new experiences. Honoria, fourteen, and Baoth, eleven, would bring new energy to the ranch while their younger brother Patrick remained at the family's Hook Pond cottage in East Hampton, Long Island, to fight for his strength.

Although Ernest typically didn't enjoy children until they were old enough to communicate, he had instantly liked the Murphy children upon meeting them years ago. He had once hoped for a daughter of his own, but with Gregory's birth and the doctor's instructions that Pauline could not survive another pregnancy, that was not to be. Instead, Ernest had found himself calling young women he was fond of, like Jane and Honoria, "daughter" as a term of affection.

Ernest and Lawrence Nordquist had been hunting in the high country, and when they returned to the ranch, the Murphys had arrived. The friends had a happy reunion at the ranch, and Chub and Ivan prepared the horses and provisions for a pack trip to Crazy Lakes, where they would fish and camp during the next several weeks.

HONORIA IN LOVE

EACH MORNING AT 5:00 AM, Honoria and Baoth shook off sleep and went with the cowboys to round up horses. At first Honoria worried that a weathered-looking cowboy named Hal was mean, but it turned out he was very kind, teaching her and younger brother Baoth all the words to "Red River Valley," the first song of the American West she'd ever heard.

The Murphys were assigned horses, and Honoria felt sorry for hers because his mane was so tangled. She brushed it for three days until it was "smooth as a girl's hair," then she braided it, an act that amused the hardcore cowboys. She became so horse crazy that her father joked that she might turn into a horse.

The group of six—Sara, Gerald, Honoria, Baoth, Pauline, and Ernest—set out on a pack trip to Crazy Lakes, where Ernest promised "the trout would be plentiful." Nose to butt, their horses made their way on a narrow trail through densely packed forests. Honoria worried that the horses could not fit between the small clumps of pines, but Ernest told her the sure-footed horses knew the mountains.

"Don't be afraid, daughter. You can do it," he assured her.

The riders reached camp in mid-afternoon, and the wranglers unloaded saddle bags, tended horses, pitched tents, and prepared steaks and potatoes for supper. After dinner, the group sat around the fire as Ernest wore a silly Tyrolean hat and told stories about his hunting adventures. As evening set in, Honoria became afraid.

"Will grizzlies come into our camp?"

"There aren't any around," Ernest said. "Only raccoons and rock chucks."

Honoria believed him, and she was no longer afraid.

———————

Ernest had been in Honoria's life since she was seven, and he was one of her favorites of her parents' friends. Goofy and fun to be around, and when he spoke to her and her brothers, he gave them his full attention. The first morning at camp, as the group set out for a day of fishing, Ernest offered to take Honoria with him in a little two-person motorboat. He cut the motor when they reached an area where he thought it might be good fishing.

While Honoria trolled her line behind the boat, Ernest gently rowed.

A tug! Honoria reeled in the line with Ernest's encouragement, landing a large trout that flopped around the boat.

"Watch while I take the hook out of his mouth," Ernest said, holding the fish firmly in his hand while he removed the hook.

Honoria was not interested in the next step—cleaning a dead fish— and when he tried to show her, she waved him away, disgusted.

"Now daughter," Ernest said. "Let's grow calm while I explain to you the beauty of this creature of the water." He taught her about the scales and how to scrape them off, and that fish are clean, eating only things that live in the water.

"Can you see how the inside of its gills look like pink coral? Can you appreciate its beauty? Look at the silver shine of its underbelly and the fine feathery lines of its fins. Don't they look like lace?"

This was only the first catch of the morning—Honoria and Ernest caught many more—but it was the largest catch from their boat. When they reunited with Pauline and the Murphys, they all had caught many trout and were in a happy mood, soon helped along by the whiskey the grown-ups drank.

Chub Weaver was their camp cook, and he fried the trout over an open flame. Honoria thought they tasted unlike any fish she had ever eaten, "sweet like nectar." When Honoria and Baoth were tucked into their tent for the night, they heard Dow-Dow—their pet name for their father—singing as he strolled through the woods. When he heard them laughing, he came to their tent and serenaded them until they fell asleep.

PERFECTION

GERALD MURPHY DID NOT SHARE Honoria's love for the freshly caught trout. In a letter to his friend Archie MacLeish, he complained that "streams are overflowing with trout, some up to two pounds but the fish are adequately and not badly cooked—but somehow neutralized." The local beef proved equally disappointing. Yes, Gerald had been all over the world, and yes, he had eaten many fine meals, but he didn't feel that he had a "jaded palate." He simply felt that the ranch meals were cooked with indifference; the staff simply didn't care.

When Sara dared to complain to Ernest after being served an iceberg lettuce salad with a dollop of mayonnaise and fruit cocktail, Ernest scolded her and accused her of being snooty. Though he usually admired Sara's direct observations, he was upset that Sara had offended the cook.

Still, Gerald thought Ernest's chiding was, in a way, a sign of his affection for Sara. Ernest was never difficult with people he didn't care about. Only the few people that he had admitted into his inner circle were given his attention, "for good or bad." And Gerald felt he was not in the same class of friendship with Ernest; he felt Ernest kept him at a distance. Both Sara and Gerald had noticed a change in their old friend, who seemed more irritable and distant than the Ernest they used to know.

Ernest had shared his world with the Murphys many times. When they'd first met, he invited them to ski at Schruns, where he taught Gerald to ski. (Dos Passos was there too, hopeless because of his bad eyesight, preferring to slide down the mountain on his rear.) He took them to Pamplona, and Gerald had even joined him in the bullring, barely escaping a bull's horn by waving his raincoat. And on the ranch, Ernest had taken Gerald up to check on a dead mule that was being used for bear bait.

In Paris, Ernest had entrusted Gerald and Sara with an advance copy of *The Sun Also Rises*, which they had absolutely loved, recognizing his genius. "My dear boy . . . we love you, we believe in you in all your parts, we believe in what you're doing," Gerald had written. Sara wrote a separate note: "In the end you will probably save us all, by refusing (among other things) to accept any second rate things. Bless you and don't ever budge."

And yet here it seemed he was accepting second-rate things. Gerald was in awe of the Absaroka Mountains and felt the people who lived here "hardly noticed their vast and spectacular surroundings." There were numerous horses to choose from, but they were "most indifferent to ride because nothing has been demanded of them." Gerald's horse was a gelding with thoroughbred blood and sire to four colts on the ranch. One of the colts had been broken the previous year, and Ernest had given it to Pauline. Yet it was only a good horse, not a horse "approaching perfection." In short, nothing on the ranch approached perfection.

Ernest was wonderful with the Murphy children. Gerald appreciated how kind and patient he had been on this trip with Honoria. But it annoyed Gerald to hear Ernest call her "Daughter." That was something that belonged to Gerald—she was his daughter. Besides the nickname his children gave him, Dow-Dow, Gerald had always called himself "Papa" too, and now Gerald noticed Ernest doing the same.

Ernest left the Murphys and Pauline at the ranch while he drove to Cody to pick up Charles Thompson, his Key West friend coming out to hunt. From Cody they would drive to a private pheasant reserve before returning to the L Bar T. Gerald hoped that the pheasants they brought back were tastier than the bland fish and beef they'd been eating.

COUNTING SHEEP

IT WAS TIME for the Murphys to return to New York; they were packing for the trip home when Charles and Ernest arrived at the ranch. Although he'd enjoyed the time with them, Ernest was looking forward to his next adventure. The bighorn sheep season opened on September 15, giving Charles only one day for his sea-level blood to acclimate to the high altitude.

The hunting party of Pauline, Charles, and Ernest headed out, riding straight up the sharp spike of the mountain where Ernest had shot the old ram on his previous trip in 1930. They stalked nineteen sheep over four days; the difficult terrain gave Charles hell as he struggled with the altitude. The ledge work was the "damnedest" Ernest ever saw—you had to be a good climber to get near the sheep. At one point, he had to take off his shoes for about two miles on a rock slide, and he fell nine times. The wind raged above tree line, blowing Pauline's Stetson off her head. And while they found sheep, the animals spooked before the hunters could get close enough for a shot.

Finally, the disappointed and fatigued party headed back down. Ernest felt it was a crime Pauline hadn't gotten a sheep after what she'd been through. She would be returning to Key West soon to work on their new home and await Jack's arrival. Ernest hoped a letter from Jane would be waiting for him at the ranch finalizing the details for Jack's trip.

WOMAN'S WORK

PAULINE EXPERIENCED MANY emotions as she packed up. She'd ridden hard all summer, caught many trout, and hunted bighorn sheep in challenging conditions. And she'd had a lovely time with Ernest. But much work awaited her at their new home on Whitehead Street, which remained a fixer-upper "haunted house."

With Uncle Gus's help, they'd been transforming the rundown house into a grand home. Pauline was supervising the addition of a bathroom in the master suite, removing partitions and plastering walls, and she wanted to get it ready for Ernest's return in a month. Patrick and Gregory would continue to stay in Piggott for the meantime. She'd stop to say hello, but there was no place for a rambunctious toddler and infant in a construction site.

She would be back in Key West in time to meet Jack when he arrived from France, though Ernest still was working on the particulars of his return. Ernest said he would contact Pauline with the details after she reached Key West.

Before leaving, Pauline wrote a note to Max on one of Ernest's letters to him, saying that she and Ernest had enjoyed a superb summer and that Ernest was in "noble" condition, "galloping about on a large black horse with a big black beard." She knew Ernest was in his element out West, playing mountain man—part of the public persona he had created. She, on the other hand, was ready to return to civilization, looking forward to seeing their sons and to creating a nest where her family would all be happy together. But she lamented that she would no longer have Ernest to herself. In Key West and Havana, he had many friends awaiting his return.

REVIEWS

THE DAY AFTER PAULINE LEFT, Ernest and Charles rode thirty-five miles to a cabin at Timber Creek that Chub and Ivan had built to protect hunting parties from cold and snow. While they were hunting, a blizzard struck, and Ernest noticed how, in a snowstorm, there was a white cleanness, and in the peacefulness "It seemed like there were no enemies."*

But Ernest knew that he did have enemies, critics who had it out for him. Despite the storm, Ernest rode back to the ranch to check the reviews of *Death in the Afternoon*, which had been published on September 23. During the ride, he'd spotted a moose in an open meadow, but couldn't shoot it because he didn't have a license. He stopped along the way to shoot six sage grouse. Old Bess trembled and breathed hard through her nostrils when Ernest fired his Colt Woodsman. He brought the sage grouse to Olive at the ranch, made himself a whiskey sour, and sat down to read the reviews.

---

* Hemingway described this 1932 snowstorm years later in *For Whom the Bell Tolls*.

181

AND THE CRITICS SAY . . .

Meh.

DISAPPOINTMENT

THE TWO REVIEWS in the mail were both disappointing. Robert M. Coates, the *New Yorker* critic, wrote in the October 1, 1932, issue calling Ernest out for attacking other writers and for his use of "obscene" language. R. L. Duffus in the *New York Times Book Review* thought Ernest's "style was too dense" and not as good as his previous work.

What had Ernest expected? He had a love-hate relationship with critics, and he had almost dared them not to like this book. Their comments would affect sales when he needed *Death in the Afternoon* to sell well.

In addition to the reviews, he found a letter from Max, who said that although the publishing business was bad, in his opinion, *Death in the Afternoon* was selling well. The reviews were good from a publisher's standpoint, even though Max knew they included commentary that Ernest would hate.

In addition to the reviews, Ernest saw two obstacles standing in the way of this book's success: the Great Depression and Scribner's advertising budget. Published on September 23, 1932, selling for $3.50 per copy, the first printing had consisted of 10,300 copies. Sales had been encouraging, and two weeks later there had been a second printing, with 12,000 copies sold—strongest in cities like New York and Chicago.

But maybe common readers, people who lived in smaller towns across the country, didn't care about bullfighting. One reader wrote a "Letter to the Editor" in the *New York Times Book Review* that included, "I have never so much as seen the cover of one of the 2,000-odd Spanish books and pamphlets on the subject nor after reading the utter maudlin tosh distilled by Mr. Hemingway nor do I desire to do so."

Scribner's editorial staff had created advertising copy they thought would help smooth the way for Ernest's fiction fans to buy a nonfiction book about bullfighting. Ernest had thought their strategy a mistake, asking them to revise the advertising copy to more accurately reflect the book's content. He worried that, as with his past books, Scribner's ramped up advertising before publication and then dropped it, moving on to promoting their next new book.

After reading the reviews, Ernest dashed off a cable to Jane and Hadley, still trying to coordinate Bumby's transport on the *Majestic*. After Gregory's birth the previous December, Hadley had written to him and wished him the merriment of the holidays with "better eyes, more books, and no more infants." With her pending marriage to Paul, she would no longer be his responsibility, but she would always be his friend. She still signed her letters to him with his nickname for her, "Kat," short for Feather Kat.

During that last trip to Paris, when Ernest had seen Hadley, he'd realized the city had forever changed for him—it was no longer his city. With Hadley about to remarry, the Paris apartment that he and Pauline had leased now vacated, friends who had moved on, and friends who were no longer friends, he understood that it was a young man's city. He had a new home and life in Key West, and in becoming a father for the third time, it seemed to him that nothing would ever be the same.

After writing to Hadley, Ernest sent Pauline a cable with instructions on what to do about Bumby. He was trying to find out if his oldest son had sailed on the ship, and who would meet him in New York to put him on the train to Key West.

CHARLES SHOOTS A BEAR, ERNEST SHOOTS A BIGGER BEAR

BEFORE RETURNING TO THE HUNTING CAMP, Ernest encountered Huck Mees—a legendary mountain man known for making the first ascent of Pilot Peak. Ernest asked him if he'd seen the mule bait on Pilot Creek that Ernest and Gerald had set. Huck told him the mule had been eaten entirely, the larger bones piled up neatly with the skull on top. It looked as if three bears had feasted there, including one with a track eleven inches long. It had dug a foxhole beside the bait for protection while it dined.

Ernest rode with Ivan the thirty-five miles back to Timber Creek in the lingering storm. While Ernest was away, Charles had shot a large black bear and Ernest wasn't leaving until he got his own bear.

For a week, Ernest hunted in blizzard conditions to no avail. Finally, on October 11, he rode up Pilot Creek with Lawrence where additional bait had been placed. At dusk, a black bear emerged from the thicket and began devouring the horse meat. Ernest crawled to get a good shot at it. When he was seventy-five yards away he fired, but the shot hit the bear too high, and the bear bellowed and ran into the woods. Ernest trailed it into the semidarkness by the blood track.

Ernest's mother liked to tell the story that when Ernest was a boy, he'd say, "'fraid a nothing." He had faced death in a war, in the bull-fighting arena, and in a car crash. Now, in the fading light, he crept into the emerging darkness, ready to face whatever awaited him. He was just twenty feet from the injured bear when he fired a second shot that brought the bear down. The bear was the color of Ernest's beard and weighed five hundred pounds, measuring eight feet from paw to outstretched paw, much bigger than the one Charles shot.

Satisfied that he had outhunted Charles, Ernest was pleased with their tally for the season: Charles had shot a bull elk, Ernest and Charles had shot one together, and Ernest had shot one alone. Charles had also killed two fine bucks and a bear, and Ernest had "killed a hell of a big bear."

They had such an abundance of game meat that Ernest and Charles gave some to Ivan and Chub, who were both getting married that fall, to serve at their wedding receptions. They returned to the ranch and feasted on elk and venison before preparing for the long drive back to Key West.

Ernest with two trophy elk racks and a massive black bear he shot, 1932.
Ernest Hemingway Collection, John F. Kennedy Presidential Library and Museum, Boston

LETTERS BEFORE LEAVING

ERNEST NEEDED TO WRAP UP correspondence with friends before hitting the road. It was time to set things straight with Mike Strater about calling off the safari. He'd heard that Mike's feelings had been hurt that Ernest hadn't told him about the safari earlier himself—he'd had to learn about it from Archie.

Ernest wrote to Mike, apologizing and doing his best to explain why he hadn't written sooner, that since the four men weren't in one location it made it difficult to tell them all at once, so Ernest had written them one by one—no slight intended. He hoped Mike would still be able to join him with Archie and Charles when they went to Africa the following spring.

The season for fishing and hunting was over, trout had dropped into the deep pools, deer migrated to their winter range, and elk moved into the park. Ernest wrote Lawrence Nordquist a check on October 16 for $1,629 to cover his stay at the ranch, then he packed up and drove to Cody with Charles to spend the night at the Chamberlin Hotel.

The next morning, he left fourteen letters and a manuscript—all his summer correspondence—in a mailbag at the Studebaker Garage to be mailed to Max, asking him to forward the letters to their intended recipients. When they left Cody on October 17 for the trek to Key West, Ernest wasn't sure if he would return to this part of the country. An African safari was on his mind—his next big adventure—and this land was becoming too settled. Snow swirled as they drove, making visibility nearly impossible. They had to burn a candle in a can near the

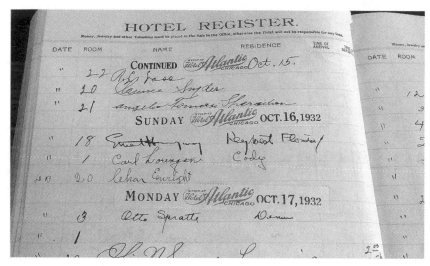

A guest register of the Chamberlin Hotel in Cody, where Ernest stayed with Charles Thompson in 1932. Renamed the Chamberlin Inn in 2005, the hotel has been renovated and remains open for business today. *Courtesy the Chamberlin Inn*

windshield to melt the ice so Ernest could see. It took them three days to outrun "un-Christly blizzards" across Wyoming and Nebraska, which Ernest described as a nightmare.

Sunny Key West would be an oasis to come home to after 2,000 miles of driving. He would write more stories and enjoy some deep-sea fishing as he considered his next project this winter. And his warm bed with Pauline awaited him.

Part IV

1936

What Ernest Loved About Pauline

Keen editorial eye
Her family became his family: Jinny, Mother Pfeiffer
Uncle Gus's support
Figure was lovely, better all the time
Strong
"Someone to feel swell with" after a day's work
The "feeling of us against the others"
Willing to join him on adventures
Believed in the "promotion of masculine society"
~~Never worried like other wives~~
~~Vowed to always let him have his way~~
~~She could give him "little Pilar"~~
~~Her throat never got sore like his~~
~~Spontaneous lovemaking~~

AFTER AFRICA

IT HAD BEEN more than two years since they'd returned from Africa, but Pauline often recalled that trip. The Serengeti had been so hot that the sun had drained the color from her nail polish in just a few hours. Driving over bumpy, dusty roads, hiking up mountains—some nights Pauline was so tired she skipped dinner and went straight to bed at camp, where she slept in huts with mosquito netting.

Pauline wasn't a fan of hunting from the car, nor did she even enjoy killing large animals that could kill her, but she'd offered to come on the safari when both Archie and Mike had bowed out, leaving just Ernest and Charles Thompson. She knew Ernest would need an audience for his trophy kills. Archie had claimed financial difficulties, and Mike said he couldn't leave work, but the real reason might have been Ernest's behavior—he'd had arguments with both men before the safari.

Africa had a unique beauty. The land's rolling plains were green from the rains, Kilimanjaro rose up in the distance, and the wildlife was magnificent—a lioness with a beautiful coat, "flocks of wildebeest," and zebras racing to cross in front of the car. Pauline wrote in her journal with a pencil, capturing their days as they traveled across the country and keeping a list of the wildlife they saw: Grant's gazelles, impalas, Thomson's gazelles (or "tommies"), giraffes, a large warthog, guinea fowl, and many other birds.

Charlie, Ernest, and Pauline had sailed from Marseilles on the *General Metinger* on November 22, 1933, traveling for seventeen days before checking in at the New Stanley Hotel in Nairobi to await the arrival of their guide, Philip Percival, who had come highly recommended by Jane Mason. It gave them time to explore the area and acclimate to the higher altitude, as they socialized with other well-heeled guests like Alfred Vanderbilt and Winston Guest, also acquaintances of Jane's.

They began the safari on December 20, 1933. One day of hunting blended into the next as Charles went out with his gun bearer and Ernest went with Mr. Percival. Some days there was friction between the men, as Ernest always wanted to shoot the biggest and best trophy and Charles was besting him. Pauline described the routine: the men went off hunting, and when they returned there were "drinks, baths more drinks [and] dinner in pajamas."

There'd been moments of tenderness, like on Christmas, when Ernest had surprised Pauline with a dustproof, waterproof watch she'd admired in Paris before departing for Africa. She'd been so touched by his thoughtfulness, and it had helped her through Christmas, missing the boys.

In the party of forty men, there were assistant hunters, gun bearers, drivers, cooks, and others. Overwhelmed by the dust, fleas, and strange noises at night, on February 3 Pauline wrote that she "felt rather dreary and men ridden." One night an animal, maybe a pack rat, bit Pauline's toe through the covers while she slept, giving her quite a start.

But her negative moods never lasted long. They visited Colonel Dick Cooper's charming tea plantation, "high and cool and swimming in flowers and vines, with a lovely view of Lake Manyara. . . ." They "played the gramophone and drank on the veranda" and slept in a big double bed.

Ernest had experienced a close call on the trip when he'd left his rifle on top of the car and it fell off and discharged—it was a miracle no one was killed. Then he had developed dysentery, suffering from diarrhea and piles, and had to be airlifted to a hospital in Arusha, where he recovered before returning to camp. When he returned, he'd lost weight, becoming very thin, but Pauline thought he'd looked extremely handsome.

With the rains coming near the safari's end, the hunting party had been pressured to leave before the roads became impassable. But Ernest had not shot a kudu, the last animal on his trophy list. Things were getting tense at camp, especially because Charles had killed a beautiful enormous kudu. They were out of time, and for Ernest, still no kudu.

On their last morning, Pauline was awakened by a racket of shouting by the hunting party, and found Ernest rejoicing. At last he'd killed a kudu. Two, in fact.

After leaving the Serengeti, they checked into the lovely Palm Beach Hotel in Malindi, where Pauline would stay for two weeks while Ernest, Charles, and Mr. Percival continued their fun with a fishing trip before heading home. It wasn't until the first week of March that they boarded the ocean liner *Gripsholm* for the long voyage to Paris before returning home to Key West.

Along the way, Lorine Thompson met them in Haifa. She brought photos of Gregory and Patrick, moving Pauline to tears. "Poor little lambs, I can see they miss Mummy," Pauline said. She had last seen Gregory on August 4, 1933, before leaving the States, and Patrick as he returned from France with Jinny on November 22.

She had known her parents wouldn't approve of leaving the boys for so long, so she'd waited until the very last minute to tell them—they thought she was only going to Paris to help outfit Ernest for the trip and would be returning home after he left on the safari. When her mother learned that Pauline was going too, Mary Pfeiffer wrote, "And so you are to journey to Africa in the near future? What part please? Just Africa is pretty indefinite. I have been looking at it on the map. Have also purchased a globe to better keep you located."

Ernest and Pauline had spent two weeks shopping in Paris before returning to the United States, arriving in New York City on April 3, 1934, where Uncle Gus hosted a reception in their honor. Ernest's reputation now included "big game hunter," publicity he approved of, as newspapers featured photos of him with his lion kill and the headline SITTING DOWN IS THE BEST WAY TO SHOOT A LION. They returned with "four lions, two leopards, three cheetahs, two rhinoceroses, and four buffaloes. Their trophy kills also included gazelles, wildebeests, impalas, klipspringers, zebras, oryxes, bushbucks, reedbucks, waterbucks, roan antelopes, topi, elands, sables—and kudus."

Despite their time away from Key West, Ernest was not ready for life as usual. Now that the safari was over, he was looking for his next new thing. He'd been thinking about buying a boat, so he and Pauline stopped at the Wheeler Shipyard in New York, where he used a $3,000 advance from *Esquire* as a deposit on a thirty-eight-foot cabin cruiser. The hull would be painted black with the name *Pilar* in white letters, the secret name Ernest had called Pauline when they were courting, and also the name for their daughter, if they'd had one.

Looking back on the safari—the scale of it, the panoramic scenes, and the time with Ernest—it was an experience Pauline would always cherish. They returned to Key West, and Ernest settled down to work on his book about their experience, *Green Hills of Africa*.

In the book, he'd written about her, "The only person I really cared about, except the children, was with me." He described her as "very desirable, cool and neat-looking in her khaki and her boots, her Stetson on the side of her head."

She'd gone with him because she knew he needed an audience; she'd wanted to make her husband happy. She got her reward when she read Ernest's manuscript: ". . . and I had no wish to share this life with anyone who was not there, only to live it, being completely happy and quite tired." She was married to the greatest writer in America, and he'd written those words about her.

When they'd returned from safari in 1934, Jane Mason had been preoccupied with her latest adventures, which included her new friend Dick Cooper, the married Wyoming oil magnate who owned the tea plantation they'd visited in Africa. If it bothered Ernest, he didn't say. He'd been consumed with his new plaything, the *Pilar*, and he'd discovered a new place, Bimini, for his entertainment. The whole family, including Jinny, nurse Ada, and the boys, had gone there in June. But after returning home to Key West, Ernest announced he wanted to go to Wyoming. He contacted Lawrence Nordquist, telling him that he was bringing Pauline and the boys to the ranch, arriving in two weeks.

Pauline was good at pivoting; just as she had put her own life on hold to accompany Ernest to Africa, she was flexible about changing plans with little notice. She went into action, packing their Western clothes, outfitting Jack and Patrick for the ranch, and making arrangements for Gregory to stay with the boys' nurse, Ada. Finally, they all piled into the car and drove out of Key West.

WYOMING AFTER ALL

CIVIL WAR HAD BROKEN OUT in Spain on July 3, 1936, and Ernest was absorbed in radio news reports as they drove to Wyoming with Pauline in the front seat and Patrick and Jack in the back. His beloved Spain, the setting for two of his novels and a number of stories, and it was being torn apart by war.

The popular front called the Loyalists, composed of republicans, trade unionists, socialists, and some leftists, had been elected by a majority. The rebel coalition, the Nationalists—made up of the officer class in the army, the police, the church, and the aristocracy—refused to accept the results. Ernest had friends on both sides and wanted to remain neutral in his public position, but he was itching to head to Spain to write about it. First, though, he had a novel to finish.

While he was in Bimini, writing short stories and waiting for a new book idea, Arnold Gingrich, his *Esquire* editor, had visited. He'd shown Arnold some of his stories, and Arnold had been very excited by what he'd read, recommending that Ernest expand one of the stories about a broke fishing boat captain into a novel. This was just the encouragement Ernest needed and he had already written thirty thousand words. He decided to go ahead and finish the book out West, where it was cool.

On August 10, they drove through the stand of quaking aspens and onto the open meadow of the Nordquist Ranch, with its sweeping view of the valley. Since his last visit, Ernest had been to bullfights in Spain, hunted lions in Africa, and discovered a new playground in Bimini, but Wyoming was always on his mind. While he was in Africa, he thought

199

about climbing the steep terrain with Pauline and Charles to hunt sheep, and the time a gale blew Pauline's Stetson off her head. The exertion of sheep hunting in challenging conditions had helped prepare Pauline, Charles, and him for the steep terrain in Africa.

He had enjoyed time with the Murphys on the last trip to the ranch. Now poor Baoth was dead. Ernest realized they were "entering the time of life when they would start to lose people of their own age," a reminder to live life a day at a time. They had all been worried about Patrick Murphy and tuberculosis, but it was Baoth who, at fifteen years old, contracted meningitis and died. Ernest realized that the only people who really mattered to him were his wife, Jinny, and his sons.

At least Prohibition had ended. They would no longer need to import moonshine from Red Lodge and could now legally buy a drink. Despite his bitterness at the new highway, Ernest had to admit that it would make it easy to drive to a Cooke City bar.

He would follow his tried-and-true schedule of working in the morning and fishing in the afternoon and, later in the season, taking time for some grizzly hunting. But the book about the broke fishing boat captain was his focus. Writing was going well. He had worried that Max would be disappointed to learn he wasn't working on the book of short stories but on a novel instead. On the contrary, Max was delighted and thought it was much better to have the novel come out first.

CHANGING COURSE

PAULINE ENJOYED BEING back in the Sidley cabin, with its roomy layout, spacious enough to accommodate Ernest's writing and the two boys. She had become adept at moving into new environments upon Ernest's whims, whether it be returning to rugged Wyoming or experiencing his latest infatuation, Bimini.

Bimini had been lovely; they had stayed at a luxurious home owned by Mike Lerner, one of Ernest's new friends on the island. The Hemingway clan included Jack (still called Bumby at times, despite his objections), Patrick (called Mouse), Gregory (nicknamed Gigi), Jinny, and Ada. Even with Ada and Jinny's help, the boys were a lot to handle. Jack, a passionate animal lover, kept a wild bird flying freely in his room, and Patrick had set his room on fire. Pauline and Ernest had to write a large check to cover the damages. Gigi, at five, was still too small to cause much trouble.

On Cat Cay, they spent time with a young couple Ernest had met from Palm Beach, Tommy and Lorraine Shevlin, who, like Mike Lerner, were part of the "millionaire" set. Arnold Gingrich had flown in from New York to join them, and Jane Mason was there too, talking about her newest friend, "her Mr. Cooper," as she called him.

Just as Pauline had prayed for, Jane turned out to be one of Ernest's passing infatuations—albeit a long one. Pauline's strategy to look the other way instead of giving him an ultimatum had proved wise. She realized that Ernest's love of women was part of his writing, and she didn't take his flirtations seriously.

Still, she had noticed that for the past eight months, Ernest had been extremely irritable, whether from lack of female companionship or because he was between books. He picked fights with friends and acquaintances alike. In Key West, he'd heard that the poet Wallace Stevens had said some unflattering things about him, so he marched over to where Wallace was staying nearby and knocked him to the ground, breaking Wallace's hand. Another time, when Ernest couldn't open the front gate to their home, he had a fit, kicking it so hard he broke his toe. While on the *Pilar* with Katy and Dos, he shot himself in both legs when his rifle discharged and the bullet ricocheted. Katy was so disgusted by his recklessness that she stopped speaking to him. (Luckily for him, the wounds were minor.)

In Bimini, he seemed back to his normal self, happy to have an entourage. When Pauline needed to return to Key West to finish some projects on their home, she left Jinny there to keep an eye on him. She could trust Jinny to report back to her about any funny business. Pauline appreciated the deep friendship between Ernest and her sister, knowing that Jinny was one of the few people Ernest allowed to stand up to him. Ernest had returned home, leaving Jinny behind in Bimini to carry on with the fun, but he said he missed her, one of the few people he truly cared for.

Ernest and Pauline had celebrated their birthdays in Key West. On July 21 he turned thirty-seven, and the next day, Pauline turned forty-two. With Jane out of the picture, Pauline had Ernest's complete attention again. She knew he wasn't happy with her adherence to Catholic doctrine regarding birth control, but despite that challenge, she felt she had a good marriage. Ernest liked her to experiment with her hairstyles; she'd grown it out to a chin-length bob, and although she'd been wearing it blonde like Jane's, she went to an ash blonde—something he had approved of.

Now at the ranch, without a salon for miles, she'd cropped it short like a boy's again. She worked to stay in shape, holding steady at 113 pounds, playing tennis and swimming. On safari Ernest had compared her to "a little terrier"—although she preferred to be thought of as "a wolfhound, long and lean and ornamental."

While Pauline unpacked their bags in the cabin, the boys charged like wild horses down the hill, Jack to the river and Patrick to the corral.

Freedom and fresh air would be good for Patrick, as would be playing with the other children on the ranch. And Jack's big brother influence was always welcomed. He had grown into being such a lovely child, "not spoiled or self centered or silly," Pauline had told Ernest, "but a handsome, considerate, well-mannered intelligent fellow with a fine sense of humor."

BLACK ASS MOODS

ERNEST NEEDED TO PRODUCE A WINNER. Although the early numbers of *Death in the Afternoon* had been encouraging, sales had dropped off a month later, totaling just 20,780 copies—versus the 101,675 copies of *A Farewell to Arms* that had sold.

Winner Take Nothing (1933), a book of short stories, had received a mediocre reception. He had really thought *Green Hills of Africa* (1935) would put him on the map again, but to his disappointment the critics had been confused by his hybrid style. Was it nonfiction or a novel?

A few critics, including Edward Weeks from the *Atlantic*, liked *Green Hills of Africa*, finding it absorbing, and in *Time* the reviewer was touched by the way Ernest wrote candidly about his love for his wife.

But others were not as complimentary. Edmund ("Bunny") Wilson, the critic Ernest had once trusted, said the book was weak. Another critic encouraged Ernest to find more important themes than "the pursuit and dismemberment of animals and fish no matter how big."

Comments like these hurt his book sales, compounded by a too steep price tag and insufficient advertising by Scribner's. When he had returned to Key West following the release of *Green Hills*, he sunk into one of his "black ass moods," telling Sara Murphy he should blow his bloody head off. He couldn't remember feeling so low, and he had written his mother-in-law to say that the experience had made him "more tolerant of what happened to my father."

Eventually Ernest figured out that his depression was caused by not enough sleep and exercise, and the pressure he was feeling to write something that people liked. After the first of the year he had ramped up his physical activities and lost ten pounds. Lacking female distraction, Ernest searched for new inspiration and found it in the *Pilar*, which would be a key character in the new novel he was writing. Spending time on the water, on the *Pilar*, had been his salvation, and sometimes he was gone for months at a time.

The creative juice was flowing again at the ranch as he worked on the new novel about a man who carries a shipment of dynamite between Cuba and Florida and the consequences of this activity. During the first two weeks at the ranch, Ernest did little fishing, instead sitting at the desk in the Sidley cabin and producing eighteen thousand words. Unlike previous summers when the rains came and the streams were muddy, the weather this summer was ideal, with clear skies and sunshine providing a strong temptation to go fishing. He finally took three days off to hunt antelope and one more day to fish before returning and writing twenty thousand more words.

FRENEMIES

ERNEST AND SCOTT FITZGERALD, once real friends, had become friendly enemies. Ernest recognized he had behaved badly with Scott—he had even admitted it to Max—but still he let Scott get under his skin. Their relationship had deteriorated through the years as Ernest saw Scott wasting his talent due to his drinking and his crazy wife, Zelda, whom Ernest loathed.

When Scott gave *Green Hills of Africa* a lackluster review, Ernest was infuriated. Why did Ernest care what Scott said, when he considered him washed up? Earlier in the year, Ernest had been embarrassed for Scott when he read a series of articles in *Esquire* by Scott, "The Crack-Up," about his mental breakdown. What the hell was he thinking, airing his problems for the world to read?

To Max, who deeply cared about his writers, Ernest tried to keep up the pretense of caring about Scott. After all, it was thanks to Scott that Ernest had made the switch from his small publisher Boni & Liveright to Max and Scribner's. But when Scott's *Tender Is the Night* was published in 1934, a novel loosely based on the Murphys, and Scott had sent the manuscript to Ernest, anxiously awaiting his opinion, Ernest had blasted him. Rather than creating real characters, Ernest accused him of providing "faked case histories."

Not everyone felt that way. Critics had liked Scott's book, further irritating Ernest. In "The Snows of Kilimanjaro," a short story that was published in the August edition of *Scribner's Magazine*, Ernest couldn't resist getting in another dig at Scott accusing him of admiring and glamorizing the rich.

After Scott read the story, he demanded that Ernest "lay off him" in print and remove his name in any future reprints of the story. It had seemed like a strange reply to Ernest, from a man who had just totally exposed himself to the world. Didn't he know this challenge would make Ernest even more determined to write about whomever he pleased if it furthered his story?

In her book *The Autobiography of Alice B. Toklas*, Gertrude Stein had called Ernest "yellow" and a "slob." He'd paid her back in *Green Hills of Africa* without actually naming her, saying that it was a shame that she had wasted her talent by turning to malice and self-importance. Ernest was much happier without those Paris friends, no longer relevant in his life, and it wasn't his problem if people got their feelings hurt. For five years he hadn't written about anyone he knew because he felt sorry for them, but time was short and he was going to stop being a gentleman and focus on being a novelist.

It wasn't just Scott and Gertrude that Ernest had taken literary shots at; in the novel he was currently at work on, he again created characters inspired by real people. Helene Bradley—a tall, blonde beauty who took writers, painters, and big game hunters as lovers—was remarkably like Jane Mason. Other characters closely resembled Dos and Katy, Tommy and Lorraine Shevlin, and even Pauline.

THE BOYS

BEING BACK ON THE RANCH with Patrick and Jack, Pauline recalled the last visit with the Murphy children. Sara was still beside herself with grief a year after Baoth's death; does a mother ever recover from grief like that? Pauline could relate in a way with the pain she had felt about the loss of her own young brother, Max. Being thirteen years older, she had been like a second mother to him, and his death at age eleven from the Spanish flu had devastated her family.

Pauline knew that had Baoth's death had been hard on Ernest, too. He had taught Honoria and Baoth to fish, and had entertained them with songs and stories around the campfire. Even though Ernest told people that he considered parenting a part-time job, Pauline saw his patience with his sons. He'd taken Patrick with him on the *Pilar* and bragged to Pauline's mother that Patrick was a good companion, and, admitting that he might be prejudiced, but he thought Patrick was very smart. Ernest told her that Gregory was still too young to tell much about yet.

Pauline realized it appeared she preferred Patrick's company to little Gigi's, but that was because at age eight, Patrick could hold a conversation with an adult. Gigi, at five, was not able to keep up with his brother yet and was sometimes misunderstood.

Jack was often with them on school breaks since returning to the United States, after Paul Mowrer had become managing editor of the *Chicago Daily News*, making it much easier to coordinate his travel than when they had been arranging transatlantic passage from Paris. Jack was an important part of the family, and Pauline had asked Uncle Gus to make a trust for Jack like he'd done for the rest of the family.

When Jack had first visited the ranch, he could hardly contain his excitement at being a wrangler and learning to fish, and Pauline now saw the same excitement in Patrick. He didn't come down off his horse for twelve hours except to eat. Ernest had joked that Patrick would be bowlegged after this season.

Her parents didn't approve of splitting the boys up, sending Gregory off with Ada to Syracuse while Patrick visited them in Piggott, nor did they understand the amount of time Pauline and Ernest left the boys in others' care. But her parents were getting older and were from a different time. Pauline and Ernest had other friends in their circle, like the Coopers, who left their children with relatives while they traveled the world. It wasn't uncommon in well-traveled families like theirs.

With freedom from caring for Gregory—as Patrick and Jack explored the ranch on their own—Pauline could make sure to be available for rides and picnics and fishing whenever Ernest finished work. Jane might not be in the picture, but Ernest's new love, the *Pilar*, had been taking him away from Pauline for months at a time as he fished in Havana and Bimini. Finally, she had him all to herself again, smoothing the way for whatever he needed, even though sometimes he bristled at her doting on him.

In the years since they'd returned from Africa, she took comfort in what he'd written about her in *Green Hills of Africa*. But in his new short story, "The Snows of Kilimanjaro," published just this month in *Esquire*, his words were not as flattering. The protagonist's wife, Helen, shared some of Pauline's attributes, and not always in a good way. She told herself it was only fiction and that was just how Ernest wrote, basing characters on real people but then fictionalizing them. At least that's what she tried to believe.

THE RICH

ERNEST WAS STARTING to feel bitter about the wealthy people who surrounded him, like his in-laws and his new friends on Bimini. This bitterness was showing up in his writing.

In "The Snows of Kilimanjaro," Harry Walden has contracted gangrene on safari and is dying in an African camp while his wife, Helen, helplessly watches. He blames Helen and her money for making him soft.

When Ernest finished writing the story, he created a list of possible titles:

"The End of a Marriage"
"Marriage Is a Dangerous Game"
"A Marriage Has Been Terminated"
"Through Darkest Marriage"

Ernest's greatest fear in life was losing his talent—writing was what gave him pleasure in life—and as he waited to have another hit novel, he blamed others for his lack of recent success. In the seven years since *A Farewell to Arms* was published, Pauline had become even stricter in her observance of Catholic prescriptions. She was still paying for her guilt over having had an affair with him when he was a married man and going against the church, and she was motivated to be even more pious as years passed—a great inconvenience. In addition, he felt her money wasn't good for him, and he was conflicted over enjoying the wonderful things money could buy versus living without the benefits of Pauline's wealth.

In Bimini, Ernest had discovered a playground for the superrich like Mike Lerner and Tommy Shevlin and Bill Leeds, whose yacht the *Moana* was too large for the harbor. Of course, there were wealthy people in Key West, but not like the Bimini group. In Oak Park, Ernest had grown up around affluent families and had wanted to be part of them, but this was a whole new class, and he found himself conflicted. He enjoyed their company and considered them friends, but at the same time he despised their wealth, writing about them in "The Snows of Kilimanjaro."

His felt that his own relatives, the Pfeiffers, couldn't resist reminding him that he had benefited from their generosity, and it made him resentful. When Mary Pfeiffer mentioned in a letter that he had "a fairy godfather," referring to the financial help Uncle Gus had given him, or when Uncle Gus asked him to return the small refund check from the safari, these little digs reminded him who held the purse strings.

Ernest had published another story about the rich, "The Short Happy Life of Francis Macomber," in the September issue of *Cosmopolitan*. It was the story of American sportsman Francis Macomber and his wife, Margot, on safari in Africa. When confronted with a wounded lion, the husband shows his fear, and his cowardice disgusts his wife. She leaves their bed in the middle of the night to join their hunting guide Wilson in his bed—Wilson had bravely killed the lion. Some readers felt that the character of Margot Macomber, described as having a perfect oval face and wearing her hair in a knot at the nape of her neck, sounded similar to Jane Mason.

Maybe what he liked about the ranch was the simplicity of the people who lived there, straight shooters like Lawrence Nordquist and Chub Weaver, whom Pauline and Ernest had hired for seventy-five dollars a month to be their "cook, factotum, and outdoor instructor for the young" during this stay. Hard-working, down-to-earth people—so different from the Bimini jet-setters.

And yet, Ernest liked to have an audience when he played mountain man, and the rich had idle time on their hands to drop everything and come to Wyoming for sport. He found ready adventurers when he invited Tommy and Lorraine Shevlin to join Pauline and him in September to hunt antelope, elk, and grizzlies.

TOMMY BOY

IN BIMINI, TOMMY SHEVLIN spotted Ernest at the Fountain of Youth bar. Tommy had read *Death in the Afternoon*, and he recognized Ernest, so he approached him. "Aren't you Mr. Hemingway?"

"Nobody calls me Mr. Hemingway here," Ernest replied.

"We've spent the summer watching bullfights in Spain and I've read your book and thought it was marvelous," Tommy said. But he had to disagree with Ernest on his opinion about one of the bullfighters in the book.

Ernest set down his drink. "How many bullfights did you see?"

"Possibly twenty."

"You can talk to me when you've seen maybe three hundred," Ernest said, and turned his back.

"I'm sorry, I didn't mean to criticize at all," Tommy said.

"Oh shut up about it and let's have drinks."

That's how their friendship had started. Later that day the two men sparred on the beach. Tommy realized Ernest was a puncher, a slugger. Ernest told Tommy, "You live under your left shoulder."

Tommy and Ernest shared a love of the sporting life, and Tommy admired Ernest's intelligence and his confidence in the field and fishing. But Ernest could be awkward socially. He wouldn't have gone to a Palm Beach society party for anything in the world, partly because he was shy, and also because he didn't care anything for those people.

Tommy recognized that Ernest had a wonderful sense of humor, but you didn't want to play practical jokes on him. He didn't like to be

213

laughed at, and he had a hair-trigger temper that you needed to watch. When Ernest invited Tommy and Lorraine to the Nordquist Ranch, Tommy accepted, looking forward to experiencing a new part of the country.

When the Shevlins arrived they found Ernest clean-shaven and trim. Tommy and Ernest rode horses into the mountains to fish at Granite Creek, where they caught six rainbow trout over sixteen inches long and four rainbows over eighteen inches. Then they moved down country to hunt antelope, and Tom admired Ernest's shooting prowess. Ernest shot two bucks; Pauline shot a nice buck too, and Tommy shot a doe.

They'd been getting along well until Ernest asked Tommy to read the manuscript of the new novel. Tommy had been flattered but had misunderstood what Ernest wanted from him. He carefully read the manuscript and wrote notes telling Ernest exactly what he thought: "I like some parts of the book, including the main character. But I dislike other parts of the book . . ."

Ernest read Shevlin's remarks, becoming very angry, and threw the manuscript out the window into the snow. Ernest hadn't really wanted his comments; he wanted his praise. He left the pages out in the snowdrift for three days. Finally, Ernest dug them out of the snow and apologized to Tommy.

"I don't write," Tom said. "And just because we're good friends, why did you ask me to criticize it?"

"Well I'll be goddamned if I know," Ernest replied. "I'll never do it again."

THE ELUSIVE GRIZZLY

THE GREATEST PREDATOR in North America, the grizzly, had eluded Ernest, and he wanted to kill one. Ernest figured that Tommy wouldn't give him much competition on the grizzly hunt—he was like a lot of rich kids who can't shoot because he never practiced. In Ernest's mind, Tommy had become a big game hunter without burning the necessary cartridges, as though Ernest would declare himself a polo player just by knowing how to ride a horse. But he was a good kid whom Ernest liked.

Jack needed to return to Chicago for the start of school, so Ernest and Pauline took him to the train in Cody while Tommy and Lorraine were sent to check on the grizzly bait Lawrence had set near Crandall Creek. Would they know what to do if they ran into a grizzly? Ernest wasn't sure, but when the Hemingways returned from Cody, Pauline, Patrick, and Ernest rode into the high mountains with Lawrence and Chub to meet the Shevlins at camp and find out.

After getting settled, late one afternoon Ernest and Lorraine hiked up the trail to the confluence of Crandall Creek to check on the bait while Tommy rode up high on a ridge as a lookout. When Lorraine and Ernest heard a crashing sound through the woods they moved low behind a rock to hide.

Ernest had expected an elk would come running out but instead saw three grizzlies. The biggest one reared up on its hind legs and looked straight at them. Ernest shot two with a 30.06 rifle, one right after the other. He regretted killing two, as they were so beautiful with their bristling silver coats, but he didn't have time to decide—he'd had to act quickly.

From left: Pauline, Patrick, Tom and Lorraine Shevlin, and Ernest with the grizzly Tom shot, 1936. *Ernest Hemingway Collection, John F. Kennedy Presidential Library and Museum, Boston*

Tommy killed a grizzly two days later, even bigger than Ernest's two. Ernest insisted that they eat some of it. When Ernest was a boy, he and his friend had killed a porcupine that was terrorizing the neighborhood, and he'd proudly brought the creature home, thinking his father would be delighted. On the contrary, his father had scolded him, telling him it was wrong to kill any animal that a person didn't eat. Was Ernest remembering his father's words as he cut some steaks from the bear and cooked them medium, then made sandwiches with the rank and stringy meat between pancakes smeared with orange marmalade? Ernest devoured the sandwich with pleasure, bear fat shining on his face.

Damn if it wasn't like the kudu and Charles in Africa all over again. When Charles had returned to camp with the massive kudu that dwarfed Ernest's meager animal, Ernest had behaved badly and made Charles feel terrible. But Charles had been a damn good hunter, and Ernest hadn't expected Tommy to provide that level of competition.

To make himself feel better, Ernest challenged Tommy to a horse race back to the ranch, betting $500 that he would win. It was snowing hard. At first, Ernest was ahead, but in the final four-mile stretch, Tommy broke away, gaining the lead. It was "slippery as a bastard on the road," and the hooves of the horse in front threw mud back into the face of the rider in the rear. When they dismounted, they looked like mud statues. Pauline actually used a trowel to get the mud off Ernest.

Tommy had won the race, but Ernest was determined to beat him at something, so he challenged him to a game of craps that night. Ernest lost $900.

All told, the Shevlins were on the ranch nearly a month, and when they finally returned to Palm Beach at the end of September, Ernest was ready for them to go. They'd had a fine time despite his worries that the good hunting country had burned out; their hunting season had been a success. They'd shot antelope, two fine elk, and three grizzlies. Now Ernest wanted to get back to work.

A CHANGE OF SEASONS

THE GRIZZLY HIDE WAS BEAUTIFUL, like silver-tipped fox but thicker and longer, the hair blowing "beautifully in the wind." Unfortunately, the hair slipped when the man who was curing it didn't do it properly and ruined the hide. Ernest, who had pictured it as a wonderful rug, was terribly disappointed, but at least he had the second hide as a prize. It turned out to be lucky that had shot two grizzlies instead of one, or he wouldn't have a hide to show for his effort.

With a successful grizzly hunt under his belt and the weather turning cold, it was time to leave the ranch. He trimmed his thick black beard with nail clippers, transforming from mountain man to Key West writer once again. Ernest packed up his novel of the struggling boat captain, 353 pages written in longhand, still with much work to do on it this winter. On October 27, Ernest wrote Lawrence a check for $1,934.73 to pay their bill at the ranch, then packed up the car for the drive, stopping in Piggott for a quick visit before returning to Key West.

Although he had concentrated on his novel, Spain remained heavy on his mind. He was interested in writing about the war's effect on common people, and he was determined to make it to Spain when he finished this book, if the war wasn't over by then. He had promised Max that before leaving for Spain, he would secure the completed manuscript in a vault to ensure it would be safe in case anything happened to Ernest.

NEW YORK

In Piggott, they arrived to find that Jinny had left for New York to find an apartment—a disappointment to Pauline, who always looked forward to seeing her sister. She thought it odd that Jinny had left before the Hemingways arrived. Why didn't she wait to see them? Although Jinny had spent time with the family and Ernest in Bimini, Pauline had hoped to see her and catch up.

Jinny's letter awaiting Pauline didn't explain her decision to leave for New York, but she did ask if Pauline could help her move into her new apartment. Jinny had always dropped everything to help Pauline and her family—babysitting, interior decorating, being available at a moment's notice whenever they needed her—so Pauline could hardly say no. Gregory could continue to stay with Ada, while Ernest would return to Key West with Patrick. They had learned that it was easier to deal with one boy at a time while traveling. Even one could be challenging, so Ernest hired a local Piggott man, Toby Bruce, as his driver for the trip home, while Pauline prepared to go to New York.

With Jane out of the picture, she wouldn't worry about who Ernest was spending time with in Key West during her absence. She had her friends Charles and Lorine Thompson to keep an eye on him. But she knew it wasn't a woman that threatened to capture Ernest's attention now; it was the war. Ernest's talk about covering the Spanish Civil War was worrisome.

Of course, she didn't want him to go to war, and her parents were dead set against it too. He was a father and husband, and his family

221

needed him. But she knew Ernest craved the excitement he had felt years ago in Italy, and nothing could stop him once he made up his mind to do something. She had married a writer. She knew Ernest probably better than anyone else did, and despite her objections, she knew he would base his decision on what was best for him as a writer.

HELLO, ERNEST?
THIS IS WAR CALLING . . .

As ERNEST READ NEWS in the Havana paper of the Spanish Civil War, including a daily casualty count, it was becoming harder not to choose between Franco's fascist rebels, supported by the Roman Catholic Church, and the leftist reform government composed of anarchists, communists, and socialists. One of his young writer friends in Key West referred to Ernest as a Catholic writer, "because he had friends on both sides," but Ernest had set the record straight by saying that when he wrote, he tried to write without personal bias because he had friends on both sides of the war. He would make up his mind on the war in Spain when he got there and saw it with his own eyes. However, he could never support a government intent on wiping out the Spanish working class.

Things were tense at home. Pauline was back from New York and didn't want him to go to Spain. In addition, she took issue with his comments about priests and the Roman Catholic Church—like most Catholics, she leaned toward the conservative side with the church hierarchy and supported the rebels. But when the North American Newspaper Alliance asked him to report on the war for the news service, Ernest took the job.

Ernest's in-laws were surprised he would even consider such a thing as traveling to a foreign war when he had responsibilities at home. Max had also told Ernest he wished he wouldn't go, and that he hoped nothing would get in the way of the novel's publication that spring. Ernest knew he needed to finish the novel before he left—he was nearly done with revisions to his story about the fishing boat captain. He had sent it to Arnold Gingrich at *Esquire* for his opinion, and Arnold cautioned that he felt Ernest had libeled himself; the characters Helene and Tommy Bradley were too close to the real-life Jane and Grant Mason. Ernest thought Arnold's comments, protective of Jane, were biased. He suspected that Arnold and Jane had begun a secret affair after meeting in Bimini.*

As he continued work on the book, with plans to deliver it to Max Perkins in New York after the first of the year, Ernest and Pauline stopped talking about Spain to avoid fighting.

On a December afternoon, while sitting at Sloppy Joe's Bar, a chance meeting with three tourists provided a stroke of luck for Ernest. An older woman, a golden-haired young woman wearing a black cotton sundress, and a young man—possibly the young woman's husband—entered the bar. Introductions were made, and he learned the young woman was Martha Gellhorn, a writer from St. Louis—a funny coincidence that she came from where Hadley and Pauline had both gone to school many years ago. Martha was traveling with her mother and her brother. She'd recently published a book, *The Trouble I've Seen*, to acclaim, and she'd even quoted Ernest in her book, using his phrase "Nothing ever happens to the brave" as an epigraph for her novel. As they spoke, he learned she too was interested in covering the Spanish Civil War.

---

* They did have an affair and married years later in 1955 after Jane's third marriage ended.

A WOMAN WALKS
INTO A BAR . . .

LORINE AND CHARLES THOMPSON waited with Pauline for Ernest to arrive. The Thompsons had been invited for a crawfish dinner at the Hemingway home, and after a round of drinks without Ernest, Pauline asked Charles to go to town and find him. Charles headed to Ernest's hangout, Sloppy Joe's, and returned shortly, but he was alone.

Charles reported that Ernest was talking to a beautiful blonde in a black dress. Ernest had asked him to relay a message that Ernest and his new friends would meet them after dinner at Pena's Garden of Roses.

The Thompsons had become very close to Pauline and Ernest. Lorine had helped them find their home on Whitehead Street, and she and Pauline spent much time together while their husbands hunted and fished. It wasn't the first time Ernest had been late to meet them, detained by a fan or fellow fisherman, so the group carried on with dinner without him.

Later that evening, they met up with Ernest and his new twenty-eight-year-old friend. Lorine watched as Pauline tried to make the best of the evening—Pauline had seen attractive women flirt with her husband in the past. "What she felt underneath, nobody knew," Lorine later said. After events took their course, Lorine reflected that despite the story of the "chance encounter" at the bar that Martha and Ernest told, perhaps Martha had come to Key West to make a play for Ernest.

Part V

1938–1939

What Ernest Loved About Pauline

~~An excellent editor, the only person he trusted with his work~~

~~Her family became his family: Jinny, Mother Pfeiffer~~

~~Uncle Gus's support~~

~~Figure was lovely~~

~~Strong~~

~~"Someone to feel swell with" after a day's work~~

~~The "feeling of us against the others"~~

~~Willing to join him on adventures~~

~~Believed in the "promotion of masculine society"~~

~~Never worried like other wives~~

~~Vowed to always let him have his way~~

~~She could give him "little Pilar"~~

~~Her throat never got sore like his~~

~~Spontaneous lovemaking~~

A HERO'S WELCOME

PAULINE HAD BEEN surprised to receive Ernest's cable announcing he'd be coming back home from Spain in May. She typed a response, with news of the boys, the weather, the garden, and the brick wall she was building, finishing with: ". . . life here is going on just the same as when you were here and it was unattractive to you, and it won't be any different when you get back. So if you're happy over there don't come back here to be unhappy." She added in pen, "but hope you can come back and we can both be happy."

During his stint in Spain, Ernest had returned to Key West for three brief visits—each time irritable, edgy, itching to go back—making life miserable. Jinny told Pauline rumors about the Hotel Florida in Madrid where Ernest stayed with other journalists, filmmakers, and Martha. Jinny and Ernest had had a terrible row when he had visited her in New York on his way to Spain, and she had told him she could no longer condone his womanizing and demeaning treatment of her sister. Ernest had switched from telling people she was one of the people he cared about most to saying she was spreading rumors about him and trying to ruin his marriage.

Worried about Ernest's behavior, Pauline even made a desperate attempt to check on him for herself, arranging to meet him at Christmas in Paris for what she had hoped would be a wonderful reunion. Instead she sat alone in a hotel room as he claimed to be detained by the war. "War" became one of Pauline's names for Martha. When he finally arrived at the hotel one week later, their fighting was explosive, raging for two weeks—hardly the romantic getaway Pauline had planned. They returned

229

to the States together aboard the *Gripsholm*, and Ernest remained in Key West only a month before heading back to "war."

Pauline made a decision that life must go on when he was away; he'd been home a mere eleven weeks out of the past seventeen months. So she made an effort to develop new friendships in Key West, hosting cocktail parties at their new swimming pool, which had been financed by Uncle Gus. She went to nightclubs and out to dinner, gardened, and played tennis. On the outside it appeared she had a full, busy life. In reality, all she wanted was for her husband to be at home with her.

When Ernest's plane landed at the Key West airport at the end of May, Pauline loaded up the Ford with Patrick, Gregory, and the family driver and friend Toby Bruce, hoping to avoid a confrontation by bringing an entourage. But once again, their happy reunion was interrupted, this time when a WPA worker's jalopy collided with their car on the drive back from the airport, and Ernest and the man got into a heated argument. The police arrived and arrested the two men, hauling them into police court before sending them home.

There was a period after coming home when he seemed happy. He wrote in the mornings in his studio, and swam in the new pool during the afternoons, or fished on the *Pilar*. Pauline almost believed it, telling her parents, "Ernest seems very content to be at home. . . . I am beginning to wonder if he isn't TOO quiet." And she was right. As predictable as the arrival of monsoon season, his bad temper came. One day when he found his studio locked and the key missing, he grabbed a pistol and shot the lock off the door; Pauline sent Ada and the boys to the Thompsons, safe from the fray. Later Ernest barged into a costume party with Pauline and her friends, starting a fight with the man Pauline was dancing with, breaking furniture, and mortifying Pauline.

Friends knew Ernest could be difficult. Katy Dos Passos called him the "Monster of Mt. Kisco," and he had broken off his friendship with Dos after disagreeing on politics in Spain. In addition to Jinny and Dos, he had blown up his relationship with Archie MacLeish, too, over the financing of the film *The Spanish Earth*.

After Ernest's outrageous behavior at the costume party, Pauline could no longer keep the peace. She and Ernest began battling constantly.

She'd made it clear, without actually giving him an ultimatum, that he needed to give up Martha if he was going to live with her and the boys. She believed in her marriage and would continue to fight for it, but she couldn't stand by and watch as he openly carried on an affair. Friends knew about Martha—Ernest and Pauline's bullfighter friend Sidney Franklin, and Dos and Katy, just to name a few. Pauline realized she had made a huge strategic error by not insisting on going with Ernest to Spain when he went to cover the war.

One day in July, as the Key West heat and humidity continued to build, Ernest announced that he was taking the family to Wyoming. Pauline thought the change of scenery might do them all good and embraced the plan, making a to-do list: "pack Papa's western gear, two rifles, three shotguns, one pistol, and four different sizes of ammunition; fix the cork in the water jug"; and have the new Buick (that they purchased to replace the wrecked Ford) checked out for road.

HOME, SOMEWHAT SWEET HOME

When Ernest's contract with the North American Newspaper Alliance had ended in mid-May, Martha had continued on assignments of her own, covering stories in Czechoslovakia, England, and France for *Colliers*. He didn't want to be alone, so he had no choice but to return to Key West.

As Ernest headed back to the United States, he put up a good front, telling friends, "Am going home to see Pauline and the kids and take them wherever they want to go. . . . Have neglected my family very badly this last year and would like to make it up."[1] But he was very aware of what he was doing. In February he'd told Max that he had gotten himself into a tremendous jam.[2]

During the past year, he had walked a tightrope between two lives. When he was in Europe, he could forget he had a wife and family. He was living in the moment—it was dangerous and thrilling to be a war correspondent, when each moment could be your last—with a beautiful mistress. It was so easy to forget he was married that he had suggested marriage to Martha, while domesticity and the demands of being a father and husband awaited him back in Key West.

He hadn't known if Pauline would welcome him back, and he didn't know exactly what she knew and what Jinny might have told her. When he'd gotten into the argument with Jinny at her apartment, she'd said he was "like a porcupine which sticks anyone who gets too close" and Ernest accused her of being the one sticking in the barbs.

233

His ship, the *Normandie*, arrived in New York City on Memorial Day, and he stayed in town briefly before heading home, visiting his friends the Allens. They had recently seen Pauline when she had been in New York, and Ernest asked if they thought she'd take him back. They weren't very encouraging.

Pauline and the boys met him at the airport and he got settled at home, resuming his routine of writing in the morning and physical activity in the afternoon. But shortly after arriving, he started to feel irritable. After living his own life in Spain, and the freedom he'd experienced, homelife felt oppressive.

Old friends had disappointed him, starting with Jinny and her gossip, as if she'd made it her mission to ruin him. Archibald MacLeish was another friend Ernest had confronted, over financial dealings during production of *The Spanish Earth*, the movie Ernest and Martha had worked on with Joris Ivens. Ernest ended his relationship with John Dos Passos in a scathing letter because Dos continued to support Jose Robles, who had been executed for treason. Ernest accused Dos of being a fascist.

It was hot and getting hotter by the day in Key West as Ernest read galleys for his latest book, a collection of all forty-seven short stories he'd written in one volume. Ernest had also written his first play, *The Fifth Column*, inspired by his experience in Spain, and he recommended to Max that they add the play to the book of short stories.

When his novel *To Have and Have Not* was published, readers and critics had complained that it was too short. Ernest wanted to counter that criticism with a book that was long with lots of good reading, a book that gave readers their money's worth.

Wyoming had always been a good place to work, and so Ernest determined they would begin the drive shortly. Before setting out, though, he sent Max the play with the promise to send the rest of the short-story galleys either en route or once he reached the ranch.

NO HOLDING BACK

THEY PACKED UP THE BUICK V8 and began the drive on August 3 with Gregory, Patrick, Jack, and Ada. Their first stop would be Jacksonville, to drop Gregory and Ada at the train for Syracuse, where they would stay with Ada's family while the rest of the family headed west.

Shortly after departing, near Palm Beach, Gregory accidentally scratched the pupil of Ernest's bad eye—the fourth time the eye had been injured. They checked into the Hotel Washington and stayed there for two days in a darkened room while Ernest's eye healed. When they resumed the trip, Ernest wore an eyepatch and dark glasses.

They made it to Jacksonville, and Gregory, at seven years old, didn't understand why he couldn't come to Wyoming too. But for now, it worked well for Gregory to go with Ada, freeing Pauline to work with Ernest on his manuscript while the two older boys enjoyed themselves on the ranch.

Two years earlier, when they'd driven across the country with Patrick and Jack, they had listened to the radio and stories about the Spanish Civil War. War, Pauline was sick of war. She had been sitting in Havana when gunshots broke out during the revolution. And she had seen the Spanish war take her husband away.

On this trip, in the front seat of the Buick, a different kind of war raged as Ernest and Pauline quarreled. When Pauline attempted to give Ernest directions, which he mostly ignored, he blamed her if he took

a wrong turn.* They fought when Ernest expressed his new disapproval
of the Roman Catholic Church and how it had betrayed the Loyalists,
with Pauline defending the Catholic church. In Denver, they ran out of
money and Ernest had to wire Max for cash.

The real reason they fought was the uninvited guest in the car: "Miss
Einhorn," as Pauline liked to call her. They had not openly discussed
Ernest's relationship with her, but Pauline had made it clear before Ernest
returned that he was welcome at home only if he was coming home for
good. Pauline prayed that Martha, like Jane, was a thing of the past.

Rain stampeded down the valley as they finally approached the
L Bar T. Despite the downpour, Pauline was confident that the boys
would find plenty to entertain themselves. She would focus on typing
and editing the story galleys with Ernest, hoping to work through the
damage that had been done.

---

* Is this unusual behavior for a man?

WORK MATTERS MOST

THE RAIN BEAT steadily down upon the cabin roof, eliminating any temptation to go fishing when the trout would hide in holes and the fishing wouldn't improve until the stream cleared. Ernest had a singular focus; sending the short stories to Max. He'd originally hoped to send the manuscript to Max by July, but he'd been waiting to hear if it would be possible to include his play *The Fifth Column* in the book—and here it was August.

When *A Farewell to Arms* had been adapted as a play, it had flopped. But he hadn't been involved in the production at all; the producers had just bought the rights from him. He hadn't even seen the play before it closed.

This was different; it was the first time Ernest had written an actual play. He'd written it in Spain, but it had seemed cursed from the start. One producer died, the second couldn't raise the money, and it didn't look like any other producers were interested at the moment, so he was considering publishing it with the short stories. He was anxious to put it behind him.

When *To Have and Have Not* debuted in October 1937, the reviews had been unenthusiastic, and he'd felt it was partly his fault. He admitted that he'd been "snooty," and he knew the critics despised you for that. His last successful book had been *A Farewell to Arms* in 1929. Since then he'd fought with critics each time he published a book.

It frustrated him to read their snide comments about his work and then to read accolades about his friends' work. When Dos published his

U.S.A. trilogy, critics loved it, noting that parts were inspired by James Joyce's *Ulysses*. Ernest felt the root of the problem was that the reviewers were jealous of him; they all wanted to be him. Plus, he knew his political views alienated some.

It had been a while since his North American Newspaper Alliance contract had ended and he'd received a paycheck. The extra days in Palm Beach for his eye to heal added expense and also delayed his efforts to get the galleys to Max.

At the ranch, he wrestled with the order of the stories and the play in the book. Should the play come before the short stories, or after? Ernest knew the right order was important to the book, and for two weeks he wrestled with the stories' order finally deciding:

"The Fifth Column"

"Short Happy Life"

"Capitol of the World"

"Snows of Kilimanjaro"

"Old Man at the Bridge"

"Up in Michigan"

"On the Quai at Smyrna"

followed by:

the Boni & Liveright version of "In Our Time"

"Men Without Women"

"Winner Take Nothing"

Ernest and Max continued to argue over "Up in Michigan." Max was worried because authorities in Detroit had suppressed *To Have and Have Not* for objectionable material. There were still censors for obscenity; why give them reasons to suppress this book? The phrase he was concerned about was still included in the story. Couldn't they just remove it?

But Ernest didn't budge. The story needed the phrase; without it, the story was pointless.* And though cutting the story from the collection would solve the problem, Ernest was against that because it was supposed to be a collection of all the stories he'd written so far. Without "Up in Michigan," it would be all his short stories minus one.

_____

* The phrase was, "Oh, it's so big and it hurts so."

Another request Max had made was to amend "The Snows of Kilimanjaro," taking out the passage about F. Scott Fitzgerald. Instead of deleting it, Ernest wanted to retain "Scott" but would take out his surname—would that satisfy Max?

Once Ernest heard back from Max on whether he agreed to the order of the play and stories, he would start work on the final piece of the book, the preface. During the first weeks on the ranch, he'd worked hard with Pauline on getting the stories ready to send—no matter how much they fought, they were able to put their differences aside to work together. He still trusted her editing skills above anyone else's.

A CAUSE FOR CONCERN?

OLIVE AND LAWRENCE NORDQUIST, their dear friends, had divorced; Lawrence was now seeing Olive's niece. The Roman Catholic Church didn't allow divorce, and it certainly wasn't something Pauline wanted— she would do whatever it took to weather the current storm. She believed that Martha, like Jane, was just a phase that would soon pass.

She'd read what Ernest had written about men and infidelity in his novel *To Have and Have Not* with interest: "But they aren't built that way. They want some one new, or some one younger, or some one that they shouldn't have, or some one that looks like someone else. Or if you're dark they want a blonde. Or if you're blonde they go for a red-head. . . . The better you treat a man and the more you show him you love him the quicker he gets tired of you." As a writer's wife, she knew not to take his words personally. Pauline tried to keep his interest, in part by staying fit and changing hairstyles: she was blonde again with a bob like Martha's.

Reading his new play, she had additional cause for concern. The play was about a secret agent, Philip Rawlings, working for the Loyalists. His cover is that of a journalist who walks like a gorilla, eats raw onions, and is plagued by insomnia and nightmares. He is in love with a beautiful American correspondent, Dorothy Bridges.

Some passages resonated, like when he wrote about the places he's been—the Crillon and the Ritz, Nairobi, the long white beaches at Lamu, Sans Souci on a Saturday night in Havana—all places he'd been with her. "But I've been to all those places," says Philip, "And I've left them

241

all behind. And where I go now I go alone, or with others who go there for the same reason I go."

Pauline was trying to look toward the future. They had worked for two weeks on the short stories, as Pauline typed his corrections. With limited access to the outside world, he was for the moment all hers. Until the afternoon he received news from the North American Newspaper Alliance.

HITLER THREATENS

WEEKS AFTER THEIR ARRIVAL, the rain still fell in the valley, and in the high country, the peaks were dusted with snow. For the first time since he'd been coming to the L Bar T, Ernest didn't keep a fishing log recording the river conditions and fish he'd caught. The weather made it easy for him to continue to stay inside and put finishing touches on the book. On August 17, he packaged the story corrections typed by Pauline with a letter to Max, along with a handwritten dedication for the book, "To Marty and Herbert with Love," and mailed the package.*

Once he sent the preface to Max, the last piece, his work would be finished, and he would need a new project to consume him. But until then, he could hunt and fish after the weather cleared.

His plans changed abruptly, however, after he was contacted by the North American Newspaper Alliance. Adolf Hitler and his Nazi Party were continuing in their quest to reunite the German Fatherland. When the map had been redrawn after the Great War and Czechoslovakia was formed, three million Germans had found themselves living there. These Germans had begun protests and provoked violence from the Czech police. Hitler used that unrest as an excuse to place German troops along the Czech border. The North American Newspaper Alliance

---

* The dedication was to Martha Gellhorn and Herbert Matthews, the *New York Times* reporter Ernest covered the Spanish Civil War with. Ernest was making a statement to the world about his relationship with Martha. However, in the end, the dedication did not appear in the published book.

wanted Ernest to cover Hitler's actions and the possibility of another world war.

The assignment provided Ernest with the perfect exit from the ranch. Pauline had been sitting by the fire when he told her, and she had begged him not to go. Explaining that it was something he felt he had to do, he promised her he wouldn't engage in combat. Not even his love for Wyoming and the L Bar T could keep him away from Martha's pull. He had already arranged for her to meet him in Paris. He couldn't stand to be away from her for another minute.

Max wrote to him one last time before Ernest left the ranch. He felt Ernest had amended the reference to F. Scott Fitzgerald in "The Snows of Kilimanjaro" very "neatly." However, he wished Ernest could completely remove Scott's name altogether. He had asked two people to read Ernest's revision, and they agreed that Scott might still feel badly. He told Ernest they'd discuss the matter in person when Ernest delivered the preface while he was in New York.

Ernest departed for New York in late August, leaving his family behind. He and Pauline were no longer two halves of the same person. Ernest wanted to go alone. Or in the very least, if not alone, without Pauline.

TIME WITH THE BOYS

AFTER THE SHOCK of Ernest's departure settled, Pauline reluctantly accepted it. What choice did she have? He was doing important work and he must go; but his absence shouldn't stop her from enjoying her time with the boys. Ernest had arranged for Toby Bruce to come to the ranch in September to pick them up, and she would enjoy her time until then.

The rains had finally ceased, and they were free to enjoy the activities they loved—riding, fishing, and exploring. Jack had rescued a little owl with an injured wing before Ernest left, and he continued to tend to it by feeding it mice while it recovered. All the boys loved animals, and Pauline tried to accommodate their interests whenever she could. In Key West they had a menagerie, including dogs, cats, goldfish, peacocks, and flamingos, so caring for a little owl didn't faze her. Patrick was a little more needy than his independent brother, complaining of a stiff neck and that he didn't have anyone to play with. Pauline thought it would be good for him to get back in school with other children. She was proud to see him growing into such a nice boy; one morning he surprised her by going out fishing by himself and catching a trout for her breakfast.

She went out riding every day and had even gone sage grouse hunting. It was odd: after a summer of fighting, when Ernest left she felt very calm about the future of their marriage. He sent her two cables, a thirteen-page letter, a postcard, and Evelyn Waugh's new book, *Scoop*—hardly the actions of a man who might be considering leaving a marriage. She wrote him a loving letter in return, thanking him and telling she missed him very much. "But I do hope you won't stay away too long. A husband should not stay away from a loving wife too long. I won't say this again as I do not want to hurry you."

Before leaving the ranch, Pauline sent Ernest one last, hastily written letter telling him that she was feeling optimistic about their future in a "fine solid way, founded on quiet confidence that everything is going to be fixed up good." She promised to write more when they reached Piggott, and closed by saying, "My you are a lovely man, and we had a lovely time out here—hate to go." On September 6, Toby packed up the car and they departed, first stopping in Lincoln, Nebraska, to drop Jack at the train for Chicago.

———————

Ten days in Piggott with the family gave Pauline plenty of time to consider her next steps. She wasn't ready to go back to Key West—September was still hot there—instead deciding to rent an apartment in New York through Thanksgiving. She would be near Jinny and could connect with her friends like Dawn Powell, friends she had lost touch with through the years. Uncle Gus and Aunt Louise would be nearby, and she could participate in culture that she missed, like going to the ballet and theater. Jack was attending the Storm King School in Connecticut, and he could come to New York for the weekends. The more she thought about it, the more excited she became.

She sent Ernest a letter telling him of her plans and inviting him to join the family there when he returned from his assignment. She let him know that she was trusting him to be doing the things he was telling her he was doing, and that "she does not hear from strangers where her husband is and with whom."

PARIS

PARIS WITH MARTHA WAS WONDERFUL, but she often traveled on assignment, a role reversal from when Ernest had lived in Paris with Hadley and was often the one leaving her behind while he was on assignment. With Martha away, he worked on some stories, sending Arnold Gingrich "Night Before Battle" as his final piece for *Esquire*. And he'd started a new novel about the Spanish Civil War.

Pauline was living in New York in a large apartment with room for Gregory, Ada, Patrick, and Jack on weekend visits. She'd written to him sharing news about her activities in the city and about his brother Leicester, who had moved with his wife to New York and gotten a job at *Country Home* magazine.

When *The Fifth Column and the First Forty-Nine Stories* was published, Pauline couldn't find a single copy on display in the Scribner's window. She was angry when she reported to Ernest about the lackluster book promotion that he wasn't there to deal with it himself. "Perhaps my dear fellow you should be shifting from your mistress—shall we call her War—to your Master."

Critics pointed out that there were only four new stories in the book, along with a political play that was propaganda. Ernest didn't hide his Loyalist sympathies, and if the critics took issue with it, so be it. His obligation was to write the truth, and his biggest obligation was to his work. He buried himself in his new novel, returning to New York on November 24, where he would stay with Pauline and the family at the apartment until the lease ran out at the end of the month. Then Ernest and Pauline would return to Key West separately.

THE MOMENT HAD PASSED

A NEW YEAR, 1939, arrived in Key West, and Pauline could not predict what it would bring, despite her clairvoyant powers. After Ernest had returned from covering Hitler's approach, she'd realized that the moment she'd felt at the ranch, her optimism about the future of their relationship, was gone. He was sullen in the New York apartment, then came to Key West only briefly before returning to New York for the premiere of *The Spanish Earth* without her. He returned to Key West for clean clothes and then immediately left for Havana. He arrived for the sake of appearances when Uncle Gus and Aunt Louise visited, or his mother, or Jack, who was there for spring break from school. But the truth was that he'd been living at the Hotel Ambos Mundos in Cuba for months, ostensibly to work on the novel, but Pauline suspected he was consumed by something else.

She continued to write newsy letters from home to him, keeping up the pretense of a marriage: he'd left behind some things he might need—underwear, swimming trunks, and she was sending him by courier the new deck shoes he'd wanted. She also sent sample menus for a nice lunch he could make with leg of lamb and mint sauce, along with details about the boys' dentist appointments, observations on the weather, and a description of her garden.

As summer approached, and she was making plans for the boys, she ran an idea past Ernest. She had been feeling overwhelmed, she wasn't sure why, but she wrote to Ernest saying that she wanted to send the boys to camp for the summer so that they could be with other children.

It would be cheaper than her renting a home in Nantucket for all of them, and it would give her some freedom. She had found a nice camp run by Australians where the boys could fish, ride, build dams, and have fun during June and July.

Ernest, however, had not been receptive, accusing her of "dumping off the boys"—quite brash coming from a man who had very little involvement in day-to-day parenting.

HAVANA NIGHTS

ERNEST HAD LEFT for Havana after New Year's, checking into a hotel to work five or six hours a day on the novel he'd started in the fall. The more pages he wrote, the more excited he became about the work, his best since *A Farewell to Arms*. This novel could be the one that readers were waiting for.

He was still waiting to hear from Max on the latest sales figures from *The Fifth Column and the First Forty-Nine Stories*, but he knew they weren't what he'd hoped. It was hard to make money as a writer when the jealous critics were all out to get you. He needed money, and he still shared an account with Pauline, but he hated asking her to send him checks. Money was one thing it seemed they were constantly discussing. When he came back from Paris, he'd thought they had $4,000 in their account, but he discovered it was down to $400; it turned out living in New York was very expensive.

He had fifteen thousand words written on the new novel—it was bad luck to talk about it—but he was going to write until it was finished. In Cuba, he would start writing at 8:30 AM and finish at around 2:00 PM, and he planned to stay there to work, no matter what. He was feeling very fit, down to 198 pounds, healthy, and happy—he had that good feeling each day after a productive day of working on a long book. It was the same feeling he'd had when things were going well on *A Farewell to Arms*.

A distraction arrived in March when Martha came to Havana to find them a place to live. He was still married to Pauline, so he continued to receive his mail at the Hotel Ambos Mundos address for propriety's sake. But Martha had found them a lovely home on a hill ten minutes from Havana.

Since being back in the States, he and Martha had spent just a few stolen encounters together, including the New York premiere of *The Spanish Earth*, to which Ernest had even invited Jack to join them. Jack couldn't believe that his father would be in the company of such a young gorgeous woman.

Ernest and Martha made plans for her to join him in Havana, and it had been his job to find a place for them to live. But he'd been too busy with his writing. He could tell "Marty" was disappointed when she arrived. Not content to share his slovenly accommodations at the hotel, she set out to find them a place of their own while he worked.

When Ernest had received Pauline's letter about sending the children to summer camp, he'd accused her of trying to get rid of them for the summer. He didn't hear from her for a while after that, until she called the hotel to tell him that she'd had a health scare, rectal bleeding that the doctors thought might be cancer. He listened sympathetically and told her although he hated to stop work on his novel that was going so well, of course he would do it for her if she needed him to. He told her he'd call her the next day to hear the results of the diagnostic tests. And he also asked her to send him some blank checks; he had run out.

As Ernest hung up the phone, a lightning bolt shot through the wires and knocked him ten feet across the room. He was left temporarily speechless, with his neck and left arm paralyzed for a short time. It scared the hell out of him.*

---

* Karma.

STRUCK BY LIGHTNING

ERNEST DIDN'T CALL the next day as he'd promised. Instead, Pauline called Ernest to tell him the good news: the cancer test results were negative. The doctor thought her condition could possibly have been stress related. Ernest had seemed relieved that everything had worked out, and that he didn't have to stop writing to join her. Most of the call was spent talking about him and how he had been struck by lightning. He seemed more concerned about himself than if she had cancer.

Their African safari guide Philip Percival was in New York, and Pauline had relayed a message that he wanted to see Ernest while he was visiting. She invited Ernest to come to New York; perhaps they could go to the Louis–Galento fight together. But Ernest hadn't wanted to take time away from writing while it was going well. Infuriated that Ernest couldn't find time in his schedule to see his former safari guide— a man who had been so marvelous to them in Africa and who had become their good friend—Pauline told Ernest in no uncertain terms that she was not happy. She followed with a letter saying their plans "would be quite simple . . . and you were say a brick layer instead of a woman layer and a writer. . . . My God Papa, but you have made things complicated with this Einhorn business. There is something rotten somewhere."

He responded with a letter of his own. He didn't appreciate her tongue-lashing; maybe the lightning should have killed him and made it easier for Pauline.

Frustrated by fighting with Ernest, feeling relieved by her clean bill of health, and finding free time on her hands after finally receiving Ernest's assent to enroll the boys at camp, Pauline decided impulsively to go on a European tour with her friends Paul and Brenda Willert. She had recently received a $10,000 inheritance after the death of her uncle Henry Pfeiffer that she could use to finance her trip. She asked Charles Thompson to stop by the Key West house and retrieve her passport since Ernest was away in Havana.

On the afternoon of July 9, she wrote to Ernest, "Relax and enjoy Miss Einhorn and here I am off your hands temporarily at best. Love Pauline."

Then on the way to the ship on July 12, she wrote in great haste, "Dearest Papa, Very excited, rather frightened and certainly wish you were going. Maybe next time you will be."

THE REAL REASON

ERNEST KNEW THE REASON why Pauline was in Europe. He'd been keeping up the pretense that he lived in a Havana hotel, but the truth was that he was living with Martha at a villa she'd found, Finca Vigía ("the lookout house"), above the working-class town of San Francisco de Paula. Pauline had finally confronted him, realizing that Martha was more than a passing affair.

He was still keeping up appearances with friends and family, telling them that Pauline was "prettier all the time." Not ready to burn the bridge with his in-laws quite yet, he wrote them that he had supported her plans to go to Europe; she needed to have some fun after the cancer scare. With war threatening to break out, it could be years before they could go back to Paris. He added that he'd been working hard so he had plenty of money to send Pauline on the trip after selling *To Have and Have Not* to the pictures. (He didn't mention that she was using her own inheritance money for the trip.)

With Pauline out of his hair, he was free to live his life with Martha, but the heat was making it harder to work in Havana. He decided to take all three boys to the ranch this summer, a guy's trip. He wrote to Hadley to make arrangements to meet Jack in August at the Nordquist Ranch with Patrick and Gregory.

Typically, Pauline scheduled their complicated travel plans, but this time Ernest would do it himself. Jack knew how to get there, through the park to Cooke City, or on the new road if it was finished. Hadley responded that she and Paul were going to be vacationing near Cody at the Crossed Sabres Ranch. Ernest felt plans falling into place. Picking up Jack in Cody and driving together to the ranch would be terrific.

He and Martha would leave from Key West, he would drop her off at her mother's home in St. Louis, and then he would drive to Wyoming. Toby Bruce could take the train to pick up the boys at Camp Te Whanga in New Preston, Connecticut, and they'd all be together for some hunting and fishing at the L Bar T: fifteen-year-old Jack, eleven-year-old Patrick, and eight-year-old Gregory—his first time at the ranch.

Ernest sent a letter to his sons at summer camp telling them that he was working on his new book, writing about a snowstorm, and he realized, why not go out West and see a snowstorm? He told the boys Toby would pick them up, and they should be very good on the train. He closed the letter sending them much love and telling them he would see them soon.

THE REUNION

Shortly after his fortieth birthday on July 21, Ernest returned to Key West, packed the boys' Western clothes, hunting gear, and fishing rods in the Buick, and began the long drive to Wyoming. After dropping off Martha in St. Louis, he continued alone, giving him plenty of time to think.

He was on page 342 of the new novel about the Spanish Civil War, and he knew it was good. War was on his mind, as it looked like another world war might soon break out in Europe. During an interview with a reporter for the Key West newspaper, he stated that if war broke out, he would go to Europe. On the home front, the battle continued to rage as he found himself still married to Pauline, though he had asked Martha to marry him and they were working together to renovate their home outside Cuba.

It was all Pauline's fault. Her Catholicism had ruined their sex life. Her fragile health had prevented him from having the daughter he wanted. And if she'd gone to Spain with him while he covered the war, maybe things would have been different—he wouldn't have looked for warmth in a lovely correspondent's bed.

Her spending habits drove him crazy. He joked to Max about her trip to Europe that he'd probably need an advance to cover her spending in Paris. Just when he thought they had money in the account, he'd find it was all gone.

He owed Hadley money for Jack's schooling, and she had been understanding. Ernest had continued to feel affection for her—she was such a good woman. When he wrote to her about Jack coming to the ranch, he told her he admired her. He reminisced about some of the good times they had shared in the Dolomites, and the Black Forest, and the forest of the Irati—heaven on earth. He signed his letter with his nickname, "Tatie."

Driving past sagebrush-covered plains and fence posts that went on and on, he finally reached Cody, stopping at Crossed Sabres Ranch to meet up with Hadley, Paul, and Jack. The staff at the lodge informed him that the Mowrers were fishing at Grebe Lake, so he drove there to see if he could find them. He was in his car, parked at the end of the fire trail, listening to the radio about Germany's invasion of Poland and imminent declarations of war, when Hadley and Paul emerged from the woods.

He had not seen Hadley for eight years, since the time they sat in her Paris apartment and she asked his opinion about marrying Paul. Seeing her now, she looked well, with her red-gold hair and her face unlined.

Once, when they were married, he had taken the train from Paris to Schruns, where she and Bumby were waiting for him at the station. He recalled the sun streaming on them and how in that moment he had wished he had died before he ever loved anyone but her. But he had been returning after spending time in Paris with Pauline, and he had fallen in love with her.

The innocent love he had experienced with Hadley had been lost. They had been in Paris, with their whole life ahead of them. Hadley hadn't deserved it. She had never caused him a lick of trouble—he blamed Pauline. It was the oldest trick in the book when a wife's best friend seduces the husband. Now he felt Pauline was getting what she deserved. After all, she'd deliberately broken up his happy home life with Hadley. He'd been seduced by Pauline's money, something that Hadley didn't have, at least not at the level of wealth the Pfeiffers had.

Over time, he'd learned it was impossible to replicate that wonderful feeling he'd had with Hadley. He was not a player, as some thought; he couldn't handle more than one woman at a time. But he had gone from one to another, unsuccessfully trying to re-create that feeling.

Ernest thought Hadley and Paul made a grand couple. The three of them had talked together by the trail for an hour, discussing Jack's school progress, and what a fine young man he had become. They were on the subject of the war when Jack came down the trail—he had stayed behind at the lake for one more cast. How happy he looked to find them there together as they awaited his arrival.

Before driving back to the lodge, Paul gave Ernest a mess of grayling from their catch that day. The Mowrers drove back to the lodge to pack for their return drive to Chicago while Ernest and Jack headed to the L Bar T.

HOPE IN A LETTER

PAULINE HAD BEEN OVERJOYED to receive a lovely birthday telegram and letter from Ernest. She wrote to thank him and to tell him how pleased she was that he would be taking the children to the ranch out West, and how happy she was to be in Paris again. She was "renewing my youth and all my memories, and learning the streets and the land marks again." Once, it had been their Paris, and being back, remembering the good times, brought her happiness. She had even run into one of their old acquaintances on the street.

She had been observing the mood of the British, Germans, and French and their attitudes toward the political arena. Still, she didn't think there was a war on the horizon, despite stories in the newspapers about German mobilization.

The next day she added more thoughts to the letter, describing the trip, and "trying to give you an idea of how exciting and sportif" the Tour de France was, with pages recounting the scenery and hills, the crowds, and the masses of wildflowers. Still not finished, she set the letter aside, only to finish it on August 7, in time to send it out on the *Normandie*. She finished by adding, "DO have a good time out there with the children. Please tell me about everything if the big ones are biting and if the river is muddy and who is shooting well and how every body is. When I was unpacking yesterday at the bottom of my bag there was a little fly fish hook. Don't know HOW it got there."

When she had discovered the little hook, she had burst into tears. How did things get to be this way? Europe had not provided the healing tonic Pauline had hoped for. On the contrary, memories of Ernest were everywhere: Paris, the Tour de France, Austria, Bavaria, too many memories of their times together.

TALKING WITH BEARS

JACK AND ERNEST drove around the north end of Yellowstone National Park and out the northeast entrance through Cooke City. Along the way they stopped "to talk to two bears, one a cinnamon and the other black with a white blaze on its chest." Ernest enjoyed talking to bears, and Jack thought they responded to Ernest's voice and regarded him cheerfully and alertly while he spoke.

"Hey, Bear, you're looking awful damn fat. Must've been a good summer, eh?"

Sometimes they looked embarrassed when he scolded them. "Bear, you dumb son of a bitch, aren't you ashamed of yourself begging when other bears are out making an honest living, working? Bear, you're no damn good."

Jack tried talking to them too, but they ignored him. The bears seemed to know "which of us in the car was the figure of authority, and possibly, a fellow bear."

Now that Jack was nearly sixteen, Ernest treated him like a man—as when he introduced his son to Martha at the opening of *The Spanish Earth*. Jack thought Marty was nice; he also appreciated that she could cuss with the best of them, a trait he admired in a woman.

Ernest and Jack arrived at the ranch, where Patrick and Gregory were waiting for them. They all settled into the Sidley cabin, and Jack looked forward to weeks ahead of fishing and riding with Papa and his brothers.

WAR

FOR THE FIRST TIME, Ernest had all three of his sons with him at the ranch, a platoon of male company. They developed a rhythm, fishing in the morning and then, writing by the light of a kerosene lamp, he would work on his novel until late in the night.

Work on the novel came to a temporary halt early in the morning of September 3, 1939, when Ernest heard the news on his radio and ran to the lodge, shouting "The Germans have marched into Poland! World War II has started! This could not have happened if America had helped Spain!" Ernest invited ranch guests back to the Sidley cabin to listen to the news reports on his old radio that he'd carried with him throughout his time in Spain.

News of the war was a distraction, but he knew he needed to finish the novel before war took him away again. He was enjoying having his sons with him and was in no hurry to leave. As much as he moaned about the new Beartooth Highway, he could easily drive to Cooke City, Red Lodge, and Billings—ninety miles away—where he picked up Chub Weaver and brought him back to the ranch for a visit. When they reached the L Bar T, it was late at night, and they could be heard singing cowboy songs as they drove across the meadow toward the lodge. The two men had been friends for nine years.

The society of male companionship was interrupted mid-September when Ernest received an unexpected phone call from Pauline. She had returned to the United States and decided to fly out to join him. Could he pick her up at the Billings airport?

CASUALTIES

PAULINE HAD CONTINUED to write letters to Ernest during his frequent absences in the past year like a loving wife would do, choosing to believe that she still had a marriage and that her husband was working hard in Cuba on his next novel, rather than shacking up with his young mistress. But sometimes she couldn't help herself, and the words of her frustration flowed.

"Oh Papa, darling, what _is_ the matter with you. If you are no longer the man I used to know, get the hell out, but if you are, stop being so _stupid_."

On her European tour, she spent a lot of time thinking about Ernest. It had been nearly six months since they'd been in the same place together. She decided to surprise him and the boys at the ranch, the place where they had enjoyed many wonderful times. Although her attempt at a romantic reunion in Paris had been a disaster, perhaps this surprise visit would be just what their marriage needed. Either way, it was time to have a discussion. They couldn't go on like this, staying married, while Ernest lived a completely separate life from the family. She had made her feelings clear in her letters to him and was hopeful he would choose her and his sons over Miss Einhorn.

When she reached New York, she called to ask him to meet her in Billings. However, on the plane ride to Billings, she'd become ill—raw throat, fever, aching—feeling worse by the minute. Fate conspired against Pauline's happy plans.

The drive to the ranch with Ernest was long, and she felt miserable. In addition, the weather was rainy and damp, not helpful for her condition, and they were stuck inside the cabin. At first, Ernest tried to attend to her, acting as though she was a distant relative instead of his wife. He went through the motions, trying to cook some food for her while she huddled under a blanket, drinking rye whiskey for medicinal purposes. But his rote actions made it clear that she wasn't wanted there.

Trying her best to be with her family, Pauline had struggled to get out of bed, to unpack some of her clothes. But when she found the wax buttons on her favorite Paris suit melted through the fabric, it was the last straw. All her frustrations and sadness came out as she sobbed uncontrollably while Patrick tried to comfort her.

She knew Ernest was not good at caring for sick people, but this time it was different. He was restless and complained that there was nothing for him to do after work each day. Then one September day, he announced he simply couldn't do it any longer.

It was miserable, with the boys witnessing their parents' breakup, Pauline lying sick in bed as her marriage imploded. Ernest arranged for Toby to come to Wyoming and drive Pauline and the boys back to Piggott later in September. He packed his bags, loaded the Buick, and drove across the log bridge one last time, away from the ranch, to Martha's arms.

Toby picked up Pauline and the boys at the ranch, and she had the three thousand miles back to Key West to gather her thoughts. During her years with Ernest, she had given up her own ambitions at *Vogue* and made Ernest her career—as he'd gone from an unknown writer to the great writer of his time, producing nine books and numerous articles and short stories. She'd been his typist, editor, and critic, as well as his patron, providing financial support from her family.

She could see now that she had made a mistake giving up everything for him: her career, her friends, even her relationship with her boys. She had even betrayed some of the teachings of her faith to be with him, an affair with a married man, and she continued to make amends for those actions.

Now she would need to work to rebuild those relationships. But, at least, she hoped they were reparable. She had been finding Key West dull, and conversations were so limited. Perhaps she would move to New York or San Francisco, or even Paris.

She'd had eight wonderful years with him (out of twelve). But she realized that when he made up his mind to marry someone else, there was nothing she could do to stop him. She had once been the other woman; it was ironic that she had missed the early signs that it was happening to her. She had underestimated this affair with Martha. It was like Ernest's story "The Snows of Kilimanjaro," when the hunter thought he had a little thorn scratch but it turned out to be gangrene. She had thought Martha was just a little scratch.

She still loved Ernest, and she did not want to be divorced, but he had answered her question when she had asked, "If you are not the man I think you are, then you should get the hell out." Obviously he was not the man she had thought he was.

WHEN HE CAME UP
FOR AIR

SUN VALLEY, A NEW RESORT in Idaho being developed by Averell Harriman, the chairman of the Union Pacific Railroad, was actively courting a celebrity clientele, and Ernest was on the top of their list. He picked up Martha at the Billings airport and they drove through the otherworldly Craters of the Moon— craggy black volcanic rocks and acres of scorched earth—arriving in Sun Valley and checking into their suite. Ernest, enjoying the momentum he was experiencing on his Spanish Civil War novel, hunched over the typewriter while Martha entertained herself the best she could. But six weeks later she left for Finland on an assignment from *Colliers*, leaving him alone.

When he came up for air, looking around at his empty room, it was November. Ernest realized it was time to head south and give some thought to the holidays. He thought he might spend Christmas with Pauline and the boys in Key West, thinking perhaps she'd be agreeable to that. But on the contrary, Pauline wrote to him that he wouldn't be welcome if he was planning to return to Martha after the holidays.

Ernest wrote to Hadley to find out what Jack's Christmas plans were. Maybe he could have Christmas with him? The Mowrers were staying in Chicago for Christmas, but he would be welcome to join them, Hadley said, but Ernest didn't want to impose. He wanted to have Christmas with his family in Key West.

When Toby arrived at Sun Valley to drive Ernest back to Key West, he told Ernest that this time Pauline meant business. She and the boys would not be in Florida. Instead, they were going to New York to spend Christmas with Jinny.

Despite Toby's warning, Ernest showed up at the Whitehead house in Key West and found Pauline and the boys were gone, the house deserted. The staff had been given a paid Christmas holiday. Only Jimmy the gardener remained, living in the pool house. Ernest couldn't believe she was really gone, denying him the opportunity to be with his children, leaving him to spend Christmas alone.

EPILOGUE

1940

What Ernest Loved About Marty

Her spunk
She was a damned good writer
Not afraid to swear
Spontaneous and open
"Bravest woman he'd ever met"
"Would never be a dull wife who just forms herself on [him] like
  Pauline and Hadley"
Young—not an older woman like Agnes or Pauline or Hadley
Paid her own way
Friends with Eleanor Roosevelt; took him to the White House
Could maybe produce a daughter
Beautiful
She made him "so damned happy"
~~Independent~~

SUCCESS

ERNEST'S DIVORCE FROM PAULINE had been official on Labor Day, but he had made a deal with the Miami Associate Press Bureau to hold off on the news until after his new novel *For Whom the Bell Tolls* debuted on October 21, 1940. He didn't want any possible negative publicity to interfere with the book's success. The media was fascinated with his personal life, portraying him as a womanizing cad, and that wasn't the headline he wanted people to read in the news. He wanted the story to be about his new book.

In Sun Valley with Martha he had nervously awaited to hear the world's opinion of a book he felt was one of his best. The reviews were favorable! Critics called it an important addition to American literature. Edmund Wilson wrote in the *New Republic*, "Hemingway the artist is with us again. It's like having an old friend back." At the Sun Valley lodge a private switchboard was assigned to take the Hemingway calls, and a special bell-man delivered the Hemingway mail. A movie deal starring Gary Cooper was in the works for the highest price ever paid to a book for film rights.

When the reviews came out, in many ways it was a happy time, but Ernest was still smarting over his divorce negotiations with Pauline. She had not made things easy for him, the way Hadley had done; she was demanding (egged on by Jinny) a virtual pound of flesh. She didn't need the money, but she demanded it as punishment, succeeding in squeezing $500 a month support out of him for the boys. And she would keep the house in Key West, though he retained ownership of 40 percent. But most importantly, he got his freedom.

The more Pauline had delayed the divorce, extending the proceedings, the more he'd raged. She was standing in the way of his marriage to Martha. But what did Pauline think would happen? She had stolen him from Hadley, and "those who live by the sword, die by the sword." Now she knew how Hadley felt.

He and Martha had their own pet names: she called him Rabby or Rabbit, and he called her Bongie. Ernest enjoyed Martha's independence to a degree, and it was ironic that she was also a journalist and like Pauline had worked for *Vogue* in Paris. But she'd been traveling for her work too much for his liking—she had spent a whole month in New York. For a while he wondered if she really was going to marry him, and if not, he considered delaying divorce proceedings with Pauline—maybe he could get a better deal. But at last the divorce was finalized, and he and Martha were in Sun Valley on November 4, 1940, when the Associated Press ran the story.

The path was clear for their own nuptials. Anxious to get to New York City to soak up the praise about his new book, Ernest and Martha left Sun Valley on November 20, 1940, stopping in Cheyenne, Wyoming, to get married in the Union Pacific Railroad dining room with a justice of the peace presiding over the ceremony. It was almost exactly four years since they first met at Sloppy Joe's in Key West.

New York was abuzz with talk of Ernest's new novel, a literary triumph; the accolades all he had dreamed of. He and Marty attended receptions and parties while he soaked it all up, the praise, the toasts. Unlike the disparaging comments in *The Sun Also Rises*, *To Have and Have Not*, "The Snows of Kilimanjaro," and "The Short Happy Life of Francis Macomber," based on the women in his life, in *For Whom the Bell Tolls*, the hero, Robert Jordan, says: "You never had it before and now you have it. What you have with Maria . . . is the most important thing that can happen to a human being."

Everything in his life had gone better with Marty, and he was so damned happy. Ernest had found the fire he had needed to write. He had found his muse at last.

In the words of his character Jake Barnes in *The Sun Also Rises*, at least it was "pretty to think so."

AUTHOR'S METHOD

My path to this book was not a straight line; I started out writing one book and ended up writing another. I wanted to share the story of the time Ernest Hemingway spent in Wyoming near my home, but as I dug deeper in my research a voice kept chiming in, and that voice was Pauline's. As I read about her role in his life and his work from 1926 to 1940, I was hooked—by a story that began back in the United States after Paris, after the birth of Patrick, their first son, that began in Wyoming's Bighorn Mountains and ended eleven years later at a cabin in the northwest corner of Wyoming. Pauline Pfeiffer could be known as "the invisible wife" compared to Hadley Hemingway, Ernest's first wife, also known as the "Paris wife"; and Martha Gellhorn, his third spouse, the war correspondent/journalist wife—both of whom have many books written about them. Mary, Ernest's fourth and final wife, assured her place in history by writing her own book.

Since most of the people I'm writing about in *Cockeyed Happy* are deceased, I drew on their correspondence to re-create their story in their words when possible. Conversations in my book often came from letters published in *The Letters of Ernest Hemingway, Vol. 3: 1926–1929*, and *Vol. 4: 1929–1931*, Cambridge University Press; or from unpublished letters at the JFK Library, which I relied heavily upon for the period from 1931 to 1940. Unfortunately, many of Ernest's letters to Hadley and Pauline did not survive. Hadley burned many of his letters, and Pauline's stated wishes asked that Ernest's letters be burned after her death. (She died in 1951.) I included quotes from letters and other documents in this book exactly as they were written, with the writers' original spelling and grammar.

Obtaining digitized versions of Ernest Hemingway's letters was often challenging. Working remotely, I could see the dates of letters but not the content in the folders at JFK, so when I requested a batch of letters it would be hit or miss what I might find. Often they had not been transcribed, appearing in his own downward slanting script with words underlined and crossed out—challenging to decipher, but also thrilling to read in his actual handwriting.

Other sources that I depended upon include Judy Slack's *Ernest Hemingway: His 1928 Stay in the Bighorn Mountains of Wyoming,* a book compiled of news clippings, photographs, and diary entries found in The Wyoming Room, Sheridan County Fulmer Public Library. In Cody, Wyoming, Robyn Cutter provided me with a legal folder of research about Hemingway's time at the Nordquist Ranch, as well as contacts of family members who had relatives who had worked at the L Bar T.

The book that I relied upon for much of Pauline's point of view was Ruth Hawkins's *Unbelievable Happiness and Final Sorrow: The Hemingway-Pfeiffer Marriage.* Hawkins has written the most thorough work encompassing Pauline's life. Labeled as the "husband stealer," Pauline had been mostly scorned or ignored before Hawkins's book, although she was the wife with him during arguably the most productive years of his life and one of the few editors he trusted, a story that wasn't fully told until Hawkins's book.

Other books I mined for details include Carlos Baker's *Ernest Hemingway: A Life Story*; Jack Hemingway's *Misadventures of a Fly Fisherman*; Honoria Murphy Donnelly's *Sara & Gerald: Villa America and After*; Linda Patterson Miller's *Letters from the Lost Generation*; and Denis Brian's *The True Gen.* You'll find a complete list in the bibliography.

Writing a book about Ernest Hemingway is challenging in the best of times, but even more challenging when you are finishing your research during a worldwide pandemic. In a single week the libraries I was depending on closed and employees worked remotely, hours were cut, emails often went unanswered. Luckily for me the majority of my research had been done by March 2020 when the JFK Library closed, but I had to make do with the resources available to finish the book. I can't thank the JFK librarians enough for their help; it was a fabulous experience to work with them.

I am only an amateur scholar compared to the numerous biographers who have put Hemingway's life on paper, however, my time spent at Goucher College earning an MFA in creative nonfiction was invaluable in this process. Thanks to the unfailing instruction of Lee Gutkind, Lisa Knopp, Phil Gerard, and Suzannah Lessard, I learned that creative nonfiction—a term some feel is confusing—means writing a nonfiction story using such common fiction tools as scene and dialogue. You don't make things up, you don't play with timelines, you tell the real story—but in a way that reads like a novel. This book is my attempt at using this challenging genre to tell the true story of Ernest and Pauline's time in Wyoming.

Note: In a crazy coincidence, when I was conducting my research, I found a series of articles written in the 1970s by Lee Gutkind, my Goucher instructor, about Hemingway in Wyoming, something he never mentioned to me in all the years I've known him. Lee's articles and research were extremely valuable in recreating Hemingway's Wyoming days.

ACKNOWLEDGMENTS

I WANT TO THANK THE PEOPLE in my life who have accompanied me on the journey to write this book. It often became a literal journey, beginning in my hometown of Sheridan, Wyoming, and traveling to Paris, then back to the Bighorn Mountains and a remote corner near Yellowstone. Lifelong thanks to my parents, Darlene and Jerry Worden, who endured having a writer in the family, accepting my choices even if they didn't always understand them, and my daughter, Anna Skrabacz, for her tireless support and boots-on-the-ground research with me, and for writing the bibliography for this book.

More family to thank for their interest in my work and words of encouragement: Daniel Skrabacz, Carolyn and Mark Skrabacz, and my dear aunt Dorothy Green. And to Anne Parsons, my friend, researcher, advisor, and editor extraordinaire—thank you for always making my work better. To the Yayas, my girlfriends since junior high: Sandy Suzor, Cyndi Lich, Heather Vanderhoef, Rita Camp, and Julie Mason—thanks for always waiting until noon to call because you knew I was writing in the morning. You are more sisters than friends; you know all my best stories. And to friends Eliza Cross, Susan Dugan, Shari Caudron, Dan Buchan—how lucky I am to have writers as friends; your valuable input helped shape this book.

To the writers of books about Ernest Hemingway who kindly answered my questions, I appreciate your generosity: Ruth Hawkins, Valerie Hemingway, Steve Paul, Chris Warren. And to Lee Gutkind—my friend, professor and writer—who knew our paths would cross again in this way? And I wouldn't have written this book if not for my literature professor at the University of Colorado, Dr. Victoria McCabe, and my high school teacher, the late Peg Weaver, both encouraging my Hemingway interest and making a difference in my life.

People who kindly provided research, contacts, photos, and help along the way include Patricia Kennedy and Joe Ban, Brian Gaisford, Lynn Houz, and Judy Slack in the Sheridan Library's Wyoming Room; Linda Fasano for taking me to Folly Ranch; Katherine Wonson for showing me the Hemingway cabin at the Bar BC; Sharon Dynak at the Ucross Foundation; and John Sutton at Sheridan College; as well as friends Povy Kendal Atchison, always my go-to photographer; Abbie Kozik; and Amy Stark. Thank you, too, Michelle Asakawa, for your superb skills copyediting my manuscript. To Paul Balaguer and Joe Yates, thanks for allowing me to join you in your love of all things Hemingway all those years ago.

The librarians at the Ernest Hemingway Collection, John F. Kennedy Presidential Library and Museum, and Sheridan Fulmer County Wyoming Room contributed the materials that became the foundation for this book, sending digitized photos and letters—with a special thanks to Kim Ostermeyer and Debra Raver for going the extra mile in their assistance. And Robyn Cutter at Park County Archives provided a treasure trove of articles, interviews, and research.

I owe a debt of gratitude to the pros at the Dystel, Goderich & Bourret agency, Jane Dystel and Miriam Goderich, for believing in my book concept, as well as Amy Bishop and Melissa Melo; and to my editor at Chicago Review Press, Jerome Pohlen, for making this book a reality, along with the rest of the team at CRP: Benjamin Krapohl, for guiding me through the process, Jonathan Hahn, for his work on the cover, and Jen DePoorter and Hailey Peterson, for their efforts on marketing and publicity.

Gratitude to my Wiesner Media family and friends at *Mountain Living* who have checked on my progress, offering words of encouragement as I finished the book. And more to the Left Bank Writers Retreat of Paris, who share my Hemingway interest and have accompanied my many visits to Hemingway's haunts in the City of Light: Sarah Suzor,

Travis Cebula, and the writers from around the world who have joined us each June.

To John Berry, at the Hemingway Foundation, Kirk Curnutt at the Hemingway Society, and Yessenia Santos at Simon & Schuster, thank you for your assistance as I navigated the circular world of permissions and for helping me obtain the materials I needed.

CREDITS

NOTES

Part I: 1928

Keen editorial eye. Ruth Hawkins, *Unbelievable Happiness and Final Sorrow: The Hemingway-Pfeiffer Marriage* (Fayetteville, AR: University of Arkansas Press, 2012), 59.

Strong again: EH to Waldo Peirce, early September 1928, *The Letters of Ernest Hemingway, Vol. 3: 1926–1929*, eds. Rena Sanderson, Sandra Spanier, and Robert Trogdon (Cambridge: Cambridge University Press, 2015), 429.

"Someone to feel": EH to Pauline, December 2, 1926, *Letters, Vol. 3*, 170.

"feeling of us": EH to Pauline, December 3, 1926, *Letters, Vol. 3*, 173.

"promotion of masculine": Pauline to EH, March 15, 1927, Ernest Hemingway Collection, John F. Kennedy Presidential Library and Museum, Boston (hereafter cited as JFK).

Vowed to always: Hawkins, *Unbelievable*, 71.

She could give: EH to Mary Pfeiffer, July 2–3, 1928, *Letters, Vol. 3*, 402.

Her throat never: EH to Pauline, March 28, 1928, *Letters, Vol. 3*, 376.

Explorers Come West

they reminded him: EH to Waldo Peirce, August 9, 1928, *Letters, Vol. 3*, 420.

Ernest recorded mileage: EH to Peirce, August 9, 1928, 420.

corner of Nebraska: Virginia K. Moseley, "Hemingway Remembered," *Barrington Courier Review*, September 27, 1979.

go out to Idaho: EH to Evan Shipman, July 6, 1928, *Letters, Vol. 3*, 408.

enormous amount of trout: EH to Waldo Peirce, July 6, 1928, *Letters, Vol. 3*, 404–406.

"Do me a favor": Moseley, "Hemingway Remembered."

in the autoambulanzia: EH to Waldo Peirce, July 6, 1928, *Letters, Vol. 3*, 405.

He'd been nineteen: Moseley, "Hemingway Remembered."

dangerously ill: EH to Henry Strater, July 6, 1928, *Letters, Vol. 3*, 407–408.

fill up the car: Moseley, "Hemingway Remembered."

one of the first: Hawkins, *Unbelievable*, 87.

"tourist cabins": Hawkins, 92.

"bloody book": EH to Archibald MacLeish, July 15, 1928, *Letters, Vol. 3*, 411–412.

six feet tall: Hawkins, *Unbelievable*, 39.

"just as much explorers": Moseley, "Hemingway Remembered."

Shit: EH to Waldo Peirce, August 9, 1928, *Letters, Vol. 3*, 420–422.

Strength in the Afternoon

"Mother is a dragon": Pauline to EH, July 31, 1928, JFK.

"or a corpse": EH to Mary Pfeiffer, July 2, 1928, *Letters, Vol. 3*, 402.

bellow, and they can drive you: EH to Waldo Peirce, July 23, 1928, *Letters, Vol. 3*, 413–414.

hunt quail: Hawkins, *Unbelievable*, 97.

"promotion of masculine": Pauline to EH, March 15, 1927, JFK.

pressed tin ceilings: Hawkins, *Unbelievable*, 21.

"praying to Saint Joseph": Pauline to EH, November 2, 1926, JFK; Hawkins, *Unbelievable*, 30.

"ambrosial": Hawkins, *Unbelievable*, 3.

alone in the kitchen: Hawkins, 3.

"locked out": Pauline to EH, October 30, 1926, JFK.

"cockeyed happy": Pauline to EH, November 22, 1926, JFK.

"Pauline has sent": Hadley Richardson Hemingway to EH, December 12, 1927, JFK.

regaining her strength: Hawkins, *Unbelievable*, 97.

"I'm not allowed": Pauline to EH, July 29 (misdated July 8), 1928, JFK.

"With you away": Pauline to EH, July 31, 1928, JFK.

"We have a little slogan": Pauline to EH, July 31, 1928, JFK.

meant to be together: Bernice Kert, *The Hemingway Women* (New York: W. W. Norton, 1983), 203.

Fifteen Girls

"shot all to hell": EH to Pauline, December 3, 1926, *Letters, Vol. 3*, 173.

"I think perhaps": EH to Hadley Richardson Hemingway, November 18, 1926, *Letters: Vol. 3*, 153.

"Give Pauline my love": Hadley Richardson Hemingway to EH, July 12, 1928, JFK.

"pure folly": Judy Slack, *Ernest Hemingway: His Stay in the Bighorn Mountains of Wyoming* (Sheridan, WY: The Wyoming Room, Sheridan County Fulmer Public Library, 2011), 149.

"all very attractive": Gaylord Donnelley letter, October 1990, in Slack, *Bighorn Mountains of Wyoming*, no page number.

"both the matador": Moseley, "Hemingway Remembered."

"Horney, that's the place": Moseley.

social event: *Sheridan Journal*, August 3, 1928.

guests had to step back: *Sheridan Journal*.

Wyoming Wine

cold beer: I constructed this scene by compiling details from Lee Alan Gutkind, "Sheridan Couple Put in Story," *Billings Gazette*, October 18, 1970; EH to Evan Shipman, August 10, 1928, *Letters, Vol. 3*, 424; and Ernest Hemingway, "Wine of Wyoming," *The Short Stories of Ernest Hemingway*, the Modern Library Edition (New York: Random House, 1938), 548.

under the table: Hemingway, "Wine of Wyoming," 548.

didn't have any beer: Hemingway, 548.

drunk at Brasserie Lipp: EH to Evan Shipman, August 10, 1928, *Letters, Vol. 3*, 424.

arrested twice: Slack, *Bighorn Mountains of Wyoming*, 138.

"light and tasting of grapes": Gutkind, "Sheridan Couple Put in Story."

"never had problems": A. E. Hotchner, *Papa Hemingway* (New York: Random House, 1966), 51.

They Got It Wrong

"Among Miss Donnelley's guests": *Sheridan Journal*, August 3, 1928.

believe everything: EH to Clarence and Grace Hemingway, February 5, 1927, *Letters, Vol. 3*, 200.

"wrote a book" and *"Seldom has a book"*: Percy Hutchinson, "Mr. Hemingway Shows Himself Master Craftsman in the Short Story," *New York Times*, October 16, 1927.

"filthiest books": Grace to EH, December 4, 1926, *Letters, Vol. 3*, 201n2.

wonderful ability: Clarence to EH, December 13, 1926, *Letters, Vol. 3*, 201n2.

"master in a new manner": Hutchinson, "Mr. Hemingway Shows Himself."

"eased off" advertising: Maxwell Perkins to EH, April 19, 1928, *Letters, Vol. 3*, 383n7.

"getting rich": EH to Maxwell Perkins, May 31, 1928, *Letters, Vol. 3*, 387.
"war was the best": Carlos Baker, *Ernest Hemingway: A Life Story* (New York: Charles Scribner's Sons, 1969), 161.

A Clean, Well-Lighted Ranch

"someone to feel swell": EH to Pauline Pfeiffer, December 2, 1926, *Letters Vol. 3*, 170–171.
"like fog": EH to Pfeiffer, December 2, 1926, 170–171.
"Started" meant Hadley: Hawkins, *Unbelievable*, 56.
"cockeyed happy": EH to Pauline Pfeiffer, December 2, 1926, *Letters, Vol. 3*, 170–171.
"Last fall": EH to Pauline Pfeiffer, November 12, 1926, *Letters, Vol. 3*, 140.
"I love you so": EH to Pauline Pfeiffer, December 3, 1926, *Letters, Vol. 3*, 173.

Wedding Pants

"wedding pants": Hawkins, *Unbelievable*, 98.
"If you will": Pauline to EH, March 23, 1927, JFK.
"a duffel bag with feet": Hawkins, *Unbelievable*, 98.

Taxi Service

"With a swell cook": Moseley, "Hemingway Remembered."
"to grubstake him": Moseley.
cast him as the heavy: Moseley.
"because he was smarter": Moseley.

A Visit to Oak Park

"a love pirate": EH to Clarence, September 9–14, 1927, *Letters, Vol. 3*, 286n3.

Maximum Insurance

"It cost me": Pauline to EH, August 9, 1928, JFK.
he drank nearly a gallon: EH to Maxwell Perkins, August 12, 1928, *Letters, Vol. 3*, 426.
"sheepherder's madness": EH to Isabelle Godolphin, August 12, 1928, *Letters, Vol. 3*, 425.
Always concerned: EH to Maxwell Perkins, August 12, 1928, *Letters, Vol. 3*, 426.

Angel Child

"Hurry up": Pauline to EH, July 31, 1928, JFK.
"He didn't make a noise": Pauline to EH, August 16, 1928, JFK.
Jinny had stopped: Hawkins, *Unbelievable*, 98.

Fatherhood

"shits": EH to Waldo Peirce, July 23, 1928, *Letters, Vol. 3*, 413.

Improvising

"not much worse": Gaylord Donnelley letter, in Slack, *Bighorn Mountains of Wyoming*, no page number.

Waiting for Pauline

"Mrs. Ernie": *Folly newsletter*, Sunday, August 19, 1928.

Fresh Mountain Air

ruled the household: Hawkins, *Unbelievable*, 101.
"handsome eyes": Hawkins, 101.
Dutch product: Hawkins, 101.
liked to push Patrick: Hawkins, 101.
based on Lady Duff Twysden: Hawkins, 99.

The End

Ernest would put: EH to Maxwell Perkins, April 21, 1928, *Letters, Vol. 3*, 382.

Seeing D'America

"writer of prominence": *Sheridan Journal*, August 24, 1928.
"sweet old guy": EH to Waldo Peirce, early September, 1928, *Letters, Vol. 3*, 429.
"furious foe": Maxwell Perkins to EH, June 18, 1928, *Letters Vol. 3*, 394n2.
"three big ones": EH to Waldo Peirce, September 23, 1928, *Letters, Vol. 3*, 440.

A Lady in the Car

"Now, now": Moseley, "Hemingway Remembered."

A Farewell to Wyoming

"knocking on wood": EH to Maxwell Perkins, September 28, 1928, *Letters, Vol. 3*, 457.

Part II: 1930

other wives: EH to Waldo Peirce, June 2, 1930, *The Letters of Ernest Hemingway, Vol. 4*, eds. Miriam Mandel and Sandra Spanier (Cambridge: Cambridge University Press, 2018), 304.

The L Bar T

"Have been drinking": EH to Waldo Peirce, June 2, 1930, *Letters, Vol. 4*, 303.
Uncle Gus told Ernest: GA Pfeiffer to EH, June 3, 1930, JFK.
"fishing is simply": Bill Horne to EH, March 2, 1930, *Letters, Vol. 4*, 238n1.
famous for wildlife: "North Absaroka Wilderness," Shoshone National Forest (website), United States Department of Agriculture Forest Service, accessed March 16, 2021, https://www.fs.usda.gov/recarea/shoshone/recarea/?recid=80897.
"I'm a writer": Lee Alan Gutkind, "Fishing, Writing, Drinking," *Billings Gazette*, October 25, 1970.

Jack's Room

bank president's step-grandson: Jack Hemingway, *Misadventures of a Fly Fisherman* (Dallas: Taylor Publishing, 1986), 13.

Pauline's Respite

"hobo" and "I don't know": Hawkins, *Unbelievable*, 121.

The World Changed

heaven would be: EH to F. Scott Fitzgerald, July 1, 1925, *Letters, Vol. 2*, 358–359.
"Taty, I felt so sorry": Kert, *Hemingway Women*, 215.
"I have finished": James Aswell, "Sunday Supplement," *Richmond Times Dispatch*, October 6, 1929.
"Hemingway's A Farewell to Arms": John Dos Passos, *New Masses*, December 1, 1929.
"belly up": EH to Waldo Peirce, June 2, 1930, *Letters, Vol. 4*, 303–304.
retail and wholesale: EH to Allan Tate, June 3, 1930, *Letters, Vol. 4*, 310.

Then There Were the Distractions

"couldn't learn anything": Gutkind, "Fishing, Writing, Drinking."
"fishing is going to be": Gutkind.

Flaying Dead Horses

"stop and flay": EH to Maxwell Perkins, July 24, 1930, *Letters, Vol. 4*, 334.
"a bear with carbuncles": EH to Clarence and Grace Hall Hemingway, July 15, 1928, *Letters, Vol. 3*, 409–410.
"I want it to be the book": EH to Maxwell Perkins, July 24, 1930, *Letters, Vol. 4*, 334–336.
"This is a good place": EH to Perkins, July 24, 1930, 334–336.

Letters from Piggott

Pauline received a letter: Mary Pfeiffer to Pauline and EH, July 30, 1930, Princeton University Library Special Collections, Princeton, NJ (hereafter cited as PUL).
"Get a good strong anchor": Pfeiffer to Pauline and EH, July 30, 1930, PUL.
would become delirious: Hawkins, *Unbelievable*, 111.
Her mother had recommended: Mary Pfeiffer to Pauline, June 5, 1929, PUL.
"swimming and loafing": Pauline to Virginia, September 16, 1929, *Letters, Vol. 4*, 100.

Jack at the Ranch

the leather quirt: Hemingway, *Misadventures*, 17.
"You know, Schatz": Hemingway, 17.
nearly dying with impatience: Hemingway, 17.
using his pockets: Hemingway, 2.
"were so beautiful": Hemingway, 18.

Biographical Crap

"to at once remove": EH to Maxwell Perkins, July 31, 1930, *Letters, Vol. 4*, 340.
not to answer questions: EH to Grace Hemingway, October 12, 1929, *Letters, Vol. 4*, 120.
"So HeLp Me GoD": EH to Maxwell Perkins, July 31, 1930, *Letters, Vol. 4*, 340.
no copies had yet been: Maxwell Perkins to EH, August 6, 1930, *Letters, Vol. 4*, 343n.

Vive la Marriage

"from the first moment": John Dos Passos, *The Best Times* (New York: The New American Library), 200.

Her Catholic beliefs: Hawkins, *Unbelievable*, 188.

a good trait: EH to Waldo Peirce, *Letters, Vol. 4*, 304.

"Sure we are going": Bill Horne to EH, March 2, 1930, JFK.

The Man Who Invented Montana

"straight legged": Moseley, "Hemingway Remembered."

"on the bum": EH to Milford Baker, August 12, 1930, *Letters, Vol. 4*, 344.

"the river was about": Moseley, "Hemingway Remembered."

"Ernest sat in the sun": Moseley.

The Cow-Eating Bear

"everything but shooting elephants": EH to Henry Strater, June 12, 1930, *Letters, Vol. 4*, 314.

"fear of busting": EH to Archibald MacLeish, August 31, 1930, *Letters, Vol. 4*, 352–353.

The men headed: Chris Warren, *Ernest Hemingway in the Yellowstone High Country* (Helena, MT: Riverbend Publishing, 2019), 45.

Dr. Trueblood: Warren, 45.

for medicinal purposes: Warren, 45.

"Ernest Hemingway was brought": *Cody Enterprise*, August 20, 1930.

Ernest told Ivan stories: Lee Alan Gutkind, "Bearskin Tempting," *Billings Gazette*, October 20, 1970.

"I haven't read": Addison Bragg, "In the Legend," *Billings Gazette*, November 15, 1970.

"If you want": Gutkind, "Bearskin Tempting."

Sparing Goofy: EH to Archibald MacLeish, August 31, 1930, *Letters, Vol. 4*, 352–353.

When he arrived: Gutkind, "Bearskin Tempting."

Big Game Hunter

Plus, he was still: EH to Maxwell Perkins, September 3, 1930, *Letters, Vol. 4*, 354.

"skinning dead horses": EH to Perkins, September 3, 1930, 354.

Girl Friday

"Damn," he said, "I forgot": Lee Gutkind, "Hemingway's Wyoming," *Casper Star Tribune*, October 19, 1970.

"You're dead!": Hemingway, *Misadventures*, 6.

On Stage and Screen

"an awful mess": Milford Baker to EH, September 24, 1930, PUL.

Dos Passos in the High Country

"watching Hem": Dos Passos, *Best Times*, 205.

Admittance Clerk

"Occupation?" she asked: Dan Burkhart, "Hemingway in Billings," *Billings Gazette*, February 22, 1998.

SOS Max

"PLEASE FORWARD": EH to Maxwell Perkins, November 3, 1930, *Letters, Vol. 4*, 395.

Pauline Takes Dictation

more time to practice: EH to Henri Strater, mid-November 1930, *Letters, Vol. 4*, 396.

"Why don't you have Scribner's": EH to Maxwell Perkins, November 17, 1930, *Letters, Vol. 4*, 400.

"It is fine": EH to Perkins, November 17, 1930, 400.

No More Guns

"any former address": EH to Mike Strater, November 23, 1930, *Letters, Vol. 4*, 410.

"faking romanticist": EH to Maxwell Perkins, December 1, 1930, *Letters, Vol. 4*, 416.

A Rotten Time

She encouraged Max: Pauline to Maxwell Perkins, December 1, 1930, *Letters, Vol. 4*, 415.

"The lines": EH to Archibald MacLeish, December 4, 1930, *Letters, Vol. 4*, 420.

"Well. Mac,": EH to MacLeish, December 4, 1930, 420.

Montana in the Rearview Mirror

leaving Montana: PUL, Cable, Western Union destination receipt stamp 1930 DEC 18 PM 12 17.

Part III: 1932

Lovely figure: EH to Guy Hickock, October 14, 1932, *Hemingway Selected Letters, 1917–1961*, ed. Carlos Baker (Great Britain: Panther Books, 1985), 372.

Recovery

bringing her: Michael Reynolds, *Hemingway: The 1930s* (New York: W. W. Norton, 1997), 64.

CHICAGO WOMAN: *Key West Citizen*, March 19, 1931.

The View Ahead

"a certain amount": Hawkins, *Unbelievable*, 141.

"Take good care": EH to Jane and Grant Mason, July 9, 1932, JFK.

Motherhood

"You are the punctuation": Kert, *Hemingway Women*, 233.

Mary Pfeiffer felt Patrick: Mary Pfeiffer to Pauline, June 7, 1932, JFK.

"Hemingway's Death"

"Hemingway's Death": EH to Maxwell Perkins, July 27, 1932, Baker, *Selected Letters*, 364.

"the regular rule": Maxwell Perkins to EH, July 7, 1932, *The Only Thing That Counts: The Ernest Hemingway-Maxwell Perkins Correspondence*, ed. Matthew J. Bruccoli (New York: Simon & Schuster, 1996), 172.2.

If he had included: Form letter EH wrote for Scribner's, undated, Bruccoli, *The Only Thing*, 179.

Ernest told Max: EH to Maxwell Perkins, June 28, 1932, Baker, *Selected Letters*, 361.

The Five-Year Itch

she flattered Ernest: Hawkins, *Unbelievable*, 140.

"Lovelier than anyone": Pauline to EH, November 30, 1931, JFK.

A Pilgrimage to Powell

MRS. HEMINGWAY IS: *Key West Citizen*, January 27, 1931.

best shooting: EH to Maxwell Perkins, August 9, 1932, Bruccoli, *The Only Thing*, 176.

No Word

"Poor Old Papa": EH to Jane and Grant Mason, Summer 1932, JFK.

The Murphys

"the man in the silver suit": Honoraria Murphy Donnelly and Richard N. Billings, *Sara & Gerald: Villa America and After* (New York: Times Books, 1982), 23.

Honoria in Love

"smooth as a girl's hair": Donnelly and Billings, 66.

so horse crazy: Gerald Murphy to Archibald MacLeish, September 8, 1932, *Letters from the Lost Generation, Gerald and Sara Murphy and Friends*, ed. Linda Patterson (New Brunswick, NJ: Rutgers University Press, 1991), 65 (hereafter *Lost Generation Letters*).

"the trout would be": Donnelly and Billings, *Sara & Gerald*, 66.

"Don't be afraid": Donnelly and Billings, 67.

no longer afraid: Donnelly and Billings, 67.

"Watch while I": Donnelly and Billings, 67.

"sweet like nectar": Donnelly and Billings, 67.

Perfection

"streams are overflowing": Gerald Murphy to Archibald MacLeish, September 8, 1932, *Lost Generation Letters*, 65.

"for good or bad": Murphy to MacLeish, September 8, 1932, 65.

"My dear boy": Gerald and Sarah Murphy to EH, Miller, fall 1926, *Lost Generation Letters*, 23–34.

"hardly noticed": Gerald Murphy to Archibald MacLeish, September 8, 1932, *Lost Generation Letters*, 65.

"approaching perfection": Gerald Murphy to Archibald MacLeish, September 8, 1932, *Lost Generation Letters*, 63.

Woman's Work

"galloping about": Pauline to Maxwell Perkins, September 21, 1932, JFK.

Reviews

Old Bess trembled: Ernest Hemingway, "A Paris Letter," *Esquire*, February 1934.

Disappointment

"obscene" language: Miriam Mandel, *A Companion to Hemingway's Death in the Afternoon* (Rochester, NY: Camden House, 2009), 36.

"style was too dense": Mandel, 36.

"I have never": "Letter to the Editor," *New York Times Book Review*, October 9, 1932.

"better eyes": Kert, *Hemingway Women*, 238.

Charles Shoots a Bear, Ernest Shoots a Bigger Bear

"fraid a nothing": Baker, *A Life Story*, 5.

"killed a hell of a big bear": EH to Henry Strater, October 14, 1932, Baker, *Selected Letters*, 369.

Letters Before Leaving

trout had dropped: Hemingway, "A Paris Letter."

"un-Christly blizzards": EH to Guy Hickok, October 29, 1932, Baker, *Selected Letters*, 375.

Part IV: 1936

After Africa

mosquito netting: Ernest Hemingway, *Green Hills of Africa*, The Hemingway Library Edition (New York: Scribner, 2015), 204.

"flocks of wildebeest": Hemingway, 204.

"drinks, baths": Hemingway, 206.

"felt dreary": Hemingway, 230.

"high and cool": Hemingway, 230.

"Poor little lambs": Hawkins, *Unbelievable*, 164.

"to journey to Africa": Mary Pfeiffer to Pauline, October 31, 1933, PUL.

Sitting Down: Guy Hickock, "Sitting Down Is the Best Way to Shoot a Lion,"
    Brooklyn Daily Eagle, April 25, 1934.
"four lions": Hawkins, *Unbelievable*, 165.
"The only person": Hemingway, *Green Hills*, 40.
"very desirable": Hemingway, 152.
"and I had no wish": Hemingway, 40.
the greatest writer: Hemingway, 19.
new plaything: Hawkins, *Unbelievable,* 166.

Wyoming After All

the time a gale: Hemingway, *Green Hills*, 60.
"entering the time of life": EH to Sara and Gerald, March 19, 1935, *Lost Generation
    Letters*, 118.
the only people who really mattered: Reynolds, *The 1930s*, 234.

Changing Course

he missed her: Reynolds, 234.
"a little terrier": Hemingway, *Green Hills*, 45.
"not spoiled": Pauline to EH, June 14, 1935, JFK.

Black Ass Moods

the reviewer was touched: Carl Van Doren, "Hunter's Credo," *Time*, November 4,
    1935, 81; Kert, *Hemingway Women*, 273.
"the pursuit and dismemberment": Kert, *Hemingway Women*, 273.
"black ass moods": Hawkins, *Unbelievable*, 183.
"more tolerant": EH to Mary Pfeiffer, January 26, 1936, PUL.

Frenemies

it was a shame: Hemingway, *Green Hills*, 46.
no longer relevant: Hemingway, 47.

The Boys

He didn't come down: Baker, *A Life Story*, 292.

The Rich

"a fairy godfather": Hawkins, *Unbelievable*, 172.
"cook, factotum, and outdoor instructor": Warren, *Yellowstone High Country*, 79.

Tommy Boy

"Aren't you Mr. Hemingway?": Denis Brian, *The True Gen* (New York: Grove Press, 1988), 97.
"Oh shut up": Brian, 100.
"I don't write": Brian, 98.
"Well I'll be goddamned": Brian, 98.

The Elusive Grizzly

"slippery as": EH to Archibald MacLeish, September 26, 1936, Baker, *Selected Letters*, 452–453.
used a trowel: Baker, *A Life Story*, 294.
Ernest lost $900: Baker, 294.

A Change of Seasons

"beautifully in the wind": EH to AM, September 26, 1936, Baker, *Selected Letters*, 452–453.

Hello, Ernest? This Is War Calling . . .

"because he had friends on both sides": Brian, *True Gen*, 103.
without personal bias: Brian, 103.
supported the rebels: Brian, 103.
Arnold cautioned: Baker, *A Life Story*, 300.
"Nothing ever happens": Hawkins, *Unbelievable*, 194.

A Woman Walks into a Bar . . .

"What she felt": Brian, *True Gen*, 102.

Part V: 1938–1939

An excellent editor: EH to Maxwell Perkins, ca. January 14, 1940, in Bruccoli, *The Only Thing*, 277.

A Hero's Welcome

"life here": Pauline to EH, April 29, 1938, JFK.
"Ernest seems": Pauline and EH to Paul and Mary Pfeiffer, June 11–13, 1938, PUL.
Pauline realized: Hawkins, *Unbelievable*, 203.
"pack Papa's western gear": Reynolds, *The 1930s*, 293.

Home, Somewhat Sweet Home

"Am going home": EH to Mike and Helen Ward, May 26, 1938, JFK.
tremendous jam: Baker, *A Life Story*, 335.
had suggested marriage: Kert, *Hemingway Women*, 316.
Ernest accused her: Hawkins, *Unbelievable*, 196.

No Holding Back

he blamed her: Hawkins, *Unbelievable*, 210.

A Cause for Concern?

"But they aren't built": Ernest Hemingway, *To Have and Have Not* (New York: Scribner, 2003), 244–245.

Hitler Threatens

"To Marty and Herbert": Baker, *A Life Story*, 333.
he promised her: Reynolds, *The 1930s*, 294.

Time with the Boys

"But I do hope": Pauline to EH, September 2, 1938, JFK.
"fine solid way": Pauline to EH, September 6, 1938, JFK.
"My you are a lovely": Pauline to EH, September 6, 1938, JFK.
"she does not hear": Pauline to EH, September 17, 1938, JFK.

Paris

"Perhaps my dear fellow": Pauline to EH, October 18, 1938, JFK.

Havana Nights

As Ernest hung up: Hawkins, *Unbelievable*, 218.

Struck by Lightning

"would be quite simple": Pauline to EH, July 8, 1939, JFK.
"Relax and enjoy": Pauline to EH, July 9, 1939, JFK.
"Dearest Papa": Pauline to EH, July 9, 1939, JFK.

The Real Reason

"prettier all the time": EH to Thomas Shevlin, April 4, 1939, Baker, *Selected Letters*, 483.

The Reunion

he had wished: Ernest Hemingway, *A Moveable Feast*, the Restored Edition (New York: Scribner, 2009), 218.

Hope in a Letter

"renewing my youth": Pauline to EH, August 5–7, 1939, JFK.
"trying to give you an idea": Pauline to EH, August 5–7, 1939, JFK.
"DO have a good time": Pauline to EH, August 5–7, 1939, JFK.

Talking with Bears

"to talk to two bears": Hemingway, *Misadventures*, 35.
"Hey, Bear": Hemingway, 35.
"Bear, you dumb": Hemingway, 35.
"figure of authority": Hemingway, 36.

War

light of a kerosene lamp: Warren, *Yellowstone High Country*, 106.
"The Germans have marched": Warren, 107.
drove across the meadow: Warren, 107.

Casualties

"Oh Papa, darling": PH to EH, August 11, 1939, JFK.
when he made up his mind: Hawkins, *Unbelievable*, 224.

When He Came Up for Air

Pauline wrote to him: EH to Hadley Mowrer, November 24, 1939, Baker, *Selected Letters*, 496.
what Jack's Christmas: EH to Mowrer, November 24, 1939, 496.
welcome to join: Baker, *A Life Story*, 344.

Epilogue: 1940

"Bravest woman": Kert, *Hemingway Women*, 299.

"Would never be": Hawkins, *Unbelievable*, 225.

Paid her own way: Kert, *Hemingway Women*, 326.

Friends with Eleanor Roosevelt: EH to Mary Pfeiffer, August 2, 1937, Baker, *Selected Letters*, 459–460.

Could maybe produce: Baker, *A Life Story*, 355.

"so damned happy": Kert, *Hemingway Women*, 342.

Success

"Hemingway the artist": Edmund Wilson, "Return of Ernest Hemingway" (Review of *For Whom the Bell Tolls*), *New Republic* CIII, October 28, 1940.

"Those who live": Kert, *Hemingway Women*, 422.

"You never had it": Ernest Hemingway, *For Whom the Bell Tolls* (New York: Charles Scribner's Sons, 1940), 315.

"pretty to think so": Ernest Hemingway, *The Sun Also Rises* (New York: Scribner, 2006), 220.

BIBLIOGRAPHY

Adams, J. Donald. "Ernest Hemingway's First Novel in Eight Years." *New York Times*, October 17, 1937.

Baker, Allie. "Hadley Talks About the Lost Manuscripts." The Hemingway Project April 18, 2013. https://www.thehemingwayproject.com/2018/08/22/hadley-talks-about-the-lost-manuscripts/.

Baker, Carlos. *Ernest Hemingway: A Life Story*. New York: Charles Scribner's Sons, 1969.

Baker, Carlos, ed. *Ernest Hemingway: Selected Letters, 1917–1961*. New York: Charles Scribner's Sons, 1981.

Baker, Carlos. *Hemingway: The Writer as Artist*. Princeton: Princeton University Press, 1972.

Blume, Lesley M. M. *Everybody Behaves Badly: The True Story Behind Hemingway's Masterpiece* The Sun Also Rises. Boston: Houghton Mifflin Harcourt Publishing, 2016.

Boyle, Kay, and Robert McAlmon. *Being Geniuses Together: A Binocular View of Paris in the '20s*. New York: Doubleday & Co., 1968.

Bragg, Addison. "In the Legend." *Billings Gazette*, November 15, 1970.

Brian, Denis. *The True Gen*. New York: Grove Press, 1988.

Bruccoli, Matthew J., ed. *The Only Thing That Counts: The Ernest Hemingway– Maxwell Perkins Correspondence*. New York: Scribner, 1996.

Bruccoli, Matthew J., and Margaret M. Duggan, eds. *Correspondence of F. Scott Fitzgerald*. New York: Random House, 1980.

Burgess, Anthony. *Ernest Hemingway and His World*. New York: Charles Scribner's Sons, 1978.

Burkhart, Dan. "Hemingway in Billings." *Billings Gazette*, February 22, 1998.

Callaghan, Morley. *That Summer in Paris*. New York: Coward-McCann, 1963.

Cannell, Kathleen. "Scenes with a Hero." In *Hemingway and the Sun Set*, edited by Bertram D. Sarason, 145–147. Washington, DC: NCR, Microcard Editions, 1972.

Carpenter, Humphrey. *Geniuses Together: American Writers in Paris in the 1920s.* Boston: Houghton Mifflin Company, 1988.

Carr, Virginia Spencer. *Dos Passos: A Life.* New York: Doubleday & Co.,1984.

Clark, Edwin. "Scott Fitzgerald Looks into Middle Age." *New York Times*, April 19, 1925.

Daugherty, John. *A Place Called Jackson Hole.* Moose, WY: Grand Teton National Park Service, 1999.

Diliberto, Gioia. *Paris Without End: The True Story of Hemingway's First Wife.* New York: Harper Perennial, 2011.

Donnelly, Honoria Murphy, and Richard N. Billings. *Sara & Gerald: Villa America and After.* New York: Times Books, 1982.

Dos Passos, John. *The Best Times: An Informal Memoir.* New York: New American Library, 1966.

———. *The Fourteenth Chronicle: Letters and Diaries of John Dos Passos.* Edited by Townsend Ludington. Boston: Gambit, 1973.

Fitch, Noël Riley. *Literary Cafés of Paris.* Montgomery: Starrhill Press, 1989.

———. *Sylvia Beach and the Lost Generation.* New York: W. W. Norton, 1985.

———. *The Letters of F. Scott Fitzgerald.* Edited by Robert Turnbull. New York: Charles Scribner's Sons, 1963.

Fitzgerald, F. Scott. "The Crack-Up." *Esquire*, February 1936, 41.

Galantiere, Lewis. "There Is Never Any End to Paris." *New York Times*, May 10, 1964.

Griffin, Peter. *Less Than a Treason: Hemingway in Paris.* New York: Oxford University Press, 1990.

Gutkind, Lee Alan. "Bearskin Tempting." *Billings Gazette*, October 20, 1970.

———. "Fishing, Writing, Drinking." *Billings Gazette*, October 25, 1970.

———. "Sheridan Couple Put In Story." *Billings Gazette*, October 18, 1970.

Hawkins, Ruth A. *Unbelievable Happiness and Final Sorrow: The Hemingway-Pfeiffer Marriage.* Fayetteville, AR: University of Arkansas Press, 2012.

Hemingway, Ernest. "The Art of Fiction XXI." Interview. *Paris Review*, Spring 1958.

———. "The Art of the Short Story." *Paris Review*, Spring 1981.

———. *The Complete Short Stories of Ernest Hemingway.* The Finco Vigia edition. New York: Charles Scribner's Sons, 1987.

———. *Death in the Afternoon.* New York: Charles Scribner's Sons, 1932.

———. *A Farewell to Arms.* New York: Charles Scribner's Sons, 1929.

———. *A Farewell to Arms.* The Hemingway Library edition. New York: Scribner, 2012.

———. *The Fifth Column and Four Stories of the Spanish Civil War.* London: Arrow Books, 2013.

———. *For Whom the Bell Tolls.* The Hemingway Library edition. New York: Scribner, 2019.

———. *For Whom the Bell Tolls.* New York: Charles Scribner's Sons, 1940.

———. *Green Hills of Africa.* New York: Scribner, 2003.

———. *Green Hills of Africa.* The Hemingway Library edition. New York: Scribner, 2015.

———. *In Our Time.* New York: Scribner Paperback Fiction, 1996.

———. *Men Without Women.* New York: Charles Scribner's Sons, 1927.

———. *A Moveable Feast.* New York: Charles Scribner's Sons, 1964.

———. *A Moveable Feast.* The Restored Edition. New York: Scribner, 2009.

———. "A Paris Letter." *Esquire,* February 1934.

———. *The Short Stories of Ernest Hemingway.* The Modern Library edition. New York: Random House, 1938.

———. "The Sights of Whitehead Street: A Key West Letter." *Esquire,* April 1935.

———. *The Sun Also Rises.* New York: Scribner, 2006.

———. *The Sun Also Rises.* The Hemingway Library edition. New York: Scribner, 2014.

———. *To Have and Have Not.* New York: Scribner, 2003.

———. *Winner Take Nothing.* New York: Scribner's Sons, 1970.

Hemingway, Jack. *Misadventures of a Fly Fisherman: My Life with and Without Papa.* Dallas, TX: Taylor Publishing Co., 1986.

Hemingway, Valerie. *Running with the Bulls: My Years with the Hemingways.* New York: Ballantine, 2005.

Hendrickson, Paul. *Hemingway's Boat: Everything He Loved in Life, and Lost.* New York: Vintage Books, 2012.

Hotchner, A. E. "Don't Touch 'A Moveable Feast.'" *New York Times,* July 19, 2009.

———. *Hemingway in Love, His Own Story.* New York: Saint Martin's Press, 2015.

———. *Papa Hemingway: A Personal Memoir.* New York: Random House, 1966.

Hutchinson, Percy. "Mr. Hemingway Shows Himself Master Craftsman in the Short Story." *New York Times*, October 16, 1927.

Kert, Bernice. *The Hemingway Women: Those Who Loved Him—The Wives and Others*. New York: W. W. Norton, 1986.

Loeb, Harold. *The Way It Was*. New York: Criterion Books, 1959.

Lynn, Kenneth S. *Hemingway*. Cambridge, MA: Harvard University Press, 1987.

Mandel, Miriam. *A Companion to Hemingway's Death in the Afternoon*. Rochester, NY: Camden House, 2004.

Mellow, James L. *Hemingway: A Life Without Consequences*. London: Hodder & Stoughton, 1993.

Meyers, Jeffery. *Hemingway: A Biography*. New York: Da Capo Press, 1985.

Moorehead, Caroline. *Selected Letters of Martha Gellhorn*. New York: Henry Holt and Co., 2006.

Moseley, Virginia K. "Hemingway Remembered." *Barrington Courier Review*, September 27, 1979.

Patterson, Miller. *Letters from the Lost Generation, Gerald and Sara Murphy and Friends*. New Brunswick, NJ: Rutgers University Press, 1946.

Paul, Steve. *Hemingway at Eighteen: The Pivotal Year That Launched an American Legend*. Chicago: Chicago Review Press, 2018.

Reynolds, Michael. *Hemingway: The Paris Years*. New York: W. W. Norton, 1999.

———. *Hemingway: The 1930s*. New York: W. W. Norton, 1997.

Sarason, Bertram D. *Hemingway and the Sun Set*. Washington, DC: National Cash Register Company, 1972.

Sindelar, Nancy. *Influencing Hemingway: People and Places That Shaped His Life and Work*. Lanham, MD: Rowman & Littlefield, 2014.

Slack, Judy. *Ernest Hemingway: His 1928 Stay in the Bighorn Mountains of Wyoming*. Sheridan, WY: The Wyoming Room, Sheridan County Fulmer Public Library, 2011.

Spanier, Sandra, Albert J. Defazio III, and Robert W. Trogdon, eds. *The Letters of Ernest Hemingway, Vol. 2: 1923–1925*. Cambridge: Cambridge University Press, 2013.

Spanier, Sandra, Rena Sanderson, and Robert W. Trogdon, eds. *The Letters of Ernest Hemingway, Vol. 3: 1926–1929*. Cambridge: Cambridge University Press, 2015.

Spanier, Sandra, and Miriam Mandel, eds. *The Letters of Ernest Hemingway, Vol. 4: 1929–1931*. Cambridge: Cambridge University Press, 2018.

Stein, Gertrude. *The Autobiography of Alice B. Toklas.* London: Penguin Books, 1966.

Warren, Christopher. *Ernest Hemingway in the Yellowstone High Country.* Helena, MT: Riverbend Publishing, 2019.

White, William, ed. *By-Line Ernest Hemingway: Selected Articles and Dispatches of Four Decades.* New York: Charles Scribner's Sons, 1967.

Wilson, Edmund. "Return of Ernest Hemingway." *New Republic*, CIII, October 28, 1940.

INDEX

What the Cat Saw

Berkley Prime Crime titles by Carolyn Hart

DEATH COMES SILENTLY

WHAT THE CAT SAW

What the

BERKLEY PRIME CRIME, NEW YORK

Cat Saw

CAROLYN HART

THE BERKLEY PUBLISHING GROUP
Published by the Penguin Group
Penguin Group (USA) Inc.
375 Hudson Street, New York, New York 10014, USA
Penguin Group (Canada), 90 Eglinton Avenue East, Suite 700, Toronto, Ontario M4P 2Y3, Canada
(a division of Pearson Penguin Canada Inc.) • Penguin Books Ltd., 80 Strand, London WC2R 0RL,
England • Penguin Group Ireland, 25 St. Stephen's Green, Dublin 2, Ireland (a division of Penguin
Books Ltd.) • Penguin Group (Australia), 250 Camberwell Road, Camberwell, Victoria 3124, Australia
(a division of Pearson Australia Group Pty. Ltd.) • Penguin Books India Pvt. Ltd., 11 Community
Centre, Panchsheel Park, New Delhi—110 017, India • Penguin Group (NZ), 67 Apollo Drive,
Rosedale, Auckland 0632, New Zealand (a division of Pearson New Zealand Ltd.) • Penguin Books
(South Africa) (Pty.) Ltd., 24 Sturdee Avenue, Rosebank, Johannesburg 2196, South Africa

Penguin Books Ltd., Registered Offices: 80 Strand, London WC2R 0RL, England

This book is an original publication of The Berkley Publishing Group.

This is a work of fiction. Names, characters, places, and incidents either are the product of the author's
imagination or are used fictitiously, and any resemblance to actual persons, living or dead, business
establishments, events, or locales is entirely coincidental. The publisher does not have any control over
and does not assume any responsibility for author or third-party websites or their content.

FIRST EDITION: October 2012

Library of Congress Cataloging-in-Publication Data

Hart, Carolyn G.
What the cat saw / Carolyn Hart.—1st ed.
p. cm.
ISBN 978-0-425-25274-1 (trade pbk.)
1. Cats—Fiction. 2. Extrasensory perception—Fiction. 3. Murder—Investigation—
Fiction. I. Title.
PS3558.A676W44 2012
813'.54—dc23
2012022450

PRINTED IN THE UNITED STATES OF AMERICA

10 9 8 7 6 5 4 3 2 1

ALWAYS LEARNING   PEARSON

To Trent and Adrienne with love, always.

— 1 —

On the upside, the airport was small. On the downside, a blustery wind took Nela Farley's breath away as she stepped out of the terminal, pulling her small wheeled bag. She shivered in her light coat. She'd expected cold temperatures, but she'd not expected a wind that buffeted her like a hurried shopper in a crowded mall. She'd also known she wouldn't be met. Still, arriving in a strange place without anyone to greet her was a reminder that she was alone.

Alone . . .

She walked faster, hurried across the double drive to a parking garage. Chloe's call this morning had been even more fragmented than usual. ". . . on the fourth level, slot A forty-two. Leland's car is an old VW, I mean really old. Pink stripes. You can't miss it."

In the parking garage elevator, Nela opened her purse and found the keys that had arrived by overnight FedEx from her sister. They dangled from what seemed to be a rabbit's foot. Nela held it gingerly.

In the dusky garage, she followed numbers, chilled by the wind whistling and moaning through the concrete interior.

She spotted Leland's VW with no difficulty. Why pink stripes? The decals in the rear window would have been distinctive enough. In turn, they featured a mustachioed cowboy in an orange cowboy hat and orange chaps with *OSU* down one leg, a huge openmouthed bass fish, a long-eared dog with the caption, *My Best Friend Is a Coonhound*, and a gleaming Harley with the caption, *Redneck at the Ready*.

Nela unlocked the driver's door. Soon she would be off on an Oklahoma adventure, all because Chloe had roared off one sunny California day on the back of her new boyfriend's Harley, destination the red dirt state. Plus, Nela had lost her job on a small SoCal daily and was free to answer Chloe's call that she come to Craddock, Oklahoma.

Nela was both irritated with her sister—one more call for a rescue, this time to protect her job—and grateful to have somewhere to go, something to fill leaden days. As for Chloe's job, she would have been pleased if she'd had an inkling of what to expect, but in her usual fashion, Chloe had spoken of her job only peripherally.

Nela expected she'd manage. It definitely would be different to be in Oklahoma. Everything was going to be new, including subbing at Chloe's job, whatever it was. Knowing Chloe, the job could be raising guppies or painting plastic plates or transcribing medical records. Only Chloe could hold a job for several months and, despite hour-long sisterly confabs on their cells, always be vague about where she worked or what she did. Nela had a hazy idea she worked in an office of some kind. On the phone, Chloe was more interested in talking about what she and Leland had done or were going to do. *The wind blows all the time, but it's kind of fun . . . Hamburger*

Heaven really is . . . There's a farm with llamas . . . went to see the Heavener Runestone . . . However, she'd promised to leave a packet full of "stuff" on the front passenger seat.

Nela popped her suitcase in the backseat. She breathed a sigh of relief as she slid behind the wheel. Indeed, there was a folder and on it she saw her sister's familiar scrawl: *Everything You Need to Know.* Nestled next to the folder was a golden box—oh, she shouldn't have spent that much money—of Godiva. A sticky note read: *Road treats.* Confetti dangled from the rearview mirror. Taped to the wheel was a card. She pulled the card free, opened the envelope. The card showed an old-fashioned derrick spewing oil. She opened it. Chloe had written: *I gush for you. Nela, you're a life saver. Thanks and hugs and kisses—Love—Chloe*

Nela's brief irritation subsided. She smiled. She wished her little—though so much taller—sister was here and she could give her a hug, look into those cornflower blue eyes, and be sure everything was right in Chloe's world. So long as she could, Nela knew she would gladly come when her sister called.

She picked up the folder, opened it to find a garage parking ticket, a letter, and a map with directions to I-35.

. . . turn south. It's an hour and a half drive to Craddock. They say Hiram Craddock, a rail gang supervisor for the Santa Fe railroad, took a horseback ride one Sunday in 1887 and saw a cloud of butterflies stopped by the river. When the tracks were laid, he quit his job to stay and build the first shack in what later became Craddock. This fall when the monarchs came through, I loved thinking about him seeing them and saying, This is beautiful, I'll stay here. He married a Chickasaw woman. That was real common for white men who wanted to be able to stay in the Chickasaw Nation.

He opened a trading post. Anyway, I don't know if I explained about staying at Miss Grant's apartment after she died. I did it as a favor and I know you won't mind. It's because of Jugs. You'll love him. In case your plane's delayed, there's plenty of food and water, but the last I checked, your flights were on time. Anyway, it's sad about Miss Grant but I didn't mind helping out. Nobody knows you're coming in today and I didn't take time to explain but I left a note and said Jugs was taken care of. But they do expect you Monday morning and there are directions in the folder. The key with the pink ribbon is to Miss Grant's place. Oh, I left my car coat in the backseat. I won't need a coat in Tahiti! There's a pizza in the fridge. Anchovies, of course, for you. (Shudder.) When you get to Craddock . . .

Nela scanned the rest of the disjointed message, obviously written in haste. But Chloe could have a day or a week or a month at her disposal and her communications would still careen from thought to fact to remembrance to irrelevance. Nela retrieved Chloe's map and the ribbon-tagged key. She placed the map on the passenger seat and dropped the key into her purse.

Nela drove out of the garage into a brilliant day. She squinted against a sun that was surely stronger than in LA. Whatever happened, she intended to have fun, leaving behind the grayness now that was LA, and the sadness.

Bill wouldn't want her to be sad.

Occasional winter-bare trees dotted softly rolling dun-colored countryside. Nela passed several horse farms. Cattle huddled with their backs to the north wind. The usual tacky billboards dotted the roadside. Nela felt more and more relaxed. The little VW chugged sturdily south despite its age. The traffic was fairly heavy and it was nearer two hours when she turned onto the exit to Craddock. After checking the map, she drove east into town, passing red-brick shops, several banks, and a library, and glancing at Chloe's directions, turned off again to the south on Cimarron. Ranch-style houses predominated. After a few blocks, the homes grew more substantial, the lots larger, the houses now two and three stories, including faux colonials, Mediterranean villas, and French mansards.

Nela noted house numbers. She was getting close. She came around a curve. Her eyes widened at a majestic home high on a ridge, a Georgian mansion built of limestone with no houses visible on either side, the grounds stretching to woods. Nela slowed. Surely not . . . Chloe had clearly written of a garage apartment.

Nela stopped at stone pillars that marked the entrance and scrabbled through Chloe's notes.

. . . so funny . . . I use the tradesman's entrance. Keep going past the main drive around a curve to a blacktop road into the woods. It dead ends behind the house. That's where the old garage is and Miss Grant's apartment. It's kind of prehistoric. You'll see the newer garages, much bigger, but they kept the old one. It isn't like Miss Grant rented it. People like Blythe Webster don't have renters. Miss Grant started living there when she first came to work for Harris Webster. He was Blythe's father and he made a fortune in oil. That's the money that funds everything. She went from being his personal assistant to helping run the whole deal. Now that she's gone, I imagine they'll close up the apartment, maybe use it for storage. Anyway, it's a lot more comfortable than Leland's trailer so it's great that someone needs to be with Jugs. Be sure and park in

the garage. Miss Webster had a fit about the VW, didn't want it visible from the terrace. No opener or anything, just pull up the door. It's kind of like being the crazy aunt in the attic, nobody's supposed to know the VW's there. It offends Miss Webster's "sensibilities." I'll bet she didn't tell Miss Grant where to park! Anyway the Bug fits in next to Miss Grant's Mercedes. Big contrast. The apartment's way cool. Like I said, nicer than a trailer, but I'd take a trailer with Leland anytime. So everything always works out for the best. I mean, except for Miss Grant.

Even with the disclaimer, the message reflected Chloe's unquenchable cheer.

Nela pressed the accelerator. Names bounced in her mind like errant Ping-Pong balls . . . Grant, Webster, Jugs . . . as she chugged onto the winding road. If delivery trucks actually came this way, their roofs would scrape low-hanging tree limbs. In the second decade of the twenty-first century, Nela felt sure that FedEx, UPS, and any other delivery service would swing through the stone pillars into the main drive. Tradesmen entrances had gone the way of horse-drawn buggies, milk bottles, and typewriters.

As the lane curved out of the woods, she gazed at the back of the magnificent house. A rose garden that would be spectacular in summer spread beneath steps leading up to a paved terrace. Lights blazed from huge windows, emphasizing the gathering winter darkness that leached light and color from the dormant garden. Lights also gleamed from lantern-topped stone pillars near the massive garages Chloe had described as new. Almost lost in the gloom was an old wooden two-door garage with a second-floor apartment. The windows were dark.

Nela coasted to a stop. She put the car in park but left the motor running while she pulled up the garage door. The Bug fit with room to spare next to the Mercedes coupe. She glanced at the elegant car as she retrieved her suitcase. Very sporty. It would be interesting to see Miss Grant's apartment. It would be odd to stay in the apartment of a woman whom she'd never met. But ten days would speed past.

And then?

Nela shook away any thought of the future. For now, she was hungry and looking forward to pizza with anchovies and taking sanctuary in a dead woman's home. *Miss Grant, wherever you are, thank you.*

She didn't take time to put on Chloe's coat, which surely would hang to her knees. She stepped out of the garage and lowered the overhead door. Pulling her suitcase, carrying Chloe's coat over one arm, she hurried to the wooden stairs, the sharp wind ruffling her hair, penetrating her thin cotton blouse and slacks.

On the landing, she fumbled in her purse until she found the ribbon-tagged key, unlocked the door. Stepping inside, she flicked a switch. She was pleasantly surprised. Despite January gloom beyond the windows, the room was crisp and bright, lemon-painted walls with an undertone of orange, vivid Rothko matted prints, blond Danish modern furniture, the sofa and chairs upholstered with peonies splashed against a pale purple background. A waist-high blond wood bookcase extended several feet into the room to the right of the door.

Her gaze stopped at car keys lying there next to a Coach bag. Had the purse belonged to Miss Grant? Certainly Chloe had never owned a Coach bag and, if she had, she wouldn't have left it carelessly in an empty apartment. Nela shrugged away the presence of the purse. The contents of the apartment were none of her business.

As for Miss Grant, she wasn't the person Nela had imagined. When Chloe wrote, *Too bad about Miss Grant*, Nela knew she'd been guilty of stereotyping. Miss Grant was dead so she was old. Until she'd read Chloe's note, Nela had pictured a plump elderly woman, perhaps with white curls and a sweet smile. This apartment had not belonged to an old woman.

So much for preconceived ideas. Nela closed the door behind her. She set the suitcase down and turned to explore the rest of the apartment. She took two steps, then, breath gone, pulse pounding, stared across the room. She reached out to grip the back of a chair, willing herself to stay upright. She began to tremble, defenses gone, memory flooding, not hot, but cold and dark and drear.

The cat's huge round eyes seemed to grow larger and larger.

Lost in the intensity of the cat's gaze, she was no longer in a strange apartment half a continent from home. Instead, numb and aching, she was at Bill's house with Bill's mother, face etched in pain, eyes red-rimmed, and his sobbing sisters and all of his huge and happy family, which had gathered in sorrow. Bill's brother Mike spoke in a dull monotone: *He was on patrol . . . stepped on an IED . . .*

Unbearable images had burned inside. She had turned away, dropped into a chair in the corner of the room. Bill's cat was lying on the piano bench, looking at her. Splotches of white marked Big Man's round black face.

Big Man stared with mesmerizing green eyes. "*. . . He's gone . . . dead . . . yesterday . . . legs blown away . . . blood splashing . . .*"

Through the next frozen week, Big Man's thoughts recurred like the drumbeat of a dirge. But, of course, they were her thoughts, too hideous to face and so they came to her reflected from the cat Bill loved.

The next week an emaciated feral cat confronted her in the alley behind the apartment house. Gaunt, ribs showing, the cat whirled toward her, threat in every tense line. She looked into pale yellow eyes. "*. . . starving . . . That's my rat . . . Get out of my way . . .*"

Rat? She'd jerked around and seen a flash of gray fur near the Dumpster. Back in her apartment, she'd tried to quell her quick breaths. Her mind had been jumbled, that's all. She'd seen a desperate cat and known there was garbage and of course there might be rats. She had not read the cat's thoughts.

Of course she hadn't.

Like calendar dates circled in red, she remembered other episodes. At the beauty shop, a cuddly white cat turned sea blue eyes toward her. "*. . . The woman in the third chair's afraid . . . The redhead is mean . . . The skinny woman's smile is a lie . . .*" At a beach taco stand, a rangy black tom with a white-tipped tail and a cool, pale gaze. "*. . . rank beef . . . People want the baggies from the blue cooler . . . afraid of police . . .*" On a neighbor's front porch swing, an imperious Persian with a malevolent face. "*. . . I'm the queen . . . I saw the suitcase . . . If she boards me, she'll be sorry . . .*"

Now, a few feet away from her, a lean brown tabby with distinctive black stripes and oversize ears stood in a circle of light from an overhead spot—of course the cat chose that spot seeking warmth from the bulb—and gazed at Nela with mournful eyes. "*. . . Dead . . . Dead and gone . . . She loved me . . . board rolled on the second step . . .*"

Nela fought a prickle of hysteria. She was tired. Maybe she was crazy. Boards didn't roll . . . Unless he meant a skateboard. Skateboards were rolling boards. Was that how a cat would describe a skateboard? Was she losing her mind? Cats and a board that rolled and skateboards. How weird to think of a skateboard on a step. She hadn't thought of skateboards in years. Bill had done the best ollies in the neighborhood. His legs were stocky and strong. The IED . . . Oh God. Maybe it was because the cat had such distinctive black stripes. Bill's skateboard had been shiny orange with black stripes. She had to corral her mind, make her thoughts orderly. No one saw what was in a cat's mind. She was making it up. From a board that rolled to skateboards. Maybe she needed to see a doctor. No. This would pass.

The cat gave a sharp chirp, walked across the parquet flooring.

She backed away, came up hard with her back against the front door.

The cat looked up. "*. . . Hungry . . . Feed me . . . We're both sad . . .*"

With the beauty of movement peculiar to cats, he moved swiftly past her toward the kitchen.

We're both sad . . .

Nela looked after him. Slowly her frantic breathing eased. The cat—he had to be Jugs with ears like those—was not a threat. She was fighting to keep away memories that hurt. It made sense that she'd ascribe sadness to a cat with a dead mistress. Cats needed attention. Maybe he'd let her pet him. As for imagining his thoughts, her mind was playing a trick. Maybe she wasn't quite crazy. She struggled to remember the professor's droning voice in Psych 1. What had he said? Then she remembered. Displacement. That's what she was doing. Displacement. She clung to the word.

It took every fiber of her will but she quieted her quick breaths, moved with deliberation toward the kitchen. Food would help and the welcome distraction of finding her way about in a strange place.

Next to the refrigerator, she spotted a sheet of paper taped to a cabinet door. Chloe had printed, neatly for her:

Feed Jugs a.m. and p.m., one-half can and one full scoop dry food.
Fresh water. He's a sweetie. He adored Marian. Of course I called
her Miss Grant at the office. You remember Marlene Dietrich in a
black pillbox in No Highway in the Sky? *That was Marian Grant,*
a cool blonde, always efficient, knew everybody and everything and
scared everyone to death.

Jugs stood on his back paws, scratched at the cabinet door.

Now she was able to look at the cat without a sense of dread. They were fellow creatures, both of them hungry, both of them grieving. "All right, Jugs." As Nela gently opened the door, Jugs dropped to the floor and moved toward his bowl. She emptied a half can into a blue ceramic bowl with *Jugs* painted in white on one side. Nela placed the bowl on newspaper already spread on the floor. She added a scoop of chicken-flavored dry pellets to a yellow bowl with his name in blue. She poured fresh water in a white bowl.

Nela found, as promised, pizza in the fridge. In only a moment, thanks to the microwave, she settled at the kitchen table with two slices of hot crisp anchovy pizza, a small Caesar salad, and a glass of iced tea.

Jugs thumped onto the other end of the table. He made no move to come toward the food. Instead, he settled on his stomach, front paws flat on the table.

Nela studied him gravely as she ate. "You are obviously a privileged character. But you have very good manners. Did Miss Grant allow you to sit on the table when she ate?"

The cat blinked. "*. . . She was worried . . . She didn't know what to do . . .*"

Determinedly, Nela looked away. That was the human condition.

Worry about the rain. Worry about cancer. Worry about war. Worry about money. Worry about . . . The list could go on and on, big worries and little, everyone had them. Whatever worries had plagued Marian Grant, she was now beyond their reach. Nela felt puzzled. Chloe spoke of Miss Grant as if she'd seen her recently at the office but she'd made no mention of illness. If Marian Grant hadn't been old or sick, how had she died? Why had she been worried?

Nela finished the second slice. She'd do the dishes and look through the rest of Chloe's notes. Surely, tucked in somewhere, she'd left directions to her job and explained what she did.

Nela carried Chloe's folder into the living room. She looked around the room at colorful Rothko prints. Nela's gaze stopped at a bright red cat bed near the desk. Jugs was curved into a ball, one paw across his face, taking an after-dinner snooze. She was, of course, wide awake. It was almost ten here and darkness pressed against the windows, but her body was still on California time. Oh well, she was in no hurry. No one expected her to do anything until Monday morning.

No one would call who really mattered to her. Not since Bill died . . .

Nela hurried to the chintz sofa, sank onto one end, opened the folder, looked at a haphazard pile of loose sheets. She began to read the handwritten notes, glad to push away remembrance.

. . . different world. You know, the rich. They really are different. If I had Blythe Webster's money, I'd go around the world. But I guess she's been there, done that. She's pretty nice. She just started spending a lot of time at the foundation last fall. Blythe's around forty, kind of stiff and prim. Think Olivia de Havilland . . .

Nela's stiff shoulders relaxed. It was almost as comforting as pulling up one of her grandmother's afghans. She and Chloe had grown up on old movies, the free ones on Turner Classic Movies.

. . . in The Heiress, *dark hair, one of those cameo-smooth faces, neat features, but something about her makes you remember her. It's probably all that money. You think? She's looked washed-out since Miss Grant died. I don't know if she can handle things by herself. Miss Grant's the one that made the place go.*

Nela felt a spurt of exasperation. What place, Chloe? Nela scanned more tidbits about people.

. . . Abby's soooo serious. I mean, you'd think Indian baskets were like religious relics. Sure, the mess was a shame but a basket's a basket. If she'd use a little makeup, she has gorgeous eyes, but with those sandy brows you kind of don't notice them. Of course, Miss Grant took everything seriously, too. Maybe that's why she ran four miles every morning. You'd think handing out money would be easy as pie. I could hand out money and not act like I had boulders on my shoulders. Anyway, everything's been kind of nuts since the fire alarm and the sprinklers. I was afraid Louise was going to have a stroke. Usually she's pretty nice. The director's kind of like James Stewart in The Shop Around the Corner. *When he walks by women, it's boobs up, butts tucked. They don't even realize they're doing it!!!*

Nela smiled at the triple exclamation points though she'd chide Chloe for her language. Or maybe not. Chloe was Chloe.

. . . He's tall and angular and has this bony appealing face. I'm pretty sure I glimpsed lust even in the eyes of the T. People call Miss Webster the T because she's the trustee. Not to her face, of course. I wonder if the job description for director of the Haklo Foundation stipulated: Only handsome dudes need apply.

Nela seized on the clue: Haklo Foundation. A few sentences later, she hit pay dirt.

. . . It's a five-minute drive. Kind of quaint after LA. Hills and trees and cows and stuff. The foundation's a yellow stucco building with a red-tile roof. When you leave the apartment, turn right on Cimarron and keep going. You can't miss it. Leland's dad—his mom's dead—had me over to dinner when we got to Craddock. His dad had some connection to the foundation. He tried to get me a job there but they didn't need anybody. Louise told him if anything opened up, they'd be glad to have me. When Louise's assistant quit, I got the job. Louise is the top dog secretary. I was lucky there was an opening. She probably wouldn't have left except for the car fire. She shouldn't have left her car unlocked. I didn't know there was any place in the world where people didn't lock their cars. Of course, she wasn't in the car when it happened and I think the foundation got her a new car. At least that's what Rosalind told me and she always knows everything and she loves to talk. She's a sweetheart. Anyway, I'll bet it was just somebody raising hell, though Rosalind thinks the point was to screw things up for the T. She's kind of under fire from some of the old hands because she's the one that brought in the new director and has made a bunch of changes. But I mean, that's a pretty roundabout way. Anyway, I got the job and Leland

drops me off and picks me up. How about that! Chauffeur service
and . . . Oh well, you get the picture.

Nela's lips curved. In a perfect world, she'd like to see Chloe
walking down the aisle with a regular guy, not hopping on the back
of a vagabond's Harley. On a positive note, Leland had brought her
to his hometown and introduced her to his father. As usual, Nela
wasn't clear what Leland did—if anything—but Chloe always
sounded happy when she called. Besides—one of Chloe's favorite
words—her sister's boyfriends might have their quirks, from a veg-
etarian chef to a treasure hunter, but so far they'd all turned out to
be nice men. Otherwise, Nela would have been worried about a
faraway jaunt to Tahiti with a guy Chloe had known only since last
summer.

Nela closed the folder. Tomorrow she'd scout around, spot the
foundation, do some grocery shopping.

A creak startled her.

She looked up in time to see a cat door flap fall as lean hindquar-
ters and a tall black tail disappeared into darkness through the front
door. So Jugs was an indoor-outdoor fellow. He'd had his nap and
was ready to roam.

An in and out cat. That meant he went down the garage apartment stairs. That's how he would see if a board rolled on the second
step . . . Nonsense. Boards didn't roll and that's all there was to it.

Except for skateboards.

"That's enough, Nela." She spoke aloud. That was enough, more
than enough, of her odd and silly imaginings about the thoughts of
cats. She forced herself to focus on what she felt was an improve-
ment. She and Jugs were sharing space. That was definitely a step

in the right direction. Thankfully, he'd remained aloof. Maybe the next time she looked at him, she'd be able to discipline her mind. Maybe his presence would help prove she had nothing to fear from cats. Maybe she'd finally be able to face what was in her mind, come to grips with grief.

Bill . . .

She pushed up from the couch, willing away memory. She walked swiftly to the bookcases that lined one wall, looked at titles to try to force other thoughts into her mind. It hurt too much to think of Bill and their plans that ended in blood and death. The phone rang.

Startled, Nela turned. After a moment's hesitation, she walked swiftly to the cream-colored phone on the desk near the bookshelves. "Hello." Her answer was tentative.

"Nela, you're there! How's everything? Did you find the pizza? Isn't Jugs a honeybunch?"

Nela had felt so alone when she arrived. Hearing Chloe's husky voice was like a welcoming hug. "He's great. I'm great. How about you and Leland?"

"Oooooh." It was halfway between a squeal and a coo. "You can't believe how gorgeous everything is. We had to catch a red-eye to get to LA in time for our flight but we made it. We just checked in and we're leaving to ride an outrigger. Doesn't that sound like fun? He's already downstairs so I better scoot. Thanks, Nela. You're the best."

Nela shook her head as she replaced the receiver in the cradle. Talking to Chloe was like trying to catch a shooting star. None of her questions were answered: What was the job? Exactly where was it? What happened to Miss Grant? Perhaps she should follow Chloe's example and let the good times roll. In Chloe's world, everything seemed to work out. Nela smiled. *Have fun, sweetie. Be happy. Love him because . . .*

Again there were images to block, pain to forestall. She swung again to the bookshelves. She'd find a weighty tome, read until she felt sleepy. Midway through the first shelf, she pulled out a large picture book and carried it to the sofa. The cover photograph featured a marble statue of a tall, lean man. Even in cold stone, the hard-ridged face compelled attention. Deep-set eyes, a beaked nose, and jutting chin proclaimed power, strength, and ruthless determination. Behind the statue rose wide steps leading to a pale yellow stucco building. The title was in red Gothic letters: *The Haklo Foundation, the Story of Harris Webster and the Fortune He Shared.*

She thumbed through the beautifully crafted book. No expense had been spared in its production. She turned back to the introduction. Harris Webster was the descendant of an early Craddock family. Caleb Webster arrived in the Chickasaw Nation in 1885. After his marriage to Mary Castle, a member of the Chickasaw Nation, he began to prosper. He wrangled horses for her father, later opened an early dry goods store, apparently on very thin credit. He prospered, added a livery stable, and established a bank. His son, Lewis, increased the family's wealth with a cattle ranch. The Websters were one of Craddock's leading families, but the great wealth came from Caleb's grandson, Harris, a hugely successful wildcatter in the 1950s and '60s. He sold Webster Exploration to Exxon for one hundred million dollars in 1988. Harris Webster married Ellen White in 1970. Their first child died at birth. A daughter, Blythe, was born in 1973, and a second daughter, Grace, in 1985. Ellen died in 1987 from cancer.

Webster set up a trust, establishing the foundation in 1989 with an endowment of fifty million dollars. He served as the sole trustee until his death in 2007. His designated successor as sole trustee was his oldest daughter, Blythe.

The following facing pages featured portraits in oval frames. Caleb Webster's blunt, square-jawed face looked young and appealing, the black-and-white photo likely taken when he was in his late twenties. His hair was parted in the middle, his collar high and stiff. Mary Castle's dark hair was drawn back in a bun, emphasizing the severity of her features: the deep-set eyes, high-bridged nose and high cheekbones, thin lips pursed. She had looked gravely into the camera with a questioning gaze. The rest of the portraits were in color. Lewis Webster was dark-haired and narrow-faced with a strong chin. A merry smile curved the lips of his round-faced, blond wife, Lillian.

Harris Webster's color portrait, taken possibly when he was in his forties, exuded vigor and strength. Unlike the other photographs, he was pictured outdoors against a leafy background, a breeze ruffling thick black curls. Bronze skin suggested hours spent under the sun. His brown eyes stared confidently into the camera. His smile was that of a man who met any challenge with complete expectation of victory. His pale blond wife Ellen appeared fragile. Her expression was pensive, a woman turned inward.

The portraits of the Webster daughters hung side by side, affording an interesting contrast. Blythe Webster looked intelligent, imperious, and reserved. Ebony hair framed an oval face with a pleasant, though aloof, expression. The straight, unwavering stare of her dark brown eyes hinted at unknown depths. Her much younger sister Grace was blue-eyed with a fair complexion. Strawberry blond hair cascaded in thick curls. Her smile was amused, possibly wry, but there was something in the cast of her face which suggested a will that would not bend.

Nela bunched a pillow behind her and began to read.

— 2 —

Fasten seat belt sign . . . nattering shrill voices behind her . . . rain like tears . . . cat's eyes . . . alone, alone, alone . . .

Nela moved restlessly, swimming up from the depths of sleep. She'd tossed and turned for hours before drifting into fitful slumber. Her eyes opened. She stared at unfamiliar shadows, felt the strangeness of the bed. She blinked at the luminous dial of the bedside clock. Almost half past one. One in the morning. In a dead woman's apartment.

She'd chosen a guest room. There was no way she would use Miss Grant's bedroom where a red silk robe lay across the arm of the empire sofa. Had Miss Grant dropped the robe there with no thought that there would not be time ever again to straighten the room?

Nela had firmly shut the door to the guest bedroom in case Jugs was accustomed to sharing a bed, though surely when he came back inside he would seek out Miss Grant's room.

A splintering crash sounded from the living room.

Nela jerked upright, heart pounding. Had the cat knocked something over? But cats were agile, moving silently through time and space.

A heavy thud.

Nela swung her legs over the bedside. A line of light shone beneath the closed bedroom door. She had turned off the living room light before she came into the bedroom. Someone had turned on that light. Someone was in the apartment.

Fully awake now, adrenaline charged her mind and body. In one swift movement, she was on her feet and moving across the floor. An uncle who was an LA cop had drilled into his young nieces: React. Move. Don't freeze. Fight. Scream. Yell. Run.

Nela's mind closed in on the first necessity. Lock the door. Set up a barrier. Don't make it easy.

More crashes.

Nela reached the door. Her hands touched cold wood. The door panel was smooth. Guest rooms did not come equipped with deadbolts. She slipped her hand down, found the knob, pushed the button lock.

Now for her cell . . . Her purse was on the dresser. She turned, moved through the velvety darkness, hands outstretched. She tried to judge where she'd left her suitcase. She veered a little, but one knee caught the case. Losing her balance, she tumbled forward. Scrambling up, she thudded into the chest, but her purse was there. She yanked out the cell phone, opened it. As the cell phone glowed, she punched 911.

Not a breath of sound came from beyond the closed door but

she sensed menace. She felt threatened not only by the alien presence in the living room, but the darkness that surrounded her. She hurried to the wall and turned on the overhead light, welcoming the brightness.

A brisk voice. "Craddock nine-one-one. What is your emergency?"

"Someone's broken in." Her voice was shaky but forceful. "Send the police."

"Ma'am, please speak louder. Where are you?"

"Oh God, I don't know the address. I'm in a garage apartment behind a big mansion on Cimarron." She scrambled to remember. "The Webster house on Cimarron. Blythe Webster. Behind the house there's a garage apartment. Call the Craddock police. I need—"

The doorknob rattled.

Nela backed away. "I'm in a bedroom. Someone's trying to get inside. Send help." *Fight. Scream. Yell.* She lowered the cell, shouted, "The police are coming. They're on their way."

"Ma'am, try to be calm. We need the address."

"The garage apartment behind the Webster house on Cimarron." Again, she held the phone away, yelled, "The police are coming."

In the background behind the responder's calm tone, she heard a male voice. "Ten-sixty-seven. Ten-seventy. Possible four-fifty-nine."

"I have that, ma'am. Residence listed to Marian Grant." Her voice fainter, the responder spoke quickly, "Garage apartment One Willow Lane behind residence at Nine-thirteen Cimarron."

In the distance, a man's voice repeated her words. "Officers en route."

The woman's calm voice was loud and clear. "Help is on the way, ma'am. Can you describe the intruder?"

Beyond the door, there was a thud of running feet.

The responder continued to speak. "Officers will arrive in less than three minutes. Tell the intruder help is on the way."

Nela's shouts hurt her throat. "The police are coming. They're coming."

She heard the slam of a door. She was breathless as she spoke to the responder. "I think he's leaving. Hurry. Please hurry."

The responder continued to speak calmly.

Nela held the phone but she scarcely listened. Finally, a siren wailed. Nela approached the bedroom door, leaned against the panel, drawing in deep gulps of air. More sirens shrieked.

A pounding on the front door. "Police. Open up. Police."

In the bedroom, Nela took time to grab a heavy silver-backed hand mirror from the dresser, then turned the knob. She plunged into the living room, makeshift weapon raised high, ready to dart and squirm.

She moved fast, focused on the door. She turned the lock, yanked open the front door.

Two policemen entered, guns in hand.

Nela backed up until she was hard against the wall. "He got away. I heard the door slam."

The older officer, eyes flicking around the room, spoke into a transmitter clipped to his collar. "Cars two and three. Search grounds for prowler." He nodded at his younger companion. "Cover me." He glanced at Nela, his eyes cool. "Stay where you are, ma'am." With that warning, he moved warily across the room, alert, intent, ready for trouble.

Nela shivered, was suddenly aware of her cotton pj's. The night air was cold. As she turned to watch the officers, her eyes widened at the swath of destruction in the once cool and elegant room.

The officers moved fast. Doors banged against walls. They were in the kitchen. One of them muttered, "Nobody here. Window secure."

They moved back into the living room, oblivious to her. At the closed door to Miss Grant's bedroom, the lead officer shouted, "Police," flung back the door, stood to one side as he flipped on the light. There was silence in the bedroom. Cautiously, he edged inside, his backup advancing with him.

Outside, car doors slammed and men shouted. Cold night air swirled through the open front door.

Finally, the officers returned, guns put away. The tall man stopped in front of her, his face impassive, his hooded eyes moving around the room. "You hurt, ma'am?" His voice was gruff but kind. The younger officer closed the front door, but the room was already achingly cold.

"I'm fine." Maybe not fine. Maybe still a little breathless, pulse racing, but standing in the trashed room, she felt safe, safe and grateful for the quick response of the Craddock police.

"Check the living room windows, Pierce."

The stocky officer began a circuit of the windows.

The officer in charge cleared his throat. "Ma'am, can you describe the intruder?" He looked into her face, his eyes probing.

Nela clasped her hands together. "I never saw him. I heard him. I was in the guest bedroom." She realized she was shaking with cold. "Please, let me get my jacket. It's right by the door." She moved fast and yanked Chloe's long car coat from a coat tree near the front door. She shrugged into it, knew she looked absurd in the big floppy coat, bare legs and feet sticking out below the hem.

When she turned back, the officer held a small electronic notepad in one hand. "Name?"

"Nela Farley. Actually, it's Cornelia, but I'm called Nela." With every moment that passed, she felt more assured.

"Cornelia Farley." He spelled the name as he swiped the keys. His questions came fast. She answered, wishing she could be more help, knowing that all she had to report was noise.

Shouts and calls sounded outside. Officer Pierce made a slow circuit of the room, making notes.

The inquiring officer's nose wrinkled above a thin black mustache. "So you got here tonight. Anybody know you were here?"

"My sister."

He nodded. "I got it. You're in town to take her job. Anyone else know you're here?"

"They're expecting me at her office Monday."

"Do they know"—he was patient—"that you're staying here?" He jerked a thumb at the room.

"No." Chloe hadn't mentioned that Nela would be in Miss Grant's apartment.

The officer's gaze was intent. "You know anyone at the office?"

"Not a soul. I don't know anyone in Craddock."

"So, nobody came here because you're here." He surveyed the litter. The computer was lying on the floor. Drawers were pulled out and upended. Glass from a smashed mirror sparkled on the floor. The cracked mirror hung crookedly on a wall. "More than likely, somebody saw the death notice in the *Clarion* and thought the apartment was empty." He sounded satisfied. "Did the intruder make this mess?"

Nela nodded. "The noise woke me up."

"I'll bet it did. Wake anybody up." His tone was dry. "Looks like the perp got mad. Tossed that little statue and totaled the mirror. Maybe he didn't find cash. Or whatever he was looking for."

Nela, too, looked at the broken mirror. Lying on the floor was a crystal statuette of a horse that had been on the desk.

A woman's imperious voice rose above the hubbub outside. Footsteps rattled on the steps. "Of course I can go upstairs." The voice was rather high and thin and utterly confident. "The place belongs to me."

The front door opened.

Nela and her inquisitor—she noted his name tag: Officer T. B. Hansen—looked toward the open doorway.

A slender woman strode inside. Blue silk pajama legs were visible beneath a three-quarter-length mink coat. She wore running shoes.

She was followed by a middle-aged, redheaded patrol woman who gave Officer Hansen a worried look.

He made a slight hand gesture and the officer looked relieved.

The newcomer held her fur coat folded over against her for warmth. Her black hair appeared disheveled from sleep, but her stare at the officer was wide awake and demanding. "What's going on here?"

Officer Hansen stood straighter. "Reports of a prowler, Miss Webster."

The woman's eyes widened in surprise. "Here?" She glanced around the room. "Who made this mess?"

The officer's tone was noncommittal. "The young lady said an intruder is responsible."

The woman stared at Nela with narrowed eyes. "Who are you?" Her tone was just this side of accusing.

Nela took a quick breath. "Nela Farley, Chloe's sister."

The woman raised one sleek dark eyebrow in inquiry. "You don't look like her."

"No." Nela glimpsed herself in the remnants of mirror. Not only did she not resemble her tall, willowy sister, she looked like a bedraggled waif, dark eyes huge in a pale face, slender bare legs poking from beneath the overlarge coat. "I'm five-four and dark haired. She's five-nine and blond."

Miss Webster asked sharply, "Did Chloe give you Marian's keys?"

Nela nodded. "She asked me to stay here and take care of Jugs. I flew in this afternoon and drove down. I arrived about six. I'm driving Chloe's boyfriend's VW. Chloe told me to park the VW in the garage."

"Oh." Miss Webster's tone was considering now, not hostile. "That car. God knows that monstrosity should be kept in a garage. Or driven into a lake." She sped a quick smile toward Nela. "Thanks for putting the VW in the garage. I didn't know you were staying here. I hadn't thought about it." Her tone was careless. Clearly, the habitation of employees was not her concern. "Louise told me the cat was taken care of. I didn't ask how." Also clearly, the care of a dead employee's animal was not her responsibility. These kinds of things were handled by others. "I suppose this is a convenient place to stay while you're visiting, and having you here puts off deciding what to do with the cat. We have to find him a home. Marian was crazy about that animal." She shook her head, looked abruptly sad. "I can't believe she's gone. And to have someone break in her home makes me furious. Did you see the burglar? I heard the sirens. By the time I reached a window, police were milling around with flashlights and yelling. I thought I was in the middle of a war zone."

Once again Nela told her story, climbing from the deep pit of sleep, bangs and crashes in the living room, hurrying to lock the bedroom door, calling for help, the turning of the knob, the arrival of the police.

Blythe Webster's eyes glinted with anger. "Someone must have read about Marian's death in the newspaper and come like a vulture to pick over her things. Look at this mess. I'm glad you were here. Who knows what might have happened to the rest of her things if you hadn't been here? It would be awful to think of a robber stealing from Marian. So everything's worked out for the best."

The echo of Chloe's favorite phrase was strangely disturbing to Nela. Was it all for the best that she'd known moments of dark fear?

Blythe must have sensed Nela's reaction. She turned over a hand in appeal. "Forgive me. It's dreadful that you have come to help us and run into something like this. Thank you for being here and calling for help. I don't know what we should do now." She looked at Officer Hansen in appeal. "What do you suggest?" Her gesture included the shattered mirror and the emptied drawers.

"Nothing for the moment. We'll send a tech tomorrow to see about prints. But I doubt we'll find anything helpful. Would you"— he directed his question to Blythe Webster—"know if anything is missing?"

"I have no idea about Marian's belongings. I guess they were looking for money." Her gaze settled on the Coach purse atop a bookcase near the front door. "That's Marian's purse. Why didn't a thief grab the purse?" She looked at Nela. "I guess he must have intended to take it but got scared when he heard you. He must have been shocked out of his pants when he realized someone was in the bedroom. Well, no harm done apparently, except for a bad introduction to Craddock for you." Her glance at Nela was sympathetic. "I'm sorry you've had such a rough welcome. We'll make it up to you. By the way, I'm Blythe Webster. I own all of this." She waved a casual hand. "Marian worked for me. I run the foundation. I'll be seeing you there." She turned toward the patrolman. "Send me a report." She moved to the door, looked back at the police officer, a faint frown on her face. "How did the thief get in?"

Hansen said carefully, "We haven't found evidence of a break-in." His hooded gaze settled on Nela. "When we arrived, the front door was locked. Ms. Farley opened the door for us."

Blythe Webster looked puzzled. "If nobody broke in and the door was locked, how did someone get in?"

Nela felt her face tighten. "I don't know." She didn't like the searching looks turned toward her. "Maybe someone had a key."

Blythe Webster's brown eyes narrowed. "I suppose somewhere up at the house we may have a key in case of an emergency. I'll ask my housekeeper. But I can't imagine that Marian passed out keys to her apartment. That would be very unlike her."

The officer turned to Nela. "Are you sure you locked the front door?"

"Positive."

He didn't appear impressed. He'd probably been told many things by many witnesses that turned out to be mistaken or false. "There was a real nice story in the *Clarion* about Miss Grant and a funeral notice. The intruder counted on the place being empty. Maybe he found the door unlocked."

Nela started to speak.

He forestalled her. "Or maybe he didn't. Maybe he jiggled a credit card, got lucky. It's an old door. Once inside, he locked the door to keep anyone from surprising him. When he heard you calling for help, he ran out and slammed the front door behind him." He glanced toward the door, gave a satisfied nod. "It's an old lock, one where the lock doesn't pop up when the inside handle is turned. Then it took only a minute to get down the stairs and disappear in the dark." He looked from Nela to Miss Webster. "Did either of you hear a car?"

Nela shook her head. Inside the apartment, she had been acutely aware of sounds from outside, waiting for the police to arrive. She hadn't heard anything until the sirens rose and fell.

Blythe Webster was dismissive. "I was asleep. The sirens woke me. But most cars don't make much noise these days."

Officer Pierce yanked a thumb toward the front door. "They haven't found any trace outside. It looks like he got clean away."

"Whoever came is long gone now." Blythe sounded relieved. She turned to Nela. "As soon as the police finish, you can lock up and feel quite safe. Can't she, Officer?"

Officer Hansen's face was studiously unexpressive. "You may be right, Miss Webster."

Officer Pierce, who had arrived with Hansen, spoke quickly. "Right. Once you scare 'em away, they won't come back."

The redheaded patrol woman, who had followed Blythe Webster inside, nodded in agreement.

"I locked the door." Nela was insistent.

Blythe Webster nodded. "You thought you did." Her tone was understanding. "Anyway, these things happen. I'm glad you're fine. I expect you're very tired. As for me, I'm ready for a nightcap . . . Oh, here's Jugs."

Nela distinctly remembered engaging the front-door lock. She would have objected again, continued to insist, but at the mention of the cat, she swung to look toward the doorway.

The big-eared brown tabby strolled past them, his gaze flicking around the room.

Nela looked into the cat's huge pupils, still dilated for night vision. ". . . *Cars . . . strangers . . . like the day She died . . . lying on the concrete . . ."* The cat moved away, heading straight for the open door to Marian Grant's bedroom.

Blythe Webster's face abruptly tightened, cheekbones jutting. "Do you suppose he's hunting for Marian? I hate that." There was a quiver in her voice. "Anyway, now that everything's under control, I'll say good night." In a flurry, she was gone.

Nela scarcely heard the clatter as Blythe Webster hurried down the wooden steps. . . . *lying on the concrete . . .* There was a square of concrete to one side of the apartment stairs, possibly at one time intended for outdoor parking.

Officer Hansen adjusted his earpiece, spoke into the lapel transmitter. "Officer Hansen. Garage apartment behind Webster home. Possible intruder. No trace of perp. Search of living room apparent. Unknown if any valuables are missing. Alarm raised at one thirty-five a.m. by guest Cornelia Farley. She didn't see anyone but heard sounds in living room. Search of grounds yielded no suspects or witnesses." He stopped, listened. "Yes, sir. I'll do that, sir. Ten-four." He was brisk as he turned toward Nela.

She stood stiffly, watching as Jugs disappeared into Marian's bedroom.

"Ma'am—"

Nela felt a surge of irritation. Why did he call her ma'am? She wasn't an old lady. "I'm Nela."

His eyes flickered. "Ms. Farley"—his tone was bland—"a technician will arrive at nine a.m. tomorrow to fingerprint the desk and the front door and the materials on the floor. Sometimes we get lucky and pick up some prints. Usually, we don't. If you have any further trouble, call nine-one-one." He stared to turn away.

Nela spoke sharply. "I locked the door. Someone had a key."

His pale brown eyes studied her. "The chances are the intruder knew Miss Grant was dead and thought the apartment was empty. Now it's obvious the place is occupied. I don't think you'll have any more trouble." He gestured toward the desk. "It looks like somebody was interested in the desk and not looking to bother you." He cleared his throat. "To be on the safe side, get a straight chair out of the kitchen, tilt it, and wedge the top rail under the knob. Anybody who pushes will force the back legs tight against the floor. Nobody will get in. Tomorrow you can pick up a chain lock at Walmart."

"That's good advice, ma'am." The redheaded policewoman was earnest. "I was in the first car the morning Miss Grant died. The housekeeper told me she ran up the steps to call from here because it was quicker. She didn't have a key. She used a playing card she always carries in her pocket. The seven of hearts. For luck." The officer raised her eyebrows, obviously amused at the superstition. "Anyway, she got inside. Like Officer Hansen said, it doesn't take much to jiggle these old locks. Not that it made any difference for Miss Grant that we got here quick."

"What happened to her?" Nela glimpsed Jugs in her peripheral vision.

The redheaded patrol woman was brisk. "She fell over the stair rail last Monday morning, straight down to the concrete. I was in the first car to arrive." The redheaded officer—Officer L. T. Baker—gestured toward the opening into darkness. "The housekeeper found her beside the stairs. It looked like Miss Grant tripped and went over the railing and pretty much landed on her head. Broken neck. Apparently she jogged early every morning. When we saw her, it was obvious she'd taken a header over the railing. Massive head wound. She must have laid there for a couple of hours."

Nela's eyes shifted to Jugs.

The cat's sea green eyes gazed at Nela. "*. . . They took Her away . . .*"

31

Paramedics came and found death and carried away a broken and bruised body. Nela didn't need to look at the woman's cat to know this.

"A header?" . . . *board rolled on the second step* . . . Nela felt a twist of foreboding. "Did you find what tripped her?"

Officer Baker shrugged. "Who knows? The stairs are steep. Accidents happen. She was wearing new running shoes. Maybe a toe of a shoe caught on a step."

No mention of a skateboard. "Did you find anything on the ground that could have caused her to fall?"

The policewoman waved a hand in dismissal. "These grounds are tidy. Not even a scrap of paper in a twenty-foot radius from the stairs."

"She probably started down the stairs too fast." Officer Hansen shook his head. "She was a hard charger. She always helped at the Kiwanis pancake suppers, made more pancakes than anybody. There were a bunch of stories in the paper. She was a big deal out at the foundation. Anybody looking for an easy way to make a buck would have known her place was empty." His look was earnest. "Craddock's a real nice place, Ms. Farley, but we got our no-goods like any other town. It seems pretty clear what we had here tonight was intent to rob. Now that the perp knows you're here, you should be fine." He gave a brief nod to officers Pierce and Baker and they moved through the doorway. He paused on the threshold long enough to gesture toward the kitchen. "Wedge that chair if you're nervous. I guarantee you'll be okay."

—3—

Jugs wrinkled his nose, cautiously sniffed the Walmart sack on the bookcase near the front door.

Nela inserted a nine-volt battery into a doorstop alarm. When shoved beneath the bottom of the door, the wedge prevented anyone from opening the door, with or without a key, plus any pressure activated an alarm. She didn't feel she could install a deadbolt in an apartment that, as Miss Webster had made clear, belonged to her.

Nela felt as though she'd been in the garage apartment for an eon with only the short foray to Walmart as a respite. She glanced around the living room, wished she found the decor as appealing as when she first arrived.

In her peripheral vision, she was aware of the shattered mirror. Slowly she turned her head to look at it fully. The crystal horse still lay among shards of glass. There was something wanton in that destruction. If she had the money, she'd move to a motel. But she didn't have enough cash to rent a room for a week. Besides, the cat needed to be cared for.

The blond desk held only a few traces of powder. The police technician, a talkative officer with bright brown eyes and a ready smile, had arrived punctually at nine a.m., fingerprinted the front doorknob inside and out, the desk, the scattered drawers, the tipped-over chair, the statuette. He cleaned up after himself. He'd kept up a nonstop chatter. He'd quickly identified Miss Grant's prints from a hairbrush in the master bath. "Lots of hers on the desk and some unidentified prints, but the drawer handles are smudged. Good old gloves. It takes a dumb perp to leave fingerprints. Usually we only find them at unpremed scenes." He'd departed still chatting. ". . . Not too many prowler calls . . . usually a bar fight on Saturday nights . . ."

Now she was left with the mess and her new defense against invasion.

Jugs batted at the sack. The plastic slid from the table and the muscular cat flowed to the floor. He used a twist of his paw to fling the bag in the air.

She ripped off the doorstop plastic cover and threw it across the room, a better toy than a plastic sack.

Jugs crossed the floor in a flash, flicked the plastic, chased, jumped, rolled on his back to toss his play prey into the air, then gripped the plastic with both paws.

"Pity a mouse. Staying in shape until spring?"

Ignoring her, Jugs twisted to his feet and crouched, the tip of his tail flicking. After a final fling and pounce and flurry, Jugs strolled away, game done, honors his.

She stared after him as he moved toward the front door. Every time she saw him, she remembered that searing moment yesterday when their eyes had first met. She blurted out her thought while berating herself for what was rapidly becoming an obsession. "There wasn't a skateboard," she called after him. Her voice sounded loud in the quiet room. "They would have found a skateboard."

Her only answer was the clap of the flap as Jugs disappeared through the cat door.

Now she was talking out loud to a cat. Possibly he wondered what the weird-sounding syllables—skateboard—meant. More than likely his thoughts were now focused on a bird, a rustle in a bush, the scent of another cat.

Anyway, what difference did it make?

The difference between sanity and neuroses.

No matter what made her think of a skateboard, there was no connection between the vagrant thought, a pet cat, and the accidental death of a woman who moved fast.

Nela felt cheered. Monday she would go to the foundation, try to please Chloe's boss, and enjoy the not-exactly holiday but definite departure from her normal life. The normal life that an IED had transformed from quiet happiness to dull gray days that merged into each other without borders, without hope.

Nela looked down at the doorstop. There was no need to put the piece in place now. She shoved the doorstop into the corner between the door and the wall. So much for that. At least tonight she would feel safe.

She still felt unsettled by the knowledge that Marian Grant had fallen to her death. The police seemed competent. If there had been a skateboard in the vicinity of the body, the police would have found it. There hadn't been a skateboard—a board that rolled—on a step. Certainly not. But the image persisted.

She turned, walked restlessly across the room, stopped and stared at the desk and the litter on the floor and the upended drawers. Why rifle a desk? Did people keep money in desks? Maybe.

However . . . She turned back toward the front door. Only two items lay atop the waist-high blond bookcase to the right as a visitor entered. A set of keys. A black leather Coach bag. Last night Blythe Webster said the purse belonged to Marian Grant.

When the intruder had turned on the living room's overhead light, he couldn't have missed seeing the expensive purse, especially if the purpose of entry was to steal. Wouldn't a petty thief grab the purse first? Maybe he had. Maybe he'd rifled the purse first, then searched the desk. They hadn't looked inside the purse last night. Wasn't that an oversight?

Nela stopped by the bookcase. She reached out for the purse, then drew her hand back. She hurried to the kitchen, fumbled beneath the sink, found a pair of orange rubber gloves, and yanked them on. She didn't stop to sort out her thoughts, but fingerprints loomed in her mind. She had no business looking in the purse, but she would feel reassured if there was no money, if a billfold and credit cards were gone.

Nela carried the purse to the kitchen table. She undid the catch. The interior of the purse was as austere and tidy as the apartment. She lifted out a quilted wallet in a bright red and orange pattern. It took only a moment to find a driver's license. She gazed at an unsmiling face, blond hair, piercing blue eyes: Marian Denise Grant. Birth date: November 16, 1965. Address: One Willow Lane. As Blythe had said, the purse belonged to Marian Grant, had likely rested atop the bookcase since she'd arrived home the night before she died.

Nela pulled apart the bill chamber. Two fifties, four twenties, a ten, three fives, seven ones. Four credit cards, one of them an American Express Platinum. She and Chloe always lived from paycheck to paycheck but, after she'd lost her writing job, she'd waited tables at an upscale restaurant in Beverly Hills and she remembered snatches of conversation over lunch at a producer's table, the advantages of this particular card, automatic hotel upgrades, delayed four p.m. checkout times, free access to all airline hospitality suites, and more.

An intruder could not have missed seeing the purse, but instead of rifling through the billfold, taking easy money, the intruder had walked on to the desk.

Nela placed the quilted billfold on the table. One by one, she lifted out the remaining contents: lip gloss, a silver compact, comb, small perfume atomizer, pill case, pencil flashlight, BlackBerry, Montblanc pen with the initials *MDG*.

Resting on the bottom of the purse was a neatly folded pair of women's red leather gloves. She almost returned the other contents, but, always thorough, she picked up the gloves. Her hand froze in the air. Lying in a heap at the bottom of the bag, hidden from view until now by the folded gloves, was a braided gold necklace inlaid with what looked like diamonds. Nela had a quick certainty that the stones were diamonds. They had a clarity and glitter that faux stones would lack.

Nela held up the necklace, felt its weight, admired the intricacies of the gold settings. A thief would have hit pay dirt if he'd grabbed the purse as he ran. She returned the objects to the interior compartments and carried the purse to the bookcase. She replaced the bag precisely where it had earlier rested.

And so?

There were lots of maybes. Maybe the thief planned to take the purse but her 911 call induced panic. Maybe the thief knew of something valuable in the desk. Maybe Marian Grant collected old stamps or coins. Maybe Marian Grant had a bundle of love letters the writer could not afford for anyone to see. Her mouth twisted. Maybe there was a formula for Kryptonite or a treasure map or nothing at all. Lots of maybes and none of them satisfactory.

The cat flap slapped.

Nela turned to face Jugs. He sauntered past her, beauty in motion, sinuous, graceful, silent.

"It's your fault that I'm worried." Her tone was accusing.

The cat flicked a glance over his shoulder. ". . . *My territory* . . . *I showed him* . . ." He disappeared into the kitchen.

Nela wondered if he had vanquished a neighboring tom or if she was simply thinking what he might have done when outside. What difference did it make whether the thought was hers or Jugs?

A big difference.

Either the cat remembered a board that rolled on a step or she had dredged up a long-ago memory of a teenage Bill on a skateboard in happy, sunny days.

What if the cat was right? What if Marian Grant hadn't seen a skateboard on the step when she hurried out to jog early that January morning? The police surmised she'd caught a toe on a steep step, that she'd been going too fast. There had been no skateboard near the stairs when her body was discovered. But there could be reasons. Maybe some kid lived in that big house. Maybe the house-keeper saw the skateboard and either unthinkingly or perhaps quite deliberately removed it. Maybe the cat was thinking about some other skateboard on some other steps. Maybe the cat wasn't think-ing a damn thing.

Moreover, a skateboard on the steps might explain why Marian Grant fell, but again so what? She fell because she caught her toe or slipped on a skateboard or simply took a misstep. Her death had been adjudged an accident. To think otherwise was absurd.

Then why did someone creep into the dead woman's apartment last night and search the desk?

This was the easiest answer of all. As Officer Henson said, every town had its no-goods and last night one of them had taken a chance on finding something valuable in a dead woman's apartment.

Still . . . Why the desk and not the purse?

The apartment was utterly quiet. She felt a light pressure on her leg. She looked down. Jugs twined around her leg, whisking the side of his face against her, staking claim to her. She reached down, paused to remove one rubber glove, and stroked his silky back.

His upright tail curved slightly forward. "*. . . You're all right . . . I like you . . .*"

Nela felt a catch in her throat. "I like you, too."

The sound of her voice emphasized the silence surrounding them. There was no one to see them. With a decisive nod, she walked toward the door, retrieved the doorstop, pushed it beneath the door. Moving around the living room, she closed the blinds in the windows. She pulled back on the rubber glove and crossed to the desk.

She wasn't sure why she was wearing the gloves now. Maybe she had the instincts of a crook. After all, wasn't it reasonable for her to clean up the mess around the desk, make the room presentable again?

Although Nela was sure she was unobserved, she worked fast as she stacked papers. The cleanup turned out to be reasonably easy. In keeping with Chloe's judgment of Marian Grant as efficient, each folder had a neat tab and it soon became apparent that the drawers had been emptied but the papers had fallen not far from the appropriate folder and showed no signs of having been checked over.

Nela was looking for something to explain what drew an intruder past an expensive purse to this sleek desk. She started with the drawer emptied nearest the desk, turned it right side up. She restored Miss Grant's personal papers to the proper folder—insurance policies, a car title, medical records, bank and credit card statements, travel receipts, copies of tax submissions. Near the next drawer, she found clips of news stories about individuals, research programs, fellowships, and educational institutions. Each person or group featured had received a grant from the Haklo Foundation. She was getting good at her project and quickly placed clips in the correct folders. The second drawer slid into its place.

Doggedly, Nela continued until the floor was clear, the drawers replaced with the proper contents.

When she'd finished, she stared at the desk with a puzzled frown. She had a conviction that the searcher had emptied the drawers not to mess up the papers or even to check them, but to be sure there wasn't something hidden among the folders.

She looked across the room at the Coach bag. Instead of finding reassurance, she felt more uneasy. Had the searcher been hunting for that obviously expensive necklace? If so, why not look in the purse? Why the desk? But who knew what a thief thought or why?

Nela stripped off the rubber gloves, returned them to the kitchen. She found a broom closet, picked up a broom and dustpan. Soon the last of the broken mirror had been swept up and dumped into the trash container. Lips pressed firmly together, she carefully eased the frame with the remnants of the mirror from the hook on the wall. When she'd placed the frame inside Miss Grant's bedroom, she returned to the living room. She opened the blinds, welcoming bright shafts of winter sunlight.

Yet the apartment held no cheer. She had rarely felt so alone, so cut off from human contact. She wouldn't be around anyone until she went to Chloe's job Monday. The job . . . There probably wouldn't be anyone at the foundation on a Saturday but she could take a drive, find the way, make Monday morning easier. She grabbed her purse and Chloe's coat.

She was almost to the door when she paused. The Coach purse now seemed huge to her because she knew that it contained a large sum of cash and an obviously expensive necklace. She yanked wool gloves from Chloe's pockets. She put them on and picked up the Coach bag.

In the kitchen, she knelt by the cabinet that held Jugs's canned food. In only a moment, the purse rested snugly behind cans stacked four high. Maybe a thief would head unerringly for the cat food cabinet. But she felt better. Monday at work, she'd find out how to contact Marian Grant's sister and suggest that the purse, bank books, and other obvious valuables be removed from the apartment. She didn't have to admit she knew the purse's contents to suggest that it be put away for safekeeping.

She was considerably cheered as she stepped out on the high porch. The wind had died down. The day was cold, possibly in the thirties, but brilliant sunshine and a pale winter blue sky were exhilarating.

As she started down the steep steps, a streak of dark blue on the second baluster caught her gaze. She stopped and stared. An oblique line marred the white paint about sixteen inches above the step. The scrape on the wood indicated that something had struck the baluster, leaving an uneven mark on the paint.

Nela pictured early-morning darkness and a woman in a hurry, moving fast, not thinking about a familiar stairway. Likely her right foot would have come down on the first step, her left on the second.

A skateboard could have flipped up to strike the baluster while flinging her sideways to tumble over the railing.

The police had searched the area and found nothing, certainly not a skateboard.

The streak looked new and fresh. Nela was abruptly irritated with herself. Since when was she an expert on a marred surface on a white post? Since never. The scrape might have been there for months.

She started down the steps. Carefully.

HAKLO FOUNDATION glittered in faux gold letters in an arch over stone pillars. Nela turned in. Leafless trees bordered well-kept grounds. Winter-bare branches seemed even more bleak in contrast to a green lawn of fescue. The velvety grass emphasized the Mediterranean glow of the two-story golden stucco building atop a ridge.

At the foundation entrance, an impressive portico covered shallow stone steps. The imposing statue of Harris Webster gazed into infinity at the base of the steps. The red tile roof made Nela feel homesick. There were so many Spanish colonial buildings in old LA. Even the ornate stonework on oversize windows seemed familiar, but there should have been palm trees, not leafless sycamores.

A discreet sign with an arrow pointed to the right: PARKING.

Obediently Nela turned right. She passed a line of evergreens. The short spur ended at a cross street. A sign to the right announced: GUEST PARKING. The guest parking lot was out of sight behind the evergreens. A sign to the left: STAFF ONLY.

She turned left. A wing extended the length of the drive. At the end of the building, she turned left again. A matching wing extended from the other side with a courtyard in between. Arched windows overlooked a courtyard garden with a tiled fountain, waterless in January. A cocktail reception could easily spill out into the courtyard in good weather. She glanced about but saw no parking areas. Once past the building, another discreet sign led to the staff parking lot, also screened by evergreens. Beyond the evergreens, a half dozen outbuildings likely provided either storage or housed maintenance. On the far side of sycamores that stood sentinel alongside the building, she glimpsed several rustic cabins.

She was a little surprised to see a car in the lot, a beige Camry. Nela turned into the parking area and chose the slot next to the Camry. It would take only a minute to spot the entrance she should use Monday.

When she stepped out of the VW and closed the door, the sound seemed loud, the country silence oppressive. She wasn't accustomed to stillness. There was always noise in LA. She followed a covered walkway to the end of the near wing The walk ended in a T. To her left was a doorway helpfully marked: STAFF ONLY. To the right, the sidewalk led past the sycamores to the cabins.

There were two keys on Chloe's key ring. One fit the VW. Nela assumed the other afforded entrance to the building. The key to Marian Grant's apartment had been separate, identifiable by a pink ribbon.

However, the foundation locks might be rigged so that any entrance outside of work hours triggered an alarm. As Nela hesitated, the heavy oak door opened.

A middle-aged woman with frizzy brown hair peered out. Pale brown eyes, magnified by wire-rim glasses perched on a bony nose, looked at her accusingly. "This is private property. The foundation is closed to the public until Monday. I heard a car and if you continue to trespass I will call the police."

Nela had no wish to deal further with law enforcement personnel. She spoke quickly, embarrassed and uncomfortable. "I'm Chloe Farley's sister, Nela. Chloe gave me directions and I came by to be sure I knew the way on Monday."

"Oh." The brown eyes blinked rapidly. "I should have recognized you. Chloe has a picture on her bookcase. But so many things have happened and I'm here by myself. Oh dear. I hope you will forgive me. Please come in. I'm Louise Spear, the executive secretary. I'll show you around." She held the door wide. "That will make everything easier Monday. Do you have a key?"

As she stepped inside, Nela held up the key ring. "Is the bronze one the key to the staff entrance?"

Louise peered. "That's it. Did you intend to try it to be sure?"

Nela smiled. "No. I thought I could knock Monday morning if necessary. I was afraid to use the key after hours in case it triggered an alarm."

Louise shook her head. "Only broken windows sound an alarm. We can go in and out with a key at any time. The key works for all the outer doors." She closed the door.

Nela looked up a wide marbled hallway with office doors on one side and windowed alcoves overlooking the courtyard on the other. The marble flooring was a swirl of golden tones. Between the alcoves, paintings of Western scenes hung on the walls.

Louise reached out, touched a panel of lights. Recessed lighting glowed to illuminate the paintings. She was proud. "Isn't it beautiful? The paintings in this hall are from various places in Oklahoma. Our state has an amazingly varied terrain, everything from hills to prairies to mesas. There are beautiful paintings all through the foundation. I'm glad I can show you everything today when we don't have to hurry. Mondays get busy. There's a staff meeting at eleven.

It's very responsible of you"—her tone was admiring and mildly surprised—"to make the extra effort to locate the foundation today. I will confess I wasn't sure what to expect from Chloe's sister. Chloe is"—a pause—"casual about things."

Nela well understood. Chloe was not only casual, but slapdash and last minute.

"Though," Louise added hurriedly, "she's a nice girl and somehow everything gets done."

Nela gave her a reassuring smile. There was no point in taking umbrage because truth was truth. "Chloe moves quickly." That was true, too.

Louise smiled in return. "Yes, she does. I'll show you her office, but first"—she began to walk, gesturing to her right—"these small offices are for summer interns. We also have a new position this year." A faint frown touched her face. "For an assistant curator. The new director thought it would be good to put one person in charge of overseeing artifact donations. Haklo is unusual among foundations because we not only provide grants, we create our own programs to celebrate Oklahoma history. Thanks to Haklo, many schools around the state now have displays that we have provided, everything from memorabilia about Will Rogers to women's roles in early statehood to Indian relics." The frosted glass of the office door read:

ABBY ANDREWS

ASSISTANT CURATOR

Louise moved to the next door. "This is Chloe's office." She opened the door and flicked on the light.

Nela felt her sister's presence as they stepped inside. Chloe had put her personal stamp on a utilitarian room with a gray metal desk and a bank of filing cabinets. There on the bookcase was a picture of Nela and Chloe, arm in arm on a happy summer day at the Santa Monica pier. Four posters enlivened pale gray walls, an aerial view of Machu Picchu, a surfer catching a big one in Hawaii, a tousle-haired Amelia Earhart in a trench coat standing by a bright red Lockheed Vega, and the shining gold-domed ceiling of the Library of Congress.

Louise followed her gaze to the posters. "Has your sister been to all those places?"

"In her dreams." When Chloe was little, Nela had often read Dr. Seuss to her. She sometimes wondered if a little girl's spirit had responded to the lyrical call of places to go and things to see. If Chloe couldn't go there—yet—in person, she'd travel in her imagination.

"I suppose that's why she went to Tahiti." Louise's voice was almost admiring. "I don't think I'd ever have the courage, but she doesn't worry, does she?"

"Sometimes I wish she would," Nela confided. "She always thinks everything will work out and so far"—her usual quick prayer, plea, hope flickered in her mind—"they have. But I'll be glad when she and Leland get home."

Louise's glance was sympathetic. "I know. I always worried so about my son. I always wanted him safe at home and that's when he died, driving home from college in an ice storm. Maybe Tahiti is safer." Her voice was thin. "Certainly nothing's seemed secure here lately. Chloe keeps telling me not to worry. But I can't help worrying."

Worry.

Nela pictured Marian's brown tabby looking up forlornly. . . . *She was worried . . . She didn't know what to do . . .*

"What's been wrong?"

It was as if Louise stepped back a pace though she didn't move. Her face was suddenly bland. "Oh, this and that. Things crop up. The foundation is involved in so many activities and sometimes people get angry."

Nela was abruptly alert. Someone had been angry last night in Marian Grant's apartment, angry enough to pick up a crystal statuette and fling it at a mirror. Nela wasn't reassured by Louise's smooth response. The intrusion in the dead woman's apartment last night had been wrong, and there seemed to be something wrong here at the foundation, but Chloe's boss obviously didn't intend to explain. Was the search last night related to things cropping up, whatever that meant, at the foundation? The secretary's threat to call the police because of Nela's unexpected arrival had to be based on some definite concern.

"Here is the connecting door to my office." Louise gestured toward an open door. "Unless I'm in conference, I leave the door open between the offices and that makes access easier. Chloe handles my correspondence and takes care of filing. We're having a meeting of the grants committee later this month and Chloe is about halfway through preparing one-page summaries of applications. Tomorrow, you can be sure the conference room is ready for the staff meeting, fresh legal pads and a pen at each place. There's a small galley off the main conference room. About ten minutes after everyone arrives, you can heat sweet rolls and bring them in with coffee. The foundation has the most wonderful cook."

She was now businesslike with no hint of her earlier distress. As they approached the front of the building, the size of the offices grew. Louise walked fast and talked fast. Names whirled in Nela's mind like buzzing gnats. ". . . These offices are provided as a courtesy to the members of the grants committee." She rattled off several names. They reached the front hall.

"The main hallway"—she made a sweeping gesture—"runs east and west. This is the west hall." She pointed across the spacious marble hallway. "The corner office belongs to Blythe Webster. She's the trustee of the foundation."

Louise flicked several switches, illuminating the magnificent main hallway. "There are only two front offices, one at each corner. Now for our beautiful rotunda." She looked eager as she led the way. "I love the fountain behind the reception desk."

Water gurgled merrily, splashing down over blue and gold tiles.

Louise stopped next to a horseshoe-shaped counter opposite the huge oak front door. She patted the shining wooden counter. "This is the reception desk. Rosalind McNeill takes care of the phones."

Nela was pleased to recognize another name. Chloe had mentioned Rosalind in her letter. Rosalind apparently had filled Chloe in on things that had happened at the foundation.

Louise pointed at the high ceiling. "Rosalind has the best view in the building."

Nela looked up at a series of huge frescoes, magnificent, fresh, and vivid.

Louise beamed. "The paintings reflect Haklo Foundation's encouragement of crop rotation. The first panel is wheat, the next is canola, and the third is sesame."

Nela felt swept into a new world as she admired the vivid frescoes, the three distinctly different crops, grazing cattle, a champion bull, an old field with ranks of wooden derricks.

"We're very proud of the frescoes. They were painted by one of our very own scholarship students, Miguel Rodriguez. The sculptures on either side of the fountain"—she pointed to alcoves in the stuccoed walls—"are members of the Webster family. That's Harris Webster's grandmother, Mary Castle, who was a Chickasaw. The Webster family goes way back to Indian Territory days when Caleb Webster married Mary Castle. Mr. Webster—"

There was reverence in her voice and Nela had no doubt she referred to the foundation's benefactor, Harris Webster.

"—honored his Chickasaw heritage when he named the foundation Haklo. That's Chickasaw for *to listen*. That's what we do. We listen to the requests from our community and respond. Our grants fund agricultural research, rancher certification programs, wildlife and fisheries management, biofuel studies with an emphasis on switchgrass, seminars of interest to farmers and ranchers, and, of course, we support the arts, including grants and scholarships to students, artists, musicians, a local nonprofit art gallery, and particular programs and faculty at Craddock College. And we have our wonderful outreach with the historical exhibits that we create ourselves."

Pink tinged her cheeks. Her eyes glowed with enthusiasm. She gestured at the east wing. "That way is the director's office and conference rooms and the foundation library. The catering office and kitchen are at the far end. The other staff offices and an auditorium are upstairs. Aren't the stairs beautiful?"

Twin tiled stairways with wrought iron railings curved on either side of the fountain area.

They left the rotunda and walked toward the end of the main cross hall. "In the morning, I'll take you around early to meet—"

A rattle of footsteps clicked behind them on one of the curving stairways.

Louise stiffened. Her eyes flared in alarm.

Nela realized the executive secretary was afraid. Louise had said she was alone in the building.

A man spoke in a high tenor voice, the ample space of the rotunda magnifying the sound. ". . . don't know what the bitch will do next."

Louise exhaled in relief but again bright pink touched her cheeks, this time from dismay.

A softer, more precise male voice replied. "Let it go, Robbie."

"I won't let it go. I won't ever let it go."

Louise gripped Nela's elbow, tugged, and began to speak, lifting her voice, as she hurried Nela back toward the reception desk. "I forgot to show you the sculpture of Mr. Webster."

Two men came around the curve of the stairwell. The older man's silver hair was a mane, matched by an equally dramatic silver handlebar mustache. A black cape swirled as he moved, accentuating the white of a pullover sweater and matching black flannel trousers and black boots.

Nela was reminded of a drama professor from summer school between her junior and senior years. When he quoted from a play, a character came alive, robust, individual, memorable. He had been fun and she'd enjoyed every moment of the class.

His companion was younger, with perfectly coiffed thick blond hair and a smoothly handsome face now soured by a scowl. He was more conventionally dressed in a black turtleneck and blue jeans.

Nela knew instantly that they were a couple. There was that sense of physical connection that imbued all unions, whether heterosexual or homosexual.

Louise bustled forward to meet them at the foot of the stairs. She smiled at the older man. "Erik, it's wonderful to see you." She gestured toward Nela. "I want you to meet Nela Farley. She's taking her sister's place this week while Chloe is on her great adventure. Nela, this is Erik Judd and Robbie Powell." There was the slightest hesitation and a flick of a glance at Erik, then Louise said hurriedly,

"Robbie is our director of public relations." She looked at the younger man. "Robbie, you scared me. I didn't know anyone else was here. I didn't hear your car come into the lot."

"We're in Erik's Porsche. He insisted on parking in the visitors' lot." Robbie's tone was petulant.

Louise looked dismayed. "Oh, Erik, you are always welcome here."

Erik smoothed back a silver curl. "Since we're in my car, I thought it was more appropriate to park in the visitors' lot. I use the visitors' lot now when I do research here." But his smile was friendly. "It's good to see you, Louise, and to meet Nela." His nod was gracious.

Robbie managed a smile for Nela. "Thanks for filling in for Chloe. I hope you'll enjoy your time with us."

The two men walked toward the front doorway, Robbie leading. As Robbie opened the heavy door, a gust of cold air swirled inside. Erik Judd's cape billowed.

Louise turned back to Nela and picked up their conversation as if there had been no interruption. "Rosalind will buzz you about midmorning Monday to deliver the mail. She'll have everything sorted. Start with Miss Webster."

Clearly, Louise had no intention of discussing Erik and Robbie or explaining the odd emphasis on the visitors' lot.

"Now"—Louise sounded brighter—"let's look at the east wing."

Nela's grasp of who worked where was hazy. However, there was no doubt of the pecking order. Miss Webster had the big front office at the west end of the central hall. Whoever worked in the east front office must also be a major player.

Nela gestured at the door. "Is that the director's office?"

Louise drew in a sharp breath. "That was the office of our chief operating officer. She passed away last week. A dreadful accident."

Nela felt a moment of surprise that Marian Grant had outranked the foundation director in status. "Miss Grant's office?"

Louise stared at her, eyes wide.

Of course, Chloe hadn't bothered to explain where Nela would stay so Louise was startled by Nela's knowledge. "I spent the night at Miss Grant's apartment. Since Chloe e-mailed with Miss Grant's sister in Australia about arranging matters here, Chloe volunteered to stay in the apartment and take care of Miss Grant's cat until a home is found for him. I'm there while Chloe's gone." *Unless*, she qualified in her mind, *someone tries to break in again.* Nela almost told Louise about the entry in the night, but the secretary was staring at the office door in such obvious distress Nela didn't want to add to her unhappiness. Certainly if she grieved for her lost coworker, it would upset her more to think the dead woman's home had been invaded. And it would be unkind to ask Louise to take care of the Coach bag. A woman's purse is very personal and Louise would have seen the bag many times.

"Her belongings"—Louise's voice shook a little—"need to be gathered up. Perhaps you can take care of that for us. I'll arrange for some cartons. I can't bear to think about it. Her personal trinkets . . ." She stopped and pressed her lips together. Louise cleared her throat. "We need to find out if Marian's sister wants to have everything stored or shipped to her or perhaps disposed of." She paused, said dully, "Disposed of . . . It's dreadful to talk of Marian's belongings that way. She was such a competent person. She knew everything. I don't know how the foundation will manage without her. Her death is a huge loss. And to think of Marian of all people falling from her stairs! Marian skied and jogged and climbed mountains. She wasn't the least bit clumsy." Her voice quivered with emotion, almost a touch of anger, as if Marian Grant had let them down. "But there's nothing we can do about it."

Steve Flynn slid into the last booth in a line of red leatherette booths at Hamburger Heaven. On a Sunday night, choice for dinner in Craddock was limited to the usual suspects: McDonald's, Sonic, Braum's, Applebee's, Olive Garden. The hometown restaurants closed after Sunday brunch except for Hamburger Heaven.

The crowd was sparse. Sunday was a family evening. Steve was getting used to eating out alone. He dipped a French fry in the side of ranch dressing that he always ordered with his cheeseburger. He felt a flicker of amusement. Living on the wild side, ranch dressing instead of Heinz. His hand froze midway to his mouth.

A dark-haired woman in her early twenties slipped onto a wooden seat at a nearby table. She was a stranger. Not that he could claim to know everyone in Craddock, but he knew most of her age and class. He had never seen her before, of that he was certain. He would not forget her. She wasn't conventionally pretty. Her face was too thin with deep-set eyes, narrow nose, high cheekbones, and a delicate but firm chin. There were smudges beneath her brilliantly dark eyes. She carried with her an air of melancholy.

She sat at a table close to him, but he had no doubt that though she was physically present, her thoughts were far away.

His image and hers were reflected in the long mirror behind the counter, two people sitting by themselves, a burly redheaded man in an old sweater, an aloof and memorable dark-haired woman in a thin, cotton blouse.

He didn't know if he'd ever felt more alone.

— 4 —

Nela used to love Monday mornings, especially a Monday when she was on her way to work. Since Bill died, the world had been gray. She did what she was supposed to do. Sometimes she was able to plunge into a task and forget grayness for a while. Maybe taking over Chloe's job, doing something different, would brighten her world. Sunday had been a long, sad day. She'd wandered about Craddock, ended up at Chloe's Hamburger Heaven. But sitting there, eating food that she knew was good but that had no savor, she'd accepted the truth. Old sayings didn't lie. Wherever you go, there you are. It didn't matter if she was in LA or a small wind-blown town half a continent away, there she was, carrying with her the pain and sadness. At least today she had a job waiting for her among people with tasks and accomplishments. She would concentrate on the people she met, think about the things they did, push sadness and pain deep inside. She turned into the Haklo grounds, following a short line of cars.

In the lot, she parked next to a sleek blue Thunderbird. At the same time, an old beige Dodge sputtered to a stop on the other side of the VW.

"Good morning." A plump sixtyish man with a mop of untidy white hair stepped out of the Dodge and bustled toward her, blue eyes shining.

Nela waited behind the Thunderbird. She noted the tag: ROBBIE.

Her welcomer's genial face reminded her of Edmund Gwenn in *The Trouble with Harry.* "You must be Nela, Chloe's sister. You look just like your picture."

Nela knew her dark curls were tangled by the wind. The day on the pier had been windy, too.

"Welcome to Haklo." He spoke as proudly as a man handing out keys to a city. "I'm Cole Hamilton." He spoke as if she would, of course, know his name.

Nela responded with equal warmth. "It's a pleasure to meet you, Mr. Hamilton."

"Oh, my dear, call me Cole. Everyone does."

Heavy steps sounded behind them. A deep voice rumbled, "Good morning, Cole." Despite his size, well over six feet and two hundred plus pounds, the huge dark-haired man moved with muscular grace. "Francis Garth. Good morning, Miss Farley. I knew you immediately when you pulled up in that car. It's good of you to help us out while Chloe is gone."

They were moving toward the walkway to the building, an oddly assorted trio, Francis Garth towering above Nela and her bubbly new friend. Cole was chattering, ". . . Chloe told us you were a reporter. That must be an exciting life. But the pressure . . ."

Nela had thrived on deadlines. It was the only life she'd ever wanted, talking to people, finding out what mattered, getting the facts right. She'd written everything from light fluffy features to a series on embezzlement at the city treasurer's office. She'd learned how to dig for facts. More importantly, she'd learned how to read faces and body language. She wasn't a reporter now. She'd lost her job more than six months ago. Last hired, first fired. Print journalism jobs were as scarce as champagne-colored natural pearls. She'd once done a story about a woman who had spent a lifetime collecting pearls of many shades, white, black, green, purple, and greatest prize of all, the golden tone of champagne. After her last newspaper job, Nela had waited tables at a swell café on Melrose Place in Hollywood. That job, too, was gone. But someday she would find an editor who would give her a chance . . .

Immersed in her thoughts, she'd taken a good half-dozen steps before she realized that Cole's high tenor had broken off in midsentence.

Voices rose on the sidewalk from the cabins and around a curve came a very pretty girl and a lanky man in a light blue cashmere sweater and gray slacks. Nela knew him at once. Chloe's description had been right on. *The director's kind of like James Stewart in* The Shop Around the Corner . . . *He's tall and angular and has this bony appealing face.* His companion looked up at him with a happy face and her words came quickly. ". . . I haven't seen the Chihuly exhibit either. That would be such fun."

Perhaps it was the stillness of the trio standing by the building steps that caught their attention. Abruptly, light and cheer fled from her delicate features. The director's face reformed from boyish eagerness to defensive blandness. Nela wasn't personally attracted, but many women would find his cleft-chinned good looks irresistible.

Nela sensed antagonism in the men beside her, though outwardly all was courtesy and good humor.

"Good morning." Francis Garth's deep voice was pleasant and impersonal. "Nela, here is our director, Hollis Blair, and"—his dark eyes moved without warmth to the blonde's delicate face—"our new assistant curator, Abby Andrews."

In the flurry of greetings, Cole Hamilton hurried up the steps, held the door. "Almost eight o'clock. We're all on time this morning." The dumpy little man with thick white hair suddenly looked as if his blue suit was too large for him.

As the door closed behind them, Hamilton veered toward a door marked STAIRS. "Have to see about some things." He was subdued with no echo of the pride that she'd heard when he'd greeted her in the parking lot.

The new grant applications are in the first filing cabinet. The applications are made online but we print out copies for our records"—Louise gestured at the filing cabinet—"and we make copies for the members of the grants committee. Marian says they can look at them online but as a courtesy we also provide printed copies. The committee meets every fourth Thursday of the month. We have fifteen new applications to consider. Whenever a new application is received, Chloe prepares a one-page summary. I placed the remaining applications that need summaries in Chloe's in-box. The top folder holds one Chloe had already prepared and you can look it over for the format. You can—"

"Louise." The deep voice was gruff.

Francis Garth stood in Nela's doorway, making it look small. His heavy face was stern. He held up several stapled sheets. "There is an error in today's agenda."

Louise's face registered a series of revealing expressions: knowledge, discomfort, dismay, regret.

Francis raised a heavy dark eyebrow. There was a trace of humor in a sudden twisted smile, but only a trace. "I take it there was no mistake. Why was the proposal removed?"

Louise cleared her throat. "I understand the director felt that opposing the wind farms was at odds with the foundation's support of green energy."

"Wind farms can ruin the Tallgrass Prairie ecosystem. Isn't that a green"—it was almost an epithet—"concern? Hasn't Haklo always respected tribal values? The Tallgrass Prairie is the heart of the Osage Nation."

"Oh, Francis, I know how you feel about the Tallgrass Prairie. But Hollis persuaded Blythe that it was important for Haklo to rise above parochial interests to fulfill its mission of nurturing the planet." Clearly Louise was repeating verbatim what she had been told.

"Nothing in this world should be permitted to defile the Tallgrass Prairie." He spoke slowly, the words distinct and separate. He didn't raise his voice but there was no mistaking his passion. He turned, moving swiftly for such a big man.

Louise stared at the empty doorway, her face troubled.

Nela had no idea what the Tallgrass Prairie meant. But whatever it was, wherever it was, Francis Garth was clearly furious.

Louise took a deep breath. "Let's make the rounds, Nela. I want to introduce you to everyone."

"I met several people coming in this morning, the director and the assistant curator and Mr. Hamilton and Mr. Garth. I met Miss Webster Friday night at the apartment." It wasn't necessary to explain the circumstances.

"Wonderful. We'll run by all the offices so you'll know where to take the mail and we can drop in and say hello to Peter and Grace."

As they reached the cross hall, Louise slowed. She looked puzzled. "Blythe's door is closed. Usually everyone keeps their doors open. Webster wanted everyone to feel free and easy at Haklo." She looked forlorn. "That's the way it used to be."

Nela doubted Louise realized how revealing her statement was. So Haklo was not a happy place. Not now. Was Louise's dismay because of the death of a colleague? Nela wished that Chloe had been more attuned to the place where she worked, but Chloe was Chloe, not self-absorbed in a selfish way but always focusing on fun. Nela knew her sister well enough to be sure that all kinds of emotions would have swirled around Chloe without leaving any impression.

"But we still"—and now she was walking faster—"make such a wonderful difference in so many lives."

They reached the horseshoe-shaped reception desk in the rotunda.

A plump woman with a round cheerful face beamed at them. "Hi, Louise. And you must be Nela. I'm Rosalind McNeill." She eyed Nela with interest. "You sure don't look like Chloe." There was no hint of disparagement in the soft drawl, simply a fact mentioned in passing.

Nela smiled at the receptionist. "That's what everyone says."

Rosalind's brown eyes sparkled. "Chloe's very nice. You look nice, too."

Nela imagined that Rosalind always found her glass half full and that her presence was as relaxing to those around her as a sunny day at the beach. In contrast, tightly coiled Louise exuded tension from the wrinkle of her brows to thin shoulders always slightly tensed.

"I'm taking Nela around to introduce her. If the mail's ready, we can deliver it."

Rosalind shook her head. "I'm about half done. Lots of calls for Miss Webster this morning. Something's got the members of the grants committee riled. They called, bang, bang, bang, one after the other. I've heard happier voices at wakes. I don't think Miss Webster was hearing love notes. If I had one, I'd toss in a bottle of bath salts with her letter delivery." She grinned. "I've been rereading Victorian fiction. Ah, the days when gentle ladies fainted at the drop of a handkerchief to be revived by smelling salts. Did you know they're really a mixture of ammonia and water? That would revive anybody. From the tone of the callers, I'm betting Miss Webster could use a sniff."

Louise looked ever more worried. "I'd better see what's happened. Rosalind, you can finish sorting the mail, then give Nela the room numbers." She turned to Nela. "I'm sorry you haven't met some of the staff yet."

"Meeting new people has always been what I enjoy most about working on a newspaper. I'll be fine."

Louise gave her a quick smile, which was replaced almost immediately by a furrow of worry as she turned and hurried toward the trustee's office.

Rosalind's glance was admiring. "Chloe said you were a reporter. That must be exciting."

"It can be. I'm looking for a job right now." She refused to be defensive. Everybody knew somebody who'd lost a job. She didn't mind waiting tables in the interim, but someday, somehow she would write again. Bill wouldn't want her to give up. The only happiness she'd known in this last dreary year was when she was writing. That became a world in itself, arranging facts, finding words, creating a story.

Nela came behind the counter. A vase of fresh daisies sat on the corner of Rosalind's desk. A foldout photo holder held pictures of three cats, a bright-eyed calico, a thoughtful brown tabby, and a silver gray with a Persian face.

Rosalind saw her glance. "My gals, Charlotte, Emily, and Anne. They can't write, but they snuggle next to me when I read. Funny thing"—there was an odd tone in her voice—"and you probably won't believe me, but every time I sit down with *Jane Eyre*, Charlotte rubs her face against the book. Of course, she's making it hers, but it's only that particular book. Go figure." As she talked, she flicked envelopes with the ease of long practice into a long plastic tray. Dividers were marked with recipients' names. "I've added the mail for Miss Grant to Dr. Blair's stack. I guess Chloe told you about the accident. That was a shocker." She slapped the last of the letters in place. "The trustee's mail is always delivered first."

When Nela lifted the plastic tray, Rosalind gave a half salute. "If you need reinforcements, I'll be at The Office."

Clearly Rosalind's tone was wry, but Nela dutifully inquired, "The Office?"

"That's Craddock's home-away-from-home watering hole. Coldest beer, hottest wings." A grin. "When things get too hairy here at Haklo, we always kid around and say you can find us at The Office." A sigh. "In my dreams."

Blythe Webster's door was still closed.

Nela shifted the tray on her hip. She'd been instructed to deliver the mail. She would do so. She knocked lightly on the panel, turned the knob, and pushed the door open.

". . . have to investigate." The man's voice was loud, stressed.

The door made a sighing sound.

Nela immediately realized she'd intruded at a stressful moment. Blythe Webster stood behind her desk, face drawn down in an intense frown. Louise Spear stood a few feet away. Eyes huge in a shocked face, Louise twisted her hands around and around each other. The lanky director moved back and forth, a few steps one way, then back again, clearly distraught.

Nela obviously had interrupted a grim conversation. The sooner she departed, the better. "Excuse me. I have the morning mail for Miss Webster." She remained in the doorway, poised for a quick withdrawal.

Blythe lifted a hand to touch a double strand of pearls. Her face was set and pale. "Put the letters in the in-tray."

Nela quickly crossed to the desk, deposited several letters and mailers.

Blythe managed a strained smile. "Nela, this is Dr. Blair, director of the foundation. Hollis, this is Nela Farley, Chloe's sister. Nela is taking Chloe's place while she's on her holiday."

"Thank you, Miss Webster. I met Dr. Blair earlier." She began to move toward the door.

"Wait a minute." Blythe's tone was sharp. She glanced at a diamond-encrusted watch. "It's almost ten. We must deal with this immediately. Nela, as you deliver the mail, inform each staff member that the meeting has been moved to ten o'clock. Attendance is mandatory."

—5—

Louise looked at the grandfather clock in the corner of the conference room. The minute hand stood at twelve minutes past ten. The golden oak of the clock matched the golden oak paneling. In the glow of recessed lights, the granite conference tabletop added more serene colors, streaks of yellow and tangerine against a wheat background.

A sense of unease pervaded a room where no expense had been spared to create a welcoming environment. In the mural on one wall, monarchs hovered over reddish orange blooms on waist-high grasses that wavered in a wind beneath a cloudless blue sky. On the other wall, a buffalo faced forward, dark eyes beneath a mat of wiry black curls in a huge head framed by curved horns, massive shoulders, short legs, and shaggy brown hair.

Nela sat to one side of the conference table in a straight chair. Six black leather swivel chairs were occupied, leaving a half dozen or so empty at the far end of the table. The delivery of the mail had given her the chance to meet both Grace Webster, Blythe's sister, and Peter Owens, the director of publications. It had been interesting when she issued Blythe's summons to each staff member to be in the conference room at ten o'clock instead of eleven. She would have expected surprise. There had been wariness, but no surprise.

In what kind of workplace was a peremptory summons treated as if it were business as usual?

She looked with interest around the room. Cole Hamilton fiddled with a pen, making marks on the legal pad. Francis Garth sat with his arms folded. He reminded her of the buffalo in the far mural. All he lacked were horns and short legs.

Her gaze paused on Abby Andrews. Nela thought that Chloe's description of the new assistant curator didn't do her justice. Abby was a classically lovely blonde with perfect bone structure. Her brows could have used a bit of darkening, but her deep violet eyes were striking. At the moment, she sat in frozen stillness as if she might shatter if she moved.

Why was she so tense?

Nela had no doubt that Blythe's younger sister Grace was trouble waiting to happen. Grace tapped her pen on the tabletop. *Tap. Tap. Tap.* Her rounded face was not unpleasant, but she was clearly combative.

The quarter hour chimed.

Robbie Powell brushed back a lock of brightly blond hair.

Nela made a quick link. Tab Hunter in *Damn Yankees* but with longer hair. She knew Chloe would agree.

"I'm expecting a call from a Dallas newspaper. I may be able to place a feature story on that research into antibiotic overuse in stock.

I had to change the time. And now we're sitting here, waiting." Robbie kept his tone light. "I assumed something important had occurred, but neither the trustee nor the director have shown up after the imperial summons." Robbie straightened a heavy gold cuff link in his blue oxford cloth shirt. His blue blazer was a perfect fit. He had the patina of a man at home in meetings, always sure to know everyone's name, quick with a smile and compliment.

Nela was good at reading moods, and beneath Robbie's surface charm, she sensed anger.

Louise was placating. "They'll be here soon. There's been an upsetting development."

The faces around the table were abruptly alert. There was unmistakable tension.

Francis cleared his throat. "What development?"

Louise didn't meet his gaze. "It will be better for Blythe to explain."

Peter Owens shifted in his seat. "Ah, well, we're on company time." His comment was smooth, but he, too, looked uncomfortable. A lean man with black horn rims perched in wiry dark hair, he had wide-set brown eyes, a thin nose, and sharp chin. His good quality but well-worn tweed jacket with leather elbow patches made him look professorial. "How about some of Mama Kay's sweet rolls? A little sugar will lift your spirits, Robbie."

Louise looked at Nela. "Please serve the sweet rolls and coffee now. Except for Blythe and Hollis."

Nela warmed the sweet rolls and carried the serving plate to Louise. Nela poured coffee into Haklo Foundation mugs, gold letters on a dark green background, and served them.

Peter nodded his thanks, then lifted his mug. "Ladies and gentlemen, a toast to our newest addition. Welcome to Haklo Foundation,

Nela. We enjoy your sister. She's definitely a breath of freshness in this fusty atmosphere. Have you heard a report from Tahiti?"

Nela responded to his genuine interest. "Just a call Friday night to say they arrived safely and everything was fantastic."

"Fantastic in all caps?" But his voice was kind.

Nela smiled. "Absolutely."

He nodded toward her chair. "Pour yourself some coffee, too. I highly recommend Mama Kay's raspberry Danish. The foundation is beyond good fortune to have her as our chef."

Nela glanced at Louise, who nodded.

Nela settled at her place with a plate. The sweet roll was indeed excellent, the flaky crust light, the raspberry filling tart and perfect.

Peter spoke in a mumble past a mouthful of pastry. "Speaking of travelers, I suggest we vote on a staff conference in Arizona. Surely there is something useful we could survey there. Or possibly Costa Rica. Francis, you're very good at sniffing out development prospects for Oklahoma beef. How about Costa Rica?"

Francis turned his heavy head. He looked sharply at Peter's smiling face, then said quietly, "In the past we've done good work gaining markets for Oklahoma beef. But the new budget doesn't support that kind of outreach."

Peter shrugged. "Your office has had a very good run." His face was still pleasant, but there might have been a slightly malicious curl to his crooked lips.

As he drank from his mug, Nela wondered if she had imagined that transformation.

Francis folded his arms. "Things change." His deep voice was ruminative. "I played golf with Larry Swift the other day. You know him, Swift Publications. He's pretty excited to be invited to submit a bid to handle the design of a pictorial history of Carter County."

Peter's face tightened. "I've been talking to Blythe. I think she understands that in-house design is cheaper and, of course, better quality."

"Does she?" Robbie's tone was ingenuous. "She asked me about Swift Publications the other day. I had to say they do swell work."

"Nela, please take the carafe around, see if anyone wants more coffee. My, I hope the weather doesn't turn bad . . ." Louise chattered about the awfully cold weather, and had they heard there was a possibility of an ice storm?

Nela poured coffee and wondered at the background to the ostensibly pleasant but barbed exchanges.

The door swung open. Blythe Webster hurried inside. Her fine features looked etched in stone. Hollis Blair followed, his lips pressed together in a thin, hard line. He was Jimmy Stewart after he lost his job at the little shop around the corner.

Chairs creaked. There was a general shifting of position.

"My, my, my. What's happened?" Cole Hamilton's rather high voice quavered. Francis Garth's heavy bushy eyebrows drew down in a frown. Abby Andrews's lips trembled and she seemed even more fragile. Grace Webster's blue eyes narrowed as she studied her sister's face. Robbie Powell looked apprehensive. Peter Owens leaned back in his chair, gaze speculative, arms folded.

Nela half expected Louise to dismiss her from the meeting. This no longer seemed an occasion for her to serve pastries and coffee. But the secretary never glanced her way. In the stress of whatever prompted the earlier meeting, Louise wasn't thinking about Nela and her function. It wasn't Nela's job to remind her.

Blythe Webster stopped behind the end chair. "Sit down, Hollis."

Nela thought her tone was brusque.

Hollis Blair dropped into the empty seat to her right. He hunched his shoulders like a man preparing to fight.

Blythe remained standing, resting a green folder on the chair back. She made no apology for their late arrival and gave no greeting. "This morning I received calls from Alice Garcia, Kay Drummond, and Jane Carstairs. In today's mail, each informed me she had received a letter on Dr. Blair's letterhead which contained obscene material." She looked toward the director. "I immediately spoke with Hollis. He assures me he had no knowledge of the letter." The words were spoken evenly, suggesting neither acceptance nor denial of the director's involvement.

Hollis Blair's head jerked up. "Obviously I didn't send the letters. I know nothing about them. Someone obtained my letterhead and used it without permission."

Robbie Powell flapped his well-manicured hands. "We have to get those letters back. This could be a nightmare. Can't you see the headline in the *Oklahoman? Prurient Letter Linked to Haklo Director.*"

"It isn't his fault." Abby blurted out the words angrily, a flush staining her pale cheeks.

Hollis looked toward her, his blue eyes suddenly soft. "It's all right, Abby. We'll find out who's responsible."

Peter Owens spoke quietly. "If there's no proof Dr. Blair sent the letters, the foundation can disclaim any responsibility. Since there have been other random acts of vandalism—"

It was like a picture that had been askew righting itself. Now Nela understood the reason why Louise spoke nostalgically about happy times at Haklo. Moreover, none of the staff had seemed surprised at a peremptory summons.

"Doesn't sound too damn random." Francis's voice was gruff. "Obscene letters sent to members of the grants committee suggests the recipients were chosen quite specifically. Of course"—he looked at Blythe—"you may soon be receiving other calls."

Blythe shook her head. "I don't think so. The calls came ping-ping-ping as soon as the morning business deliveries were made. I checked with Bart Hasting's secretary. He has a letter from the foundation from Dr. Blair. I asked her not to open it. Bart and his family are skiing at Vail. If anyone else in town had received a letter, I'd know by now. So, the damage can be contained. Since no one on the committee wishes harm to the foundation, they will keep this confidential." She glanced at the wall clock.

Cole Hamilton looked distressed. "This is a serious matter. A suggestion of immorality could taint the foundation forever."

"I'm afraid women with a juicy bit of gossip never keep it to themselves." Robbie shook his head in regret.

Nela wondered if there was a hint of malicious amusement in his light voice.

"Really?" Grace was dismissive. "I'm sure you never gossip, do you, sweetie?"

Robbie stared at her. For an instant, the handsome youngish man looked old and beaten. "I was misquoted, my words taken out of context."

"Grace, that matter is closed. Robbie apologized." Blythe's tone was sharp.

Grace laughed aloud. "Oh, my charitable sister. No matter if an employee is overheard describing her as Head Bitch at the foundation. But maybe truth is a defense."

For a long instant, the sisters stared at each other.

Cole Hamilton fluttered his hands. "Girls, girls. I know your father would move swiftly to correct the current dreadful situation here." His eyelids blinking rapidly, he spoke in a rush. "It is shocking how calamities have engulfed the foundation since Dr. Blair took over last fall."

Peter Owens cleared his throat. "Let me see, we had some road-kill out in front of the foundation last week. I guess that's Hollis's fault as well."

Cole's face creased in stubborn lines. "You can't pretend there aren't problems."

Blythe made an impatient gesture. "No one is pretending there aren't problems. Hollis has instituted inquiries into each incident."

Robbie raised a thick blond brow. "What has he found out? Who set that girl's car on fire? Who destroyed the Indian baskets? Who set off the indoor sprinklers and drenched my office? Who turned on the outdoor fountain and the pipes froze and it's going to cost thousands to fix it? Who took the skateboard from Abby's porch? Next thing you know, the vandal will strap a bomb to it and roll it up the main hall one night. Who stole your necklace? I find it puz-zling"—his green eyes flicked toward Hollis—"that our director didn't call the police, and that necklace must be worth thousands of dollars with those heavy gold links and those diamonds. And now these letters . . ."

Nela remembered too clearly the heavy weight of the necklace, the glitter of the stones. Somehow she managed not to change expression. She had the same sense of unreality that an earthquake brought, jolted by one shock and then another. A missing skateboard. A stolen necklace. She pushed aside thoughts of a skateboard. That was her invention, extrapolating what a cat meant by a rolling board. But the gold necklace heavy with diamonds that rested at the bot-tom of Marian Grant's purse was real, not an invention. Up to this moment, she had been engaged as an observer. Now, with abrupt suddenness, she was as intensely involved as any of the Haklo staff.

"I"—Blythe's tone was imperious—"instructed Hollis to arrange for a private investigation about the necklace. I do not want the disappearance of the necklace to become a police matter. Inevitably, if there is a police report, there would be a story in the *Clarion*. We've had enough stories. I'm still getting questions about that car fire and the fountain. However"—she glanced at her watch—"if all of these incidents are connected, the person who wishes harm to the foundation may have been too clever. Within a few minutes, I expect to know whether one of our computers generated the message. Obviously the writer would have deleted the file but IT assures me that any deleted file can be found. At this moment, our IT staff is checking every computer. Penny Crawford will bring the results to me. As we wait, we will proceed with our regular meeting. Hollis."

Dr. Blair gave an abrupt nod. "I will be sending out a memo to staff today in regard to our annual . . ."

The words rolled over Nela without meaning. How many heavy gold-link necklaces studded with diamonds could be floating around Craddock? But if the jewelry had been stolen, why was it in Marian Grant's purse? From everything she'd heard about Marian Grant, the idea that she'd commit a theft was preposterous. But the necklace was in the purse.

Maybe that's what the intruder was looking for Friday night. Yet the person who entered had ignored Marian Grant's purse, instead slammed through her desk.

Whatever the reason for the search, Nela knew she had to do something about the purse that now rested behind a stack of cat food in Marian Grant's kitchen cabinet. Nela's situation was untenable. If she admitted she'd searched Miss Grant's purse and not mentioned to anyone what she'd found, it would be difficult to explain the fact that she'd hidden the purse. If she kept quiet, it would be devastating if anyone found the hidden purse.

A knock sounded on the door.

"Come in." Blythe spoke firmly.

The door opened and a dark-haired young woman stepped inside. She kept her gaze fastened on Blythe's face. "Miss Webster, I found the file."

Blythe's fingers curled around the double strand of pearls at her throat. "Which computer, Penny?"

The young IT tech looked uncomfortable. "The computer is in the office assigned to Abby Andrews."

Abby gave a choked cry. Her face flushed, then turned pale. She came to her feet, held out a trembling hand. "I never wrote anything like that. Never. I wouldn't hurt the foundation." She ignored Blythe, turned instead toward Hollis Blair, her gaze beseeching.

Hollis stood, too. His bony face flushed. "Of course you didn't. Someone else used your computer, Abby."

Blythe studied Abby. Her gaze was interested, neither supportive nor accusing. "Sit down, Abby, Hollis." She waited until both of them took their seats. Blythe's cameo-perfect face was composed.

Nela wondered if it was inherent in Blythe's nature to exercise control. She also wondered if the trustee knew that she was diminishing both Hollis and Abby with her cool instruction. *Sit down, children.*

Blythe continued in a measured voice. "Remain calm. There's no proof Abby created the file. There's no proof Abby didn't. Let's explore the possibilities." She nodded at the IT staffer. "When was the file created?"

"Thursday at eleven oh eight p.m." Penny Crawford carefully did not glance toward Abby.

"I was in my cabin." Abby's voice was defiant. "I was by myself. I had no reason to come here at night."

Cole Hamilton peered at the assistant curator. "It requires a password to access a computer." The question was implicit.

Robbie looked relieved, almost complacent. "They say you always leave an electronic footprint. This may explain all the trouble we've had this winter."

Abby swung toward him, her thin face stricken. "I didn't create that file. It's a lie. Why would I do something like that? If anyone had reason to cause trouble for Dr. Blair, it's you. You and your boyfriend."

Nela realized that the usual office veneer had been stripped away. It was an unpleasant scene, but she watched each one, hoping that one of them might reveal something to explain the necklace in Marian's purse.

Robbie's smooth face turned to stone. "If Cole's worried about the taint of immorality, maybe we should start at the top. With our new director and his girlfriend."

"Let's all stop saying things we'll regret." Peter Owens's voice was calm.

"Don't be a bore, Peter." Grace was amused. "This is more fun than *The View*. What's wrong with some home truths? Everybody knows Robbie's as inflated with venom as a puff adder since Erik got canned. The psychology's a little twisted to tag Abby as the villainess but these days nothing surprises. She's the director's adoring slave even though the rest of us aren't sure he's up to the job. Of course, he responds. Maybe Abby caused the troubles so she could console him." She turned to Abby. "You are living in one of the foundation's guest cabins. I saw his car there very late one night. I told Blythe. But she didn't do anything about it. Of course"—she shot a questioning look at her sister—"you were hell-bent to hire Hollis and you never, ever make a mistake, do you, Sister?" Grace didn't wait for an answer. "It's too bad Dad isn't still around. Dad always had a rule about women in his office. He told everyone, 'Don't fool with the working stock,' and in case you want to know what that means, a man in charge doesn't screw the secretaries. They didn't have assistant curators in those days. But the rule should be the same."

Hollis's voice grated. "My private life and Abby's private life have nothing to do with you or with the foundation. The suggestion that she'd create any kind of situation that would harm the foundation is absurd. That's a nasty, twisted idea. If we're going to consider who might be angry with the foundation or"—his glance at Blythe was measuring—"with Blythe, we don't have far to look." He looked directly at Robbie Powell.

Robbie's boyish face hardened. "What's that supposed to mean?"

Grace laughed. "Come on, Robbie. Skip the hurt innocence. Be a big boy." Her tone was chiding. "You started the toe-to-toe with Hollis when you suggested Abby was vandal-in-chief. Our director may not be able to keep his pants zipped, but he's not a fool. If anybody wants to make a list of people pissed off at Blythe, you and your boyfriend clock in at one and two. Speaking of, how is our former director?"

Robbie's voice was clipped. "Erik's working diligently on a definitive history of the foundation."

Nela sorted out the players in her mind. It was Erik in the cape who had opted to park in the visitors' lot. Now she knew why.

Robbie looked at Blythe. "The foundation should be ready to sign a contract for its publication."

Grace gave a hoot. "Don't be a pushover, Blythe. Robbie's trying to make you feel guilty because you booted Erik."

"Grace, please." Blythe frowned at her sister. "It was time for the foundation to have younger leadership, a more forward-looking vision." The words were smooth, automatic, meaningless.

Robbie was strident. "Erik gave the best years of his life to the foundation. What thanks did he receive?"

Grace looked amused. "I rest my case. Who hates you the most, Blythe? Erik or Robbie? I'd say it was a tie. We know Robbie can get in and out of the building. You can bet Erik still has his keys. Or he could easily filch Robbie's."

"You have keys." Robbie's tone was hard. "You've been furious ever since Blythe vetoed the grant to the Sutton Gallery. The vandalism began the very next week. I hear the gallery might have to close down."

Nela moved her gaze from one cold face to another.

"The gallery won't close." Grace spoke with icy precision. "I will make sure of that."

Blythe was impatient. "I insist we remain on topic. We have to deal with the file in Abby's computer." She turned toward the assistant curator. "An emotional response isn't helpful. We will deal with facts."

Abby sent a desperate glance toward Hollis. She looked helpless, persecuted, and appealingly lovely.

Nela didn't know these people but the idea seemed to be that Abby and Hollis were lovers. If ever anyone had the aura of a heroine adrift on an ice floe, it was Abby. Her need for support could be genuine or could be calculated to bring out the defending male response of chivalry. There was no doubt the handsome, lanky director was charging to Abby's defense. He gave her a reassuring smile. "We'll get to the bottom of this. It's unpleasant, but it has nothing to do with you, Abby."

Abby's eyes never left his face.

A skateboard disappeared from Abby's porch. Whose skateboard? When did it disappear? Before Marian Grant fell to her death?

Blythe wasn't deflected. She tapped the folder. "Who knows your password?"

Abby's voice shook. "I don't know. Someone must have gotten it somehow."

Blythe's gaze sharpened. "Did you tell anyone your password?"

"Never. Someone got it somehow." Her violet eyes were dark with misery.

Blythe looked skeptical. "How?"

Francis Garth shifted his big body, rumbled, "Stop badgering her, Blythe."

Blythe massaged one temple. "My password's written on a slip of paper in my desk drawer. Maybe—"

Louise clapped her hands together. "Don't you remember, Blythe? Marian kept a list of current passwords in case a computer needed to be accessed." Louise looked excited. "We can check." She turned to Nela. "Go to Marian's office. She kept a small notebook with tabs in her right-hand desk drawer. Marian was always organized. Look under *p*s for password."

Nela closed the conference room door behind her. It was a relief to be outside that emotionally charged atmosphere. Maybe she would find an answer that would help Abby. The assistant curator was upset for good reason. To be accused of sending out a sleazy message on the director's letterhead was bad enough, but obviously she and Hollis were more than employer and employee. All the dictums of good sense warned against an office romance, but dictums didn't matter to love. A casual friend had warned her against dating Bill, pointing out, for God's sake, he's in the army, and what kind of life is that? Good advice, but her heart didn't care. Bill hadn't planned to stay in the army. He was going to go back to school . . .

Nela jerked her thoughts back to Abby. Abby's wavering denials did nothing to prove her innocence. Nela walked faster. Abby couldn't prove her innocence and Nela couldn't prove she'd had good intentions when she found that necklace in Marian's purse.

In the main hall, Rosalind looked up from the reception desk. "Hey, is the meeting over? I've got a backlog of calls."

It wasn't Nela's place to say the meeting might go on forever and all hell was breaking loose. She forced a smile. "Still going. They sent me for something from Miss Grant's office."

She felt hopeful when she reached the office door. Maybe she would find the notebook and possibly offer at least a sliver of succor to Abby. If Marian had indeed recorded computer passwords, someone might have obtained Abby's password. The sooner Nela returned, the sooner the meeting would end. By then it would be nearing lunchtime. She'd go back to the apartment and do something about that damned necklace.

She opened the door to chaos. One word blazed in her mind. *Fury.*

—6—

"Why didn't you ask?" Blythe Webster flung out a hand. "I should have been consulted." Her face was tight with anger.

Rosalind McNeill looked upset and uncertain. "I'm sorry, Miss Webster. Nela stopped in the doorway and I knew something dreadful had happened. I hurried over there. When I saw the mess, I raced to my desk and called nine-one-one. Then I ran to tell you and now you're all here." She gestured toward the staff members, who milled about near Marian's office.

The sound of approaching sirens rose and fell.

Blythe pressed her lips together, finally said brusquely, "I understand, Rosalind. Of course you did the right thing." The words clearly came with an effort at civility. "It's just that we've had so much dreadful publicity. Now there will be more." She turned away, moved toward the front door.

Rosalind looked after her with a worried face.

"You did the right thing." Nela doubted her reassurance brought much comfort to Rosalind. "It's against the law to conceal a crime."

Nela stepped a little nearer to the open office door.

Hollis Blair stared into the trashed office with a tired, puzzled expression. Abby looked relieved. Perhaps she thought the violent destruction—drawers' contents flung on the floor, filing cabinets emptied, computer terminal smashed, art work broken or slashed, chairs overturned—benefitted her. Certainly the file on her computer was no longer the center of attention.

Nela caught snatches of conversation.

Cole Hamilton paced back and forth. ". . . grounds need to be patrolled . . ."

Francis Garth massaged his heavy chin. ". . . obviously dealing with an unbalanced mind . . ."

Grace Webster jangled silver bracelets on one arm. ". . . I heard last week that Erik still hadn't found a job . . ."

Peter Owens looked worried. ". . . suggest care in publicly discussing any grievances . . ."

Robbie Powell was businesslike. ". . . essential to prepare a press release . . ."

Outside, the sirens shrilled, then cut off.

Hollis Blair braced his shoulders, moved to join Blythe.

The heavy main door opened. A fast-moving, dark-haired woman in street clothes was followed by two uniformed officers, a thin wiry blonde and a large man with a balding head.

Nela was glad it wasn't the same pair of officers who had been at Marian Grant's apartment. Even the most incurious of police might wonder that she had called for help Friday night and today she had found a vandalized office. Logic denied a link, but swift judgments often had little connection to logic. Happily, she'd never seen either the dark-haired woman or the uniformed officers before.

Blythe was gracious. "Thank you for responding to our call." She looked past the detective and the uniformed officers. Her face stiffened at the approach of a burly redheaded man in a worn pullover sweater and shabby gray corduroy slacks. The sweater looked very old, several threads pulled loose near one shoulder. The shirt beneath the sweater had a frayed collar. Blythe's tone was sharp. "The foundation is private—"

Robbie Powell moved past her to clap the redhead on the shoulder. "Hey, Steve. We don't have a statement yet. Apparently we've had some serious vandalism but let's see what the police can discover. Guess you picked up the call on the *Clarion* scanner?"

Wiry red hair flamed above a broad, pleasant, snub-nosed face spattered with freckles. His gaze stopped when he saw Nela.

Nela felt her lips begin to curve upward, then controlled her face. It was as if she'd looked into the blue eyes of an old friend, but her reaction to the redheaded man was nothing more than a funny link, half glad, half sad, to her past. It was as if Gram were beside her, describing happy summer nights watching first-run movies outside on a moonlit pier in Long Beach with the sound of the ocean as a backdrop. Gram's favorite movie star had been Van Johnson, a chunky, appealing redhead.

Nela put the pieces together. *The Clarion*. Statement. Police scanner. He was a reporter. A print reporter obviously, because he carried a laptop and no cameraman trailed him. Maybe her instinctive positive attitude toward him was as much a recognition of a mindset like hers as a legacy of long-ago movies.

She wondered if the stocky reporter, who had given her one last searching glance before following a clutch of police officers, would ever have heard of the boy-next-door movie star so famous in the 1940s and '50s? Nela had managed to find DVRs of all of Van Johnson's films for Gram and they'd been a great pleasure to her those last few months.

"Nela, are you coming?"

She looked up, startled.

Louise gestured toward the hallway. "Detective Dugan will report on the progress of the investigation in half an hour. Then she will interview each of us individually. Blythe has arranged for lunch to be served in the conference room while we wait."

C onversation was disjointed. No one spoke to Nela. The staff seemed oblivious to her presence and that suited her fine. She tried to maintain a grave but disinterested expression even though she was focused on a matter that each of them would find supremely interesting, the diamond-and-gold necklace in Marian Grant's purse. It was too late to explain that she'd found the necklace. Perhaps after work she'd pretend she'd been curious, wondered if the purse held a clue, and immediately call the police upon her "discovery" of the necklace. That seemed like a sensible course. But the weight of her knowledge wouldn't be lifted until she could finally hand the purse over to someone in charge.

The conference room door opened and the redheaded reporter stepped inside. He nodded at the large policeman who stood near the buffalo mural, then walked casually toward the far end of the table. If he was attempting to be inconspicuous, he didn't succeed. He was too burly, too vigorous, too intense to miss. His flaming red hair could have used a trim, curling over the rim of the collar that poked above his worn sweater.

"Excuse me." Clearly Blythe addressed him. "This is a private meeting, not open to the press."

"I'm covering the police investigation into a possible theft, possible breaking and entering, possible vandalism at the foundation." He nodded toward the policeman. "It's standard procedure for officers at the scene to sequester possible witnesses. The public portion of police investigations are open to the press."

"Hey, Steve, take a seat." Robbie Powell shot a quick warning look at Blythe. "The foundation always welcomes public scrutiny. From a quick survey, it appears the foundation has been subjected again to pointless vandalism. This probably won't be of much interest to you."

Blythe pressed her lips together. She said nothing further but her irritation was obvious.

The reporter's blue eyes checked out everyone around the table, lingering for a moment when they reached her.

Again she fought an urge to smile.

His gaze moved on. "Thanks, Robbie. You may be right." He strolled around the end of the table, dropped into the chair next to Nela. She noticed that he unobtrusively carried a laptop. When he was seated, he slid the laptop onto his knees, flipped up the lid. He did all of this without dropping his eyes to his lap. His fingers touched the keyboard as he made notes.

Without warning, he looked at her. Their gazes met.

Nela gazed at his familiar, unfamiliar face, broad forehead, snub nose, pugnacious chin. Once again, she fought a deep sense of recognition. She was the first to look away.

*   *   *

The foundation chef, a mountainous woman with blue-white hair and three chins that cascaded to an ample bosom, seemed unfazed by the request for an unexpected meal. Within twenty minutes, she had wheeled a cart into the conference room. Nela and Louise bustled to help and soon an attractive buffet was set on a side table. Louise looked pleased at the array of food: chilled shrimp with cocktail sauce, mixed green salad, crisply crusted ham and cheese quiches, steamed asparagus with a mustard and butter sauce, chocolate cake, coffee, iced tea.

The large police officer remained standing by the door, declining an offer of food. With a balding head but youthful face, Sergeant Fisher might have been an old thirty or a young fifty.

The staff members returned to the seats they'd taken that morning. The meal was eaten quickly and in almost complete silence.

Francis Garth pushed back his plate and glanced at the grandfather clock. "Sergeant"—he turned to the end of the table—"will we be seen in a particular order? I need to leave for Stillwater by one o'clock. I have a meeting with a researcher on switchgrass production."

Sergeant Fisher's voice was as unrevealing as his face. "I will inform Detective Dugan."

Cole Hamilton's face once again furrowed in worry. He shot a sideways glance toward the policeman. "I'm sure all of us wish the police the very best, but why talk to us? What do we know that would be helpful? Someone broke in."

"Did someone break in?" Grace's tone was silky. "I suppose the police are checking all the ground-floor windows and doors. Of course, if any had been smashed, the alarm would sound." She flicked a glance toward the large square windows. "It would take a crowbar and maybe a sledgehammer to break in through these windows."

Nela's glance flicked to the swiftly moving fingers on the laptop.

Grace smoothed back a lock of strawberry blond hair. "It's the same in all the conference rooms and offices. Dad built this place like a fortress. The only windows that might be vulnerable are the French windows in the main rotunda. Funny thing, though. Nobody"—she looked from face to face—"noticed anything out of the ordinary when they came to work this morning. It's a little hard to believe Rosalind crunched through broken glass when she opened the French window blinds this morning and neglected to mention it."

Peter Owens poked his horn rims higher on his nose. "Your point?"

"If nobody broke in, how did the office trasher get inside?" Grace looked at each face in turn.

No one spoke.

Nela glanced around the room. Blythe looked grim, Hollis thoughtful. The reporter's freckled face was bland. His eyes never dropped beneath the rim of the table. The unobtrusive note-taking continued.

Grace's smile was sardonic. "My, what a silent class. It looks like teacher will have to explain. A key, my dears."

Beside Nela, those broad freckled hands moved silently over the electronic keypad.

Blythe's tone was cold. "It's better to let the authorities reach their own conclusions."

Hollis Blair rubbed knuckles on his bony chin. "We have to provide them with anything pertinent."

Blythe slowly turned toward Nela. There was a welter of conflicting expressions on her usually contained face: uncertainty, inquiry, and possibly suspicion.

Sergeant Fisher's curious gaze moved from Blythe to settle on Nela.

Nela's chest felt tight. She knew what was coming. These police officers hadn't connected Nela to Friday night's 911, but Blythe Webster had heard the sirens and hurried to see. Obviously Blythe was making a connection.

Nela lifted her head, spoke quickly. "Friday night someone broke into Miss Grant's apartment. The sounds of a search woke me up. I was staying there to take care of Miss Grant's cat." She heard the exclamations from around the table. Only Blythe was unaffected. Beside her, the reporter's face remained bland and interested and knowledgeable. He would have seen the police report about Friday night's break-in. Nela had herself looked at a lot of police reports. It had never occurred to her that one day her own name would be included in one.

Hollis Blair's frown was intense. "Why wasn't I told about this?"

Blythe made a dismissive gesture. "It didn't occur to me to mention it, Hollis. Friday night the investigating officers believed someone saw the obituary and thought the apartment would be empty. Marian's desk was searched."

"Searched for what?" Grace's tone was flat.

Nela shrugged. "I suppose for valuables of some kind. But I wonder if there is a connection to the search of her office." She tried to block from her mind the heavy gold necklace in the black Coach bag.

"That makes sense." Blythe suddenly sounded cheered. "Perhaps the thief went from the apartment to the foundation. This must be attempted robbery."

"I hate to throw darts at your trial balloon"—Grace was sardonic—"but there's still a pesky little question: How did a thief get into Marian's apartment and how did a thief get inside the foundation and what the hell was he trying to steal? Or she."

"That's for the police to determine." Blythe was impervious to her sister's attack. "Nela probably forgot to lock the apartment door. One officer said old door locks are easy to jiggle open and maybe someone opened it with a credit card."

Grace folded her arms. "Not even an American Express Platinum could budge a foundation door."

Francis Garth looked thoughtful. "As Grace points out, gaining access to the foundation would be challenging for someone without a key. Does anyone have any ideas?"

Louise shifted uneasily in her chair. Her hand trembled and she hastily placed her fork on her plate. "I don't see how any of us can have any information that would help the police."

Francis added a packet of sugar to his iced tea. "It may be helpful to determine when the vandalism occurred. Marian's funeral was Thursday. Friday morning I went into her office. I was looking for a file on the Rumer Co-op. I found the file. At ten forty-five Friday morning, her office was fine. Who has been in her office since that time?" He looked inquiringly around the table.

Abby Andrews, violet eyes huge, looked terrified but spoke steadily. "Friday afternoon I returned some papers that I'd borrowed the week before. It was probably about two thirty. The office hadn't been disturbed."

Louise twined the red and gray scarf at her throat around one finger. "I was in her office a few minutes before five Friday. I checked to see if she'd finished the direct bank deposits before"—she swallowed—"before she died." Quick tears misted her eyes. "They were all done. Marian always took care of things on schedule."

Francis reached for the legal pad Nela had placed on the table that morning. The big head once again rose like a buffalo surveying the plain. "Anyone else?"

Silence.

He made quick notes. "How about this morning?"

Silence.

Francis tapped his pen on the legal pad. "Her office was entered after five p.m. Friday and before approximately eleven twenty this morning when Nela"—he nodded toward her—"was sent to look for password information." His face corrugated in thought. "Marian died a week ago today. Why did the searches occur this past weekend?"

Blythe was impatient. "You'd have to ask the thief."

Nela wasn't sure it was her place to speak out, but maybe this mattered. "Chloe exchanged e-mails with Miss Grant's sister. Her sister asked Chloe to stay in Miss Grant's apartment to take care of Jugs. Chloe was there until she left town Friday. I don't think anyone knew I was going to be there Friday night."

Cole Hamilton's round face was puzzled. "How would a thief know that your sister was there during the week or that she left on Friday?"

Grace clapped her long slender hands together. An emerald gleamed in the ornate setting of a ring on her right hand. "Cole"—her tone was a mixture of amusement and affection but her eyes moved around the room, steely and intent—"do you realize what you just said?"

He turned to Grace. "I fail to see anything odd. It seems to me that some thief reading the newspaper couldn't possibly know . . ." His words trailed away.

"Bull's-eye. But there's no bull about it." Grace's eyes were hard. "Only someone associated with the foundation would know that

Chloe had been staying in Marian's apartment or that Chloe left Friday."

Nela quickly looked around the room.

Blythe's brows drew down in a sharp frown. Hollis Blair appeared startled. Eyes wide, Abby Andrews pressed fingers against parted lips. Robbie Powell's handsome face smoothed into blankness. Louise Spear shook her head, lips pressed together in negation. Peter Owens looked quizzical, his horn-rimmed glasses gently swinging from one hand. Cole sat with his mouth open, a picture of befuddlement. Francis Garth's heavy face closed into an unreadable mask.

Francis cleared his throat. "We're a long way from determining who might have known what and how either of these crimes occurred. I suggest we remain focused on timing."

"Anybody—with a key—could easily visit the foundation over the weekend. Nobody's here unless we have an event." Grace's tone was musing.

Louise looked uncomfortable. "I wish we'd gone inside Marian's office Saturday. Then we'd know if her office was entered Friday night."

Peter Owens raised an eyebrow. His glasses ceased to move. "You were here Saturday? With someone?"

Louise's thin face stiffened. "I don't have a computer at home. I was doing some genealogy research. It wasn't on foundation time. I'd already cleared it with Blythe."

Blythe waved a hand. "Of course you can use your computer on your free time. Who else was here?"

Louise nodded toward Nela. "Nela came to be sure she knew her way for Monday. I showed her around the building. And Robbie and Erik were here, too."

Robbie spoke quickly. "I can assure you that Erik and I had no occasion to enter Marian's office."

Nela saw a flurry of quick, covert glances. "I wanted to be sure I knew the way Monday." She was aware of a distancing by the staff members, as if each drew back a little, considering, thinking, wondering.

Francis's big chin poked forward. "Did you knock on the door? Or do you have Chloe's keys?"

"I have her keys." Nela lifted her chin, tried not to sound defensive. "I didn't use them. Louise came to the door."

Grace's chair creaked as she leaned back, apparently completely at ease. "Nela, you look like somebody in the water with circling sharks. I fail to see why you'd stage a break-in at Marian's apartment or trash her office. Unless Chloe asked you to do more than sub for her, I'd say you're the original innocent bystander."

Heavy braided gold necklace with diamonds . . .

The door opened. Detective Dugan strode inside and the spotlight turned. She was perhaps in her early forties. Short dark hair faintly streaked with gray framed a broad face. She wore a wine-colored cable-knit turtleneck, moderate-length black wool skirt, and black penny loafers. She might have been a Realtor or a secretary or a shop owner except for an underlying toughness evident in the dominance of her gaze and the set of a strong chin. She carried an aura of competence, suggesting she could handle anything from gang members to a sexist cop in the break room.

Nela's tense shoulders relaxed. She gave a little sigh of relief. She was no longer the center of attention. Then she felt an intent gaze. She looked at the reporter.

His bright blue eyes watched her, not the police officer.

— 7 —

Nela was the last person to be summoned from the conference room to a small adjoining office.

Detective Dugan gestured toward a straight chair in front of the borrowed desk. "Thank you for your patience, Miss Farley." She spoke in a cool voice, rather deep for a woman. Sergeant Fisher sat to one side. He held an electronic notepad.

Nela took her seat and smiled. Her smile fled when the officer's face remained unresponsive.

Dugan glanced at a second electronic pad, read in silence. When she looked up, her gaze was sharp. "When the first responders arrived Friday night, you unlocked the front door. Investigating officers found no sign of a forced entry." She tilted her head. "With Miss Webster's permission, an officer visited the apartment a short while ago."

Nela's hands clenched. Had they found the purse? She felt a pulse flutter in her throat.

"I have a report here." Dugan tapped the screen. "An officer made several attempts to engage the lock and open the door with a credit card. He didn't succeed. However"—her tone was judicious—"an intruder equipped with a plastic strip or a lock pick would likely gain entry."

"Friday night an officer told me that when the housekeeper found Marian Grant's body, she hurried upstairs and entered the apartment with a card from a playing deck." Nela felt triumphant.

There might have been a flicker of admiration in Dugan's eyes. "It isn't commonly known, but a laminated playing card is more supple than a credit card and more likely to succeed. Most people don't carry an extra playing card with them. Are you suggesting the housekeeper was the intruder Friday night?"

Nela's response was quick. "I have no idea who broke in."

"No one 'broke' in." Dugan spoke with finality. "If there was an intruder, the means of access hasn't been determined." She tilted her head to one side, like a cat watching a sparrow. "How do you think the intruder gained entry?"

"I don't know any thieves. I don't know what they carry or how they get in. I locked that door Friday night." Nela looked into Dugan's suspicious face. "Someone came in. I think they used a key."

"A key." Oddly, there was a note of satisfaction in Dugan's voice. "You have a key, both to the apartment and to the foundation."

Nela sensed a threat.

"You arrived Friday afternoon. You called nine-one-one at one thirty-five a.m. claiming the apartment of the late Marian Grant had been entered. Officers found much of the living room in disarray, suggesting an intense search. There was no sign of forced entry. Moreover, you had to unlock the front door to admit the officers. It is rare"—the detective's tone was dry—"for a fleeing intruder who has presumably jiggled a lock with a credit card or some other tool to carefully close and lock a door. That takes time. Fleeing criminals find time in short supply. Today police were summoned to find evidence of a search at Miss Grant's office." Dugan shifted forward in her chair, her brown eyes cold. "Let's say someone plans to search Miss Grant's office. There may be information in that office that someone cannot afford to be found."

Nela listened with increasing alarm. She didn't know where Dugan was going, but the detective's gaze was hard and searching.

The detective's eyes never left Nela's face. "The searcher might be aware that the foundation could not easily be broken into. In fact, the searcher must have known that no alarm was triggered by the use of a key after hours. Miss Spear reassured you about that when you came on Saturday."

Nela had thought Louise Spear liked her. But maybe she'd innocently told the detective about their conversation on Saturday.

The detective continued, her tone brusque. "It appears the searcher used a key to enter the foundation. There are a limited number of persons who have keys to Haklo Foundation. What steps could be taken by a possessor of a key to suggest innocence?" The question was as smooth as a knife sliding into butter. "Any ideas, Miss Farley?" Dugan's broad face looked heavy, formidable.

"I don't know anything about Marian Grant or her work at the foundation." But she knew Marian's purse held a stolen necklace. The necklace had to be the reason for the search. Maybe if she told the detective . . . Nela pictured Dugan's response—suspicion, disbelief, accusation.

Dugan spoke in a quick cadence. "Your sister, Chloe Farley, arrived in Craddock last September."

Nela was puzzled. What did Chloe's arrival have to do with a search of Marian Grant's apartment and office?

"The week after your sister arrived, a foundation employee's car was set on fire." Dugan leaned forward. "Gasoline was poured inside, ignited. The employee quit. The next week Chloe Farley was hired by the foundation."

Nela controlled a hot flash of anger. The interview with the detective had turned ugly. She had to think fast, try to reason with this woman. "Are you claiming that Chloe set fire to somebody's car on the chance that the woman would quit and Chloe would get her job? That's absurd. Chloe would never burn up someone's car. And how could she know the girl would quit or, if she did, that Chloe could get the job?"

The detective continued in the same clipped voice. "Your sister came to Craddock with Leland Buchholz. His father is a financial adviser who has worked with foundation investments. People get jobs because they know people. Jed Buchholz spoke to Miss Webster the week before"—she paused for emphasis—"the car fire. Miss Webster told him if they had any openings, she'd be happy to hire your sister. Let's review what has happened since Chloe Farley started to work at the foundation." Her eyes dropped to the notepad. She brushed a finger on the screen. "Tuesday, November fifteen, Indian baskets being photographed for publication were found hacked to pieces. Monday night, December five, activated sprinklers in Mr. Powell's office flooded his desk and damaged a sofa and chair. The flooring and rug had to be replaced. Friday, December sixteen, outdoor fountains were turned on, allowed to run for some period of time, then turned off, causing the pipes to freeze and break. Up to this point, everything appears to be vandalism for the sake of destruction. Then what happens? Something entirely different."

A flicker of irritation creased her face. "The police should have been immediately notified when Miss Webster's necklace—valued at two hundred and fifty thousand dollars—was stolen from her desk drawer. She discovered the theft Thursday morning, January five. However, now that we have been informed, it seems clear what happened."

Nela's voice was equally clipped. "What does any of this have to do with Chloe?"

"She's the only new employee." Dugan flung out the words like a knife thrower hitting a target.

Nela didn't try now to keep the hard edge of anger from her voice. "That's no reason to suspect her. Moreover, she isn't the only new employee. The foundation has a new director." She wasn't sure when Dr. Blair came to work but she didn't think he'd been there much longer than Chloe.

The detective was unimpressed. "This is Dr. Blair's first post as a foundation director. Should he someday seek to move to a larger foundation, his resume will have to include a description of these incidents and his inability to protect the foundation. Miss Andrews is also a new employee this fall. However, no one thinks"—her tone was bland—"that Miss Andrews would in any way jeopardize Dr. Blair's job. That leaves your sister."

"You're wrong. Besides, how could Chloe steal Miss Webster's necklace?"

"Miss Webster informed me today that it was common knowledge around the foundation that she kept the necklace in her desk drawer. The necklace was a gift from her father and a sentimental favorite. She made a point to wear it during the Monday-morning staff meetings." Dugan's face folded in disgust. "A quarter million dollars in an unlocked drawer. She might as well have hung up a sign with an arrow: Get rich here."

Nela couldn't imagine carelessly leaving a necklace worth—to her—a fortune in an unlocked desk. "She kept the necklace in her desk? That's crazy."

"Yeah. You got that right. But here's the point. That necklace rested safely in that drawer until your sister came to work here."

"Detective"—Nela's voice was icy—"you have no right to accuse Chloe. Where's your proof?"

"I don't have proof." Dugan's voice was dour. "I feel it in my gut. Your sister comes to town. She needs a job. Miss Webster says she can have the first opening. The next week, a fire scares off Louise Spear's assistant. There's a job available and your sister gets it. Nothing more happens until she's been here long enough to find out about a necklace worth big bucks. Now, if the necklace disappeared right after she came, there might be some suspicion. So she muddies up the water with vandalism. When the necklace is stolen, everybody chalks it up to just another crazy thing by somebody who has it in for the foundation. I don't buy that scenario. It stinks. Something's out of kilter here. All the vandalism accomplished was fouling up Dr. Blair's record and upsetting Miss Webster. The necklace is different. That's money. Lots of money. I checked out your sister. She's never had a regular job—"

Nela looked at Dugan. She would read the police office as steady, contained, purposeful. She had probably never had a flaky moment in her life. Would she understand that Chloe never lived for regular? Chloe frosted cupcakes, helped raise rabbits, parked cars at charity functions (*Nela, I got to drive a Jag today!*), was a magician's assistant, tracked island foxes on Catalina Island as part of an effort to protect the endangered species, worked as a kitchen hand in a gourmet restaurant.

"—and she doesn't have any money. We're checking everything

out. I saw the feature in the *Clarion* about her boyfriend winning a free trip for two to Tahiti. Maybe that's phony. We'll find out. Maybe she's got a lot of money now."

"Chloe has no money. Neither do I. Does that make us thieves?" Nela's voice was tight with fury.

Dugan's jaw set in a stubborn line. "She comes to town. All of this follows."

"She wasn't here Friday night. She wasn't here this weekend."

Dugan's hard stare was accusing. "You're here."

It was like coming around an outcrop on a mountain trail to find a sheer drop.

Dugan's stare didn't waver. "I understand you talked to her Friday night."

In high school, Nela had once gone to Tijuana with a bunch of kids. She'd not realized they were going to a bullfight. She'd hated watching the bull pricked by tiny barbs. She'd bolted from the stands, waited on a hot dusty street until the others joined her. Now she felt one sharp jab after another and, like the bull, there was no escape for her from the arena. The detective must have quizzed each of the staff members about Chloe and Nela. Louise had been kind and welcoming but it was she who must have told Dugan that Nela had a key and knew there was no burglar alarm. Even though the director of publications had seemed genuinely interested in Chloe, Peter Owens must have revealed that Chloe called Nela Friday evening. Dugan was taking innocent pieces of information and building a case against her and against Chloe.

"You know how I see it, Miss Farley? The necklace was stolen before Miss Grant's accident. What if Miss Grant knew Chloe took the necklace? What if she had some kind of proof? What if she told Chloe she was keeping that information in a safe place away from the foundation? But Miss Grant's unexpected death made things tricky."

. . . board rolled on the second step . . .

The detective's accusatory words jabbed at Nela as her thoughts raced. Nela heard them, understood them, but she grappled with a far more deadly understanding. Marian Grant either stole the necklace herself or she knew who took the necklace. It had to be the latter. That's why Marian Grant died. She must have told the thief that she had the necklace, that she'd put it in a safe place. She had not summoned the police. Perhaps she wanted to avoid more disturbing headlines about the foundation. Perhaps she wanted to use the possession of the necklace to block future attacks against the foundation. Perhaps she saw the necklace as a means of making the thief accede to her demands, whatever they might be. Perhaps she set a deadline for the thief to quit or confess. What if the deadline was Monday morning?

. . . board rolled on the second step . . .

Dugan threw words like rocks. "Maybe Chloe thought the information was in the apartment and that's why she volunteered to take care of the cat. Maybe she looked and looked with no success. Maybe she worried all the way to Tahiti and called you and said you had to look for her. Once again we get the pattern. You dial nine-one-one and claim a break-in and that sets it up for the office search to look like someone else must have done it."

Nela wanted to shout that Dugan had everything wrong. She was looking for a vandal and a thief. She should be looking for a murderer.

Marian Grant had been murdered.

Nela opened her lips, closed them. What was she going to tell this hard-faced woman? That she'd looked into a cat's eyes and seen his thoughts? . . . *board rolled on the second step* . . . She could not claim to have special information. She could imagine Dugan's response to a claim that a cat had seen a skateboard. Yet now she felt certain that she knew the truth of that early-morning fall.

Nela wasn't ready to deal with the reality that she knew what was in a cat's mind, if reality it was. Not now. Maybe never. However the vivid thought had come to her—a psychic intimation, a reporter's intuition, a funny split instant of a memory of a teenage Bill and his skateboard tangling with her climb up steep steps to a dead woman's apartment—she couldn't share that knowledge.

Yet she had to face the truth that a skateboard on the steps, removed after Marian's fall, inexorably meant that Marian Grant's death was no accident. But if Nela suggested murder, Dugan would likely add murder to the list of Chloe's supposed crimes.

Dugan was quick to attack. "You have something to say?"

"Yes, I do." Nela spoke with determination and confidence. "Chloe is innocent. I am innocent. I don't know what's behind the things that have happened at the foundation. Chloe never even mentioned the vandalism except for the girl's car. She seemed surprised that she quit."

Dugan raised a skeptical brow. "Your sister never mentioned the vandalism to you?"

Nela wondered how to explain a free spirit to the fact-grounded detective. "She talked about Leland and what they were doing. Chloe never thinks about bad things. She's always upbeat. You're right that something bad is going on at the foundation, but it doesn't have anything to do with Chloe or me. I agree"—her tone was grave—"there's something very wrong here. I think the theft of the necklace was part of the other things, not because it was worth a lot of money." And Marian Grant died because she knew the identity of the thief. But that she couldn't say, not without admitting she could, at this very minute, lead police to the necklace, which would likely result in her prompt arrest.

Dugan looked sardonic. "Nice try. Turning on a sprinkler system isn't in the same league as heisting jewelry worth a couple of hundred thou. Besides, if the necklace wasn't stolen for money, why take it? I've been a cop for a long time and, like a good coon dog, I know the real scent when I smell it."

Nela shook her head. "It isn't just the necklace. There was too much destruction in Miss Grant's office."

Dugan looked puzzled.

"There was fury. It wasn't just a search."

Dugan's smile was bleak. "Camouflage. Just like the baskets and the sprinkler and the fountains."

— 8 —

Steve Flynn's strong stubby fingers flew over the keypad. He was nudging the deadline, but he still had ten minutes. He'd fallen back into the routine as if he'd never been away, the early pages locked down around two, late-breaking news up to four. His six years on the *LA Times* until he was let go in one of the wholesale newsroom firings seemed like a mirage. Maybe they had been. Most of that life had been a mirage. Especially Gail. He felt the familiar twist, half anger, half disbelief. So much for 'til death us do part. Maybe that phrase ought to be dropped from modern weddings. Maybe the vows should read, *I'll stay until something better comes along.* Or, *been good to know you, but my way isn't your way.* When the call came about his dad's stroke, he had told her he needed to go back to Craddock to run the *Clarion.* Somebody had to do it unless they sold the newspaper that had been founded by his great-grandfather. His brother Sean was a surgeon in Dallas. Sean had never been drawn to the business while Steve had grown up nosing around the newsroom. He tried to explain to Gail about the paper and family and keeping a flame alight in the little town they loved. Gail stood there within his reach, close enough to touch, but she receded like the tide going out. Oh, she'd been kind. Or thought she had, her words smooth . . . *felt us growing apart for a while now . . . have such a great future here . . . got a callback today . . . The producer wants to see more of me . . . wish you the best of luck . . .*

He'd been back a little over a year and the divorce had been final for six months.

He returned to the screen, his fingers thumping a little too hard on the keyboard. He finished the story, glanced at the time. Four more minutes. He scrolled up.

A gold and diamond necklace valued at approximately $250,000 was stolen from the desk of Haklo Foundation Trustee Blythe Webster sometime between Jan. 4 and 5, according to Craddock Police Detective K. T. Dugan.

Detective Dugan said the necklace was an original work of art created by Tiffany & Co. for Miss Webster's father, Harris Webster, who established the foundation.

The theft was revealed Monday when police were called to the foundation to investigate a possible break-in. Detective Dugan said the foundation had been entered, apparently over the weekend, and the office of late employee Marian Grant vandalized.

Detective Dugan said Miss Webster had not previously reported the theft of the necklace because she wished to avoid further negative publicity for the foundation, which has been attacked by vandals several times, beginning in September. Incidents include a car set afire in the foundation employees' parking lot; destruction of valuable Indian baskets; activated fire sprinklers in an office resulting in property damage; and water turned on, then off in an outdoor fountain, causing frozen pipes. The car fire occurred Sept. 19 during office hours. Other incidents occurred after hours.

According to the police report, the office vandalized this weekend had been occupied by Grant, who was chief operating officer at the time of her death, Jan. 9. Miss Grant, a jogger, was found dead at the foot of her apartment stairs, apparently the victim of a fall. Police said the fall may have been caused by new running shoes. Police said Miss Grant customarily jogged early every morning.

Police received a 911 call at 11:40 a.m. Monday from Rosalind McNeill, Haklo Foundation receptionist. In the call, Mrs. McNeill reported that an office was trashed, papers thrown everywhere, file cabinets emptied, the computer monitor cracked, and furniture overturned.

According to police, Mrs. McNeill said the office had not been emptied of Miss Grant's belongings and there was no way to determine if anything was missing.

Detective Dugan declined to suggest a motive for the invasion of the office.

The detective also declined to speculate on whether the damage to Miss Grant's office was connected to a reported break-in early Saturday morning at the dead woman's apartment at 1 Willow Lane. A 911 call was received at 1:35 a.m. According to the police report, the call was placed by Cornelia Farley, a temporary employee of the foundation who was staying at the apartment to care for the late resident's cat. Miss Farley told police she awoke to hear sounds of a search in the apartment living room. She called 911. When police arrived, no trace of an intruder was found, but Detective Dugan said a desk had been searched and the living room was in disarray. Detective Dugan said it was unknown if anything had been removed from the apartment.

The Haklo Foundation issued a statement: "Operations at the Haklo Foundation remain unaffected by the series of unexplained incidents, which apparently are the work of vandals. Blythe Webster, foundation trustee, announced today a reward of $100,000 for information leading to the apprehension and conviction of the vandals. Miss Webster will personally fund the reward. No foundation monies will be used. Miss Webster emphasized that she and all the employees will not be deterred from the execution of their duties by this apparent vendetta against the foundation."

Detective Dugan said the investigation is continuing.

When he came home to the *Clarion*, Steve had insisted he was a reporter. There were five of them in the newsroom. He glanced around the room, gray metal desks, serviceable swivel chairs, maps of the county on one wall, a montage of early-day black-and-white photographs of Craddock on another.

At the far desk, Ace Busey looked older than Methuselah, with a lined face and drooping iron gray mustache. Ace still smoked, but he covered city and county politics like a burr on a horse's back, darting out of meetings long enough to catch a drag when he was certain nothing was going to pop. He'd never been wrong yet.

Freddi Frank nibbled on a cinnamon bun as she made notes. Freddi ran the Life section: houses, gardens, recipes, and women's groups, any spare inches allotted to wire coverage of the glitterati currently atop the celebrity leaderboard. Freddi was unabashedly plump and amiable, and her Aunt Bill's candy was the centerpiece of the staff Christmas party.

The sports desk was unoccupied. Joe Guyer could be anywhere: at a wrestling match, covering a high school basketball game, adding clips to his old-fashioned notebook. Joe worked on a laptop but he continued to distrust the electronic world. Balding, weedy, and always in a slouch, he had an encyclopedic memory of sports trivia, including facts large and small about the Sooners football team. He could at any time drop interesting tidbits: the first OU football game in September 1895 was played on a field of low prairie grass near what is now Holmberg Hall; the Sooners beat the Aggies seventy-five to zero on November 6, 1904 in their first contest; 1940 quarterback Jack Jacobs was known as Indian in a tribute to his Creek heritage; in 1952 halfback Billy Vessels was the first OU player to win the Heisman Trophy.

Jade Marlow rounded out the lot. Steve didn't glance toward her desk. He was aware of her. Very aware. The new features reporter, Jade was a recent J-school grad, good, quick, smart, glossily lovely, a tall slender blonde, curvy in all the right places, sure she was going big places. She'd been inviting, but he had simply given her a cool blue look and walked away and now she avoided him. That was good. He looked at her and he saw Gail—beautiful, confident, blond, smart, and a producer wanted to see more of her. How much more? Did she get the role? Or was she playing a different kind of role? He didn't give a damn. Not anymore. He wrenched his mind back to the newsroom.

Around the corner from the sports desk was the lair of the *Clarion* photographer, Alex Hill. Pudgy and always disheveled, Alex handled a Nikon D3S as delicately as a surgeon with a scalpel.

Steve felt pumped. It wasn't the *LA Times* newsroom, but, in its own way, it was better. That's why he didn't mind spending part of every day in the publisher's office. Maybe Dad would come back. Right now he still had only a trace of movement on his right side and his speech was jerky and sometimes unintelligible. It was up to Steve to make sure the *Clarion* kept on keeping on. Ads were the paper's lifeblood. He went to all the service clubs meetings. He renewed old friendships, made new ones. He rode herd on ads and circulation and the aged heating system and the printing press that might need to be replaced. A memo from the business office recommended switching paper purchase to a mill in India. He'd worry about that tomorrow. Right now he was pleased with his afternoon. A good story, would probably run above the fold.

Steve clicked send and looked across the room at a trim, white-haired woman. As the file arrived, she half turned from her computer screen to give him a thumbs-up. Mim Barlow, the city editor, had worked at the *Clarion* since Steve was a little boy. She knew everyone in town, insisted on accuracy, and sensed news like a hawk spotting a rabbit. She was blunt, brusque, stone-faced, and scared the bejesus out of kid reporters. She was tough, but her toughness masked a crusader's heart. She'd helped break a story about abuse at a local nursing home that resulted in two criminal convictions and the closure of the home. The night Mim received the Oklahoma Press Association's Beachy Musselman Award for superior journalism, she'd walked back to the table carrying the plaque and taken her seat to thunderous applause. She'd bent closer to him. "If I'd sent the reporter out a month sooner—I'd heard some stuff at the beauty shop—maybe that frail little woman wouldn't have died. Good, Steve, but not good enough. I was busy with that series on the county commissioners and that road by the Hassenfelt farm. I let little get in the way of big."

Maybe it was being around Mim that made him look at people's faces and sometimes see more than anyone realized. He'd looked at a lot of faces today. One stood out, a face he wouldn't forget. He'd seen her last night at Hamburger Heaven. He'd watched her leave with regret, wishing that someday, somehow he would see her again, damning himself as a fool to be enchanted simply because a beautiful, remote woman sat at a nearby table and her loneliness spoke to his.

Today he had seen her again.

He reached for his laptop, checked his notes. Cornelia Farley, called Nela. Pronounced *Nee-la*. Pretty name. Glossy black hair that looked as if it would be soft to the touch, curl around his fingers. He'd known last night that he wouldn't forget her face and bewitching eyes that held depths of feeling.

She'd been the last to be interviewed by Dugan. As staff members exited the police interview, Steve queried them. All had "no comment" except Robbie Powell, who promised to provide an official statement. Powell refused to confirm or deny that Blythe Webster had declared a news blackout. Steve remained in the hall asking questions, though now he knew there would be no answers.

When Nela came out of the room, she'd walked fast, never noticed him standing nearby. Her cheeks were flushed, her eyes bright. She moved like a woman in a hurry.

Last night she'd been ice. This afternoon she was fire.

He wanted to know why.

She'd moved past him. He would have followed but he had a job to do. Brisk steps sounded and he'd turned to Dugan.

"Hey, Katie." He'd known Katie Dugan since he was a high school kid nosing after the city hall reporter and she was a new patrol offi-cer. "Let's run through the various incidents here at the foundation."

The blockbuster was the revelation of the theft of Blythe Web-ster's two-hundred-fifty-thousand-dollar necklace. Katie had been grim about the fact that no report had been made at the time. She'd related the disparate incidents, including a somewhat vague refer-ence to misuse of foundation stationery. She'd balked at explaining how the stationery had been used, but she'd provided a detailed description of the necklace: diamonds set in eighteen-karat gold acanthus leaves connected by gold links. He'd come back to the office knowing he had a front-page story.

Now he'd finished his story but he couldn't forget Nela Farley. He had seen her in profile as he left Haklo, sitting at her desk, work-ing on a computer, but her face spoke of thoughts far afield. There was a determined set to her jaw. Now he looked across the room at the city desk, gave an abrupt nod, and came to his feet. As he passed Mim's desk, he jerked a thumb in the general direction of Main Street. "Think I'll drop by the cop shop."

Mim's sharp gray eyes brightened. "You got a hunch?"

"Maybe." Maybe he felt the tug of a story behind a story. Nela Farley's interview with Katie Dugan had transformed her. As a new-comer to town, her involvement at Haklo should have been periph-eral. But he knew he cared about more than the story. He wanted to know Nela Farley. Maybe he was not going to let the little get in the way of the big.

At four thirty, Louise stepped through the connecting door. Her frizzy hair needed a comb. She'd not bothered to refresh her lipstick. Her eyes were dark with worry.

Nela watched her carefully. Had the detective told Louise that Nela and Chloe were her number-one suspects? Since the brutal interview with Dugan, Nela had made progress on the stack of grant applications while she considered how to combat the accusations against her and Chloe. It was essential that she continue to work at the foundation. It came down to a very clear imperative. She had to find out who was behind the vandalism, including the theft and likely the murder of Marian Grant, to save herself and Chloe. But first she had to get rid of the necklace.

Since Dugan hadn't returned with a warrant for her arrest, Nela felt sure that the purse still remained hidden behind the stacked cans of cat food. Would it occur to the detective that the search of the apartment and the office might be a search for the necklace? Right now, Dugan was convinced of Chloe's guilt and believed the necklace had already been sold and the proceeds pocketed. That's why Dugan questioned the expensive trip to Tahiti. An investigation would prove that there had been a contest and that Leland won. No doubt inquiries were being made into Chloe and Nela's finances as well. If poor equaled honest, she and Chloe had no worries. Unfortunately, the fact that Chloe's bank account and Nela's had lean balances didn't prove their innocence.

Louise gave a huge sigh. "What a dreadful day. That horrible letter . . . At least it wasn't sent to anyone other than members of the grants committee. That's a huge relief. But I don't know what to think about Marian's office. There doesn't seem to be any point other than making a mess. Of course there wasn't any point to any of the other vandalism. And you must have been very upset when someone broke into the apartment." Her glance at Nela was apologetic. "I'm afraid I've been so busy thinking about the foundation, I didn't even stop to think how you must be feeling." Louise came around the desk, gently patted Nela's shoulder. "A young girl like you isn't used to these sorts of incidents." Louise was earnest. "I don't want you to think things like this happen much in Craddock. I've been at the foundation for twenty-three years and we never had any vandalism before September. Poor Hollis. The car was set on fire only a month after he came. What a way to begin your first big job. He'd only been an assistant director at a foundation up in Kansas for two years, and it was quite a plum for him to become head of the Haklo Foundation. Of course, it was real hard on Erik, our former director. But anyone who works for a family foundation has to remember that the family runs everything. Blythe's the sole trustee and she has complete power over the staff."

"Why did she want a new director?" Nela knew the question might be awkward, but she was going to ask a lot of awkward questions.

"Oh." It was as if a curtain dropped over Louise's face. "She met Hollis at a big philanthropy meeting in St. Louis. We attend every year. Hollis made a good impression. Fresh blood. That kind of thing." She was suddenly brisk. "Here I am chattering away. You go home early and get some rest."

As Nela left, Louise was sitting at her desk, her face once again drawn with worry. Nela forced herself to walk to Leland's VW even though she felt like running. The sooner she reached the apartment, the sooner she could decide what to do about the damnable necklace.

Steve Flynn ignored his shabby leather jacket hanging on the newsroom coat tree. He rarely bothered with a coat. Oklahomans weren't much for coats even on bitter winter days. Hey, maybe it was in the twenties today. By the end of the week, it would be forty and that would seem balmy. He always moved too fast to feel the cold, thoughts churning, writing leads in his head, thinking of sources to tap, wondering what lay behind facades.

He took the stairs down two at a time to a small lobby with a reception counter. A gust of wind caught his breath as he stepped onto Main Street. Craddock's downtown was typical small-town Oklahoma. Main Street ran east and west. Traffic was picking up as five o'clock neared. Most buildings were two stories, with shops on the street and offices above. Craddock had shared in the prosperity fueling the southwest with the boom in natural gas production, especially locally from the Woodford Shale. New facades had replaced boarded-up windows. Some of the businesses had been there since he was a kid: Carson's Drugs at the corner of Main and Maple, Walker's Jewelry, Indian Nation Bank, Hamburger Heaven, and Beeson's Best Bargains. There were plenty of new businesses: Jill's Cupcakes, Happy Days Quilting Shop, Carole's Fashions, and Mexicali Rose Restaurant.

It was two blocks to city hall. He walked fast, hoping he'd catch Katie before she went off duty. Again he didn't use an elevator. The stairwells were dingy and had a musty smell. He came out in a back hallway and went through an unmarked frosted door to the detectives' room.

Mokie Morrison looked up from his desk. "Jesus, man, it's twenty-two degrees out there. That red thatch keep you warm?" Mokie wore a sweater thick enough for Nome.

Steve grinned at Mokie, who had three carefully arranged long black strands draped over an ever-expanding round bald spot. "Eat your heart out, baldie." He jerked his head. "Dugan still here?"

"She's got a hot date with her ex. Better hustle to catch her."

At Katie's office door, he hesitated before he knocked. Katie and Mark Dugan's on-off relationship evoked plenty of good-natured advice from her fellow officers. Katie blew off comments from soulful to ribald with a shrug. Steve was pretty sure Katie would never get over her ex. Mark was handsome, charming, lazy, always a day late and a dollar short. Like Mokie had told her one night as he and Steve and Katie shared beers, "Katie, he's not worth your time." Good advice but cold comfort in a lonely bed on a winter night. Just like he told himself that he was better off without Gail and then he'd remember her standing naked in their dusky bedroom, blond hair falling loose around her face, ivory white skin, perfect breasts, long slender legs.

He knocked.

Katie looked up as he stepped inside. "Yo, Steve." She glanced at a plain watch face on a small black leather band.

"Just a few questions." He turned a straight chair in front of her desk, straddled the seat. "I was out in the hall at Haklo when you talked to the staff. I timed the interviews."

She raised a strong black brow. "That's anal. Even for you."

"Sometimes I pick up a vibe in funny ways. That's what happened today." His gaze was steady. "Some interviews lasted a few minutes, several ran about ten. You spent thirty-one minutes talking to Miss Farley."

Not a muscle moved in Katie's stolid face.

"Come on, Katie." His tone was easy. "I picked up some stuff at Haklo. Nela Farley's been in town since Friday afternoon. She's subbing for her sister, Chloe, Louise Spear's assistant. Why the inquisition?"

Katie massaged her chin with folded knuckles, an unconscious mannerism when she was thinking hard.

Steve kept his face bland.

Katie chose her words as carefully as a PGA player studying the slope of a green. "I thought it was proper to discuss her nine-one-one call from Miss Grant's apartment Friday night."

Not, Steve thought quickly, to talk about a break-in or even a *purported* break-in, but the placement of a 911 call. He kept his voice casual. "Yeah, the report said she awoke to find an intruder in the living room."

"She said"—slight emphasis—"she heard someone in the living room. She appeared to be upset." Kati's tone was even. "She unlocked the front door when the investigating officers arrived. That's the only entrance to the apartment. No windows were broken. Officers found no sign of a forced entry."

He frowned. "How did an intruder get inside?"

Katie was firm. "Investigating officers found no evidence of an illegal entry at Miss Grant's apartment."

He raised an eyebrow. "Are you saying Miss Farley lied?"

"I am saying no evidence was found to suggest a forced entry." She glanced again at her watch. "If that's all—"

He was running out of time. Work was fine but other people's problems never beat out sex, and Katie was impatient to leave. He spoke quickly. "The apartment appeared to have been searched. Miss Grant's office was searched. Do you believe both incidents are part of the pattern of vandalism, including the missing necklace?"

"Yes." Clipped. Definite. One word. *Nada mas.*

"How can Miss Farley be involved since she arrived in Craddock Friday?"

"The investigation is following several leads." Katie came to a full stop, pushed back her chair.

Steve was exasperated. "That's no answer. You talked to Miss Farley for thirty-one minutes. Is she a person of interest?"

Katie came to her feet. "At this point in the investigation, there

is not a single suspect. No premature announcement will be made."
She pulled out a lower drawer, retrieved a black shoulder bag, stood.

He rose and turned the chair to once again face the gray metal desk.

Katie was already out the door.

In the hall, he watched her stride toward the exit. Katie had been careful, circumspect, cautious, but when he connected the dots, he understood why ice had turned to fire. Nela Flynn was in big trouble.

Jugs followed Nela into the kitchen, chirped impatiently as she closed the blinds. She put the McDonald's sack on the counter. He jumped up and sniffed. "Not good for you, buddy. I'll get yours in a minute."

With the blinds closed, no one could see her. The front door was blocked by the safety wedge. She dropped to one knee by Jugs's cabinet, pushed aside the stacked cans of cat food, felt weak with relief. The black leather bag was there. She started to reach, quickly drew back her hand. If ordinary criminals were careful about prints, she wasn't going to be mutt enough to leave hers on Marian Grant's purse.

Once again attired in the orange rubber gloves, she edged out the purse, pulled the zipper, held the sides wide, moved the red leather gloves, saw the glitter of gold and diamonds. So far, so good. She took comfort that the police hadn't entered the apartment, found the stolen jewelry. But safety was illusory. She had to get rid of the necklace. ASAP.

Jugs stood on his back paws, patted at the shelf. "I know, buddy. It's suppertime and you think I'm nuts." She returned the purse to the cabinet, knowing any casual search would find it. But for now, that was the best she could do. She dished up Jugs's food, placed the bowls on the newspaper, provided fresh water.

Jugs crouched and ate, fast.

She found a paper plate for herself, opened and poured a Coke. By the time she settled at the kitchen table, Jugs was finished.

The lean cat padded to the table, jumped, once again settled politely just far enough to indicate he wasn't encroaching upon her meal. He gazed at her with luminous green eyes. "*. . . miss Her . . .*"

Nela stared into those beautiful eyes. For now, she would accept that whenever she looked at Jugs, she moved into his mind. She took some comfort from that rapport, whether real or imagined. "I'm sorry." And she was. Sorry for Jugs, grieving for lost love. Sorry for everyone lost and lonely and hurt in an uncaring world. Sorry for what might have been with Bill. Sorry for herself and Chloe, enmeshed in a mess not of their making. Sorry and, more than that, determined to do what she had to do to keep them both safe. It was, she realized, the first time since Bill died that she'd felt fully alive.

She looked into Jugs's gleaming eyes.

"*. . . You're mad . . .*"

She pulled her gaze away from his, unwrapped a double cheeseburger, began to eat. She felt a flicker of surprise. Yeah. Jugs had it right. She was mad as hell. So many paths were blocked. It was too late to report finding the necklace. She could claim it occurred to her to wonder if anything had been taken from the bag so she opened it . . . She shook her head. Nice try, but it wouldn't fly. The detective would never believe she'd found the necklace in the purse. Detective Dugan would see that claim as a lie and be convinced Chloe had stolen the necklace and left it in the apartment for Nela to keep safe. The necklace had to go.

Throw it away?

It would be her luck to toss the jewelry in a trash bin and be seen.

How about taking a drive, tossing the necklace into the woods? Two hundred and fifty thousand dollars flung into underbrush? Probably a birdwatcher would ring the police before she drove a hundred yards. If she parked and walked into the woods, maybe dug a hole, she'd leave footprints.

What did you do with something that didn't belong to you?

She ate, dipping the fries in pepper-dotted ketchup, drank the Coke, and made plans.

At Hamburger Heaven, Steve stirred onions and grated cheese into chili and beans. He spread margarine on a square of jalapeño-studded cornbread. He once again sat in his usual booth. Beyond the tables, every space was taken at the counter. A roar of conversation competed with Reba McEntire's newest country music hit. Steve shut out the lyrics about love gone wrong, picked through the nuances of his exchanges with Katie.

When he'd asked if Nela Farley was a person of interest, Katie could have made several replies. She was never shy about barking, "No comment." However, he could then have written a story saying that Detective K. T. Dugan declined to reveal whether Nela Farley was a person of interest. Any reader might reasonably assume, as he did, that Dugan's reply definitely indicated Farley was indeed a person of interest.

That wasn't the only red flag. Instead of discussing a break-in at Marian Grant's apartment, Katie talked about the 911 call and the fact that there was no proof anyone had broken in. If no one broke in, either Nela Farley had searched the room, then placed a fake 911 call—she had permitted someone to enter and leave, then ditto—or someone with a key to Marian Grant's apartment was the intruder.

If there wasn't an intruder . . .

Steve knew he wanted to believe Nela's story. But Katie was a good cop and she'd lined up Nela Farley in her sights. Why did he want to defend the girl with the intelligent, sensitive face? He knew better than most that beauty didn't count for much and a woman could look at you with love in her eyes one minute and it's-time-for-you-to-go the next. Women lied.

Why would a girl who'd never been to Craddock want to plow through the desk in a dead woman's apartment?

He always thought quickly and the answer was waiting in his mind. Nela Farley had a connection to Craddock. Her sister, Chloe, worked at Haklo. In fact, Nela was in town to sub for her sister while Chloe and her boyfriend were on a two-week freebie to Tahiti. Freddi had written a fun feature for the Life section about Leland Buchholz's contest win and his and Chloe's plans for the Tahiti holiday. Alex took some great shots, capturing the couple's happy-go-lucky attitude.

Nela could be acting on behalf of her sister. However, her sister had been in the apartment for several days and surely had time for a thorough search. Even if Chloe asked Nela to search again, Nela had no need to create an intruder. She was staying in the place as a caretaker for a cat. She could search anything at any time she wished and no one would be the wiser.

Steve ate his chili without noticing the taste.

So he didn't get Katie's emphasis on the 911 call . . .

And then he did.

If it was absolutely essential to remove something from Marian

Grant's office, a paper, a file, maybe a link to the theft of a two-hundred-fifty-thousand-dollar necklace, a previous search of the Grant apartment by an unknown intruder pointed away from Nela Farley.

But not if the police thought the 911 call was phony.

Steve pushed back the bowl. He lifted his Dr Pepper and drank.

Katie believed the apartment break-in was fake. She linked both searches to the vandalism and the theft of the necklace.

Steve gave a soundless whistle. Now he understood why Katie refused to name a person of interest. Clearly, following Katie's reasoning, the vandalism and theft had been committed by Chloe Farley and now Nela Farley was desperately trying to protect her sister.

He finished the Dr Pepper, but without his usual pleasure in the tingly burn of the pop. Katie Dugan always spoke carefully. Her final comment had been bland until he parsed the words: *At this point in the investigation, there is not a single suspect. No premature announcement will be made.*

He knew every word was true. There was no single suspect. There were two suspects, Chloe Farley and Nela Farley. There would be no premature announcement because Chloe Farley was in Tahiti, a nice place to hang out to avoid prosecution in the U.S.

Steve recalled the feature story written by Freddi. Leland was part of a prominent Craddock family. Though Freddi wrote with humor and enthusiasm, Leland and his girlfriend came across as flakes. Nice flakes, but flakes. Had a quarter-million-dollar necklace been too big a temptation?

Steve realized he'd crushed the empty Dr Pepper can. *Ease up, man. You don't know her.* But she looked like a woman of courage touched by sadness. Her image haunted his mind.

She could be innocent . . .

Or guilty.

—9—

Nela, wearing the orange rubber dishwashing gloves, carefully positioned Marian Grant's purse on the bookcase by the door. A casual observer would never suspect the purse had been moved since Marian placed it there. Nela opened the purse and fished out the necklace. The diamonds glistened in the living room light. Nela dropped the necklace into a clear quart-size plastic bag and placed the bag also on the bookcase. The plastic bag, carefully eased by gloved fingers from the middle of its box, was fingerprint free. She felt a spurt of satisfaction as she returned the gloves to the kitchen. She was turning into an old pro at avoiding fingerprints. That was easy. Now came the challenge. She would be safe and so would Chloe if she could follow—sort of—in the footsteps of Raffles, one of Gram's favorite fictional characters. Nela doubted if Detective Dugan had ever heard of Raffles. Gram had loved the short stories as well as the movies, especially the 1939 film with David Niven as the gentleman thief. Tonight, Nela pinned her hopes on doing a reverse Raffles.

She ran through her plan in her mind. She'd leave about ten. She glanced at her watch. Almost two hours to go. She was impatient. There was so much she needed to do. She'd already tried to use Marian's home computer but there was no handy password in the desk drawer. Nela didn't have a laptop. If she did, she could seek information about the staff at Haklo. Still, she could use this time profitably.

She settled on the sofa with a notebook. Jugs settled beside her. She turned to a fresh page. She always traveled with a notebook. She might not be able to dig for facts and figures, but she could sum up her impressions of the people she'd met. She didn't doubt that the vandal/thief and possible murderer was among that group. Only someone with intimate knowledge of Chloe's schedule would have been aware of her departure Friday for Tahiti, leaving Marian Grant's apartment unoccupied for the first time since her death.

Nela wrote fast.

Blythe Webster—Imperious. Possibly spoiled. Accustomed to having her way. A woman with her emotions under tight control. Attractive in a contained, upper-class way, large intelligent eyes, a rather prim mouth. Seems on good terms with everyone at Haklo.

Louise Spear—Eager to please, thoughtful, a perfect assistant. Her eyes held uncertainty and worry, a woman who wanted someone else to lead. Distress about vandalism appears genuine. No discernible animus toward anyone.

Robbie Powell—Obviously resents the new director. Emotional. Angry enough at his partner's firing to vandalize Haklo?

Erik Judd—His flamboyant appearance said it all. He lived in bright colors. No pastels for him. How much did losing his post at Haklo matter? Probably quite a lot. He had swept out the door, cloak flaring, but there was a sense of a faded matinee idol. Did parking in the visitors' lot reveal festering anger? Vandalism on a grand scale might amuse him.

Cole Hamilton—She'd had only a glimpse of him in his office but he hadn't looked as though he was engaged in any work. His round face was not so much genial as lost and bewildered. He had an aura of defeat. What was his function at Haklo?

Francis Garth— Big, powerful, possibly overbearing. Not a man to cross. The thought was quick, instinctive. Though he'd remained calm about the agenda item, clearly the Tallgrass Prairie mattered more to him than a matter of business. Did he have other disagreements with the trustee and director?

Hollis Blair—Boatloads of aw-shucks, Jimmy Stewart charm but he had run into a situation where charm didn't matter. Was someone jealous of his apparent affair with Abby Andrews? Or was his assumption of the directorship offensive to more than just Robbie Powell and Erik Judd?

Abby Andrews—She would have looked at home in crinolines holding a parasol to protect her alabaster complexion from too much sun. Was she a clinging vine or a scheming woman who engineered problems for Hollis so that she could be there to offer support?

Grace Webster—To say there was an undercurrent between the sisters was to put it mildly. Grace was by turns combative, difficult, chiding, hostile. Grace struck Nela as reckless, daring, and impulsive. Several times she had been darkly amused. Maybe she thought vandalism was a joke, too.

Peter Owens—He'd seemed like a tweedy intellectual, but she didn't think she'd imagined his pleasure in tweaking Francis Garth. There—

Jugs lifted his head. He listened, came sinuously up on his paws, flowed to the floor. He moved toward the front door.

She spoke gently. "Ready for a big night?" Words didn't matter to a cat. Tone did.

Jugs stopped a few feet from the door, stood very still.

The staccato knock came with no warning.

Nela jumped up and bolted to the bookcase. She used the edge of her sweater to pick up the plastic bag. Heart thudding, she opened Marian's purse, using another edge of the sweater, and dropped the bag inside.

The quick, sharp knock sounded again.

Nela moved to the door, taking a deep breath. She turned on the porch light, but she couldn't look out to identify the visitor. The door lacked a peephole. She opened it a trace. "Who's there?"

"Steve Flynn. *Craddock Clarion*." His voice was loud, clear, and businesslike.

Nela's tight stance relaxed. Steve Flynn, the redheaded reporter who could have been a double for Van Johnson. She'd almost smiled at him when their gazes first met. But he wasn't the boy next door.

Why had he come?

"Miss Farley, may I speak with you for a moment? About the break-in Friday night."

Nela's thoughts raced. The detective didn't believe there was a break-in. Would it be suspicious if she refused to talk to the reporter? She didn't need anyone else suspecting her of a crime. She glanced at the Coach bag, hesitated, then turned the knob.

The wind stirred his short red hair. The glare of the porch light emphasized the freckles on his fair skin. Steady blue eyes met hers. "I've been looking over the police report on the attempted burglary here. Can I visit with you for a minute?"

Cold air swirled inside. He stood hunched with his hands in his pockets, his only protection an old pullover sweater.

She held open the door.

As she closed it, his eyes noted the door wedge. He raised them to look at her.

Nela saw a flicker of interest. He didn't miss much.

She led the way into the living room, once again saw him scan the surroundings, taking in the scrape on the back of the desk chair, the discoloration that marked where a mirror had once hung.

He declined coffee. "I don't want to interfere with your evening."

"I don't have anything planned." Other than transporting a stolen necklace as far away as possible.

"Then"—his smile was quick and charming—"if you don't mind, fill me in on what happened Friday night."

On closer view, his boy-next-door face was older, more appraising, less ingenuous than she'd first thought. There was depth in his blue eyes and a hard edge to his chin. She was also suddenly aware of being near him, of his stocky build, of his maleness.

Jugs padded toward him, raised his head.

The reporter nodded at the cat. "You have to have attention first, huh? No entrance without showing proper respect, right?" A broad hand swung down to stroke Jugs's fur. He straightened. "My mom's cat was a big tabby. He thought he was the man of the house along with my dad. What's his name?"

"Jugs."

He grinned. "Those are big ears, that's for sure. Now, about Friday night—"

Nela wondered if he was one of those reporters who always takes a cop's view. It was natural. She'd been there, too. Reporters understood the hard, tough, dangerous world cops face every day. Reporters admired courage masked by black humor. Good reporters never slanted a story, but they listened when a good cop spoke.

"—what happened?"

The cat moved toward her, looked up. "*. . . wants to know you . . . not sure about you . . . doesn't trust women . . . women lie . . .*"

Nela jerked her gaze away from Jugs. "I was in the guest room. I'll show you." She turned to lead the way. Jugs padded alongside. Nela struggled for composure. What was wrong with her? Jugs couldn't know anything in the mind of this man who meant nothing to her—except that he might pose a danger.

As she opened the bedroom door and half turned toward him, their eyes met. "I was asleep."

He looked past her toward the bed.

She was intuitively aware of him, of his nearness, of the tensing of his body, of a sense of uncertainty, of a man who had been hurt and was still angry, of longing and wariness. She steeled herself. The emotions of the day had fogged her reason.

"Noise woke you?"

"Yes. Then I saw the line of light beneath the door." She shut the bedroom door, gestured toward the living room. "Come sit down and I'll tell you." She chose the easy chair, waited until he settled on the sofa opposite her. She spoke at a quick clip, wished her voice didn't sound breathless. ". . . bangs and crashes . . ." She described every-thing. "I yelled the police were coming. I heard someone leave. I didn't come out until the police knocked. Then I ran to open the door."

Those clear deep blue eyes never left her face. "The police said the door was locked when they arrived."

"The thief locked the door behind him. I think whoever came had a key."

He looked puzzled, his gaze flicking across the room toward the door. "How about the doorstop? A key doesn't do any good if that's in place."

"I bought the wedge Saturday morning. Somebody had a key Friday night. Somebody still has a key. I shove the wedge under the door now at night."

"What were they looking for?"

The necklace. She felt the answer deep in her gut. She stared at him and realized her peril. The quick sharp question had caught her unaware. Unless she knew more than she had revealed to the police, she should have quickly said she didn't know or suggested they must have been looking for money. She had remained quiet too long. When she spoke, she knew her answer was too little, too late. "I suppose whatever thieves look for. Money, valuables of some kind."

He didn't change expression, but he wasn't fooled. He was well aware that she had knowledge she had not revealed. He folded his arms, that classic posture of wariness. "Somebody with a key wouldn't be your run-of-the-mill thief."

"If you say so." She suddenly felt that they looked at each other across a divide. "I don't have any experience with thieves."

"A key makes everything different. Either someone knew her and had a key or someone knew her well enough to know, for exam-ple, that she tucked an extra key in a flowerpot."

"Flowerpot?"

For an instant, he was amused. "Metaphorically speaking. Somewhere. Under a flagstone. In the garage. People do things like that around here."

Nela considered the possibility. "If someone knew where Miss Grant kept an extra key, they must have known her pretty well. What do you know about her?"

"Smart, hardworking, type A, absolutely devoted to Haklo. She came to Craddock twenty years ago as Mr. Webster's executive secretary." He paused, gave a small shrug. "In any little town, the leading lights, and that's spelled *people with money*, are the focus of gossip. Everybody thought she was his mistress. Maybe she was, maybe she wasn't. Webster's wife was reclusive. Again it's all gossip but people said he and his wife didn't share a bedroom. In any event, Marian was a good-looking woman who never exhibited any interest in anybody else—man or woman—so the gossip may have been right. Haklo was definitely Webster's baby and pretty soon she was running it. All she cared about was Haklo, especially after Webster died. Maybe she saw Haklo as a monument to him. Maybe she felt closest to him out there. Anyway, Haklo was her life. Everybody knew better than to cross her, including the Webster daughters. Both of them were always charming to Marian but I don't think there was any love lost between them, which figures if she slept with their dad. Marian was always in charge. Anyone who opposed her ended up backed against a wall, one way or another. Marian maneuvered money and pressure from money to get the best deal possible for Haklo."

"If she found out who was behind the vandalism, she'd make them pay?"

"With a pound of flesh and smile while she was doing it." His eyes narrowed. "What are you suggesting?"

Her gaze fell. She hoped she hadn't looked toward the door. This man saw too much, understood too much. How would he feel if she blurted out that somebody put a skateboard on the second step and that's why Marian Grant died? He would demand that she tell him how she knew. She spoke hurriedly. "Nothing. I just think someone had a key to get in." Nela felt certain she had met the late-night intruder today at Haklo. "Maybe Miss Grant's office was wrecked before the thief came here. Maybe she kept a key lying in the front drawer of her desk. Maybe it had a tag on it: *Extra front-door key.*"

"That's possible. It certainly explains how someone got in here." He spoke in a considering tone. "Somebody has a key. They come in . . ." His gaze stopped at the purse on the bookcase. "Is that your purse?"

She should have put the hideous purse away. She deliberately kept her eyes away from the bookcase.

He waited for her answer.

"Miss Webster said the purse belonged to Miss Grant."

"Miss Webster?"

"She heard the sirens and came."

"Was the purse there Friday night?"

She tried to sound as if her answer didn't matter. "Yes."

"A thief walked right by the bookcase and ignored the purse?" He looked skeptical.

"I shouted that the police were coming." She had to convince him. "I heard running steps. He didn't take time to grab the purse."

"He took time to push the door lock."

"Maybe not, then. Maybe when he first came it, he locked the door so no one could surprise him." Nela figured that's what must have happened. "It's the kind of lock that has to be disengaged. It doesn't pop out automatically."

"That may be right."

"I think the thief went straight to the desk. It was a mess. Somebody was looking for something in her desk."

"Have you checked the purse? Maybe the answer to everything is there." He rose and took a step toward the bookcase.

Nela popped to her feet, caught up with him, gripped his arm. "We can't do that. We have no right. Tomorrow I'll take the purse to the foundation and ask Miss Webster to take charge of it." She pulled her hand away from his arm, remembering the muscular feel of his forearm beneath the sweater.

He remained midway to the bookcase. "I suppose you have a point there." But he still gazed at the black leather bag.

She had to get rid of him.

"That's all I have to say, Mr. Flynn. If you don't mind, I'm rather tired. It's been a long day." She opened the door.

He stared at her for a long moment.

Nela felt an odd sadness. If she didn't know better, she would think she'd seen a flash of disappointment in his eyes, disappointment and regret.

"Yeah. I'll bet you are. Thanks." He turned away, crossed the small porch in a single step, started down the stairs.

She closed the door, leaned against the cold panel, and stared at the purse.

At the bottom of the stairs, Nela waited for her eyes to adjust to the darkness. She wore Chloe's big coat and her brown wool gloves. In one pocket she'd stuffed a pencil flashlight she'd found in a utility drawer in the kitchen. The plastic bag with the necklace was in the other pocket. She'd tucked her driver's license in the pocket of her jeans along with a ten-dollar bill and Chloe's key to the employee entrance.

She gazed at the back of the Webster house. Light seeped from the edges of curtains, but there was no movement in the long sweep of gardens or on the terrace. Time to go. There could be no safety until she disposed of the necklace. She hurried down the steps. The wind was up. Knife-sharp air clawed at her face.

The garage door lifted smoothly. As she backed the VW from the garage, she clicked on the headlights. She made no effort at stealth. She had every right to run out to a 7-Eleven and pick up something. She left the car door open as she closed the garage door.

At the end of the drive, she turned left instead of right. She drove three blocks until she was out of the enclave of expensive homes. She entered a convenience store lot. As she locked the VW, one car pulled out from a line of pumps, another pulled in. She hurried inside, bought a six-pack of Cokes. In the car she placed them on the floor in front of the passenger seat.

She glanced at her watch in the splash of light from the storefront. Twenty after ten. In her mind she traced her route. She'd studied the Craddock city map Chloe had included in the packet with one of her usual sticky notes. A thin squiggly line appeared to reach the main grounds of the foundation from a road on the west side. That would be safer than using the main entrance.

The drive didn't take long. Traffic was light. There was one set of headlights behind her when she turned onto the road that ran in front of the foundation.

Nela drove around a curve and jammed on her brakes. A doe bounded across the road, her fur a glossy tan in the wash from the headlights. In another bound, the deer cleared a fence and disappeared into a grove of trees. A car came around the curve behind her, slowed.

Nela started up again. She was aware of the headlights in her rearview mirror. The car pulled out to pass, roared around the VW, and now the road was dark behind her. She continued for about a hundred yards and turned right onto a narrow blacktop road with a thick mass of trees on one side and a fenced field on the other. The VW headlights seemed frail against the country darkness. She peered into the night. If the thin line on the map indicated a road into the Haklo property, it should soon come into view on her right. She saw a break in the woods. Slowing, she swung onto a rutted dirt road. The headlights seemed puny against the intense darkness, but she dimmed to fog lights, affording her just enough illumination to follow the ruts.

A hundred yards. Another. She reached an open expanse. Dark buildings loomed to her left. Light filtered through a grove of trees to her right. That would be light from the occupied Haklo guest cabin. Nela turned off the fog lights and coasted to a stop by a long low building. Her eyes adjusted to night. She rolled down the window. She was parked next to a galvanized steel structure, which probably housed equipment and supplies for the upkeep of the foundation and its grounds. Straight ahead was the line of evergreens that marked the staff parking lot. Quietly she slipped from the car. She looked again toward the cabin. Though light glowed from the windows, there was no movement or sound.

Except for the occasional *whoo* of an owl, reassuring silence lay over the dark landscape ahead of her. Once past the evergreens, she tried to walk quietly, but the crunch of gravel beneath her feet seemed startlingly loud. It was better on the sidewalk leading to the staff entrance. She took her time, using the pencil light to light her way. All the while, she listened for sound, movement, any hint that she had been observed. Surely if the police had left a guard, someone would have challenged her by now. Every minute that passed increased her confidence that only she moved in the stillness of the country night.

The building itself lay in total darkness.

At the staff entrance, Nela held the pencil flash in her gloved left hand, used Chloe's key. In an instant she was inside, safe in a black tunnel of silence. She ran lightly up the hallway, using the tiny beam to light her way. She was almost there, almost safe. In only a moment she'd be free of the incriminating necklace.

She opened the door to Blythe's office and dashed across the room. She pulled out the plastic bag, emptied the necklace onto the center of the desktop. The stones and precious metal clattered on the wooden surface. In the light of the flash, diamonds glittered and gold gleamed.

She whirled away from the desk. In the hall, she shut Blythe's office door behind her. The tiny beam of light bouncing before her, she again ran lightly down the hallway, not caring now at the sound of her sneakers on the marble. She felt exultant when she reached the exit. She and Chloe were safe. As soon as she reached the car and drove away, there was nothing to link her and Chloe to that damnable, gorgeous, incredibly expensive necklace.

She pulled open the heavy door at the end of the hall and stepped out into the night. The door began to close.

A quick bright light blinded her.

"The image also records the time. *Temporary Employee Exits Haklo After Hours*. Interesting headline, right?" His tenor voice was sardonic. "Care to comment?" He came quickly up the steps, used a broad hand to hold the door open. "Why don't we go inside?"

Once Nela had seen a bird trapped inside an enclosed mall, flying up, seeking, not finding. Sometimes there is no escape. Numbly, she turned and stepped inside.

He followed close behind her.

When the door closed, she lifted the pocket flashlight, held the beam where she could see his face.

He squinted against the light, his freckled face grim, his gaze accusing. He looked big, tough, and determined. He cupped a cell phone in his left hand. "What's your excuse? Forgot your hankie?"

His tone hurt almost as much as the realization that she had failed Chloe. She should have done something, anything, to be rid of the necklace. Instead, she'd tried to return the stolen jewelry to its owner and now she—and Chloe—were going to pay the price. She was cornered but she wouldn't go down without a fight. "Why are you here?" But she knew the answer. He was after a story and he couldn't have any idea just how big it was going to be. "Do you make it a practice to follow women you don't know?"

If she had no right to be here, certainly he didn't belong either. So he was a reporter. So he looked like Van Johnson, an older, tougher Van Johnson. Maybe Gram would have loved him, but his presence here was as unexplained as hers. Maybe he knew much more about what had happened at Haklo than she could ever imagine. "How did you know I was coming here?"

His mouth twisted in a wry half smile, half grimace. "Pirates used to fly the skull and crossbones to scare the hell out of ships. You sent plenty of signals tonight. You're as wary as an embezzler waiting for the bank examiner. You know more—a lot more—than you want to admit. You might as well have marked Marian's purse with a red X. Once I got outside, I decided to hang around, see if anything popped. I didn't know what to expect, maybe someone arriving. Instead, you slipped down the steps like a Hitchcock heroine." There was an undertone of regret mingled with derision.

"You followed me? But I went to the Seven-Eleven . . ." Her voice trailed off.

His gaze was quizzical. "For a Hitchcock lady, you aren't very savvy about picking up a tail. Once you left the Seven-Eleven, you were easy meat. When you turned on Pumpjack Road, I knew you were going to Haklo. I was right behind you. I passed you, went around a curve, and pulled off on the shoulder. When you didn't come, I knew you'd taken the back entrance." His eyes were probing. "Not a well known route. Clever for someone who's new to town. So, shall we take a tour? See if there are any other offices trashed?"

"Would you like to hear the truth?" She flung the words at him. "Or are you enjoying yourself too much?"

His face changed, disdain melding into combativeness. "Yeah. I'd like to hear some truth from you."

In his eyes, she saw disappointment and a flicker of wariness: *Fool me once, shame on you; fool me twice, shame on me.*

She met his gaze straight on. Maybe truth would help. Likely not. But truth he damn well was going to get. "Friday night somebody searched Marian's living room. Saturday I had the same thought you did. Why hadn't the thief taken the purse? I looked inside. I found an incredibly beautiful diamond-and-gold necklace in the bottom of the bag. I left it in the purse. I knew nothing about the theft of a necklace at Haklo. Chloe never mentioned the theft when we talked. All she cares about is Leland and fun and adventure. She told me about Turner Falls and Bricktown and the Heavener

Runestone. I didn't know the necklace was stolen until the staff meeting this morning."

He listened with no change of expression.

"If you want more truth"—anger heated her voice—"I found out a stranger in town makes an easy target. The detective made it clear that Chloe is suspect number one as the thief, with me busy covering up for her. I knew Dugan wouldn't believe I found the necklace in the purse. Tonight I brought the necklace here and put it on Blythe Webster's desk."

"You put the necklace in Blythe's office?" His broad face reflected surprise, uncertainty, calculation, concentration. He stared at her for a long moment, then slid the phone into his pocket. "Show me."

The heavy silence of an empty building emphasized the sound of their footsteps on the marble floor. At Blythe's office, he opened the door and flicked on the lights. The necklace was starkly visible in the center of the desk, the diamonds glittering bright as stars.

Steve Flynn walked slowly to the desk. He stared down at the magnificent diamonds in the ornate gold settings. "I'll be double damned." He pulled his cell from his pocket. A tiny flash flared. He looked for a moment at the small screen. "You can tell the damn thing's worth a fortune even in a cell phone picture." He closed the phone, turned, and looked at Nela. Finally, he shook his head as if puzzled. "Why didn't you throw it away?"

"It would have been smarter." But nobody gets second chances.

"Why didn't you?" He was insistent.

"It wasn't mine." It was ironic that basic honesty was going to put her in jail. "The more fool I."

"Yeah. There's a small matter of property rights." He sounded sardonic. "All right, I may be a fool, too, but everything in here"—

he waved his hand around the office—"appears to be in place. You came in, you dropped the necklace, you left. Come on."

"Aren't you going to call the police?"

"No. For some crazy reason, I believe you." He jerked a thumb at the door. "Let's get out of here. We need to talk."

−10−

Steve leaned back against the plumped pillow, legs outstretched, and listened. Pretty soon he had a sense of how Haklo appeared to her: Blythe Webster imperious but shaken, and staff members who weren't just names but individuals with passions. Louise Spear grieved over Marian and Haklo's troubles. Francis Garth was furious at a threat to his beloved Tallgrass Prairie. Francis was proud of his Osage Heritage—the preserve was the heart of the Osage Nation—and Francis was a formidable figure. Robbie Powell and his partner, Erik Judd, bitterly resented the new director. Hollis Blair was in a situation where aw-shucks charm didn't help. Abby Andrews was either a wilting maiden or a scheming opportunist. Cole Hamilton appeared subdued and defeated, but his comment that emphasized the necessity of a key to Haklo might be disingenuous. Grace Webster was at odds with her sister. Peter Owens was affable but possibly sly.

When Nela revealed the existence of the obscene letters sent out on the director's letterhead, he saw another link in the chain of ugly attacks on the foundation. But this one appeared tied directly to Abby Andrews, which might tilt the scale toward schemer instead of victim.

Steve liked Nela's voice. Not high. Not low. Kind of soft. A voice you could listen to for a long time. She looked small in an oversize chintz-covered chair, dark hair still tangled by the wind, face pale, dark shadows beneath her eyes. But she no longer seemed remote as she had in his first glimpse at Hamburger Heaven.

His eyes slid from her to a photograph on the table next to her chair. A dark-haired laughing man in a tee and shorts stood near an outcrop of black rocks on a beach, the wind stirring his hair. Across the bottom of the photograph was a simple inscription: *To Nela— Love, Bill*. A red, white, and blue ribbon was woven through the latticed frame.

Steve was accustomed to figuring from one fact to another. The picture had to belong to Nela. To carry the photograph with her as she traveled meant that the man and the place mattered very much to her. He was afraid he knew exactly why the ribbon was in place and that would account for the undertone of sadness that he'd observed.

But tonight, she was fully alive, quick intelligence in her eyes, resolve in her face, a woman engaged in a struggle to survive. The brown tabby nestled next to her. One slender hand rested on the cat's back. As she spoke, she looked at him with a direct stare that said she was in the fight for as long as it took.

When he'd caught her coming out of Haklo, he'd felt a bitter twist of disappointment, accepting that Katie had been right, that she was covering up for her light-fingered sister. At that point, he had a picture of her leaving Haklo, the time electronically recorded. She was cornered. All he had to do was tie up the loose ends. It was like ballast shifting in a hull. When the heavy load tipped to one end, the ship was sure to go down.

Now the ballast was back in place. He was pretty good at keeping score and she had two heavy hits in her favor: the return of the necklace and the door wedge. Sure, she could have found the necklace at the apartment, maybe not in the purse as she claimed, decided her sister was the thief, and returned the necklace to protect her. But the smart decision would have been to fling the necklace deep into woods on the other side of town. She could easily have found some woods and jettisoned the jewelry. She took a big chance bringing the necklace to Haklo tonight, which argued she not only wasn't a thief, she was too honest and responsible to throw away a quarter of a million dollars that didn't belong to her. That was one home run. The second hinged on one small fact: The morning after her 911 call, she went out and bought a wedge to shove under the door.

She turned her hands palms up, looked rueful. "I understand if you decide to call the detective. You're a reporter. You have to be honest with the cops you know. I was a reporter, too. Trust is a two-way street."

He wasn't surprised. She had the manner of someone who was used to asking questions, looking hard at facts, winnowing out nonsense. She'd showed she was tough when he confronted her at Haklo. She'd asked if he would listen to truth. Truth was all that mattered, all that should matter to a reporter. Maybe that was why he'd felt a connection to her right from that first look. They might have lots of differences in their backgrounds, but they would always understand each other.

"If you call Dugan"—her voice was calm—"I'll tell her what I've told you. Someone came here hunting for the necklace and that's the reason her office was searched. Unfortunately, Dugan won't believe me."

He didn't refute her conclusion about Katie Dugan. If Katie learned the necklace had been in Nela's possession, she'd be sure her judgment was right. As soon as Chloe returned from Tahiti, they'd both be booked.

"Let me be sure I get it." He watched her carefully. "You arrived here Friday afternoon. Everything was fine. You went to bed, somebody got inside, hunted in the desk. You called nine-one-one. When the cops came, you had to unlock the front door. You believe someone entered with a key. That likely comes down to a small list. Marian's life was centered at Haklo. Either someone knew where she kept an extra key or maybe the intruder entered Haklo first and found a key to the apartment in her office and came here when the necklace didn't turn up in the office. Saturday morning you checked Marian's purse and found the necklace. You didn't do anything about it because you had no business snooping and no reason to think she shouldn't have a necklace in her purse. You hid the purse to protect the necklace. You went to Haklo Saturday, Louise took you around. Monday you heard about the vandalism, including the obscene letters. But that receded into the background after you found Marian's office trashed. Then you learned that the necklace was stolen property. Katie Dugan believes your sister heisted the necklace after puffing up a smokescreen with the vandalism and you are covering up for her. Tonight you decided to put the necklace on Blythe's desk. That's everything?"

She hesitated, frowning. Her gaze dropped to the cat nestled close to her.

Why wasn't she looking at him? What else did she know? Steve came upright, leaned forward, his eyes insistent. "I've gone out on a limb for you. I know you went in Haklo after hours. I know where the necklace is. If this all came out, I could be charged as an accessory. I need to know what you know."

Slowly she looked up.

He stared into dark brilliant eyes that held both uncertainty and knowledge.

"I don't have proof." Her gaze was steady.

"Tell me, Nela." He liked the sound of her name, *Nee-la.* "I'll help you. All I ask is that you don't lie to me. I've heard too many lies from beautiful women." He stopped for a long moment, lips pressed together. "Okay. I want honesty. I'll be honest. I heard too many lies from one particular beautiful woman, my ex-wife. I'm telling you this because I want you to know where I'm coming from. I'll help you—if you don't lie to me. You have to make a choice. If you can't or won't—be honest, tell me and I'll walk out of here and tonight never happened. I never came here, I never went to Haklo, I don't know anything about a piece of jewelry."

"I won't lie to you. I may not be able to tell you everything." She was solemn. "Whatever I tell you will be the truth. I think I do know something." She glanced again at the cat, then said, almost defiantly, "I can't tell you how I know."

He wanted to believe her, wanted it more than he'd wanted anything in a very long time. *Steve, you damn fool, women lie, don't let her suck you into something screwy. Why can't she tell how she knows whatever it is that she knows? Protecting somebody?* He almost pushed up from the chair. He could walk away, avoid entanglement. But he was already speaking. "All right. Keep your source."

As for how she obtained a piece of knowledge, the possibilities were pretty narrow. Either she or her sister had seen something that

Nela now believed to be important in the saga of Haklo and its troubles. He'd bet the house she was protecting her sister. He was putting himself in a big hole if he didn't report her entry into Haklo and the necklace on Blythe Webster's desk. He needed every scrap of information to dig his way out. He would be home free—and so would Nela and Chloe—if the jewel thief was caught. "What do you know?"

"Marian Grant was murdered."

The words hung between them.

Steve had covered the story. Marian Grant was a prominent citizen of Craddock. Her death was front-page news. Marian's accident had been a surprise. She had been in her late forties, a runner, a good tennis player. However, accidents happen to the fit as well as the unfit. For an instant, Nela's claim shocked him into immobility. Then pieces slotted together in his mind—vandalism at Haklo, a missing necklace in Marian's purse, a thief fearing arrest, Marian's death—to form an ugly pattern, a quite possible pattern. Still . . .

"Are you claiming somebody was here and shoved her down the steps?"

"No. I have reason to believe"—she spoke carefully—"that someone put a skateboard on the second step."

"A skateboard?" He pictured that moment, Marian hurrying out the door for her morning jog, taking quick steps, one foot landing on a skateboard. Hell yes, that could knock her over a railing. "If somebody knows that for a fact, the cops have to be told."

"They would want to know how I know. I can't identify the source."

He liked piecing together facts from a starting point. "You arrived here Friday, right? You can prove you were on a certain flight and that you were in LA until you took that flight?"

"Absolutely."

"You've never been to Craddock before?"

"No."

"Therefore, you couldn't know about a skateboard on the steps from your own knowledge. Who told you?" The list had to be short. Her sister, Chloe, had to be the only person Nela knew before she arrived.

Nela brushed back a tangle of dark hair. "I promised the truth. I'm telling you the truth. No one told me."

"If"—he tried to be patient—"no one told you and you weren't here, how do you know?"

"All I can say is that no one told me." She spoke with finality, looked at him with a faint half smile.

He understood. She wasn't going to budge. There had to be a strong reason for her silence. But she had nothing to gain from making a claim that Marian Grant had been murdered. If anything, turning the search for the necklace into a murder investigation might place her and Chloe in more peril. Once again Nela was making a moral choice: Return a quarter-million-dollar necklace. Expose murder.

"Steve—"

It was the first time she'd ever said his name. Someday would she speak to him, call him by name, and be thinking of him and not stolen jewels or murder?

"—you said I could keep my source. But we need to tell the police. Sometimes I got anonymous tips on stories. Will you tell the police you got a tip, an anonymous tip? Can't you say that somebody said"—she paused, then began again, this time in a scarcely audible wisp of sound—"Marian Grant was murdered. She knew who took the necklace. Someone put a skateboard on the second step of the garage apartment stairs . . ."

* * *

Craddock had few public pay phones left. In the parking lot of a Valero filling station, Steve stood with his back to the street, his shoulders hunched against the cold. He not only didn't have his jacket, he didn't have gloves. In fact, he didn't own a pair of gloves. He'd found a shammy crammed in the glove compartment. He dropped in the coins, pushed the buttons. The phone was answered after five rings. He listened to the entire message, waited for his extension number, pushed the buttons. He heard his own voice, waited again, finally whispered, repeating Nela's words. He hung up and used the shammy to clean the receiver.

Nela looked down at the muscular cat stretched out with his front paws flat on the surface of the kitchen table. "You look like one of those stone lions that guard the New York Public Library."

Jugs regarded her equably. *". . . You're happier today . . ."*

Yes, she was happier today. Removing the necklace from the apartment was like kicking free of tangled seaweed just before a big wave hit. "That's just between you and me, buddy. Thank God cops don't read cat minds. I'd be in big trouble."

Jugs continued to stare at her. *". . . You're worried . . . She was worried . . ."*

As she sipped her morning coffee, a faint frown drew her eyebrows down. Although she felt almost giddy with relief every time she thought about the necklace now in Blythe's office, the removal of the jewelry didn't solve the main problem. Maybe that's why her subconscious, aka Jugs, was warning her.

She pushed away the quicksilver thought that her subconscious could not possibly have known if someone had rigged the step to make Marian Grant fall. But something had to account for that searing moment when she'd looked at Jugs and imagined his thoughts. . . . *board rolled on the second step . . .* When she thought of a rolling board, the image had come swiftly, a skateboard. Saturday morning when she'd looked at the banister, a streak of paint was just where a skateboard might have struck if tipped up. That was confirmation, wasn't it? Something had hit that banister. They said violence leaves a psychic mark. Who said? Her inner voice was quick with the challenge. All right. She'd read somewhere that there was some kind of lasting emanation after trauma. If Marian had been murdered, if someone left a skateboard on her steps, that certainly qualified as a violent act. When Marian plunged over the railing, did she have time to realize what had happened?

Nela shook her head. She might as well believe in voodoo. But some people did. Maybe she'd had a moment of ESP. But she'd never had any use for so-called psychics. The explanation had to be simple. There was that gash in the stair rail. Maybe subconsciously she'd noticed the scrape when she first arrived and the shock of confronting Jugs stirred some long-ago memory of a skateboard.

She looked at Jugs, but his eyes had closed. When he'd looked at her Friday night, other thoughts had come to her mind. . . . *She was worried . . . She didn't know what to do . . .*

About a stolen necklace?

Nela thought about the last few days in the life of a woman she'd never known, a smart, intense, hardworking woman who had devoted her life to Haklo.

A vandal struck Haklo again and again.

Blythe's necklace was stolen.

The necklace was in Marian Grant's purse that she placed atop the bookcase the last night of her life.

Did Marian steal the quarter-million-dollar adornment?

The violent searches of her office and apartment after her death appeared almost certainly to be a hunt for the necklace. Dumped drawers indicated a search for some physical object, not incriminating papers suggested by Detective Dugan. The destruction in her office reflected a wild and dangerous anger on the part of the searcher when the effort to find the necklace failed. From everything Nela had been told about Marian, there was nothing to support the idea that Marian could have been a thief. Instead, it was much more likely that Marian had discovered the identity of the thief and obtained the necklace. However, she didn't contact the police. She kept the necklace in her purse.

Why hadn't she called the police?

As Steve had made clear, Marian always protected the foundation. Her decision to handle the theft by herself meant that a public revelation would create a scandal. She was a confident, strong woman. Perhaps she insisted the thief had to confess or resign or make restitution. Perhaps she said, "I've put the necklace in a safe place and unless you do as I say, I will contact the police." Perhaps she set a deadline.

Had the thief killed her to keep her quiet?

She died early Monday morning. The funeral was Thursday. Chloe had stayed in the apartment since Monday night to take care of Jugs. Whether Marian's death was accident or murder, the presence of the necklace in her purse was fact. The thief's first opportunity to search the apartment had been Friday night after Chloe had left town.

Nela welcomed the hot, strong coffee but it didn't lessen the chill of another pointer to someone on the Haklo staff. All of them knew about Chloe's trip to Tahiti. Chloe hadn't mentioned that Nela would stay in the apartment until Chloe's return. As for access to Marian's apartment, perhaps a key was, as Steve suggested, secreted in some simple place known to the searcher. Or perhaps the office was searched before the apartment and a key found in that desk.

Whatever the order, the searches were fruitless because the necklace was in Marian's purse. The treasure wasn't hidden. The necklace had simply been dropped to the bottom of a Coach bag, a safe place in the eyes of its owner. A killer scrabbled through drawers, dumped files, and all the while the necklace was within reach.

Detective Dugan's instinct was good. The necklace was the crux of everything. But Dugan was convinced that Chloe was the clever thief who'd created the vandalism as a diversion and that Nela was covering up for her. When Steve reported a tip about murder, Dugan might tab Chloe as a murderer as well as a thief.

Nela put down her mug. She couldn't count on the police investigation. But she wasn't blinded by hometown loyalties. If Dugan wasn't willing to look at the Haklo staff members as suspects, Nela was.

D etective Dugan stood with arms folded. "All right."
Steve flicked on the speakerphone, punched for messages. He listened with a sense of relief. His whisper had been very well done, the faintly heard words sexless, unaccented wraiths that couldn't be grasped. "Message received at eleven forty-two p.m. Monday: . . . Marian Grant was murdered . . . A skateboard on the

second step . . . threw her over the railing . . . She knew who took the necklace . . ."

Detective Dugan touched a number in her cell phone directory. "Mokie, get a trace on a call received at the *Clarion* last night at eleven forty-two. Send out a lab tech to One Willow Lane. Marian Grant died in a fall down the garage apartment stairs. Check for possible damage to the railing. Look for scratches, paint traces. If there is damage, get forensic evidence. Also measurements and photos. Thanks."

She turned to Steve. "Play the message again." She listened with eyes half closed. At its end, she shook her head. "Can't tell whether the caller was a man or a woman. Could have been anybody. No discernible accent." Her eyes opened, settled on Steve. "Why you?"

Steve was unruffled. "Goes with the territory. If you have a tip, call a reporter."

"Why last night?"

Steve kept his expression faintly quizzical. "A big story in yesterday afternoon's *Clarion*. It probably caught someone's attention."

Katie's face wrinkled in concentration. "I want to talk to that caller. Murder." Her tone was considering. She squeezed her eyes in thought. "I figured all along that the necklace was the key and that Grant knew who took it. That explains the search of her office. The searcher messed everything up to try and make it look like more vandalism. The point has to be the necklace. A quarter of a million dollars is serious money. Let's say Grant threatened to name the thief. People around her knew she jogged every morning. A skateboard on the steps couldn't guarantee she'd be killed but the probability was good. Okay, the thief puts a skateboard on the steps then shows up around six fifteen, taking care not to be seen. If she was still alive, pressure on the carotid would dispatch her pronto. If she's already dead, pick up the skateboard and melt away. Now, how could anyone except the murderer know about a skateboard on the steps? If someone did know, why keep quiet until now? Scared? Not sure? Maybe saw a skateboard in a weird place and decided Marian was too athletic to fall accidentally?" Her chin jutted. "I've got to find who made that call."

Steve felt uneasy. Murder made all kinds of sense, but he couldn't figure out how Nela knew. If her sister had stolen the necklace and committed murder, Nela would never in a million years have told him about the skateboard. That she had revealed the skateboard affirmed her and Chloe's innocence for him. But Nela had spent only one day at Haklo. Certainly no one would confide that kind of information to her. How the hell did Nela know?

"Maybe"—and he knew he was dealing with his own worries—"you should hunt for somebody who has a skateboard."

Katie looked sardonic. "Who on the Haklo staff does wheelies? I'll ask around."

I n the Haklo staff lot, Nela felt a tiny spurt of amusement as she parked once again between the snazzy Thunderbird and the old Dodge. The Thunderbird, psychedelic VW, and prim Dodge surely made some kind of statement. But grim worry returned when she reached the walkway to the staff entrance and saw a police officer waiting there. Even though she knew the police would be called when the necklace was found, her stomach tightened. She walked a little faster. Anyone would be curious, right? She came to a stop and looked up the shallow flight of steps.

Officer Baker's faded red hair curled becomingly under her cap. "Good morning, ma'am." She held the door open. "Please go directly to the conference room in the east wing."

Nela stopped and stared. Any innocent person would. "What's happened?"

Officer Baker was pleasant. "Miss Webster has asked that everyone report to the conference room. Detective Dugan wishes to speak with staff members."

In the conference room, Louise Spear stood at the head of the table, her brown eyes anxious. "Nela, please make coffee for us. I suppose the police know something now about Marian's office."

As Nela measured beans, placed them in the grinder of the coffeemaker, she heard low voices around the edge of the partition, several asking Louise about the purpose of the meeting. She listened, making out what words she could. So far, no one had mentioned the necklace. Nela was surprised that Blythe Webster hadn't told Louise of her discovery. Perhaps Louise knew and had been told not to mention the necklace.

While the coffee was brewing, Nela glanced around the partition. In addition to the staff members present yesterday, Rosalind McNeill, eyes bright with excitement, sat toward the end of the table next to the imposing white-haired chef. The receptionist was clearly delighted by the change in routine. The chef's brown eyes had the remote expression of someone in attendance but thinking of something else. A difficult recipe?

Nela added two more mugs. When the coffeemaker pinged, Nela filled mugs and carried the tray around the table. When she'd served those who accepted, she returned the tray and the carafe to the kitchenette, then settled on the straight chair a little to one side of the long table.

Once again Haklo staff was in place. She had a quick memory

of *Casablanca*, another of Gram's favorite movies, and Captain Renault's wry, "Major Strasser has been shot. Round up the usual suspects."

Blythe Webster looked like a woman who had received shocking news, her eyes wide and staring. The fingers of one hand plucked at the pearl necklace at her throat. Cole Hamilton's aging Kewpie doll face wavered between indignation, worry, and perplexity. Francis Garth looked immovable as a monolith, his gaze somber, his heavy shoulders hunched. Abby Andrews twined a strand of blond hair around one finger, her violet eyes uneasy as she looked from the detective to the director. Hollis Blair gave Abby a swift, warm look before his bony face once again settled into ridges of concern. Grace Webster noticed the exchange with cool disapproval. Robbie Powell wasn't as youthfully handsome this morning. His green eyes darted around the room. His face thoughtful, Peter Owens propped an elbow on the table, gently swung his horn rims back and forth. Rosalind McNeill had the air of a woman awaiting the start of a performance. The chef stared unseeingly toward the buffalo mural.

The door opened and Detective Dugan entered, trim in a stylish white wool blazer and black wool slacks. Detective Morrison followed, tape recorder in hand. In comparison with his fashionable superior, he looked down-at-the-heels in a baggy gray sweater and too large plaid wool slacks. He closed the hall door. Dugan stopped a few feet from the table and turned her gaze to Blythe.

Blythe looked at her with hollow eyes and nodded.

Dugan looked around the room, waited for silence. "Ladies and gentlemen." Her voice was smooth with no hint of threat. "We are continuing our investigation into a series of events at the foundation, including vandalism and theft. However, our investigation has taken a much more serious turn. We have received a report on good authority"—Dugan paused for emphasis—"that Marian Grant was murdered."

Louise Spear gave a cry. "That can't be." She touched her throat with a shaking hand.

"Murdered?" Grace Webster's round face was incredulous. "She fell down the stairs."

Dugan stared at the younger Webster sister. "It may be that a device placed on the stairs caused her to fall. Therefore, when I ask questions, I want each of you to understand that we are seeking information leading to a murderer. It is the duty of the innocent to answer truthfully and accurately. Detective Morrison will record this meeting. When you respond to a question, please preface your answer with your name."

If possible, Abby Andrews shrank even farther into her chair. Hollis Blair looked dazed. Cole Hamilton's face screwed up in dismay. Robbie Powell sat rigid in his chair. The horn rims in Peter Owens's hand came to a stop, remained unmoving. Rosalind's mouth curved in an astonished O. The chef remained imperturbable.

"Murder?" Cole's voice rose is disbelief. "That's impossible. How can you make such a claim? It was dark. Marian had on new running shoes. She fell."

"Forensic evidence supports the claim that her fall may have been caused by a foreign object placed on the second step." Dugan's gaze briefly touched each face.

Nela pictured that telltale scrape on the baluster. Dugan had wasted no time. Obviously, she had already received a report. Had a police officer viewed the scarred surface, possibly brought a skateboard, experimented to see if pressure on one end tilted the board enough for the tip to strike at that level?

Francis Garth cleared his throat. "Detective Dugan, I'd like to clarify our position. Is there a presumption by police that those present in this room are considered to be suspects in the as yet unproven murder of Marian Grant? If so, please explain how that conclusion has been reached."

Nela sensed both fear and indignation in the room.

"This investigation is focused"—Dugan's tone was firm—"on those who have keys to Haklo Foundation. Significant force would be required to break into Haklo. Yesterday when police arrived to investigate the search of Marian Grant's office, there was no evidence of forcible entry. We believe the search of her office was connected to the theft of Miss Webster's necklace. We believe Miss Grant had proof of the identity of the thief. This information may have led to murder. Miss Grant may have said the incident would be overlooked if the necklace was returned and the vandalism ceased. From what we understand, Miss Grant was always mindful of the Haklo Foundation's stature in the community. We think she was trying to protect the foundation. Possibly she told the thief that she had evidence hidden away and gave the thief a deadline. Since there is now evidence that her death was not an accident, we can reasonably assume a connection between her death and the search of her office."

Nela spoke out forcefully. "Someone also searched the living room of her apartment Friday night."

The detective's cold eyes paused at Nela.

Nela understood that Dugan still thought it was possible that the 911 call from Marian's apartment was phony. Dugan included Nela and Chloe among possible suspects. But if Nela and Chloe were the main suspects, what was the point of this inquiry? Did Dugan hope for some kind of damaging information about Chloe to surface? And why hadn't Dugan mentioned the return of the necklace? Nela clenched her hands, saw Dugan take note. She forced her hands to go limp, knew that movement had been cataloged as well.

Dugan continued smoothly. "We believe the person who took the necklace either searched Miss Grant's office or arranged for such a search." Again a quick glance at Nela. "That person had a key to the foundation." She glanced down at a note card. "I have here a list of every person who has a key. Three people with keys are known to have been out of town this past weekend and their absence has been confirmed. Everyone in this room has a key. The final person who may have a key or access to a key"—she glanced at Robbie Powell—"is the former director, Erik Judd."

Robbie frowned. "Erik would never use his key to enter for any reason other than work."

"He has a key?"

Robbie was bland. "Yes. He's engaged in research here at Haklo for his history of the foundation."

"I understand Mr. Judd resented being fired."

Robbie shook his head. "Actually, he's welcomed the time to be able to concentrate on his writing."

"Why was he fired?" Dugan's tone was pleasant but her eyes sharp.

There was an uncomfortable pause.

Dugan's cool gaze moved to Blythe.

Blythe looked stubborn. "Erik was getting old and he wasn't very exciting. After all, he's in his fifties." She spoke as if it were a greatly distant age. "I wanted someone to lead Haklo to a new level, give us vision. I know Erik was disappointed, but he has a pension. And we'll publish his history."

Robbie said nothing.

Nela saw the twitch of one eyelid. Robbie was keeping anger over his lover's dismissal under wraps, but she had no doubt that beneath his smooth surface he harbored intense dislike for Hollis. She needed to find out more about both Erik and Robbie.

Cole brushed back a white curl. "Erik dealt with problems quickly. I think it's disappointing that Hollis hasn't made any progress on clearing up these matters." There was a flash of malice in his eyes.

"Erik could not have done more than Hollis has, Cole." There was an edge to Blythe's voice. "Hollis is in no way responsible for the dreadful things that have happened. His energy and enthusiasm have inspired us all." Blythe gave Hollis Blair a reassuring nod. "Anyway, vandalism doesn't matter now. If someone hurt Marian, we have to find out what happened. As for that necklace, I don't care if I ever see it again."

Nela was puzzled. The necklace was on Blythe's desk this morning. Had she turned the jewelry over to the police? Was that her meaning?

"I've told Detective Dugan that we will do everything we can to find out the truth of this"—she paused—"anonymous call that claims Marian was killed. I have to say it doesn't seem likely to me. But it is now a police matter." She was somber but there was no suggestion of personal distress.

Nela studied Blythe's composed face. Where was sorrow? Where was outrage? Blythe spoke like a woman directing a meeting and a troublesome issue had arisen. Marian Grant had been a part of Haklo since its inception. She had been important to Webster Harris . . .

Nela looked toward Grace Webster. She appeared shocked and uneasy, but again there wasn't the flare of sorrow and anger that would follow after learning of a cherished friend's murder.

Louise held tight to the gold chain at her neck. "This is dreadful.

Nothing matters except Marian. Marian was part of our lives, the heart of Haklo. There's a picture in her office of Webster breaking a champagne bottle on the front pillar when the building was first opened and Marian clapping and laughing out loud. When I was with her, I almost felt that Webster would walk in the room any minute." Louise's face crumpled in misery. She looked up and down the table. "All of us have to answer the detective's questions. We have to tell the detective everything we know. For Marian."

"Of course we will," Francis responded.

Nela looked at the Webster sisters. Neither Blythe nor Grace spoke. Nela knew then that Steve had been right when he spoke of a small town's suspicion of an affair between Harris and Marian. It would be interesting to check the oil man's will. Nela had no doubt that Harris had made certain that Marian would remain as chief operating officer. Blythe and Grace had very likely long lived with hidden resentment.

Grace gave her sister a searching look, then said rapidly, "If anyone knows anything, speak up."

Blythe nodded. "Absolutely. We have a duty to aid the police."

A duty, but no impassioned call for justice from either Grace or Blythe.

The emotion came from Louise Spear. She pressed her fingertips against her cheeks. Her lips trembled. Hollis Blair's bony face looked haggard. Abby Andrews sent quick, panicked glances around the room. Francis Garth's heavy head moved until his dark eyes fastened on Peter Owens. Peter felt the glance and his professorial face hardened. Robbie Powell frowned, seemed to withdraw. Cole Hamilton was the picture of worried concern. Rosalind placed fingertips against her lips. The chef alone seemed unaffected, though her brown eyes were curious.

"We'll get started." Dugan glanced around the table. "Among those who work in this building, including any not present today, who—"

Nela sensed danger. Dugan wasn't confining her inquiry to this room. Was the expanded field—anyone with a connection to the foundation—a clever way to apply the question to Chloe?

"—possesses a skateboard or has ever been seen with a skateboard?"

Francis Garth's heavy head turned toward Abby Andrews. Peter Owens, too, stared at the assistant curator. Hollis Blair's bony face creased in dismay.

Abby pushed back her chair, came to her feet. She turned toward Hollis. "Someone's—"

"Name first." Dugan was forceful.

"Abby Andrews." She looked at the detective pleadingly. "Someone's trying to get me in trouble. They used my computer for those awful letters. And now a skateboard. Ask anyone. My little brother was here for a visit and he forgot his skateboard. It was on the porch of the cabin. It disappeared last week."

Dugan took a step nearer the table. "Describe the skateboard."

"It's black with orange stripes."

"When did you last see it?" The question came fast.

"The Saturday"—Abby looked frightened—"before Marian died."

"Where?" Curt, short, demanding.

"On the front porch of the cabin. It was propped up by the door."

"There are four cabins on the grounds west of the main building. You are the only person currently occupying a cabin."

Her violet eyes huge with fear, Abby nodded.

"When did he leave the board on the porch?"

"Craig was here the week before."

"Who would have occasion to see the skateboard on the porch?"

"Anybody. Everybody. Blythe had all the staff members out to the cabin next door to discuss redoing the interiors. They passed my cabin to go inside. The skateboard was right there in plain sight." Her voice wobbled but the challenge was clear.

Dugan turned to Blythe. "Is there anyone in addition to those present who were included in the survey of the cabin?"

Blythe's face creased in thought. "I think that's—oh, of course. Chloe Farley was with Louise."

Nela's glance locked with Dugan's. She hoped the detective read her loud and clear: *Look at these people. They're scared. I'm not. Chloe's innocent.*

The detective's face didn't change. There might have been grudging respect in her dark brown eyes, but the brief silent exchange didn't deflect her from Abby. "When did you notice the skateboard was gone?"

"Sunday afternoon. I'd found a box in the basement and I was going to pack it up to mail to Craig."

Dugan gazed at each person in turn. "Does anyone have knowledge of the skateboard between Saturday and Sunday?"

No one answered.

—11—

Nela's fingers automatically worked the computer keyboard as she prepared a summary of a grant application. Below her surface attention to the task, her thoughts darted as she tried to make sense of the tense meeting with Detective Dugan. Of course murder mattered more than theft, but why hadn't Dugan even mentioned the return of the necklace, especially since she believed the necklace might be the reason for Marian Grant's murder? Why was Dugan keeping that information quiet?

All through the rest of the morning and during lunch and the afternoon, she'd waited for word of the necklace's return to reach her. She had waited for the sound of Dugan's firm steps and the level stare that accused.

It was shortly after three when Louise Spear stood in the doorway between her office and Chloe's. Louise's face was drawn with strain. "Nela, please come here for a moment."

Nela rose and walked into Louise's office. When she stepped through the connecting door, she expected to see Dugan. Instead, she was alone with Louise.

"Close the door. Sit down."

The door into the hallway was already shut. Louise's office was paneled in gleaming oak. Bookcases filled one wall. A print of a dramatic painting by the Baranovs hung behind her desk, the magnificent colors vibrant and life affirming. Nela loved the glorious colors favored by the Russian artists. The print commanded attention. Nela wondered if, consciously or subconsciously, plain and modest Louise chose the compelling print to make herself less noticeable.

Louise stood to one side of her light oak desk. A shaft of pale winter sunlight emphasized deep lines etched at the corners of her eyes and lips. She looked fatigued and worried.

Nela sat in the plain wooden chair that faced the desk. Had Louise been deputized to fire Nela? Why hadn't the police detective talked to her first? Had the redheaded reporter informed Dugan of her after-hours visit to Haklo?

Louise's brown eyes scarcely seemed to acknowledge her presence. She was turned inward and her thoughts obviously weren't pleasant. Finally, she gazed at Nela. "Tell me about Friday night." She rubbed one thumb along the knuckles of her clenched right hand. "At Marian's apartment."

Nela described the sounds of a search and the light beneath the door and the arrival of the police.

Louise stared at Nela with wide worried eyes. "Did you see anyone when you opened the bedroom door?"

Nela knew abruptly that this was why Louise had called Nela into her office. Louise could have taken the necklace. But she could have taken the necklace many times in the last few years if she had wished. Why this fall? Did she need money? Did she resent Hollis Blair?

"Nela?" Louise appeared tense.

Nela felt suddenly that Louise was afraid of what Nela might say. "I didn't open the bedroom door until the police knocked. The thief was gone by then."

Louise's shoulders slumped. "I was hoping you might have some idea who was there. Well, I suppose if you knew anything you would have told the police."

"Yes. I would have told the police." But perhaps she'd been wiser than she knew when she'd stayed safe in the bedroom waiting until the front door slammed behind the intruder, an intruder who looked everywhere for a hidden necklace and it wasn't hidden at all. "Have the police found out anything more about the necklace?" Why had no one discussed the return of the necklace? Surely its mysterious arrival was another pointer to someone with a key. That hadn't been Nela's intent when she brought it, but maybe underlining the connection to Haklo had been a very good idea.

"Unfortunately they haven't been able to trace it. The detective said they have queries out to pawnshops." She lifted thin fingers to touch one temple. "That will be all for now, Nela."

Nela managed to nod and get up and walk into Chloe's office without revealing her shock. She settled behind Chloe's desk and stared blankly at the computer screen. The necklace was still missing. But she'd left it on Blythe's desk. Nela opened the bottom drawer, pulled out her purse. She reached for her cell, then glanced at the open door to Louise's office. She couldn't afford to be overheard when she spoke to Steve. She had to wait until she left the foundation. She dropped the cell in the purse, closed the drawer.

* * *

It was one of those days. A tractor trailer overturned on the exit ramp into Craddock. One of Craddock's leading literary lights, a much-published Oklahoma historian, died unexpectedly. A black Lab saved his family by butting against a bedroom door to awaken sleeping parents in time to gather up their five children and escape a house fire caused by a frayed extension cord on a portable heater. Every winter when the frigid days came, the *Clarion* warned readers to be wary of the dangers of frayed cords and of carbon monoxide from faulty fireplaces and wood stoves and generators. Every winter there were blazes. This one had a happy ending. Some didn't.

Steve Flynn was in and out of the office. Lunch was a Big Mac on the run. It was almost three thirty before he had time to call Katie Dugan. He punched his speakerphone.

"Hey, Steve." Of course she had caller ID.

"Bring me up to date on Haklo."

"I suppose you plan a story on the anonymous call to the *Clarion*?"

He leaned back in his swivel chair, propped his feet on the desk, balanced a laptop on his lap. "We print the news as we get it." His tone was laconic.

"I can always dream, can't I? But probably our inquiries have tipped the murderer. If there is a murderer. Which isn't clear."

"And?"

"On the record, we are pursuing inquiries into the anonymous call to the *Clarion* that claimed the death of Marian Grant was murder."

Steve typed the quote, not that he wouldn't remember. It was stock Katie-speak when she didn't intend to elaborate. "And?"

Silence.

"Come on, Katie. Surely there's movement somewhere in this story. A little bird told me there was a bad"—he drew out the vowel but Katie didn't smile—"letter that went out to members of the grants committee."

She gave a quick little spurt of irritation. He knew she was wondering where he'd picked up that piece of information. "No comment."

"Do you have a lab report on damage to the apartment stairs?"

"No comment."

She hadn't said there was no report, which meant there was a report, but she was unwilling to reveal what had been learned. "Could a skateboard—if one is found—be tested for a match?"

"No comment."

"What's the status of the search for the necklace?" That should flush the fact of its return, although he was puzzled that Katie was playing coy about the jewelry's unaccountable arrival on the desk of its owner. The anonymous tip about murder was the lead of the story he would write, but the necklace would get big play, especially since once again a key had surely been used to enter Haklo. The noose would draw tighter around Haklo employees.

"At this point in the investigation, no trace of the necklace has been found."

Steve felt like he'd been sucker punched. The blow came from nowhere. His feet swung to the floor and he sat up straight. He listened blankly to the rest of Katie's response. "Inquiries have been made and will continue to be made at pawnshops and auction houses. Although Miss Webster has so far declined to request reimbursement from insurance, the insurance company with her permission has supplied photographs and a detailed description of the jewelry. If you ask pretty please, I'll send over a jpeg."

"Yeah." It was like staring at a billboard in Czech. Nothing made sense.

"Hey, I thought you'd appreciate this puppy. Did a sexy broad just walk by your desk? I don't need a swami to tell me you've lost interest in our conversation. Ciao."

The connection ended.

He e-mailed the police department's Public Information office, requesting the jpeg. All the while, thoughts ran and nipped at each other's tails like hungry rats. . . . *She could have gone back to Haklo . . . intelligent eyes, quick on her feet . . . glossy black hair . . . promised not to lie . . . necklace gone . . . Someone took it . . . She could be telling the truth about the skateboard . . . If she didn't trust him, the smart thing was to remove the necklace . . . sure as hell must not have gotten a lot of sleep last night . . . Hurts, doesn't it, buddy? . . .*

He reached out to punch the speakerphone, slowly drew back his hand. What good would it do to call Katie Dugan? He had no proof. Yeah, he could pinpoint Nela in the doorway of Haklo after ten p.m. He had a picture of the necklace on Blythe Webster's desk. But still, it came down to his word against hers. She could swear she left with him and never returned, make it clear that he could as easily have returned for the necklace as she. Katie would believe him. Belief wasn't proof. He glanced at the clock. He had ten minutes to meet his deadline. The dog and the fire would run below the fold today. Murder trumped a feel-good story. Or was Nela's claim of a skateboard as phony as her promise not to lie? Of course, she hadn't lied yet. What would she say when he asked her about her return trip to Haklo? As for the skateboard, damned if there wasn't knowledge of one floating around Haklo. Could Nela have known about the skateboard missing from the cabin? He didn't know. As for now, he had a story to write. He typed fast, his face set in hard, angry lines. When done, he reread the piece.

An anonymous phone call to the *Clarion* Monday night claimed Haklo Foundation Chief Operating Officer Marian Grant was a murder victim. Grant died as a result of a fall down her apartment stairs early on the morning of Jan. 9.

The caller, who has not been identified, said Grant was thrown over the side of the stair rail when she stepped on a skateboard deliberately placed on the second step.

Police who investigated Grant's fall did not find a skateboard on or near the stairs. Police Detective K. T. Dugan was informed of the call by *Clarion* staff. Detective Dugan refused to comment on the investigation into the call.

The anonymous caller said Grant was killed because she had discovered the identity of the thief responsible for the robbery of a $250,000 gold and diamond necklace from the desk of Haklo Trustee Blythe Webster.

Detective Dugan said police are continuing to contact pawnshops and auction houses in hopes of tracing the jewelry. Miss Webster has offered a $100,000 reward for the arrest and conviction of the thief.

The theft of the necklace is one in a series of unexplained incidents at the foundation.

Steve ended up with a summary of the vandalism, a description of Marian's career at Haklo, and the foundation's importance to Craddock.

He finished reading, zapped the article to Mim. He stared at the phone. He didn't like being played for a fool. Besides, he'd picked up a hand to play when he hadn't called the cops last night. Now he couldn't pretend to himself that he didn't know beans about a quarter-million-dollar piece of jewelry. His options were limited. Should he call Nela? Be waiting by the VW when she got off work?

To what purpose?

Ace Busey, his plaid wool shirt emanating waves of old cigarette smoke, settled one hip on the edge of Steve's desk. "Somebody's ticked you off big time. Must be a gal. Hasn't Papa told you that dames are deadly?"

Steve looked up into Ace's saggy, streetwise face. "Just concentrating."

Ace raised a shaggy eyebrow. "You look like a prune on a hot day. Lighten up. No dame is worth it."

Steve forced a humorless smile. "That's a given."

Ace slouched to his feet. "Got to catch a smoke." As he walked away, he said over his shoulder, "Don't say Papa didn't warn you."

Nela stepped into Louise's office with grant application folders. "I've attached one-page summaries to each application." Dry words for dreams and hopes and visions boiled down to a page. She wished that everything was different, that she could be excited about the foundation's outreach, make a difference for kids at summer camps, for libraries with budgets cut to the bone, for research to help drought-stricken farmers.

Louise looked up. Her thoughts seemed to come from a far distance. "Oh, yes." She gestured at her in-box. "I'll take care of them tomorrow."

Nela placed the folders in the lower receptacle. "Is there anything else I can do?"

Louise slowly shook her head. The movement seemed to take great effort.

Nela understood the burden of grief. "I'm sorry about Miss Grant. She must have been a wonderful person."

"Friday afternoon when I went in her office, I could tell she was upset. I asked if something was wrong. There was an odd look in her eyes. She said"—Louise's face crinkled in memory—"'There's nothing wrong that can't be fixed. And I intend to fix it.' Of course, Marian believed she could handle anything." Louise massaged one temple. "Just a few days before she died, she told me she should have done something in St. Louis, that she'd known from the start it was a mistake to bring Hollis here. I knew what she meant. I was there, too. Hollis has too much charm. I know what happens when he walks into a room. Some women are more vulnerable than others." She shook her head. "And that girl chasing after him." Her eyes were huge with distress. "If someone put a skateboard on Marian's stairs and Abby's brother's skateboard is missing, there has to be a connection. Oh, I don't know what to think. I may be all wrong."

Nela looked at her sharply. "Do you have an idea who may have taken the skateboard?"

Louise drew herself up. Her voice was stiff. "I don't know anything about the skateboard." There was a ring of truth in her voice. But her eyes were still dark with worry. "It's just that I keep thinking about Marian. I can't bear to think what may have happened."

Nela knew, better than most, that outsiders couldn't lessen heartbreak. Nothing Nela did would ease Louise's sadness about Marian

Grant or restore Haklo to happier days. But she knew, too, that kindness helps. "I'm sorry you're upset."

Louise's face softened. "You're a nice girl, Nela. Just like your sister. None of this has anything to do with you—"

Nela wished with all her heart that Louise was right.

"—and I'm sorry if I've troubled you. Don't worry. I know I'm tired. Things are always worse when you're tired." She glanced at the clock. "You can go home now. Home . . ." For an instant, she pressed her lips together. "You're a long way from home. I don't think I could bear to go to Marian's apartment. Especially after someone coming inside Friday night." Once again lines of worry framed her eyes and lips. "Thank you for staying there. I know Jugs. He must miss Marian terribly. Go home early and pet Jugs for me. For Marian. Tell him he's a good cat." Louise turned away to look toward the windows.

By the time Nela reached the connecting doorway, Louise appeared lost in her thoughts, her thin face drawn and weary. In Chloe's office, Nela glanced at her watch. Only a few minutes after four. She shrugged into her coat. In the hallway, she walked fast, fumbling in her purse for her cell phone. Steve had to know about the necklace. As soon as she was safely alone in the VW, she'd call him.

Steve glanced at caller ID. He let the phone ring three times before he picked up the hand unit. "Flynn."

"Steve"—the connection was scratchy, obviously a call from a cell—"the necklace wasn't found."

"Yeah." The word was clipped.

She talked fast. "Someone took the necklace from Blythe's desk. What can we do?"

"Someone took it?" His tone was taunting.

There was silence. Finally, she spoke. "What do you mean?"

"Two people knew the necklace was there. You. Me. I didn't take it. Do the math."

"You think—" She broke off. "I see." A pause. "That's a funny thing." Her tone was bleak. "It never occurred to me to think you went back and got the necklace."

The connection ended.

"Nela . . ." He spoke to emptiness.

Nela knew what it was to be alone, to feel separated from the world. There had been a moment with Steve—more than one—when warmth seemed near again. That brief connection was broken. There was no point in wasting time thinking about a stocky man with red hair. He'd been a stranger. He was a stranger again with no reason to share what he knew about people he knew.

It was up to her now to find the devious mind behind the troubles at Haklo and she might have very little time to act. She needed the perspective of someone who knew the staff. Louise not only might wonder if Nela came back inside, but, picturing faces in her mind, Nela had no idea which staff member to contact. What would she say? But she had to do something. She opened the car door, taking care not to let the wind butt the edge against the glossy blue Thunderbird with the personalized license plate: ROBBIE. The car was as slick as the PR director. Definitely he wouldn't be the right person to ask who might have a motive to cause trouble for Haklo. Although he kept his comments within bounds, his dislike of Hollis Blair was obvious. Vandalism might have appealed to Robbie as a way of attacking Hollis.

She'd liked Erik Judd. She had sensed beneath his drama that particular empathy that often belongs to creative people.

Nela stared at the Thunderbird, slowly shut the VW door. She used her iPhone, found an address and directions.

It was a five-minute drive to a quiet neighborhood with older homes, some of them brick duplexes, others 1950s vintage ranch-style houses. A green Porsche sat in the drive of the third house on the left, a one-story rambling brick house with bay windows. The house appeared well kept, no fading paint or cracks in the drive. The window glass glistened.

Nela walked swiftly to the front porch, lifted a shiny brass knocker.

The door opened almost at once. Erik Judd stared out at her, his face anxious. "Has something happened to Robbie?"

Obviously he knew who she was, that she had taken Chloe's place, and her unexpected arrival, certainly something beyond the norm, raised fear that something was wrong.

"He's fine." Nela understood the shock of unexpected arrivals. She still dreamed about the moment that Bill's brother walked in. "The police believe Marian Grant was murdered."

Erik's eyebrows folded into a frown. "Robbie called me. But"—his gaze was suspicious—"what does that have to do with you? Why are you here?"

"Everyone at the foundation is a suspect." She looked at him steadily. Sometimes truth wins the day. If he shut the door in her face, so be it. But he might not. She might have only a little time left to do her best for Chloe. He would do what he could to protect Robbie. "That's why I came. You and I both have someone we love who may be at risk from the police. The police are suspicious of Chloe because she's new to Haklo this fall. But Robbie may have publicly taken too much satisfaction from Hollis Blair's difficulties because of the vandalism."

Erik raised a silver eyebrow. "From a bare acquaintance on Saturday, you seem to have learned a great deal about me and Robbie. But I fail to see why you are standing on our front porch."

"I'm an investigative reporter." She might not have a job right now, but that made no difference. She knew how to ask and probe and seek for a story. Now she would use her skills to save herself and Chloe.

Erik's pale blue eyes studied her. "Why do you want to talk to me?"

"You know everyone at Haklo." She saw a flicker of understanding in his watchful gaze. "I want you to tell me who could have committed the vandalism at Haklo and who would kill to avoid exposure as a vandal and a thief."

He smoothed one curling swoop of his mustache. "Aren't you a bit fearful of a private meeting with the 'disgruntled former director'?" His tone put the description in quote marks.

"Oh"—her tone was careless—"Steve Flynn knows where I am."

He was suddenly amused. "Quick thinking, my dear. But I don't believe that. However"—he held the door wide, made a sweeping bow—"enter my parlor if you desire."

She hesitated for only a moment, then stepped inside.

He led the way into a comfortable, manly den with leather furniture, a wide-screen TV, and Indian blankets hung on the paneled walls.

She skirted an easel with a half-finished watercolor of purple and gold wildflowers in a meadow, chose a cane chair.

Erik sat opposite in a red leather chair that was a dramatic setting for his curling white hair, black silk shirt, and white wide-cuffed wool trousers and black half boots. He listened, nodding occasionally as she marshaled her facts.

When she was done, he nodded approval. "Quite concise and complete. I'm aware of all the incidents. I should make it clear that I am not a recluse brooding over ill treatment. It was"—he paused, seeking the right word—"a shock when Blythe dismissed me, especially for a callow youth with no experience, except perhaps"—his mouth twisted in a wry smile—"in the useful art of charming ladies. I always assumed outstanding leadership was sufficient. I was wrong. However"—and now he sounded quite comfortable—"I have enjoyed thoroughly a return to the life of a writer. In fact, if you'd looked in the Haklo library a half hour ago, you would have found me there. I often spend the afternoon at Haklo with my research on the foundation. Robbie has remained angry even though I've assured him I am content. Now"—he leaned forward—"I want to be clear. Neither Robbie nor I have ever done anything that would be detrimental to Haklo. I devoted the best years of my life to making Haklo one of the finest charitable foundations in the country. I am sickened by the events that have occurred this fall. As for Robbie, I'm afraid he has enjoyed watching Hollis squirm, but Robbie knows that I would utterly oppose any kind of attack on Haklo. Haklo is bigger than Hollis or Blythe or me or Robbie."

"Someone there, someone with a key, must be behind the vandalism and the theft." Nela held his gaze. "If you care about Haklo, help me figure out who is guilty."

Erik frowned. One hand touched the crystal eagle that hung from a leather necklace. "From what you've told me, it does seem likely that the vandal is a staff member." His eyes narrowed. "Not Louise. Not Rosalind. I can't speak to the new director or his girlfriend or your sister." A stop. "Harris Webster used to worry about his daughters. Blythe has always been obsessive. Once she was obsessed with a young man who worked for Harris. Now she's obsessed with Haklo but the vandalism punishes Haklo. Grace is impulsive, a wild thing. She's furious that her father made Blythe the sole trustee. Francis is ruthless. Whatever is important to him is all that matters. Cole used to be a major force at Haklo, Webster's good friend. Now he's yesterday. I think it's broken his heart. Peter is fighting Blythe's ideas of outsourcing. He has a wife who likes money. But that tweedy, casual appearance is misleading. He's climbed Kilimanjaro."

As she drove away, Nela carried with her two impressions. Erik trusted Robbie, truly believed Robbie would never do anything to jeopardize the foundation that Erik loved. No doubt he would describe her visit and emphasize how he had made it clear that both he and Robbie had nothing to do with the attacks on Haklo. But if Robbie had been tempted to cause just enough trouble to harm the new director, exposure meant more than criminal action, it meant breaking the heart of the man he loved. Would Robbie be willing to kill to keep the vandalism from Erik?

—12—

Have to eat, right?" Nela tried to sound upbeat. She spooned chicken-flavored food into a freshly washed cat bowl.

Jugs looked up. ". . . *crying inside* . . ."

Nela put down the bowl. She'd pet Jugs after he ate, tell him Louise said he was a good cat. The words wouldn't matter. The tone would give him comfort. She knew she should eat as well, but her throat was tight and she wasn't hungry. She turned away, walked into the living room, dropped into the easy chair. How long would it take for the police to arrive? By this time, Steve Flynn would have contacted Dugan, showed her the photos in his iPhone.

Nela knew she had few options. Whatever she did, she wasn't going to lie. She would decline to comment and that would probably put her in jail. She glanced at her watch. Dugan was taking her own sweet time in coming. Would it do Nela any good to share Erik

Judd's views? Or would Dugan have closed her mind to everyone but Chloe and Nela?

The hospital bed still looked odd in his parents' spacious bedroom. His dad was dozing. The home health aide looked at him eagerly. When Steve came for a visit in the evenings, she could slip out for a while, a walk in good weather, now a few minutes in her room, catching up on a favorite TV show. His dad loathed TV, said if he ever got bored enough to watch TV, he'd hold a funeral service for his brain.

Steve stood beside the bed. Sometimes it seemed they took a little step forward, then two steps back.

His father's eyelids fluttered open. His eyes were as blue as Steve's. His hair, too, had once been red, but was now white. His broad face sagged a little on one side, a visible reminder of the stroke that felled him.

"Hey, Dad." Steve spoke in a normal tone. His dad despised sickroom whispers. Though his speech was still somewhat garbled, he'd made it clear to a succession of helpers. ". . . Still hear . . . Up speak . . ."

Those bright blue eyes were as perceptive as always, reflecting a quick and facile mind trapped in an uncooperative body. ". . . 'Rubble . . ."

Yeah, there was trouble. Big-time trouble. Chances were he'd been a sap over a woman. One more time. But this time, he wanted to call her. He wanted to believe her. He admired the way her chin jutted when she faced opposition. He wanted to plumb the intelligence behind her gaze. He wanted to know about her. Did she like to go camping? Had she ever trout fished? He knew some things.

She had guts. She loved words. Her face in repose suggested she knew sadness. A guy named Bill had loved her. But who else could have taken the damn necklace? Steve gave a shrug, tried to appear casual. "Hard day. Lots of stuff happening."

Maybe those blue eyes saw more because they'd had a glimpse of eternity. Maybe Daniel Flynn knew better than to waste time with niceties. His gaze was sharp, demanding. ". . . You . . ."

Steve pressed his lips together, knew his face was a road map of misery.

His dad lifted his head. ". . . heart . . . listen . . . promise . . ."

Listen to your heart. Maybe it wasn't a smart motto. Maybe he didn't give a damn about being smart. Steve reached out, touched a still muscular shoulder. "I will, Dad. As soon as I think some things through."

Jugs lay at the end of the table in his lion pose, watching as she ate.

It wasn't much of a dinner. A bowl of tomato soup and some dry crackers from a box long past its fresh date. Chloe hadn't been in the apartment long enough to leave a half-empty box of crackers. Nela was eating saltines that had been purchased by Marian Grant. Odd. But Marian wouldn't begrudge crackers to someone taking care of Jugs. Nela looked into watching green eyes and felt certain of that. She wasn't certain of anything else. "Jugs, I don't know what to do."

". . . *She was worried* . . ."

"So am I, buddy." Oh hell yes, she was worried. She ate and listened for a knock at the door, for the questions she dared not answer. She cleaned up the kitchen in only a moment. In the living room, she dropped into the comfortable overstuffed chair and looked across the silent room at the sofa. Last night he'd sat there and given her a chance. When he'd walked into the main hall of Haklo late Monday morning, wiry red hair, broad open face, bright blue eyes, stocky and muscular, she'd instinctively started to smile. It wasn't until he looked at her late last night and gravely listened to her halting explanations that she'd realized he was a man with a hard edge, a man who had been hurt and was afraid to trust.

He'd trusted her. For a little while. She fought away sudden sharp sadness. What difference did it make? She scarcely knew him. Abruptly, she came to her feet, hurried into the living room. She picked up Bill's picture. She looked at his laughing face, young and strong, alive and loving her. Carrying the picture, she sank onto the sofa. The red, white, and blue ribbon she'd wound through the latticed wood of the frame brought no comfort.

Jugs jumped up beside her, pressed against her thigh.

She massaged behind big ears. "It's up to me, Jugs." She looked again at Bill's photograph and the familiar emptiness echoed inside. Bill wasn't here. Bill wasn't anywhere.

Jugs lifted his head, turned to stare at the front door. His ears flicked forward.

A sharp knock rattled the door.

Nela slowly came to her feet. She'd known this moment was coming. She walked to the door, turned on the porch light, twisted the knob. As cold air eddied around her, she stared, her lips parted.

Once again the wind stirred his short red hair. Once again he wore no coat. Tonight he carried a folder.

She looked past him.

"Just me. Maybe you'll tell me to take a hike. I thought it over.

I didn't ask you. That wasn't fair." Now his blue eyes held hers. "Did you go back last night?"

"No."

The look between them was more than a question and answer.

His face softened. "Sorry. Sometimes now"—the words came slowly—"I expect bad outcomes. I shouldn't have jumped to a stupid conclusion. "

"It wasn't stupid. You don't know me. I found the necklace in Marian's purse, but I can never prove that it was there. I tried to see it safely back to Blythe. I feel like I've done everything I can do. But thank you for coming. It was very kind." She started to close the door.

He held up the folder. "Can I come in? I've got some stuff that may help."

Nela hesitated. "You've already done more for me than you should." He hadn't called the police when he found her coming out of Haklo. She was sure they'd broken some laws leaving the necklace on Blythe's desk, but he didn't deserve to be in trouble because of her. "I'm afraid it's dangerous to hang around with me."

"That's a chance I'll take."

Nela wanted to let him inside. She wanted him to leave. She didn't know what she wanted, but she was acutely aware of his nearness. He was alive and strong and vital. Bill—

"I don't know." She knew she must sound like a fool. "I'm sorry. I don't want to have anything else to do with what's happened at Haklo. I'm going to be here for Chloe until she returns. But she and I have nothing to do with the problems there. Let's leave it at that." She closed the door.

Now she had lied to him. She'd promised him she wouldn't lie and now she had. She couldn't walk away from the turmoil at the foundation. She was going to find out more, much more, seek the truth. For her and for Chloe.

But she didn't have to involve Steve Flynn.

She leaned against the cold wooden panel and listened to the sound of diminishing steps.

S lanting beams from passing headlights created a silhouette of leafless limbs on the bedroom ceiling, jumbled dark splotches that made no sense, formed no coherent pattern. Steve always sought a pattern. This time he was out of luck. His thoughts shifted from her rebuff to his damn fool determination to help someone who didn't want help, swung from certainty to uncertainty. Was she honest? Did he care? People did what they thought they had to do. She'd help her sister at all costs. Was that why she sent him away? Or was she running from him because she, too, felt the attraction between them when they stood close together? She carried sadness with her. He thought he knew why. Someday he would ask her about the dark-haired guy standing on a beach and the red, white, and blue ribbon that wreathed the brown wooden frame. Someday. Not now.

His mouth twisted in a wry grin. Big talk on his part. Her good night had been a pretty definite good-bye. One thing was for sure. He'd wanted for months to be free of memories of Gail. Maybe he should have remembered to be careful what he wished for. Was the god of hilarity laughing aloud? Gail was fading. Her name no longer conjured images that excited desire or bitterness. Instead, he saw Nela's intelligent, vulnerable face with lips that he wanted to kiss.

The grin slipped away. She was in trouble. She—and her sister— would be safe only if he discovered the truth behind the vandalism and the theft of the necklace. He'd made a start last evening on figuring out who could have taken the necklace from Blythe Webster's desk. Tomorrow he'd narrow the field. He might not have a white horse to ride to Nela's rescue, but he knew Craddock maybe even better than Katie Dugan.

Though Nela was weary to the bone, sleep was elusive. She kept hearing the sound of Steve's footsteps fading into silence. She pushed away thoughts of Steve. She heard Bill's voice . . . *If I don't come back* . . . Bill had wanted to tell her that if he died, she must live. She had placed her fingers on his lips, warm living lips, to stop the words she didn't want to hear. She had read the message in Bill's eyes just as tonight she'd looked into blue eyes and seen another message: *I want to know you. Give me a chance.*

She turned restlessly, tried to get comfortable. She knew what Bill had wanted for her. But not yet. Not while emptiness filled her heart.

She'd sent Steve away. She wanted him to be safe. As a reporter, he was jeopardizing his job to keep information about a crime from the police. She had involved him in a crime when he learned that she'd returned the necklace to Haklo. Detective K. T. Dugan could charge him with obstruction of justice and possibly conspiracy in regard to transportation of stolen property. Right now there was no reason Dugan should ever learn that Steve had been at Haklo last night. Nela would never tell anyone.

She began to sink into the oblivion of exhausted sleep. Faintly, Nela heard a *click-click-click* on the bedroom door. Her eyelids fluttered open as she turned her head on the pillow. Jugs . . . wanted in . . . good cat . . . lonely . . . Groggily she rolled on an elbow, sat up.

Click-click-click. She came to her feet, crossed the cold hardwood floor. She'd learned a lesson Friday night. The door would always be locked while she slept. She turned the knob, held the panel open. A dark shape flowed past. When she settled again on the bed, Jugs snuggled beside her, soft and warm. A faint purr signaled his happiness.

—13—

Steve took another bite of a glazed doughnut, washed away the sweetness with strong coffee. Not much of a breakfast, but enough. He wrote fast, his printing big and legible on a legal pad. He could have made notes on his laptop. For quick jottings, he still liked real paper. He had been in kindergarten when the *Clarion* installed computers. He remembered thick yellow copy and the clack of Remingtons and an ever-present smoky haze. Now the newsroom was silent, the walls had long ago been repainted to remove years of nicotine scum, and the copy spike on Mim Barlow's desk was a memento. He was finishing his third cup of coffee when Mim's brisk steps sounded in the newsroom.

She stopped beside his desk. "Something big?" She sounded hopeful.

"Background."

Her glance was sharp. "Let me know if I should hold space."

"Not today."

"Right. Do a follow-up on the missing necklace."

"Already sent it over."

"If everyone was as efficient . . ." She turned toward her desk.

Steve put the legal pad to one side of the screen, ready now for a summation that he could print out. He wanted to have a copy for Nela. Stubby fingers flew over the keys.

HAKLO TIMETABLE

1. *September 19.* Car set afire in employee parking lot. 1995 Camaro destroyed. Unsolved. No suspects. Anne Nesbitt, 23, owner of car, relocated to Norman, now works at the Sam Noble Museum of Natural History. No record of troubled relationships in her personal life. Police investigation concluded the fire was randomly set and not directed at Nesbitt personally.

2. *November 15.* Nine Chickasaw baskets found hacked to pieces in exhibit room.

3. *December 5.* Sprinklers activated in Robbie Powell's office.

4. *December 16.* Courtyard fountain turned on, frozen pipes.

5. *January 5.* Necklace missing from desk of Blythe Webster.

6. *January 9.* Marian Grant died from a fall down garage apartment stairs.

7. *January 14.* Nela Farley called 911 to report intruder in Marian Grant's apartment.

8. *January 14.* Nela Farley found expensive necklace in Marian Grant's purse.

9. *January 16.* According to Nela, members of Haklo grants committee received obscene material on Haklo Director Hollis Blair's letterhead.

10. *January 16.* Ditto, letter traced to file in computer of Assistant Curator Abby Andrews. Andrews denied creating file.

11. *January 16.* Search of Marian Grant's office discovered by Nela Farley. Office searched sometime after 5 p.m. Friday and before late Monday morning.

12. *January 16.* Nela Farley learned about necklace stolen from Blythe Webster and realized the necklace was in Marian Grant's purse.

13. *January 16.* Nela Farley entered Haklo after hours and placed necklace on Blythe Webster's desk.

14. *January 16.* Unidentified caller to *Clarion* claimed Marian Grant was murdered, her fall caused by a skateboard placed deliberately on the second step.

15. *January 17.* Detective Dugan informed Haklo staff of the anonymous message. Theft (or claimed theft) of skateboard from the porch of Abby's cabin revealed.

16. *January 17.* Necklace once again missing.

Steve didn't need a reminder of the incidents. He'd written too many stories to forget a single one. Instead, he focused on dates.

The car was set afire in September. After a lapse of two months, several acts of vandalism occurred. Was the car fire an anomaly, independent of the other incidents? Maybe the car fire gave someone an idea.

The fire caused no harm to the foundation. The later vandalism was clearly intended to cause problems for Haklo. The fire could have been set by anyone. The destruction of the Indian baskets, water damage in Robbie's office, theft of Blythe's necklace, and use of Blair's letterhead could have been done only by someone familiar with the foundation.

The vandalism could have had any of several objectives: To harass either Haklo or its trustee, Blythe Webster, to mar the stewardship of the new director, to make the theft of the necklace appear simply to be another in a series of unlawful acts, or as an act of revenge by a disgruntled current or former employee.

Katie Dugan settled on the fact that no vandals had ever struck at Haklo until this fall. Katie believed newcomer Chloe Farley committed the vandalism but that her goal was to take the necklace. The lapse of time between the car fire and the destruction of the Indian baskets supported Katie's theory. Chloe likely would not have known until she'd worked at Haklo for several weeks that Blythe Webster kept a quarter-million-dollar necklace lying in a desk drawer in her unlocked office.

However, Chloe was not the only new employee at Haklo since summer. He thumbed through notes. Hollis Blair arrived August first. Abby Andrews was hired August fifteenth.

Steve stared at the list. Why was there a two-month lag between the car fire and the hacked baskets? Maybe when he knew the answer to that, he'd know the truth behind vandalism, theft, and murder.

He clicked several times on his computer. The burned car had been front-page news. Who had handled that investigation?

N ela turned into the main Haklo drive. She was alert as she passed the main building and turned left to drive to the employee lot, but she didn't see any police cars. Nela parked again between the Thunderbird and the Dodge. Louise's car was also in the lot. Nela looked in every direction as she walked to the staff entrance. When she stepped inside and the door sighed shut behind her, she scanned the hallway. No trace of police. It seemed strange to be wary of the police. Her uncle Bob had been a sergeant in the LAPD, a big, ebullient, loud man. Her aunt always worried. A cop never knew when a stopped car might harbor danger, yet every day cops walked toward cars, some with tinted windows. They carried a gun in a holster, but they approached empty-handed, keeping streets safe for ordinary people.

Lights spilled from Louise's open door. In Chloe's office, Nela dropped her purse into a desk drawer. Despite the lack of a police presence, she continued to feel apprehensive. What was Detective Dugan doing now? Driving to Haklo to interrogate Nela again? But the detective had no reason to inquire into Nela's activities Monday night. Surely she was focused on a search for the missing skateboard.

Nela hung Chloe's large jacket on the coatrack, checked the clock. She stepped to the open door between the offices.

Louise's office was brightly lit. She looked up. "Good morning, Nela." Although her face was wan, she made an effort to smile. "That's a pretty skirt."

"Thank you, Louise." Nela's wardrobe was limited by what she'd managed to put in one suitcase. The long swirling skirt was silk with a pattern of blue and black circles. She added a crisp white blouse and black pumps. It was one of her best outfits, one she'd often worn when working as a reporter. If she saw Steve . . . But she wouldn't see him. She'd turned him away, listened to the fading sound of his footsteps. The thought brought a quick stab of unhappiness. She wanted to see him. She didn't want to see him.

". . . put some more application folders on your desk. After you finish the summaries and deliver the morning mail, please pick up the proofs of a new scholarship brochure from Peter." She looked a little defiant. "He sent me the brochure online but I still like to look at paper." She gave a decided nod and turned back toward her computer.

Nela settled at Chloe's computer. It was important for her to act as if Haklo's troubles didn't affect her personally. As she read and typed, willing herself not to think of Steve, she listened, alert and wary, for the brisk sound of official steps in the hallway. She felt like a fish in a barrel, easy prey. As soon as possible, she had to figure a way to discover the truth behind the tangled relationships at Haklo, what mattered and what didn't matter, who had stolen a necklace and committed murder to prevent exposure.

She'd started her investigation with Erik Judd. He'd been willing to talk to her, but would any of the rest of the staff be willing to respond?

Her fingers hung in the air above the keyboard.

Maybe there was a way to take advantage of her reporter background. She glanced up at the clock. In a few minutes, she was scheduled to deliver the mail to Haklo staff, starting, of course, with Blythe Webster. Monday morning, as soon as Blythe heard from members of the grants committee about the obscene letters with the Haklo director's letterhead, she had set in motion a thorough search. She hadn't been passive, hadn't waited for anyone else to take charge. Tuesday the police dropped the bombshell of the anonymous call claiming Marian Grant's death was instead murder. Blythe made it clear at that meeting that all staff members were to cooperate with the authorities. Yes, the police were investigating, but Blythe might see a role for Haklo itself to seek truth. And maybe Nela could help.

S teve dropped into the straight chair next to Mokie Morrison's desk. "Glad I caught you." Most of the other desks in the detectives' room were unoccupied.

Mokie was cheerful. "Katie believes in old-fashioned shoe leather. At least she didn't send me out to check with the sanitation guys to see if anybody noticed a skateboard disappearing into the jaws of death last week. In case you're wondering, the jaws of death are those big choppers that grind up garbage when the guys throw stuff in. The choppers can turn metal pylons into mincemeat, damn near. The garbage guys need to watch their elbows and hands. That's just one hazard. Do you know anybody who works harder than garbage guys? Hang on and freeze their butts in winter. Hang on and bake in summer. And, man, the smell. And they're supposed to check out the trash before it splinters? I don't think so. Anyway, Katie's frustrated. Plus too many places in this case—the apartment behind the Webster mansion and the assistant curator's cottage on the Haklo grounds—don't have any convenient nosy parker neighbors. So I got no complaints about my assignment, but Marian Grant's banker and lawyer aren't ready to chummy up with the cops. Lots of mutters about court orders, sanctity of client information. Me, I think the whole idea that Marian Grant was murdered is just another poke by the Haklo Vandal, one more way to make things awkward for the T. It's kind of a blot on Haklo's shiny bright rep if somebody bumped off the COO. The hell of it is, nobody can prove murder or accident, but once the story's out there, some people will believe in murder and think there's a big cover-up."

Steve was casual. "Maybe, but it's funny that the tip was specific, a skateboard on the second step, and then it turns out one of the Haklo people is missing a skateboard. That gives the story some legs."

Mokie leaned back in his chair. "Nah. The Haklo Vandal used a skateboard in that call you got because the Vandal spotted a skateboard on the cabin porch and then, to muddy things up even more, filched the skateboard."

"The skateboard disappeared before the call was made."

"So? Can't say the Haklo Vandal doesn't plan ahead. Anyway, what can I do for you." Mokie smothered a yawn. "Got to be more interesting than listening to lawyers and bankers talk in great big circles."

Steve pulled some folded copy paper out of his pocket. "You covered the Camaro fire out at Haklo. I know it's been a while, but I'd like to run through what you remember."

"Oh, man." Mokie's eyes gleamed and he sat up straight. "Hot stuff."

"The fire?" Weren't fires always hot?

Mokie's eyes squinted in remembrance. "Nah. The babe. Stacked." He moved his hands in a modified figure eight. "Boobs with a life of their own. Hips . . ." He sighed. "Inquiring officer couldn't touch but he could dream. At least I got to sit in the back of the patrol car with her. Inches away." He wriggled his nose. "Gardenia perfume. Like a summer night in the bushes with a babe."

Steve shook his head. "If you can get past primal appeal, tell me about the fire."

Mokie grinned. "Man, you got to remember, first things first. Wow. Drop-dead gorgeous. As for the fire"—his tone was suddenly matter-of-fact—"let me take a look." He swung around to his computer, clicked a couple of times. "Yeah. Here it is. Call came in at three fifteen, car on fire in Haklo staff lot. Arrived at three twenty-two. Bystanders wringing hands. Fire truck arrived at three twenty-four. Flames shooting from Camaro windows. Fire out by three thirty-eight." Mokie's nose wrinkled. "Pretty bad stink. Plastic seats melted by heat, interior destroyed, car turned out to be totaled. A gardener called in the alarm, tried to douse the blaze with a watering hose. The sirens brought people outside and somebody alerted the Camaro owner, who came running outside. One Anne Nesbitt." A deep breath. "Man, I wish I'd been there to see her run. Daffodil yellow cotton top, molded, tight cream skirt. Very short."

"The fire," Steve reminded gently.

"Somebody splashed the interior with gasoline, stood back, and lobbed a wad of burning rags." He raised a crooked black brow. "That was pretty clever. The arsonist was smart enough to know there could be a flash explosion so the perp used a kid's bow and arrow. The bow was in a plastic trash barrel at the edge of the parking lot. No fingerprints. A piece of a plastic shaft, all that didn't melt, was found inside the car. Arson investigators can figure out a lot from residue. Anyway, that's the theory." He raised a crooked black brow. "I always figured it was some dame who was jealous of the victim. A bow and arrow sounds girlie."

"Did you trace it?"

Mokie raised both eyebrows. "Like we can trace the sale of a Walmart toy. You know how many Walmarts there are in a fifty-mile radius? You can bet the perp didn't get the bow and arrow in Craddock. No luck there. Actually, no luck anywhere. I dug hard and didn't find a whiff of anybody who had a grudge against the babe."

"How about hard feelings on the staff?"

"Why? Because she's gorgeous?" A slight frown tugged at his brows. "Have to admit there didn't seem to be any loiterers out there that afternoon. The gardeners didn't see anybody walking around. One guy claimed nobody came in by the service road. The only other access was to park in front and either come through the main door or walk down the east road. The east road was closed off for some repair work that afternoon. The crew didn't see anybody. I asked her every which way I knew and she couldn't tell me anybody that was mad at her. I checked out which staff members were there that afternoon. You want the list?"

Steve nodded.

Mokie clicked twice. "Easier to say who wasn't there. Hollis Blair was in Kansas City at a meeting. Everybody else was on site. You can't say I didn't give it my all." His mouth slid into a suggestive smile. "I talked to her a half-dozen times. Finally"—a regretful sigh—"I had to give up. There was no rhyme, no reason." He pulled his cell phone from his pocket, slid his thumb several times over the small screen. "Take a gander."

Steve looked at the image. Mokie hadn't exaggerated. Anne Nesbitt was a babe, shining thick golden hair, delicate intriguing classic features, and, not to be missed by any male between ten and ninety, a voluptuous body.

* * *

Nela was midway through the stack of folders when Chloe's phone buzzed. "Nela Far—"

"Come to my office at once." Blythe Webster's voice was sharp with a tense undertone. The connection ended.

Nela took a steadying breath as she replaced the receiver. Obviously, Detective Dugan had shared her suspicions of Chloe and Nela with Blythe. Was Blythe going to fire Chloe and her substitute on the spot? Nela walked up the hallway with her shoulders squared.

She stepped through the open door to Blythe's office. Each time she'd been in this elegant office, there had been a background of tension. The first time she'd overheard the worried exchange between Blythe and Hollis occasioned by the arrival of obscene letters on Haklo stationery. The second time she had slipped inside with the stolen necklace, eager to leave the jewelry behind and escape. The third time Steve Flynn marched her inside, but the glitter of gold and diamonds had persuaded him that Nela—and Chloe—were innocent of wrongdoing.

Now the office was once again a backdrop to drama.

Blythe Webster stood rigid next to her desk. She wore her luxuriant dark mink coat and held a sheet of paper in one hand. On the desktop lay a white envelope that had been opened. "Shut the door. Where did this letter come from?"

Nela stared at the trustee's haggard face and realized in a welling of relief that Blythe had not called Nela into the office to accuse her or to fire her.

"The letter, where did it come from?" Blythe's voice wobbled. "Answer me."

"I didn't bring the letter. I haven't made deliveries yet this morning. I was summarizing—" She broke off. Blythe didn't care about Nela's work. She cared only about how the envelope had reached her desk.

In a jerky movement, Blythe reached toward the envelope, stopped inches away. She stared for a moment, pulled open the center drawer, picked up a pen, used the end to tip the envelope address side up. "There's no stamp. If the letter didn't come through the mail"—Blythe's words were reluctant—"someone must have put it on my desk." Her lips compressed, she turned and picked up the telephone receiver. "Rosalind, have there been any visitors in the building this morning?" She listened. "No visitors?" Her expression was grim when she replaced the receiver.

She looked at Nela. "Go to your office. Remain there. Do not discuss the letter with anyone."

S teve Flynn set a full mug of coffee on his desk. Arson of the Haklo employee's car seemed more and more like an outlier to the subsequent vandalism. His mouth twisted in an almost-smile. Mokie might be an old dog, but he hadn't forgotten the hunt. Maybe his instinct was right, some woman had set sexy Anne Nesbitt's car on fire in a jealous rage.

Steve laid out his notes on his desk, scanned them. Mokie had been thorough.

. . . boyfriend in Norman, doctoral student. No hanky-panky there. Known each other since college, never dated anyone else. Nesbitt had no known enemies . . . Acquaintances insist Nesbitt was on good terms with everyone. . . . Gardeners working on west side of

grounds claim no strange cars in or out within half an hour either side of fire . . . East-entrance road under repair that day, closed, no cars entered from that direction . . . Perp could have parked somewhere else, walked on foot, but no strangers noted . . .

Maybe no stranger did arrive that afternoon. Maybe the perp was already present, a member of the Haklo staff, the crime carefully planned, the bow and arrow, gas tin, and wad of cloth hidden near the employee lot. Yeah, there was an odd lag in time between the fire and the destruction of the Indian baskets, but he'd try to reconcile that puzzle later. For now . . . He pulled out a fresh legal pad, picked up his pen.

KNOWN TO HAVE KEY TO HAKLO

Blythe Webster, Haklo trustee; Grace Webster, honorary trustee; Hollis Blair, director; Louise Spear, executive secretary; Cole Hamilton, advisory vice president; Francis Garth, business development research fellow; Robbie Powell, director of public relations; Peter Owens, director of publications; Abby Andrews, assistant curator; Chloe Farley (and thereby Nela Farley), administrative assistant; Rosalind McNeill, receptionist; Kay Hoover, chef; Erik Judd, former director.

He'd known Rosalind since kindergarten. Some people could be badasses. Some couldn't. Rosalind couldn't. He drew a line through her name. Kay Hoover was the grandmother of his best buddy in high school. She made pralines to die for. Mama Kay thought about food. And family. And food. And family. He marked out her name. Two more quick strokes went through Chloe and Nela's names. He couldn't vouch for Chloe, but he believed Nela. If she was innocent, Chloe was innocent.

Now for a closer look at those with easy access to Haklo.

In the chair behind Chloe's desk, Nela had a good view of the portion of hall revealed by the open door. She waited and watched. The sound she had expected was not long in coming. Not more than ten minutes later, brisk steps clipped in the hallway.

Nela had only a brief glimpse, but the glimpse was telling. Detective Dugan strode purposefully past, accompanied by a somber Blythe Webster. Dugan was in all black today, turtleneck, skirt, and boots. The cheerful color of Blythe's crimson suit looked at odds with her resolute expression, a woman engaged in an unwanted task. Two uniformed officers followed, balding, moonfaced Sergeant Fisher with his ever-ready electronic tablet and a chunky woman officer in her late twenties.

Nela eased from the chair and moved to the open door. She didn't step into the hall. Instead, unseen, she listened.

"The light is on, but the office is empty." Dugan had a clear, carrying voice.

The squeak of a chair pushed back. Rapid steps sounded. Louise Spear hurried past Chloe's doorway, didn't even glance toward Nela. "What's wrong?" Her voice was anxious, held definite foreboding.

"Where is Miss Andrews?" Dugan sounded pleasant, but firm.

"Usually at this time she's upstairs in the artifact room." Louise sounded puzzled.

"Sergeant, ask Miss Andrews to join us."

"Blythe, what's going on? Why are the police here?"

Blythe sounded remote, as if she were trying to remain calm.

"The police have to make an investigation. I don't have anything to say right now. Let's see what happens."

Nela slid closer to the door. No one spoke until the officer returned with Abby.

Abby's face was fearful and pinched. She stared with wide, frightened eyes at the cluster of people outside her office. "What's wrong? Why do you want to talk to me?"

Blythe Webster spoke in a tight, contained voice. "Abby, it's necessary for the police to search your office. I have granted them permission to do so."

"Why?" Abby's breathing was uneven. "What are they looking for?"

Hurrying steps came down the hall. Hollis Blair strode forward, brows drawn in a tight frown. He looked from Blythe to Dugan to Abby. "I saw police cars. What's happening?"

Abby's voice shook. "They want to search my office."

Nela stepped into the hallway. She might be sent away, but surely it was only natural to respond to the arrival of the police.

Abby's delicate face twisted in fear. "I don't think they have any right. I haven't done anything." She lifted a trembling hand to push back a tangle of blond hair.

Hollis appeared both shocked and angry. "I'll take care of everything." He swung toward the police detective, who stood in the doorway. "Detective, I want an explanation."

Dugan was brief. "Information received necessitates a search of the office. The search will proceed."

"On whose authority?" The director bit off the words.

"Mine." Blythe Webster spoke quietly.

Abby turned toward Blythe. "I haven't done anything. Why are you—"

Dugan interrupted, "The search of the office is not directed at you personally, Miss Andrews." But Dugan's brown eyes never moved from Abby's lovely, anxious face. "Please step into the doorway and see if you notice any disarray in your office."

Arms folded, a gold link bracelet glittering on one wrist, Blythe listened, eyes narrowed, lips compressed.

Two more uniformed police came from the main hallway along with Detective Morrison.

"Disarray?" Abby repeated uncertainly.

"Anything out of place? A drawer open that you left shut? Any suggestion that an unauthorized person had been in your office?" Dugan's questions came quick and fast.

"Oh my God." Abby hurried to the doorway. In a moment, she faced her tormentors. "I don't know. I don't think so. I don't know." Her voice rose in distress. "Why? What are you looking for?"

Dugan nodded toward Detective Morrison and the two newly arrived uniformed officers, a lean, wiry man with bushy eyebrows in a pasty face and the redheaded policewoman who had come to the garage apartment when Nela called for help.

Hollis Blair glared at Blythe, his handsome features strained, his jaw rigid. "Why wasn't I notified? There better be a damn good reason for this." He jerked a thumb toward Dugan.

The trustee's shoulders stiffened. She gave him a level stare, her brown eyes cool. Her expression was not hostile, but the distance seemed to increase between them.

By now, the hallway around Nela was crowded. Louise Spear stood a little to one side, eyes huge, staring at Abby's office, her face puckered in a worried frown. Other staff members hurried toward the clump of people, likely drawn by the arrival of the police and the hubbub in the west hallway. Rosalind McNeill tried to appear grave but she almost bounced in excitement. Cole Hamilton moved back and forth uneasily, darting quick looks past Dugan. Occasionally one eyelid jerked in a nervous tic. Peter Owens, his gaze intent, looked from Blythe to Abby to Hollis. Francis Garth stood with folded arms, heavy head jutting forward, thick black brows lowered, massive legs planted solidly. Robbie Powell muttered, "Police again. This can't be good for Haklo."

Heels clicked on marble as Grace Webster arrived. She clapped her hands. "Never a dull moment."

Hollis moved nearer Blythe. "I'm the director. I should know if the police are called. And why."

"I'm the trustee." That was all Blythe said.

Hollis Blair stiffened. His angular face flushed. After a tense pause, he took two steps to stand beside Abby.

"Whoop-de-do, Blythe's in her dowager queen mode. Sis, I hate to break it to you"—Grace Webster's tone was saccharine—"but what are sisters for? That frozen face makes you look fifty, not a happy number for somebody who's barreling up on the big Four-O."

"I didn't know you were coming in today." Blythe's voice was cold.

"Can't stay away. Haklo used to be bo-ring. Not anymore." Grace yanked a thumb over her shoulder. "What's the cavalry here for?"

Blythe ignored the question, her face smooth, her eyes focused on the doorway.

Grace's look of amusement faded, replaced with anger.

The public relations director took a few steps toward Blythe. "The *Clarion* will pick up the call. We need to be prepared—"

Sergeant Fisher came to the doorway. "Detective."

The silence among the onlookers was sudden and absolute. Abby Andrews clutched Hollis Blair's arm.

Detective Dugan stepped into Abby's office. A muttered murmur, no words intelligible to those in the hall. The office door closed.

Blythe stood with a hand at her throat. Louise shivered. Abby wavered on her feet. Hollis slid a strengthening arm around her shoulders. Cole Hamilton's face drew down in disapproval. Francis Garth gazed at the assistant curator speculatively. Robbie Powell was impassive, but his eyes locked on the office door. Grace's look of defiant amusement fled.

—14—

Steve Flynn picked up a folder. He'd gathered up odds and ends of information about those with Haklo keys. Nothing had jumped out at him. No bright red arrow pointed to a vandal, thief, and murderer. Somewhere there had to be a fact that mattered. He settled down to reread the dossiers.

Blythe Webster, 39. BA in English, OU. After graduation returned to Craddock and lived at home. Younger sister still in middle school. Served as a hostess for her father. Unmarried. Craddock gossip in 2005 linked her to a handsome young landman who worked for Webster Exploration. Rumor had it that Harris Webster offered the landman a hundred thousand dollars to relocate—by himself—to Argentina. Harris told Blythe he knew a skunk when he saw one and he was saving her from an unhappy marriage. Blythe spent a year in Italy. She returned to

Craddock when her father's health worsened. At his death, she became the sole trustee of Haklo Foundation. She traveled extensively and left the running of Haklo to Marian Grant, COO. However, as trustee, she always attended the annual conference of small charitable foundations. Following the conference this past summer in St. Louis, she took a renewed interest in the foundation. In short order, she instituted a number of changes. From corporate luncheons to the bar at the country club, the locals delighted in totting up the casualties both inside and outside the foundation. Erik Judd was fired. A grant to a local art gallery wasn't renewed. Haklo ended support of a scholarship program for Native Americans at Craddock College.

Steve glanced at a photograph. Shining black hair framed an olive-skinned face. Her eyes, large and expressive, were her most compelling feature. Her lips were perhaps a little too reminiscent of her father's thin mouth. Her composed expression suggested a woman with power. He'd often dealt with Blythe Webster. She expected to be treated with deference. She could be abrupt and was reputedly wary in personal relationships. That he could understand. How did you get over knowing a man preferred cash on hand to your company? He knew odds and ends about her. She collected Roman coins and had a take-no-prisoner mentality in her dealings. She once drove a coin dealer into bankruptcy when he sold a coin she wanted to a rival collector. She played scratch golf. She was generous in her praise for employees and gave substantial bonuses at Christmas.

Grace Webster, honorary trustee, 27. A strawberry blonde who liked to have fun. Usually ebullient, though she was often caustic with her sister. Her contemporaries dubbed her the wild one.

Five colleges. Never graduated. Backpacked across Europe. A succession of boyfriends. Harris Webster was amused by her escapades. He told a friend that he never worried about Grace and men, saying she always had the upper hand, enchanting men but never enchanted. When her father died, she was angry that Blythe became the sole trustee. Everyone thought that Harris saw Grace as too young and carefree for the responsibility. Perhaps out of spite, she comes to Haklo daily when she is in Craddock and keeps up a running critique of Blythe's decisions. Their relationship is frosty. Her latest lover was a local artist, Maurice Crown, who delighted in satiric paintings. A recent painting juxtaposed the Haklo Foundation crest with gallons of crude oil gushing from a Gulf platform. Blythe promptly cancelled a grant to the gallery that featured Crown's paintings. Grace was furious, insisting foundation bylaws prohibited cancellation of grants except on the basis of criminal malfeasance. However, the trustee had all the power. Grace is markedly different from her sister, adventurous, enthusiastic, always ready to take a dare, impulsive, careless, optimistic. Perhaps the trait they hold in common is bedrock stubbornness. Each is always determined to do exactly as she chooses.

Steve had clear memories of summers at the lake and Grace's daredevil boat races. She appeared supremely pleased in her photograph, strawberry blond hair cascading to her shoulders, an exuberant smile, seductive off-the-shoulder white blouse. Her chin had the same decided firmness as her sister's.

Hollis Blair, director, 32. BBS in business, OSU. MA in art history with an emphasis on the American West, SMU. PhD in education, University of Texas. At 28, he joined the staff of a medium-size charitable foundation in Kansas City. Blythe Webster heard Blair speak at a foundation workshop in St. Louis last summer. After the session, she invited him to join her for dinner. She met with him several times during the weeklong workshop. Within three days after her return to Craddock, Erik Judd had been fired and Hollis Blair hired. He arrived August 1. He is affable, charming, outgoing, eager to please.

The photo had accompanied the press release put out by Haklo when Hollis became director. Chestnut hair, deep-set blue eyes, a bony nose, high cheekbones, full lips spread in a friendly smile. Steve had played golf with Hollis several times and found him good-humored and intelligent with perceptive questions about Craddock. The last time they'd met had been at a reception in early December for the new director of the chamber of commerce. Steve recalled a man who looked tired and worried. Hollis had brightened when he was joined by the Haklo assistant curator, Abby Andrews. At the time, Steve had thought it generous of Hollis to bring an assistant curator to a function. Apparently, he was interested in more than Abby Andrews's work advancement.

Louise Spear, executive secretary, 58. Widow. A grown daughter in Corpus Christi, three grandchildren. Louise started as a secretary at Webster Exploration in 1974, moved to the foundation when it was created. Louise is precise, careful, responsible, and follows instructions. She considered Harris Webster a great man. Haklo was second only to her family in her affections. She has taught Sunday School at the Craddock Methodist Church for 34 years. Kind, gentle, thoughtful, always ready to help.

Steve didn't bother to look at Louise's photo. He knew Louise. Casting her as a vandal, much less a murderer, was ludicrous.

Cole Hamilton, advisory vice president, 64. BBA 1969, OU. Widower. No children. Longtime crony of Harris Webster. When Haklo was formed, he left Webster Exploration to serve as senior vice president. Active in local charities, he served as a sounding board for Harris. A former member of the grants committee once said caustically, "Cole always loses at poker to Harris. That seems to be his primary qualification for his title. But he's sure he's indispensable, second only in importance to Harris." His advice always began, "Harris agrees that Haklo should . . ." A man who took great pride in being a part of Haklo. But Harris was dead and Blythe was now the trustee.

Steve turned to the screen, brought up several photos of Cole Hamilton. One had been taken with Harris Webster on the deck of a cruiser. Each man held up a string of fish. Harris's string was longer. The oilman's predatory face was relaxed. Cole beamed, basking in the moment. In a more recent picture at a November open house at Haklo, Cole's round face was morose as he stood by himself at the edge of a group.

Cole was no longer at the side of Harris Webster, the center of Haklo. After Harris's death, Marian Grant ran the foundation. Very likely Marian treated Cole kindly. Marian had been part of that close-knit group, Harris, Cole, herself, and Louise. But this summer Blythe Webster took over and soon there was a new director and Cole's title changed from vice president to advisory vice president.

Steve reached for the phone. "Louise? Steve Flynn."

"Yes." Her tone was tense.

He spoke easily. "I hear Cole Hamilton is being pushed out of his job."

"Steve, don't print that." A tiny sigh traveled over the connection. "I don't know what's going to happen about Cole. Just between you and me, Blythe has asked him to step down, but he won't turn in a resignation. I don't think Blythe wants to terminate him. In any event, he is the current advisory vice president. Let's leave it at that."

"Right. I'll wait until there's an announcement. Thanks, Louise."

The call ended. Steve looked again at Cole's pictures, such an affable, comfortable man, especially in the early photos. How much did his job, not just the work, but the prestige of being a part of Haklo, matter to a man who had no family and who had spent his life working for Harris Webster? Wasn't vandalism the kind of revenge a somewhat effete, deeply angry, and hurt man might take? Stealing the necklace was part of that pattern, striking out at the woman who was treating him badly. Cole Hamilton, soft-spoken and genial, scarcely seemed likely to kill. But murder might have been the only way to prevent exposure.

Steve looked at the next name on his list.

Francis Garth, business development research fellow, 47. BA, MA, University of Tulsa. PhD in economics, University of Chicago. Native of Pawhuska. Active as a member of the Osage Tribe. Prominent family, longtime civic supporters. Divorced some years ago, no children. Long-distance runner. Mountain climber. Taught in Chicago, a think tank in Austin, joined Haklo in 1994. A proponent of encouraging Oklahoma exports to foreign countries, especially Costa Rica. Knowledgeable about beef industry and exportable non-food crops. Instrumental in arranging grants for factory expansion. Passionate in his support of the Tallgrass Prairie.

Steve scanned the index in the annual report of the Haklo Foundation issued shortly after the end of the fiscal year in October. He flipped to the business development section. A figure jumped out at him. The business development budget last year had been two hundred and eighty thousand dollars. The current budget had been cut to one hundred and fifty thousand. Just as in Washington, money meant power. Francis Garth was an impressive man at the peak of his career, whose priorities weren't those of a new director.

Steve turned back to the computer. Burly, muscular Francis stared into the camera with a heavy, determined face. Not a man to welcome a downgrade. Would a bull of a man be likely to resort to vandalism? It didn't seem in character. But Francis Garth was highly intelligent, able to think and plan a campaign. A series of unfortunate incidents would damage Hollis Blair's resume. As for murder, Francis had the air of a man who would, without a qualm, do what he had to do.

A very different man from Robbie Powell. And Erik Judd. Steve didn't hesitate to combine their resumes.

Robbie Powell, director of public relations, 44. BA in public relations, University of Missouri. Worked at PR agencies in Kansas City and later Dallas. Joined staff at a medium-size Dallas charitable foundation, became the protégé of the foundation director, Erik Judd. Judd, 55, was a University of Cincinnati graduate in social work. Worked in social service agency in Ohio, earned his PhD in finance, joined the Dallas foundation, within ten years named director. When Judd was hired by Harris Webster as director, he brought Robbie with him. They shared a home in the older part of Craddock, a rambling ranch-style house. When an anti-gay city councilman berated Harris for their lifestyle, the philanthropist's response was forcible and pungent. "I hired Erik to run my foundation and he's doing a damn fine job. Robbie's dandy at PR. When I need a stud for breeding, I buy the best bull out there. For the foundation, I bought the best PR man available. I know the difference between the foundation and my ranch." The Webster clout made it clear that no hostility to its staff would be tolerated. That power and changing mores assured acceptance by Craddock society. Erik was highly respected for his accomplishments as was Robbie. But past success didn't matter to Blythe when she decided she wanted new ideas and younger leadership.

There were plenty of file photos taken over the years, individually and together, of Robbie Powell and Erik Judd: Robbie making a presentation at a Rotary luncheon, Erik shaking hands with a visiting congressman, Robbie handing out prizes at a livestock show, Erik in earnest conversation with Harris Webster. Robbie's young blond good looks had aged into well-preserved smoothness, hair always perfectly cut, face tanned, expensive clothes well fitted. Erik's dramatic personality might amuse some, but he always got the job done and he was known for kindness and thoughtfulness. He was also a scholar and in his free time wrote highly acclaimed essays on early Oklahoma history. Under his direction, Haklo had maintained a reputation as a conservative, well-run foundation, nothing flashy but year after year of steady growth.

Steve was thoughtful. Robbie and Erik were highly respected for their abilities. On a personal level, they were committed to each other. Until this past summer, they had very likely never imagined a cataclysmic change in their lives. Steve had seen too many men who had lost jobs in the last few years to dismiss the effect of that loss. He'd heard that Erik had withdrawn from many activities, presumably to concentrate on writing a history of Haklo. Was he depressed or was he genuinely enjoying time to be a scholar? How angry was Robbie at the injury to Erik? Erik was polished, civilized, erudite, and now diminished. Robbie was quick to react to slights and never missed an opportunity for a dig at the new director. Did the acts of vandalism cause more injury to Hollis or to Blythe?

Steve picked up the next dossier.

Peter Owens, director of publications, 38. BA, MA in media relations, University of Maryland. Wife, Denise. Owens and wife met in college, married shortly after graduation. He worked at publications in various cities, moving to accompany his wife, Denise, from one teaching post to another. She was named an assistant professor of English at Craddock College six years ago. He worked for a local horse publication and met Marian Grant when he wrote a series of articles about breeding seminars hosted by Haklo. He became director of Haklo publications three years ago. Owens and his wife have twin nine-year-old daughters who are stellar swimmers.

Steve had met both Owens and his wife. Peter was casual, understated. Denise was intense, vocal, and self-assured. There were two photos, the official photo online at the Haklo website and a picture at the college last spring with his wife and a visiting poet. The official photo was bland and unrevealing. At the university event, he stood with his hands in his trouser pockets, smiling pleasantly. He was perhaps six-two, shaggy dark hair, horn-rimmed glasses, relaxed demeanor. He stood a pace behind his petite, dark-haired wife, who was engaged in intense conversation with a heavyset, white-haired woman.

Abby Andrews was the last entry, but definitely not least, thanks to a file in her computer and a missing skateboard. However, this dossier contained very little information.

Abby Andrews, assistant curator, 23. BA in anthropology, University of Kansas. 3.7 grade point average. Active in her sorority and several campus activities, including yearbook staff and student council. Met Hollis Blair when he spoke to the anthropology club. Blair hired Abby to be his assistant in Kansas City one month later. He arrived in Craddock August 1. Abby came to Haklo August 15.

In Abby's Haklo staff photo, she stared gravely into the camera, her lovely features composed. She wore a string of pearls with a pale blue cashmere sweater. The *Clarion* always carried photos of new Haklo staff. Abby appeared very young with a smooth, unlined face.

Steve tapped impatient fingers on his desk. There was nothing odd or peculiar in her background. A nice recent college grad. Yet, an obscene letter was found in her computer and a skateboard went missing from the front porch of her cabin.

Steve's face crinkled. Why was she living in a Haklo cabin?

He speed-dialed Louise. "Just rounding up a few points. Tell me about the Haklo cabins. Their history and function."

Louise's tone was bland. "Harris thought it would be appropriate for visiting scholars and scientists to be able to stay on the foundation grounds. Eventually, it was decided the cabins would be ideal for summer interns." Full stop.

"And?" Steve prodded.

"The cabins have always been useful for guests."

"Abby Andrews isn't a guest."

"I think Hollis offered her a cabin since she is paying off student loans."

"Right. Thanks, Louise." He wasn't sure that the knowledge mattered, but it was one more out-of-the-ordinary fact about Abby Andrews. Except it wasn't out of the ordinary once her relationship with Hollis Blair was evident.

He felt great uncertainty about the importance of Abby Andrews. Surely the idea that she engineered the vandalism, which hurt Hollis, didn't make sense. But on another level, it made all kinds of sense in Katie Dugan's initial premise that the point of the vandalism was to make the theft of the necklace possible. Student debt was a crippling factor for a lot of college graduates, and a quarter-million-dollar necklace could pay off loans and then some.

As for the missing skateboard, it became important because of his whispered message. He'd based that message on Nela's insistence that there had been a skateboard on Marian's steps. How and when had Nela learned—or guessed—that Marian Grant stepped down on a skateboard and fell to her death? Nela said she could not tell him how she knew. He felt a ripple of uneasiness.

"Hey, buddy." He spoke aloud. "Don't get spooked." But his Irish grandmother would have looked at him and said softly, " 'There are more things in heaven and earth, Horatio, Than are dreamt of in your philosophy.' "

Maybe so, but he wanted to know the basis for Nela's claim. He didn't think Nela was protecting Chloe. Chloe might have known that Abby's skateboard was missing. However, it seemed unlikely that Chloe would link a missing skateboard to Marian's fall. Why would she? Was it possible that Chloe was suspicious about Marian's fall and for some reason saw Abby as a threat to Marian? It seemed very unlikely. But, as he had also learned long ago, if you want to know, ask.

He picked up his phone.

The office door opened. Her face impassive, Detective Dugan looked at Blythe. "Miss Webster, we can use your assistance."

The trustee's eyes widened. She gave a tiny sigh. Her demeanor was that of a woman whose fears have been confirmed. She pressed her lips together and moved purposefully into the office.

As Blythe stepped inside Abby's office, Dugan firmly closed the door after them.

Grace turned toward Abby. "What have you got in there?"

"I don't have anything—"

The door opened. Dugan walked out. "Miss Andrews, come this way."

Tears brimmed in Abby's violet eyes. She clung to Hollis's arm. "Why? I haven't done anything wrong."

"I have a few questions."

Hollis Blair stepped forward. He was combative. "Abby doesn't have to answer your questions."

Dugan nodded. Her voice was mild. "In the search of Miss Andrews's office, a diamond-and-gold necklace was discovered in a filing cabinet. Miss Webster has identified the necklace as the one taken from her desk. If Miss Andrews prefers, we can take her into custody for questioning in regard to grand theft." She turned to

Blythe. "Now my officers need to search the cabin where Miss Andrews resides. Do we have your permission to do so?"

"Yes." Blythe's voice was thin. She didn't look toward Abby. She turned to Louise. "Get a key. Take them there." Her words were clipped, brooked no disagreement. She didn't wait for an answer, but swung away, headed for her office.

Louise Spear stared after Blythe. Louise's face was pale and apprehensive. She was obviously upset. But she had her orders and she had taken orders for many years.

Dugan nodded at Sergeant Fisher and the plump woman officer. "You know what to look for. Call me if anything is found."

The police officers followed Louise into her office.

Abby took a step toward Dugan. "I didn't steal that awful necklace. Someone put it in the cabinet." She looked at Hollis in appeal. "I didn't take it."

Hollis Blair was grim. "Of course you didn't take it. I'll get a lawyer for you."

"I shouldn't need a lawyer." Abby's thin face, twisted in despair, was no longer pretty, but desperate and frightened. "It's all a lie."

Dugan was brisk. "We will take your statement at the station. If you wish to have counsel present, that is your prerogative. We'll go out the front entrance. This way." She gestured toward the main hallway.

Abby shot a panicked look at Hollis.

He gave her a reassuring nod.

Dugan and Abby walked together toward the main hall, Hollis a step behind. Dugan was purposeful, striding fast. Abby's shoulders hunched as she hurried to keep pace.

Grace looked puzzled. Her expression was distant, as if her thoughts were far away and not pleasant. She moved swiftly toward the main hall. Peter Owens glanced toward Louise's office. "I guess the show's over for now." He moved toward the rear stairs.

Cole Hamilton spoke in a soft aside to Robbie. "All these new people were a mistake. I told Marian it didn't look right for a man to bring a pretty girl in as soon as he gets a new job. It wasn't like there wasn't a pretty young thing in the office. Why, Anne Nesbitt was pretty enough to please anyone. He noticed her. What man wouldn't? But a nice girl. Now I wonder if Abby set her car on fire so there wouldn't be another young girl around."

He intended his comment for Robbie, but Nela was near enough to overhear.

Robbie's eyes gleamed in his old-young, pleased face. "A lust for diamonds. They say some women can't resist them. But vandalism to serve as a smoke screen was clever. I wouldn't have thought Abby was that clever."

Francis Garth's heavy voice was stolid. "She's nice. Pleasant. Pretty if you like them young and callow. But not clever. She doesn't have the nerve to be a vandal—or a murderer."

Francis's words thrummed in Nela's mind as she returned to Chloe's office, sank into the chair behind the desk. She agreed with Francis. And that put the question squarely to her. What was she going to do now?

From down the hall, Grace's strident voice carried clearly. "What's the deal? You gave the cops carte blanche to search. First Abby's office, now the cabin. How'd you know—" A faraway door slam cut off Grace's voice in midsentence. Nela wondered how forthcoming Blythe would be with her sister.

Nela knew the answer to Grace's question. Someone had placed a letter on Blythe's desk. Obviously, the message suggested a search of Abby's office for the missing necklace.

But Nela knew more than Blythe or any of the others. Nela had put the necklace on Blythe's desk Monday night. Some time after Nela's foray into the building Monday night, the necklace was removed. Today an anonymous letter on Blythe's desk indicated the necklace could be found in Abby's office.

The sound of voices and footsteps faded in the hallway. Finally, there was silence. Abby Andrews was in a police cruiser, on her way to the police station.

Nela retrieved her purse. She slipped the strap over one shoulder. She walked down the hall to the staff exit, car keys in one hand, cell phone in the other.

—15—

The connection was surprisingly clear. ". . . don't know if you remember me, Chloe. This is Steve Flynn for the *Clarion*."

Chloe's husky voice burbled with delight. "How sweet! I love the *Clarion*. You know that feature you do every Sunday, the Craddock Connection? That's the nicest thing, stories about everyday people like firemen and teachers and bricklayers. I loved the one about the lady at the nursing home who was turning a hundred and nobody knew she'd been a nurse on Corregidor during WWII. It just makes you think," Chloe Farley said solemnly. A pause and she rushed ahead, "I'm from LA and you can live in an apartment house and never know anybody. Nela always told me everybody has a story. Instead, most newspapers just write about politics. Of course, Craddock has a few drawbacks. I get tired of roosters crowing. I never heard a rooster 'til I came to Craddock but there's one in the field next to Leland's trailer. I'll bet you want to do a story about Leland

and me and our trip. Oh, you can't believe the water here in Tahiti. It's like looking through blue glass and the shells—"

Steve tried to divert the flood. "When you get back, we'll do a big story. Right now I want to ask about Marian Grant's fall down her apartment steps."

"Marian's fall?" There was no hint of uneasiness or wariness in Chloe's froggy tone. "That came as such a surprise. Why, she was so graceful—"

Nela turned the heater up full blast, but the VW was icy cold. Yet there was a deeper chill in her thoughts as she called the *Clarion*, gave Steve's extension number. Once she spoke, there was no turning back. She wasn't surprised when the message came on: *I am either away from my desk or engaged in another call . . .*

She waited until the ping. "Steve, it's Nela." She was brisk. "Blythe got an anonymous letter this morning, saying the necklace was hidden in Abby's office. Blythe called the police and they found the necklace in a filing cabinet. Dugan's taken Abby to the police station. I'm on my way there now. I'll tell Dugan how I found the necklace in Marian's purse and that I brought the necklace to Haklo Monday night and left it on Blythe's desk. I won't mention you." She clicked off the phone, put the VW in gear.

Steve ignored the call-waiting beep.

". . . hard to imagine Marian falling. She had an air, you know. Why, it would be easier to imagine Tallulah Bankhead in a pinafore." A throaty gurgle. "My gram thought Tallulah Bankhead was hilarious. Gram loved to quote her and Bette Davis. People would be surprised if they knew how women told it how they saw it even then." It was as if she spoke of a time far distant. "Of course, Marian never talked like that. Marian was serious." Chloe drawled the word. "But that's all right." Her husky voice was generous. "Marian was *somebody*. You knew that the minute you met her. I even had that feeling staying in her apartment. And Jugs is a sweetheart, which shows she had a soft side. If you need a quote, I'd call Louise Spear or Cole Hamilton. They'd known her forever. Anyway, got to go, the catamaran's ready . . ."

Steve replaced the phone. If there was any guile involved in Chloe Farley's discursiveness, he'd find a pinafore to wear. So how and where did Nela come up with a skateboard on Marian's steps? He didn't want to ask her again. Her refusal to explain had been definite. Why?

He tussled with the question as he punched listen to retrieve the message from the call he'd missed.

Y ou can sit there." The policeman—or maybe he was a detective because he didn't wear a uniform—slouched to a seat on the other side of a utilitarian metal desk. There were nine or ten similar desks across the room, some with occupants, most empty.

Nela remained standing. "I'm sorry." She was polite but firm. "I have to talk to Detective Dugan."

"She's busy. I'll take down the information. I'm Detective Morrison." He gave her a swift, admiring glance, then his narrow face smoothed into polite expectation. "Whatever it is, I can handle it."

A door rattled open behind her. Quick steps thudded on the wooden floor.

Morrison looked past her. "Yo, Steve. Haven't seen you move this fast since they handed out free gumdrops at the county extension office."

"Mokie." But Steve's voice was abstracted and he was looking at Nela.

She half turned to see the now familiar freckled face and bright blue eyes.

He stopped beside her. "I came as soon as I got your message."

She was glad and sad. Glad to know he would be with her. Sad to know she was going to cause him trouble. "You don't have to stay. You don't have anything to do with any of it." The words were quick.

He gave her a swift, lopsided grin. "I signed on Monday night. I did what I did—and I'm damn glad I did. But you're right. Katie has to know."

Mokie Morrison was looking from one to the other, his brown eyes curious and intent. "Sounds like an episode in a soap. Not that I watch soaps." The disclaimer was hasty. "My ex loved *As the World Turns*, still in mourning for it."

"I can't get in to see her." Nela's voice was anxious.

Steve turned to Mokie. "Tell Katie we've got stuff she needs to know now."

The office was small. Thin winter sunlight slanted through open blinds. Katie Dugan's sturdy frame was replicated by the shadow that fell across the legal pad and folders open on her desk. The office was impersonal, no mementos on the desktop, a map of Craddock on one wall, a map of Oklahoma and a bulletin board with wanted circulars, notes, and department directives on the other. Two metal filing cases. The detective's face was impassive as she listened and took notes.

There was tight silence when they finished.

Nela was intensely aware of Steve's nearness. They sat side by side, separated by only a few inches, on worn wooden chairs that faced Dugan's desk.

Dugan's cool gaze settled on Steve. "Why should I believe you"— a flicker toward Nela—"or her?"

Steve was affable. "How does it help either one of us to lie?" He retrieved his cell phone, touched, pushed it across Dugan's desk. "Note the date and time. Ditto the next pic. Maybe enhanced details will prove one was taken at the Haklo staff entrance, the other in Blythe Webster's office. Nela was your main suspect until the necklace was found in Abby's office. If Nela had kept quiet, she and her sister would be off your radar. Right?"

There was a touch of frost in Dugan's voice. "I'm not smart enough to see the possibility Abby Andrews was picked to be a fall guy?"

Nela felt a sickening swoop of disappointment even though she'd expected Dugan to be hostile.

Steve's face looked suddenly tough. "You know me better than that. I know you look at everything. Always. We're trying to help, Katie. Give us a chance."

"Maybe it would have been a help if you people had told me the truth from the start." Dugan's broad face was equally tough. "I got news for you, and not the kind to put in the *Clarion*. Everybody's on my radar. Including your girlfriend." Her cold gaze moved to Nela. "Maybe you found the necklace in the purse. Or maybe your sister asked you to take care of it, but you got cold feet. Maybe—"

Her phone rang. She glanced at caller ID, picked up the receiver. "Dugan . . . So anybody who took a close look would find it?" She raised a dark eyebrow, looked sardonic. "Yeah. Check for prints. Want to bet nothing doing except for the owner's? Test for a match on the stair rail. Right. Thanks." She replaced the receiver. She turned to Nela, went back to her attack. "Or maybe you decided the necklace was too damn hot to keep. I learned a long time ago that a pretty face doesn't mean squat. You could be lying your head off. Or you could be telling the truth down the line. If you are, then something strange is going on out at Haklo and that necklace is at the heart of it. If you left the necklace on Blythe Webster's desk, the water gets muddy. We found the necklace in a filing cabinet in Abby Andrews's office. The tip came in an anonymous note left on Blythe Webster's desk. Traffic has been pretty busy in and out of her office, apparently. The upshot? Anybody could be the perp." She looked steadily at Nela. "Including you."

But Nela was thinking. Paint flecks . . . "They found the skateboard, didn't they? You told Louise to take the officers to Abby's cabin and they found the skateboard there."

Dugan stiffened, like a hunter on point. "Lady, you seem to know everything. You know too much."

"You said to check for a match on the stair rail. What else could it be but the skateboard?" Nela tried to speak naturally, as if she didn't see Jugs's glowing eyes. "I read in the *Clarion* that there was a call claiming there was a skateboard on Marian Grant's stairs. Abby claimed someone took her skateboard. Now it's back. Doesn't it figure after the necklace was planted in Abby's office that the skateboard would be back?"

"Next thing I know"—Dugan's voice was sardonic—"you'll be filling out an application to be a cop. Thanks, but I can figure out what may or may not have happened. If you're telling the truth, I appreciate the fact that you came forward. If you're lying to me, I won't be fooled. Now"—and she looked from Nela to Steve and back again—"nothing said in this room is to be repeated, revealed, discussed—or printed. Go out the back way. I don't want anybody seeing you two leaving here. If either one of you gets loose lips, you'll be my guest at the county jail." She stared hard at Nela. "Ask Steve about the county jail. It makes the city jail seem like a resort."

T hey stood in an alleyway behind city hall, a few feet from a row of trash cans.

Nela hugged Chloe's coat tight, warding off not only the cold but the chill of fear. "Somebody put that necklace in Abby's office and the skateboard at her cabin. It has to be the killer. How else could the skateboard show up again? It's diabolical. Abby said the skateboard was missing and now they've found it in her cabin. You heard what Dugan said. It was some place where it wasn't hard to find."

Steve looked thoughtful. "Maybe the murderer got a little too cute. Katie will give a fish eye at how nice and easy the evidence is falling in her lap. But she won't cross Abby off her list. There's been a lot at this point, the obscene letter file in her computer, the necklace, the skateboard." He hunched his shoulders against a cold gust.

The wind was frosty on Nela's face, tugged at Chloe's big coat. "Your ears are red from the cold. You need a coat."

He grinned. "Last I heard they didn't have an ear coat in my size."

Nela laughed and felt a surge of gratitude. Steve had made her laugh when she was half scared, half mad. But the laugh died away. She reached out, gripped his arm. "I'm sorry about everything, Steve. Katie Dugan was your friend. Now she doesn't trust you."

"Katie's got a big bark. She'll figure things out. But we have to play it her way. You'd better get back to Haklo. I'll drop by the station later in the day, see what the official line is. I'll be over to see you tonight." It was a statement. He paused. "Okay?" The tone was light, but his eyes were serious.

"If you were smart"—her voice caught in her throat—"you'd stay away from me."

"Not," he said quietly, "in this lifetime." He reached out, gently framed her shoulders with big strong hands, turned her around. "Walk straight and you come out on Alcott. You can take it to Main."

She walked away without looking back, still feeling the strength of his grip on her shoulders, and knew he stood, red hair stirred by the wind, ears red with cold, hands jammed in his pockets, and watched until she reached the end of the alley.

Nela put the McDonald's sack with a cheeseburger and fries on Chloe's desk. She glanced at the clock. It was a few minutes after one. She stepped to the connecting door to Louise's office, ready to apologize for her lateness.

Louise sat at her desk, but she wasn't working. She stared out the window, her pale face lined and unhappy, unaware of Nela's presence. Indeed, she seemed to be very far away, sunk in a somber reverie. One hand fingered the collar of her pink blouse. The pink added a note of cheer to her gray jacket and skirt.

Nela said quietly, "Excuse me, Louise. I'm sorry I'm late getting back from lunch." She could eat while she worked if Louise had some tasks for her.

"It doesn't matter. I won't need you now. I'm"—she appeared to make an effort to be matter-of-fact—"going to look over some materials this afternoon. I'll need to concentrate. Please shut the door."

Nela was dismissed. She nodded and closed the door. She settled at Chloe's desk, ate without tasting the food.

Her phone buzzed. "Nela Farley."

Rosalind McNeill's words tumbled. "Everything's off schedule." Her voice dropped to a conspiratorial whisper. "After somebody dropped that anonymous letter on the T's desk, she quizzed me like she was a private eye. But she didn't waste any time calling the cops. First thing I know, they're trooping in the front door and the T's waiting for them like she's a commissar. When they found the necklace in Abby's office, I thought I was in a Brad Pitt movie. You know how the cops whisked Abby off in a cruiser? I thought they'd lock her up and throw away the key. Not so. Abby and Hollis just got back. They came in the front door, which is crazy, too, but everything's jigsaw today. Maybe if the cops take you away, the cops bring you back. I'll bet the director was right behind them in his snazzy Cadillac sports car. The T bought the Caddy for him, said it was more appropriate than the old Ford he used to drive. Anyway, they came in the front, Hollis looking like Sir Galahad and Abby clinging to his arm, pretty much in a Victorian swoon. She hung back, kept saying she couldn't bear to be here, and he was all manly and stiff upper lip that she was innocent and the innocent don't have anything to fear. So she sucked it up and they went down the hall and she turned to go to her office—"

Nela heard steps in the hall and looked up in time to see Abby Andrews walk past. Abby stared straight ahead. Porcelain-perfect face pale, shoulders tight, she looked young, vulnerable, and scared.

"—and Hollis marched into the T's office and closed the door. A closed door at Haklo means something pretty stiff. Anyway, I guess we have to keep on keepin' on. Neither hail nor sleet nor cops nor damsel in distress can stay the appointed rounds, so if you've got a minute you might drop around and get the mail. I've got everything sorted."

Nela hadn't given the morning mail delivery a thought after Blythe summoned her. "I'm sorry. I'll be right there."

The long blue plastic tray, almost three-fourths full of envelopes, rested on top of the horseshoe-shaped reception counter. Rosalind looked up with a smile and bounced to her feet, her brown eyes excited. The soft splash of water in the tiled fountain between the reception desk and the French windows to the courtyard was cheerful, a restful counterpoint to Rosalind's vitality. Before Nela could pick up the tray, Rosalind leaned on the counter, looking eager. "Did Louise fill you in on the cabin?"

"The cabin?" Everyone standing in the hallway outside Abby's office this morning heard Dugan ask for permission to search Abby's cabin, but Nela maintained a look of polite inquiry. "She didn't say anything about it."

"Well"—Rosalind looked around to be sure no one was near—"when the officers came through here, one of them—the tall, skinny one—was carrying something in a big billowy plastic sleeve and I'll bet I know what it was." She looked triumphant. She didn't wait for Nela's response. "Abby's skateboard was supposed to be missing. Well, they found it—I guess in her cabin—and I'd like to know the story behind that."

"Someone could have taken the skateboard and put it back."

Rosalind squeezed her face in thought. "Someone else here at Haklo?"

"Who wrote the anonymous letter? You can bet it wasn't Abby."

Rosalind's eyes were huge. She looked uneasy. "I guess somebody doesn't like Abby very much."

* * *

As Nela walked down the hall, the plastic tray balanced on one hip, she wondered, was there bitter enmity toward Abby? There had certainly been an effort to focus blame on her, the file in her computer, the use of her brother's skateboard to commit murder, the discovery of the necklace in her office, the reappearance of the missing skateboard. Was Abby a target simply because she made a good scapegoat? Or was she a vandal, thief, and murderer? Did she really care for Hollis Blair or was she willing to see his career jeopardized so that she could steal a quarter-million-dollar necklace? However, there was the clear fact that Abby's latest problems had been caused by an anonymous letter. Did Abby have a gambler's instinct and the guts to do a double bluff, write a note that accused her, then use the fact of the note to assert innocence? Had she decided the necklace was too dangerous to keep and well worth sacrificing to escape an accusation of murder?

Nela pictured the strained face of the girl walking toward her office. Abby had been oblivious to Nela sitting at Chloe's desk so Abby's expression wasn't formed with the expectation of presenting an air of innocence. But she had good reason to be fearful, whether innocent or guilty.

Nela stopped at Blythe's closed door. She knocked, then turned the knob. She felt an instant of déjà vu. Monday morning she'd stepped inside with the mail, interrupting a tense conversation between the trustee and the director. This afternoon, she walked in on the two of them again.

There was a decided difference today. Blythe was nodding, her expression reassuring. Hollis had the air of a man unexpectedly encountering good fortune. His bony, appealing face was grateful.

". . . appreciate your understanding. Like I told Abby, we'll get to the bottom of everything."

"Excuse me, may I leave the mail?" Nela hesitated in the doorway.

Blythe nodded and waved at the in-box. A ruby ring flashed as red as her crimson suit.

Hollis unfolded from the chair. Despite his lanky height, he looked very young as he gazed down at Blythe. "I'll tell Abby. I told her to rest for a while, then go up to the lab. She'll feel better if she keeps busy, and there are a bunch of donations to catalog. Knowing you're behind her will be a huge relief."

"Hollis, I think you may be right that Abby is innocent." Blythe was thoughtful. "Things certainly look black against her but it's silly to think she'd hide the necklace, then put a note on my desk saying the necklace was hidden in her office. And if she did hide the necklace, who could possibly have known about it?"

Just for an instant, his jaw was rigid. "The whole idea that she'd do anything dishonest is outrageous. As for the police, I think even that hard-faced woman detective is having second thoughts. We were waiting for her. Then, when she came in, she hadn't really started when someone buzzed her and she left. When she came back, she didn't say a word about Abby being a person of interest or give a warning. If she had, I would have said nothing doing 'til we got a lawyer. I still think maybe I should see about a lawyer. Instead, she said she just had a few factual questions. I thought"— he was earnest—"that it was all right for Abby to answer those. Dugan asked a few questions, then said we could go." He was like a man who receives an unexpected bonus check in the mail and wonders if it's for real. "I know you expected the worst." His lop-sided smile was rueful. "I wish you could have seen your face when I walked in and said we were back. You looked like you'd seen a ghost. So, now we have to hope the cops turn up the truth." He turned away from the desk and moved past Nela with a brief nod.

Blythe's smile faded as he stepped into the hall. She looked tired and grim.

Nela placed a half-dozen letters and several mailers in the upper box, but she didn't turn away. "Miss Webster, may I speak to you?"

Blythe looked at Nela in surprise. Until this moment, Nela knew her presence had scarcely registered with the trustee. Nela might have been a robot carrying out assigned duties. "Yes?" Her response was clipped. Clearly she was impatient, in no mood to waste time with Nela.

Nela knew she was taking a gamble, but as Gram always pointed out, "Sure, the answer can be no, but it will never be yes if you don't ask." Nela was glad she'd chosen her best blouse and the skirt that swirled as she walked. If nothing else, she felt more confident and professional. She placed the tray on the corner of Blythe's desk, noted the slight thinning of the trustee's lips. She also shed, just a little, the deference of a minimum wage employee. "Miss Webster, I was between assignments at home and I was glad to be able to come to Craddock and take Chloe's place while she's gone. I'm an investigative reporter—"

There was a flare of alarm in Blythe's eyes. Certainly Nela now had her full attention.

"—which makes me skilled at asking questions and discovering facts. I can help you protect the foundation."

Blythe frowned, her thin dark brows drawn down. Her brown eyes had a hard stare. "How?" The demand was sharp. "There have been too many stories already. I'm sick of stories about Haklo." There was a distinct chill in her tone.

Nela realized Blythe thought Nela was threatening to write an exposé revealing that only a member of the Haklo staff could have committed some, if not all, the acts of vandalism, including the destruction in Marian Grant's office.

"I'm not talking about writing a story. Here's what we"—she placed a slight emphasis on the noun—"can do."

As Blythe listened, her rigid body relaxed and she no longer looked wary.

Steve Flynn's freckled face was thoughtful. As far as Katie Dugan was concerned, he and Nela hadn't been in her office, certainly had not heard her conversation with the officers searching Abby's cabin. But she'd tipped her hand when she'd dryly commented that there likely wouldn't be any prints but to check with the paint flecks on the stair rail. Nela had instantly made the connection. Katie had neither confirmed nor denied Nela's guess that the missing skateboard had been found. To get the quotes he wanted from Katie for a story, he had to have some outside ammunition.

Steve punched his speakerphone.

"Hey, Steve. How's everything?" Robbie Powell's voice was smooth and bland.

"Doing a roundup on the latest at Haklo." Steve was equally smooth. "What's the statement about this morning?"

Robbie was too much of a pro to stammer and stutter. Instead, he was silent for an appreciable moment. Finally, he cleared his throat. "Haklo Trustee Blythe Webster this morning received an anonymous letter suggesting that her missing necklace was hidden in a staff office. Police were summoned. The necklace was found and is currently being held by police as evidence."

"Whose office?"

"That information has not been released."

"And the further search?" Robbie might assume Steve's information came from the police. But if the point ever arose, Steve certainly hadn't made that claim.

Robbie didn't question the fact that Steve knew about the second
search. "I have not spoken with a police officer. Haklo Foundation
remains confident that the police investigation will be successful."
A pause. "If you have further questions, please contact Detective
Dugan." The connection ended.

The delivery of mail afforded Nela quick glimpses of staff members, to whom, after a perfunctory nod, she became invisible,
cloaked in the comfortable anonymity of a cog in the well-oiled Haklo
machine.

Louise Spear, sunk in apathy, held a folder at which she gazed
with empty eyes. The brightness of the Baranovs' print seemed
almost shocking in contrast to the paleness of her face.

Abby Andrews hunched at a desk covered with a welter of papers
in her small, spare, utilitarian office. Her young face was pale, her
eyes red-rimmed.

In the east hallway, Hollis Blair's office was not as large as either
Blythe Webster's or Marian Grant's, but still imposing, with red vel-
vet drapes, oak-paneled walls, a broad oak desk, a sofa and several
easy chairs grouped on either side of a shiny aluminum coffee table.
Filled bookcases lined one wall. Seated at his desk, he spoke into
the speakerphone, his face grim. "I don't want a criminal lawyer.
That looks bad, like she might be guilty. You've represented the
foundation for years—"

A woman's brisk voice interrupted. "As you've explained the

circumstances, it wouldn't be appropriate for me to represent her. Of the names I suggested, Perry Womack is one of the best. And he's welcome"—the tone was wry—"in polite society. Now if you'll excuse me, I have another call waiting."

The remaining staff offices were on the second floor. Grace Webster occupied the corner front office to the west, directly above her sister's office. The difference in decor was interesting. Blond Danish modern furniture, jagged slaps of oil on unframed canvases, swirls of orange, black, crimson. A sculpture of partially crushed Coke cans, coils of rusted barbed wire, and withered sunflower stalks stood stark and—to Nela—ugly in the center of the room. A casually dressed Grace lounged on an oversize puffy pink sofa, eyes half closed as she held her cell to one ear. ". . . missed you too. Two weeks is too long. Way too long . . ."

The large second-floor east office, the same size as Marian Grant's on the first floor, had a shabby, lived-in, fusty, musty air with stacks of books, framed photographs tucked on curio stands. The desk held more pictures, but no computer monitor. There was an aura of yesterday, pictures of a young, vigorous Webster Harris and an eager Cole Hamilton with a bush of curly brown hair. There was no evidence of work in progress. He looked up from a worn book with a frayed cover, then his eyes dropped back to the page.

Robbie Powell's office was light and airy with calico plaid drapes that matched the sofa, splashes of color in photographs of outdoor scenes, and a sleek modern desk with three computers. He reclined in a blue leather swivel chair. His smooth voice was as schmoozy as a maître d' escorting high rollers to their usual table. ". . . hope you and Lorraine will mark the donor dinner on your calendars if you're not in Nice or Sydney. We'll definitely have lamb fries in honor of the Lazy Q. You know—"

The interruption over the speakerphone was brusque. "What's this I hear about somebody pushing Marian down some damned stairs?"

Robbie's face tightened, but his tone remained soft as butter. "Now, Buck, you know gossip runs wild sometimes. That's absolutely false. Now the dinner—"

"The dinner be damned. There's no getting around the fact that a bunch of strange things have been happening out at Haklo, and I don't give money if it's going to be wasted cleaning up after vandals. Or, for God's sake, killers."

Francis Garth barely glanced up from the keyboard as Nela deposited the incoming mail. His massive hands dwarfed the keys. His heavy face was somber beneath the thatch of thick brown hair. He looked like a man thinking hard and darkly. His office was bare bones, uncarpeted floor, obviously worn wooden desk, wooden filing cabinets. The only decoration was a representation of the Seal of the Osage Nation depicting a blue arrowhead against a brilliant circle of yellow. A peace pipe crossed an eagle feather in the center of the arrowhead.

Pride of place in Peter Owens's office was a low broad wooden coffee table covered with brochures, flyers, and pamphlets. Deeply absorbed with a sketch pad and a stack of photographs, he scarcely noticed the arrival of the mail. Working, he had an air of contentment, a man enjoying thinking and planning.

As Nela hurried down the stairs to the rotunda, carrying the empty tray, she hoped that she would be smart and lucky. At some time between the disappearance of the necklace and Marian Grant's fall, Marian had gained knowledge of the whereabouts of the necklace and the identity of the thief. When had she found the necklace? Surely there had been some act, some word by Marian that revealed how or when she came into possession of the stolen necklace.

Thanks to Blythe Webster, Nela could now ask questions as she wished. Nela accepted the fact that no matter how carefully she phrased her questions, she might alert a murderer. One of the persons with a key to Haklo hid ruthlessness and danger beneath a facade of civility. Nela understood the risk, but she had a chance to make a difference and she was going to take it.

She hurried across the rotunda to the reception desk. There was no better place to start than with Rosalind McNeill, who saw staff members come and go as they moved about the foundation.

At the slap of the tray on the counter, Rosalind whirled around on her desk chair. Her eyes lighted and she popped to her feet. "I saw you go in the T's office and Hollis come out. He looked like a man who just got sprung from death row. Is Abby in the clear? I figure since she and Hollis came back, the cops must have learned something to clear her. What's going on?"

"The investigation is continuing, but the detective is looking at everyone at Haklo, not just Abby." Nela thought it might cheer Abby if that word trickled back to her. "I talked to Blythe Webster and offered to help since I have a background in investigative reporting. She agreed that it would be a good thing for me to gather information from staff members." Speaking with Rosalind was the next best thing to putting up a public placard. How better to establish herself as the new eyes and ears of Haklo?

Rosalind's eyes widened. "That's cool. Gee, I wish I could perch on your shoulder." Her gaze was admiring.

"Miss Webster authorized me to speak to everyone on her behalf. Rosalind, I want you to think back to Marian Grant's last week here. Start with Thursday . . ." The day the theft of the necklace was discovered.

—16—

M okie Morrison brushed back his one strand of black hair, slanted his eyes toward Dugan's closed door. "I've seen feral hogs in a better mood."

Steve grinned. "When was the last time you were in the woods?"

"Boy Scouts. I went on a campout. Once and done. We met up with two copperheads, a cave with bats, and a feral hog. I haven't been outside the city limits since. But today"—and he was almost not kidding—"I'd pick the snakes, bats, and hog over Katie."

"Yeah. Well, I got a deadline." He gave Mokie a mock salute. His smile slid away as he knocked lightly on Katie's door, turned the knob.

She looked up from the papers spread on the desktop. "Yeah?" Her broad face was as inviting as a slab of granite.

"*Clarion*," he said gently, making his visit official. He stepped inside, closed the door, pulled folded paper from his pocket, turned it lengthwise. He already had a soft-leaded pencil in his other hand. Without an invitation, he dropped into the wooden chair. "I talked to Robbie Powell out at Haklo. He said Blythe Webster received an anonymous letter saying the stolen necklace was hidden in a staff member's office. Robbie said to check with you about the necklace and the second search."

Katie briefly compressed her lips, obviously not pleased by Steve's questions. "The necklace was found." Full stop.

"Where?"

The reply was grudging. "In a filing cabinet. Miss Webster identified the necklace, which is now in police custody."

Steve's glance was chiding. "Where was the filing cabinet located?"

"The discovery was prompted by an anonymous letter. At present, there is no proof that the occupant of the office knew of the presence of the stolen property. Therefore, the identity of the office occupant is not necessarily relevant."

"What prompted a search elsewhere on the grounds?"

"Information received in the anonymous letter."

"Where did the search take place?"

"No comment."

"Was anything found that appears to be linked to Marian Grant's fall?"

Her eyes narrowed. She knew he knew about the skateboard. "No comment."

"Is there a person of interest?"

Katie shook her head. "Not at this time."

Steve felt like high-fiving Katie. She hadn't succumbed to the lure of evidence against Abby that had been so nicely and neatly wrapped up and delivered to her. "How did the anonymous letter arrive?"

"That has not been determined."

"Did the letter come through the mail?"

"No."

"Did the contents or envelope contain fingerprints?"

"The only fingerprints belonged to Miss Webster, who opened the envelope and read the letter. She immediately notified police."

"Was the letter handwritten?"

"No."

"Was the message printed?" Should there be another search of files in Haklo computers?

"No."

Steve figured that out in a flash. Words, maybe even pictures, pasted on a blank sheet. That took time. Last night or this morning, someone from Haklo had worn gloves, patiently clipped needed words from newspapers or magazines.

"Did you send somebody through the wastebaskets out at Haklo?"

"You're quick." That's all she said.

"Katie"—Steve's voice was quiet—"you want to figure out what happened out there and whether somebody killed Marian Grant. I do, too. I want to clear up the mess. I don't want Nela Farley hurt."

Katie's eyes narrowed. "But you just met the woman. What's with the white knight to the rescue?"

Steve looked at Katie. They'd known each other for a long time. They had a careful relationship because he was a reporter and she was a cop. But they were—deep down, where it counted—friends. "You know how it works, Katie. You look at someone. Your eyes meet and there's more there than you can ever explain or describe. You and Mark. Me and Nela. Maybe everything will be good for us. Maybe not. But for now, it's me and Nela. I think she's honest. I want to help her. The best way to help is to figure out what the hell happened at Haklo. Can you and I talk it out for a minute?" He put down the sheet with notes on her desk, placed the pencil beside the paper. "Off the record."

Marian had an air. Everybody always kept on their toes around her. She was her usual self that week except"—a little frown creased Rosalind's round face—"she was really mad about the necklace. The necklace disappearing upset her even more than the vandalism. That was Thursday. Friday morning she looked distracted, as if she was thinking hard. But she looked really upset again Friday afternoon."

"Friday afternoon?" Nela prompted.

Rosalind gestured toward the French windows to the courtyard. "It's been cold since you came to town, but that week—Marian's last week—we had a couple of beautiful days. It was in the sixties that Friday. Marian loved the courtyard. Sometimes she'd take a cup of coffee and go out and sit in the sun with a book of poetry. She said poetry helped her think better. Oh, golly." Rosalind's eyes widened. "She was reading *Spoon River Anthology*. She didn't know she was going to have her own epitaph the next week." Rosalind's voice was a little shaky. She paused for an instant, then continued, talking fast, "I was on the phone with a teacher calling about a school tour group. I looked up as Marian came inside. She looked odd. I worried maybe she didn't feel well. Of course, it may just have been being out in the courtyard and seeing the fountain still messed up. Like I said, the vandalism really made her mad. But she had a weird look when she came in. She walked past me and turned to her right. She was heading for the west wing. I didn't see her again."

* * *

Hollis Blair's face crinkled in thought. He looked bemused, interested, finally eager. "Blythe's got a good idea. And she's smart to send you around to ask. You know, she's a nice person but even people who have known her for years find her a little daunting. She's been swell to me. And like she said to me, just because the necklace was in Abby's office, it doesn't mean Abby had anything to do with any of it. I know that Blythe had to call the police when she got that letter."

He gave Nela an appealing smile and his eyes were warm and appreciative. His lopsided grin had aw shucks charm. He was a big, handsome, rawboned guy. Consciously or unconsciously, he made any woman aware that she was a woman. Nela suspected he had been charming women since the day he went to kindergarten and he had probably discovered that intense looks and an air of total focus paid huge dividends.

"At least Blythe hasn't blamed me for everything that's happened." His relief was obvious, then he looked discouraged. "Everything started so well here at Haklo, then things began to fall apart. But let me think about that last Friday." His brows drew down. He shook his head. "I talked to Marian that morning. She was quite pleasant. I didn't see her that afternoon. But I can tell you one thing." He was forceful. "The idea that Abby would hurt anyone is crazy. Absolutely crazy. As for that damned necklace, somebody put it in her desk."

"Why?"

Hollis stared at her. "How would I know? To get rid of it? Abby spends a lot of time up in the artifact room. Her office is often empty. Just like those letters. It was easy to use her computer."

"You don't think someone chose Abby's desk for a particular reason?"

"I don't know why anyone would be ugly to Abby." But there was an uneasy look in his eyes.

Louise Spear's eyes widened in surprise. "Blythe said you could ask questions?"

Nela stood a few feet from Louise's desk. "When I explained my background, she agreed that I might be able to find out something useful about Marian's last week. The police now know that Marian had possession of the necklace when she died. The police believe she threatened the thief and that's why she was killed." As she spoke, she sensed the same change in perception that she'd felt in Blythe's office. To Louise, Nela was no longer simply a pleasant replacement for a flighty young assistant. It was a reminder of how easily people made assumptions about worth based on a level of employment. Nela hoped that she'd never simply relegate people to the guy who parks the car or the girl who does nails or the frail inhabitant of a nursing home. It didn't matter what people did or where they came from or their accent. Either everyone was important or no one was important. Steve would agree. The quick thought surprised her, pleased her.

"That's the week the necklace disappeared." Louise looked sick. "And then Marian died. That awful necklace."

"Do you have any idea when she might have discovered the thief?"

Louise slowly shook her head. "She was upset when the necklace was stolen. But Friday morning, she seemed more her usual self. She was busy making plans for the donor dinner. That was very special to her. She was looking ahead . . ." Louise shivered. Her face drooped with sadness.

Nela knew every word was painful for Louise. She hated to make her remember, but Marian was dead and beyond help, Abby was alive and needed help, and she and Chloe were still on the cold-eyed detective's list. "Did you see her Friday afternoon?"

Louise sighed. "The last time I saw Marian was Friday morning. She was cheerful, making lists, thinking of a speaker. She loved planning the dinner. Tables are set up in the rotunda. She always had the portrait of Webster that hangs in her office placed on an easel between the twin stairways. She never said so, but I think to her it was as if he were there. She always opened the evening with a recording from one of his last speeches. It's a very big event. It won't be the same without Marian."

Louise's description of Marian's last week tallied with Rosalind's. Nela felt convinced that she was on the right track. Marian had been upset by the theft of the necklace, but the next day she was her usual, competent, businesslike self until that afternoon. Nela knew without question that Marian had been in possession of the stolen necklace when she died. Had she found the necklace Friday afternoon?

Louise fingered the ruffled collar of her pink blouse. "What did Blythe say about Abby?"

"We didn't talk about her. I think Blythe agreed that it was important to try and discover how Marian knew who took the necklace."

"The necklace . . . I've tried and tried to understand." Louise's expression was drawn and weary. "Sometimes things aren't what they seem and it's easy"—her voice dragged—"to think you know something. But we can't get around the fact that the necklace was found in Abby's office. Abby either hid it there or someone put it there to get her in trouble." She looked away from Nela, her face tight. "She shouldn't have been there. But I saw her . . ." She sat up straighter, looked at Nela with a suddenly focused gaze. "It's good that Blythe asked you to help. That makes me feel much better. Maybe things will get sorted out after all."

Nela looked at her sharply. "Who did you see? Who shouldn't have been where?"

Louise looked uncomfortable. "That doesn't matter. It's easy to be wrong about things, isn't it? Besides, having you talk to everyone makes everything better. I'm not as worried now." She reached for the phone. "I must make some calls about the dinner."

Nela had been dismissed. She stood in the hall for a moment, heard Louise's voice. "Father Edmonds, I was wondering if you would do the invocation . . ."

As Nela walked away, she puzzled over Louise's disjointed comments. They'd been talking about Abby. Had Louise seen Abby somewhere that surprised her? Why was Louise relieved that Nela was asking questions? That fact had lifted Louise's spirits, which seemed odd and inexplicable.

Abby's office was empty. Nela took the back stairs to the second-floor west wing. As she'd expected, she found Abby in the long room with trestle tables where donations and artifacts were sorted and examined and exhibits prepared to be sent to schools around the state.

At the sound of Nela's steps, Abby looked up from a back table that held an assortment of Indian war clubs. Abby held a club with an elongated stone head. Some of the clubs were topped with ball-shaped polished stones, others with sharp metal blades, one with sharp-tipped buffalo horns. Propped against the wall behind Abby was a long board upon which she was mounting the clubs along with short printed annotations denoting the origin and tribe.

Abby watched, eyes wide, body stiff, as Nela crossed the room. As soon as Nela mentioned that Friday afternoon, Abby relaxed.

"I was working up here that day." She sounded relieved. "I don't think I ever saw Marian on Friday. Why does that matter?"

"She was upset Friday afternoon. I think she discovered the identity of the thief. She came to the west wing."

Abby spoke sharply. "She didn't come up here. I don't know what she did."

F riday afternoon?" There was a curious tone in Grace Webster's throaty voice. Even in a plaid wool shirt and jeans and boots, she reflected high gloss, Western casual at an exorbitant price. "You're here at Blythe's direction? That's interesting." She looked past Nela, seemed to focus her gaze on the jarring sculpture with its strange components. Grace's face had the hooded look of a woman studying her cards and not liking the hand she held.

The silence between them seemed to stretch and expand.

Nela said quietly, "If you saw Marian—"

"I didn't." Her gaze moved from the sculpture to Nela. "I don't think we will ever know what happened with the necklace. In any event, it's now back. Sometimes"—and Nela wasn't sure whether there was warning or threat in Grace's eyes—"it's safer not to know."

P ink stained Cole Hamilton's cheeks. "Things have come to a sad state when Blythe sends an outsider to ask questions. I don't believe any of this is true about Marian. Whoever took that necklace was just trying to make trouble for the foundation. It's been one thing after another ever since that girl's car was set on fire. I know what's behind that." His tone was sage. "She was too pretty." He was emphatic. "Too many pretty girls always causes trouble. I knew when Louise hired that girl that there would be trouble. Not that she didn't behave herself. But every man here, except those of us who know how to be gentlemen, couldn't take their eyes off of her. And before we turn around, there's another pretty girl and this one's obviously an old friend"—there was more than a hint of innuendo in his tone—"of Hollis's. Erik knew better than to hire pretty girls. But nothing's been the same, not since that bumptious young man took over. Why, he's barely thirty. As for that necklace, no one took it to sell or it wouldn't still be around. And that pretty young woman may have the brains of a feather but even she wouldn't be foolish enough to keep the thing in her office. It was just more troublemaking. How would Marian know anything about that? The whole idea's nonsense. Mark my words, someone took the necklace and put it in Abby's office to stir up more trouble. And it has, hasn't it?" He didn't wait for a reply. "Marian's fall was an accident and that's all there is to it."

Robbie's young-old face congealed into a hard, tight mask. "If anyone's asking questions, it should be me."

"Miss Webster said she was sure everyone would cooperate." Nela stared at him. "Do you object to telling me if you saw Marian that Friday afternoon?"

His green eyes shifted away, fastened on the penholder on his desk, a red ceramic frog with bulging eyes. "I caught a glimpse of her in the main rotunda that afternoon." He frowned. "I'd been down in the library. Erik was doing some research. He often comes in the afternoons. I was on my way to the stairs. Back upstairs. Marian came in from the courtyard. She didn't look as though her thoughts were pleasant. So I walked faster. I didn't want to talk to her when she was in that kind of mood."

"Mood?"

"I'd seen Marian in her destroyer mode before when something threatened her precious Haklo. I didn't know what had raised her hackles, but I knew it was a good time to keep my distance."

Nela thought he was telling the truth. But was he describing Marian's demeanor because he was well aware that Rosalind, too, would have seen Marian's obvious displeasure? Maybe he was telling the truth because he felt he had no choice.

Nela walked swiftly from Robbie's office to the stairway. She still needed to speak with Francis Garth and Peter Owens, but she wanted to see the library first. In the library, Nela stopped in the doorway.

Erik Judd sat at one of the writing tables, papers spread out around him. He had the look of a man whose mind is deeply engaged.

She glanced from him to a French window opposite the doorway that opened into the courtyard. If he lifted his head, he would have a view of the central portion of the courtyard.

"Excuse me."

He looked up at her, blinked, nodded in recognition. "Miss Farley. How can I help you?"

"I'm sorry to interrupt you, but may I ask you a question?" Since he no longer worked for the foundation, he was under no compulsion to answer simply because Blythe had authorized Nela to speak to staff. "I'm trying to find out more about Marian's last afternoon here. I will report what I learn to Blythe Webster."

He squinted from beneath his thick silver brows. "I see. Blythe is hoping someone might have information that will be useful to the police. Certainly, I will help if I can."

Erik didn't sound worried. But the mind behind the darkness at Haklo would always keep emotion in check.

"Mr. Judd, did you see Marian in the courtyard?"

There was a thoughtful pause. Finally, he spoke. "I had a brief glimpse. I'd been shelving books. When I turned to go back to the table, I saw her."

Nela knew one question had been answered. The library door had been open and Erik had glanced outside.

"She was hurrying up the center path toward the main hall. That's all I saw. I'm sorry I can't be of more help."

"Hurrying?"

"Moving with a purpose, I'd say." He frowned. "I thought something had happened to upset her."

Francis Garth's size made everything in his office seem smaller, the desk, the chairs, even the framed replica of the Seal of the Osage Nation on the wall to his right. Now he stared at Nela, elbows on the bare desktop, heavy chin resting on massive interlaced fingers. He was silent after she finished, his gaze thoughtful. He slowly eased back and the chair squeaked as he shifted his weight. "I don't think it is wise"—his voice was as heavy as his body—"to draw too many conclusions from a single glimpse of Marian on that Friday."

Nela persisted. "Marian Grant came inside the rotunda from the courtyard Friday afternoon and she was visibly upset."

Francis stared from beneath thick black brows. "Why?"

Nela shook her head. "I don't know. But everyone who saw her after that moment describes her as grim or upset."

Francis bent his big head forward. Finally, he lifted his chin. "I don't lie. But remember that truth can be misleading. I was checking on a matter with Louise, I think it was shortly after three o'clock. When I stepped out into the hall, Marian was coming out of Abby Andrews's office. She was"—he chose his words carefully—"deeply in thought. She moved past me without speaking." A pause. "I don't think she saw me."

Peter pushed his horn-rimmed glasses higher on his nose. As Nela finished, he shook his head. "I didn't see Marian Friday afternoon." He spoke absently, his thoughts clearly elsewhere.

Nela had done enough interviews to know when some nugget of information was almost within reach. Peter might not know about Friday afternoon. He knew something and was debating whether to speak.

"If you know anything that could help, please tell me."

He took off his glasses. He dangled the frames from one bony hand. "Ever since we found out that somebody killed Marian, I've been thinking about everything that's happened. I don't know anything about Marian that last Friday, but this fall she did something out of character."

Nela scarcely breathed as she listened.

"It was about a week after the car fire. She knew I was a good friend of a curator at Sam Noble." He glanced at Nela, almost smiled. "That's the natural history museum at the University of Oklahoma. You'll have to drive up and take a look at it one day. Anyway, Marian

249

came in my office and closed the door. She stood in front of my desk and"—he squinted in remembrance—"as clearly as I can remember, she said, 'Peter, I need a favor.' I said sure. She said, 'See if you can get Anne Nesbitt a job offer from Sam Noble. Do it. Don't ask me why. Don't ever tell anyone.' She turned and walked out." His smile was half wry, half sad. "When Marian said salute"—he slipped on the horn rims, lifted his right hand to his forehead—"I saluted."

Katie Dugan looked at Steve Flynn quizzically. "If the circumstances were different, I'd say Nela Farley's a nice woman. She has a nice face. Of course, nice faces don't mean much when it comes to protecting family."

Steve grinned, almost felt carefree. "Katie, that dog won't hunt. I talked to Nela's sister. I've interviewed everybody from narcissistic, guilt-ridden, emaciated movie stars to nuns who tend to lepers. I won't say I can't be fooled, but Chloe Farley is about as likely to be involved in a jewel heist as a kid running a Kool-Aid stand. Ditzy, happy, doesn't give a damn about appearances or money or status. If you knock out protecting her sister, Nela doesn't have a ghost of a motive. Right?"

A small smile touched Dugan's broad face. "Yeah. And she's got a cloud of soft black curls and a sensitive face. Man, she's pulled your string. Quite a change from that elegant blonde you married."

"Yeah." Steve had a funny squeeze in his chest. He couldn't even picture Gail's face. All he saw was a finely sculpted face that reflected intelligence and character and a shadow of sadness. He met her two days ago and he'd known her forever.

Katie reached for the thermos next to her in-box, rustled in a drawer for foam cups. When they each held a cup of strong black coffee, she raised hers in a semitoast. "Okay. Just for the sake of supposing, let's say your girl's home free along with ditzy sis. Where do you go from there?"

"Haklo. What the hell's wrong out there, Katie? I think there's been a lot of misdirection." He spoke slowly, thoughtfully. He had the ability to recall printed material as if he were looking at it, and this morning he'd outlined the start of trouble at the foundation. "Let's look at what happened in order: the girl's car set on fire, Indian baskets destroyed, office sprinklers activated, frozen pipes from water running in the courtyard fountain, stolen necklace—"

Katie interrupted. "Everything besides the necklace is window dressing."

Steve spoke carefully. "Just for now, let's keep it in the line of events, not make it the centerpiece."

Katie shrugged. "I get your point. I don't think I agree, but finish your list."

"The necklace is stolen. Then Marian Grant dies in a fall apparently caused by a skateboard, Nela Farley disrupts a search of Marian's apartment, Nela finds the necklace in Marian's purse, Marian's office is trashed, obscene letters on a Haklo letterhead are traced to Abby Andrews's computer, Nela leaves the necklace on Blythe Webster's desk, the necklace is missing Tuesday morning, an anonymous call"—he refused to worry now about Nela's source and his complicity—"links Grant's fall to a skateboard, Abby Andrews is missing a skateboard, another anonymous letter leads to the necklace hidden in Abby's office, skateboard used on Marian's stairs found in Abby's cabin." He paused to give Katie time to object but she remained silent, which he took as a tacit admission that the skateboard found in the second search at Haklo had matched the scrape on the rail of Marian's steps.

Katie sipped her coffee. "Hate to say been there, done that. I know all of this."

"What's the constant?"

She raised an inquiring eyebrow.

"Trouble at Haklo." At her impatient look, he barreled ahead. "All along, Katie, you've pitched on the necklace as the only thing that matters and, yeah, a quarter million dollars barks pretty loud. But think about the scenario. A lot of things happened before the necklace disappeared. You pitched on the idea that Chloe Farley set the girl's car on fire to scare her away and, after she got the job and had been there long enough to know about Blythe's carelessness with the necklace, Chloe decided to steal it and committed vandalism to make it appear that the necklace wasn't the objective. But if we wash out Chloe—"

Katie moved restively. "I've been a cop in this town for a long time. Haklo never had any problems 'til these new people came to town. Maybe Chloe Farley's not the perp. Maybe Abby Andrews planned everything. Sure, she's supposed to be sappy about the new director, but maybe she's sappier about a quarter million dollars. Plus every time we look, we find a link to her. But maybe she's not a dumb blonde. Maybe she figured she might be suspected so she set it up to look like she might be behind everything but there's always an out, somebody else could have used her computer, somebody took her skateboard, somebody sent an anonymous letter tagging her with the necklace. A double game."

"And she's lucky enough to go in Blythe's office and find the necklace lying on top of the desk?"

Katie wasn't fazed. "Somebody found it. Somebody moved it. Top of the list, Nela Farley and Blythe Webster. Probably Louise Spear. I'll bet she's in and out of the trustee's office a dozen times a day. As for Abby Andrews, if she's behind everything that's happened at Haklo, she'd be nervous about anybody showing up there after hours, like your girlfriend coming in the back way Monday night. Abby lives in a Haklo cabin. Maybe she saw headlights. Maybe she came out to take a look. Maybe she saw you waiting by the staff entrance and stayed to watch. She would have overheard every word. When you and Nela went inside, she followed. If she stayed out of the way, you two would never have seen her. But if she wasn't there, didn't take the necklace, it could have been anybody the next morning. People pop in and out of offices all the time. Somebody came to ask a question, do a tap dance, announce the end of the world. Hell, I don't know. But it all comes back to the fact that nothing like this ever happened until these new people came to town."

A quicksilver thought threaded through Steve's mind, was there for an instant, then gone . . . Not until the new people came to town . . .

Nela wished she'd taken time to pluck Chloe's coat from the rack in her office, but once outside in the courtyard, she shivered and kept going, looking from side to side. In spring, the courtyard would be magnificent. Flower beds bordered the walks. Benches surrounded a fountain. Even in winter it might have had an austere charm except for the back hoe and stacked copper pipe near the damaged fountain.

Nela reached the center of the courtyard, made a slow survey. Windows in the west and east halls overlooked the yard. Marian Grant could have chosen a place anywhere here for her moment of peace and poetry. However, when she came back into the rotunda, she had turned, her face set, and moved decisively toward the west wing.

Nela walked past the west wing windows, noting Louise's office, then Chloe's. Francis Garth saw Marian leaving Abby's office. She continued another ten steps. Bare yellow fronds of a weeping willow wavered in the wind that swirled around Nela, scudded withered leaves across the paved walk. Nela reached out to touch the back of a wrought iron bench, yanked back her fingers from the cold metal. The bench was turned at a bit of an angle. Someone sitting there had a clear view into the west hallway and, through the open door, into the interior of a small office. Abby's office. The desk faced the doorway.

Nela shivered again, both from cold and from a touch of horror. She knew as surely as if she'd sat beside Marian Grant that she'd lifted her eyes from her book and watched as someone stepped inside Abby's office.

Nela took a half-dozen quick steps, peered inside the window. Her gaze fastened on Abby's desk.

She looked and knew what had happened. Someone known to Marian had walked into Abby's office. Perhaps Marian had been surprised enough by the identity of the visitor to continue to watch. It seemed obvious that the visitor pulled the necklace from a pocket and placed it either in the desk or a filing cabinet. Wherever the necklace was put, Nela didn't doubt that a shaken Marian understood what was happening. She knew the theft was intended to implicate Abby and she knew the identity of the thief. She now had it in her power to protect her beloved Haklo.

K atie Dugan raised an eyebrow at caller ID. She lifted the receiver. "Dugan . . . Yeah? . . . Hold on." She covered the mouthpiece. "Blythe Webster's on speakerphone with Nela Farley. Apparently your girlfriend's been busy. Blythe wants me to hear what she found out. Since Nela will give you the lowdown anyway, I'm going to turn on my speakerphone. But you aren't here." With that, she punched. "Okay, Miss Farley, what have you got?"

Steve heard more than the sound of Nela's voice. It was as if she were in Katie's impersonal, businesslike office, looking at him with those bright, dark eyes that held depths of feeling that he wanted to understand and share. As she recounted her passage through Haklo, he gave a mental fist pump. Good going, good reporting. He made quick, cogent notes:

Rosalind McNeil pinpointed a change in Marian Grant's demeanor to her sojourn in the courtyard Friday afternoon. When Marian came back inside, she walked toward the west wing.

Louise Spear, worried and upset, focused on the necklace's discovery in Abby's filing cabinet.

Abby Andrews claimed she was upstairs in the laboratory and didn't see Marian.

Grace Webster said it might be safer not to pursue the truth about the necklace.

Cole Hamilton dismissed the idea of murder and linked the car fire and incidents around Abby to the presence of pretty young women. He said too many pretty girls always causes trouble.

Robbie Powell confirmed Marian's distraught demeanor as she walked toward the west hall.

Erik Judd claimed he caught only a glimpse of Marian.

Francis Garth saw Marian coming out of Abby Andrews's office.

Peter Owens claimed he didn't see Marian Friday. He revealed that, after the car fire, Marian asked him to arrange a job offer for Anne Nesbitt in Norman.

He and Katie listened intently as Nela continued, "I went into the courtyard. It was a pretty day that Friday and Marian went outside with her book of poetry. Not like today."

Steve knew the bricked area must have been cold and deserted this afternoon. There was a memory of that cold in Nela's voice.

"A bench on the west side has a good view of Abby's office. I think Marian saw someone walk into the office and hide the necklace. And then"—Nela's voice was thin—"I think Marian came inside and went to the office and got the necklace."

Blythe's words were fast and clipped. "Marian should have called the police." A short silence. "But she didn't. Instead, she obviously decided to handle everything herself. She should have come to me." Anger rippled in Blythe's voice. "I"—a decided emphasis—"am the trustee. I should have been informed. Oh." There was a sudden catch in her voice. "It's terrible. If she'd come to me, I would have insisted we contact the police. If we had, she would be alive now. Why didn't she realize that Haklo didn't matter that much, that Haklo wasn't worth her life? But she was Marian and so damnably sure of herself." There was an undertone of old rancor. "I suppose she accused the thief but promised she'd keep quiet if the thief left Haklo. I can see why Marian thought that was the best solution. Everyone would forget in time about the vandalism if it stopped. Instead . . ." Blythe trailed off.

Steve knew all of them pictured a dark figure edging up Marian's stairs and placing a skateboard on the second step, returning unseen in the early-morning darkness to watch a woman fall to her death, then pick up a skateboard with gloved hands and slip silently away.

"Anyway"—Blythe sounded weary—"perhaps this information will be helpful to you. Do you have any questions?"

Katie's face quirked in a sardonic smile. "That all seems clear, Miss Webster. Thank you for your call. And thank you, Miss Farley, for your report. I'll be in touch." As she clicked off the speakerphone, she raised an eyebrow at Steve. "Notice anything?"

"Yeah. Kind of interesting about the necklace. First, it's put in Abby's office. Second, Marian retrieves it. Third, the necklace is in Marian's purse. Fourth, the necklace is on Blythe's desk. Fifth, the necklace is found in Abby's office."

Katie flicked him an approving glance. "You got it. Starts with Abby, ends with Abby. What are the odds, Steve?"

S teve sat at his desk and tried to ignore the undercurrent of worry that had tugged at him ever since he'd heard Nela's report over Katie's speakerphone. Yes, she'd done good work. But there could be no doubt that she was now on the murderer's watch list. He forced himself to concentrate and maintain the coldly analytical, unemotional attitude that made him a good reporter. Figuring out what to accept and what to discard came down to more than the five *ws* and an *h*. There had to be innate skepticism that questioned motives and discounted conventional wisdom.

In the case of Haklo, there were facts. New staff members had been added, including the director. Six incidents of vandalism and a theft occurred between mid-September and this week, beginning with a car fire. Marian Grant died in a fall. There were suppositions. The vandalism was committed to detract attention from the theft of a quarter-million-dollar necklace. Marian Grant threatened the thief. Marian Grant was murdered.

Steve accepted the facts, but there were two pieces of information, one that came to him, the other picked up by Nela in her talks today with staff, that entirely recast his ideas about what happened at Haklo and why.

He glanced at the clock. Just after seven. He reached for his cell, shook his head. He'd told her he was coming. As he slammed out of the office, a couple of folders and a legal pad under one arm, the worry he'd fought to contain made his throat feel tight. He had lots to say to Nela. He hoped she would listen.

—17—

Jugs's ears tilted forward. He stared toward the front door, luminous green eyes unwavering.

Nela's heart lifted. He'd said he would come. She shouldn't feel this way. She hadn't felt this way in a long time. Not since . . . Her gaze shifted to Bill's photograph. But it was only a picture and there was, always, the desolate feeling of nothing there, nothing, nothing.

She was on her feet before the sound of a rapid knock. She'd left the porch light on. When she pulled the door back, Steve looked down at her. In the bright glare, his wiry red hair looked like a patch of flame and his blue eyes were commanding and insistent. His broad freckled face again surprised her because he wasn't now a mirror image of a smooth, always-young celluloid figure. His face was not only the face of a man who could be kind and pleasant and thoughtful, but the face of a man with a hardened worldview and a memory of loss and betrayal. He was a man who had to be reckoned with and who'd taken up space in her life in a brief span of hours. But that was how life happened. Things changed, not just in hours but in minutes. Bill had walked up a dusty road in a distant land and the world turned gray and cold for her.

Cold . . . Steve's ragged diamond-patterned sweater was familiar now. Before she thought, she blurted, "Don't you ever wear a coat?"

"Too much bother. You okay?"

The query surprised her. There was worry in his eyes, worry and concern. She felt a flicker of happiness. She'd been so alone and now she didn't feel alone anymore, not as long as he was here.

He looked into her eyes, saw her response. His smile was as warm as an embrace.

With a quick breath, Nela stepped back, knew she talked too fast. "I'm fine. Come in. Let me get you some coffee."

She felt steadied as she served fresh hot coffee in thick white pottery mugs. They sat on the sofa, Nela taking care to provide space between them, disconcertingly but gloriously aware of his nearness.

Jugs jumped to the coffee table, sliding a little on Steve's papers.

Steve grinned. "Hey, boy, you're in the way."

Jugs gazed at him for a moment, then flowed to the couch, settled between Steve and Nela.

As Nela reached down to stroke the black-and-tan striped back, Steve moved to smooth Jugs's bristly ticked coat. Her hand brushed Steve's. There was an instant's pause, the two of them still, then Steve reached for the mug, spoke rapidly.

Nela listened, trying to corral her thoughts and her feelings. Steve was so near, so big, the remembered warmth of his touch, Bill, emptiness, Chloe, Haklo . . .

". . . and here's some stuff I put together about the people who have keys, plus I was in Katie's office when you called this afternoon." He handed her several sheets of paper.

Nela read swiftly. Steve's bios added substance to her personal encounters with the staff members. She stopped reading when she turned to the sheet with the italicized head: *Nela Farley's Report to Katie Dugan.* She started to hand back the sheets.

He gently massaged behind Jugs's prominent ears, prompting a throaty purr. "Read all of it."

Everything was as expected except for one surprising twist. In Nela's report on Cole Hamilton, Steve had marked *too many pretty girls always causes trouble* with a canary yellow highlighter.

Nela repeated the sentence, looked at him inquiringly.

"That could have been an outlier. Nobody else has talked about pretty girls. But I picked up a vibe from Mokie Morrison this morning. He's the cop who tried to deflect you from Katie. Mokie is a man with an eye for good-looking women. When he talked about Anne Nesbitt"—Steve's grin was wry—"if he'd melted in a puddle right there in the squad room, I wouldn't have been surprised. Apparently she was hot." Another wry smile. "Presumably she still is. But here's what I wonder." He leaned back against the cushion. "Maybe we've been off on the wrong track, right from the start. The conventional wisdom dismissed the car fire in September, like it wasn't a part of the stuff that started happening in November. What if the car fire was part of everything? What if somebody was angry about pretty girls?"

Nela stared. "Why?"

His gaze was serious when he answered. "Short answer, sex. Long answer, people can get twisted up in knots about love or lust or whatever you want to call it. Now"—his eyes narrowed—"I'm thinking something off the wall. Not the usual triangle stuff. But how about this. Anne Nesbitt apparently packed a potent punch. There are women"—there was an undertone of grimness in his voice—"who are like pots of honey to bears. Bears can't help themselves. They have to nose around. Cole Hamilton may be old but he isn't dead and he all but said in his gentlemanly way that testosterone bubbled. Maybe one of the bears thought he had a chance with her and then Hollis Blair arrives."

"He really cares about Abby." Nela shook her head. "He wouldn't go after someone else."

"Maybe not. But he has an aura around women. Right?"

Nela understood what Steve meant. "Yes." She didn't have to say more.

"In fact . . ." He broke off, pulled out his cell, found a number. "Hey, Robbie. I got a question. You're a canny guy about people. You notice things. Think back to late last summer. I understand Anne Nesbitt was a pretty gal. Did Hollis Blair notice?" Steve listened, looked satisfied. "Pretty blatant, huh? . . . No, nothing to do with much of anything. Just a bet with a friend. We got to talking about Anne Nesbitt and I swore she was a magnet for males. Right . . . Thanks."

"Robbie doesn't like Hollis."

Steve laughed. "Despises him, actually." He was abruptly serious. "But Robbie notices things. He said every man up there but him found one reason or another for a nice chat with Anne every day. That included the director. With Hollis, I think it's pretty much automatic pilot. Hollis learned a long time ago that ladies like him and he's ready to soak up a little sun when he can. But maybe somebody thought the handsome young director had cut him out."

Nela felt a wash of horror. "And he set her car on fire? That's unbalanced."

Steve's gaze was somber. "Someone is desperately unbalanced. Step back and look at the vandalism. There's a fury in everything that's happened."

Nela wasn't convinced. "Anne Nesbitt left. Why the other things?"

"Hollis Blair is still there."

Nela slowly shook her head. "I can't imagine anyone at Haklo being that"—she looked at Steve, used his word—"twisted." If Steve was right, someone she'd met, spoken with, perhaps shared a smile with, had a monstrous ego willing to destroy, steal, and ultimately kill because of jealousy. Or was the viciousness not even prompted by jealousy? Perhaps the motive was uglier, darker. Perhaps a perceived affront would not, could not be tolerated.

"There's something bad out at Haklo." He looked uneasy. "Like a nest of rattlesnakes. That's why"—he reached out, took her hand—"I want you to back off. I've already told Katie what I think. She listened. She'll be looking at them."

Them . . .

Nela knew the list was short. If Steve was right, the vandal, thief, and killer was either Cole Hamilton, Francis Garth, or Peter Owens.

"Nela, stay in your office. Stay out of it. Leave everything to Katie."

After Steve left, Nela poured another cup of coffee, carried it to the sofa, settled by Jugs.

The cat turned his wedge-shaped face toward her.

She stared into Jugs's brilliant green eyes.

"*. . . You wanted him to stay . . . He likes me . . . I like him . . .*"
Slowly, Jugs's eyelids closed.

Nela petted his winter-thick coat. "Sure he likes you. Who
wouldn't? Cats rule, right?" She would be very alone now if it weren't
for Jugs. He was alive and warm, his presence comforting. Maybe
some evening somewhere, she and Steve would sit with Jugs between
them and they could talk of books and people and places, not of
death and murder and anger.

Did everything hinge on the theft of the necklace? If not, the
entire picture changed. If Steve was right, if the car fire was central,
the first act in an unfolding drama of passion, then it mattered very
much why the fire was set.

Had one of the men felt scorned by Anne Nesbitt and been determined to punish her? Perhaps there had been momentary pleasure
after Anne left. Nothing else happened until the attraction between
Hollis and Abby became obvious. The next vandalism destroyed
the Indian baskets precious to Abby. The rest of the incidents
caused difficulties for Hollis, his first directorship marred by the
unsolved crimes, for Blythe as the foundation trustee, and for Abby.

As for the necklace, the intent might never have been money but
a hope of implicating Abby. Marian Grant found the necklace in
Abby's office. Marian knew who had taken it. That knowledge cost
Marian her life. But when the stolen jewelry—thanks to Nela—
appeared on Blythe's desk, the necklace ended up in Abby's office.
It had never mattered that the necklace was worth a quarter million
dollars. Moreover, once again placing the necklace in Abby's office
indicated a depth of obsession. The thief should have been worried
about the return of the necklace, wondering if someone was going
to be a danger. Instead, the vendetta against Abby continued.

Nela shivered.

Jugs stirred, looked up. "*. . . Afraid . . .*"

Nela felt a catch in her throat. Yes, she was afraid. She saw faces, Cole Hamilton almost cherubic with his fringe of white curls, heavy, bull-like, massive Francis Garth with a dark commanding stare, lanky, professorial Peter Owens with his genial smile.

Which one?

J ugs gave an irritated chirp as Nela moved restlessly deep in the night. She was aware of him but only dimly. Distorted dreamlike images jostled in her sleep-drugged mind. But once, with sharp clarity, came the lucid thought: Grace warned me. Or were her words a threat? *Sometimes it's safer not to know.*

N ela carried with her a sense of danger Thursday morning. The hallway seemed cold and remote with no hint of life or movement. She walked faster, but the quick clip of her shoes emphasized the silence. She pushed open Chloe's door, turned on the light. The connecting door between Chloe's office and Louise's was open as usual, and a cheerful shaft of light spilled across the floor.

Nela crossed to the doorway.

"Good morning—" She spoke to emptiness. Louise's coat hung from the coat tree. There were papers on her desk, but Louise wasn't there.

Nela turned away. She checked her in-box. It was empty. Nela had completed the stack of applications Louise had given her yesterday. She glanced at the clock. A quarter after eight. Nela would have been glad to have tasks to do. It would be nice to be absorbed, pushing away worries about Haklo and the investigation. But surely

Katie Dugan had realized that Nela wasn't covering up for Chloe, that the necklace was only a part of a whole, and that none of the peculiar events at Haklo had anything to do with Nela or with Chloe.

Nela settled at the desk, waited. Time seemed to crawl. The minute hand moved with stately slowness. Another quarter hour passed. It was too early to make the morning round of mail deliveries. Finally, restless, Nela opened a side drawer, fished out a legal pad. She wrote a half-dozen statements in no particular order, fast. She liked, when writing a story, to pluck out the most interesting facts. Then with a quick scan, she'd rank them in order of importance and that's how she'd structure the story.

In the adjoining office, Louise's phone rang. And rang. Finally, it clicked off. Nela almost rose to go answer but she'd not been instructed to take Louise's calls and she might well prefer to later pick up messages.

Nela returned to her fast-draw observations:

Blythe Webster's active role as trustee began this summer.

Grace Webster resented her sister's appointment as sole trustee yet she made it a habit to be present at Haklo when she was in Craddock.

The vandalism began after Erik Judd was fired.

Hollis Blair seemed to effortlessly charm women.

Francis Garth was a huge man with a strong personality. Whatever course he followed, he would be formidable, either as friend or adversary.

Nela tapped the pad with her pen. Did any of these observations point to the figure behind the events at Haklo?

Chloe's phone rang.

Nela looked at caller ID: Craddock Police Department. Nela lifted the receiver. "Nela Farley."

"Miss Farley, Detective Dugan. Do you have time to talk?"

"Yes." She felt a twist of amusement. Nice of Dugan to ask. If she had questions, she could insist they be answered.

"I have a question I can't ask Steve Flynn. Wrong gender." Katie Dugan was brisk. "I know a bit more about you now. You're a reporter, used to sizing people up. I want you to consider three men: Francis Garth, Cole Hamilton, Peter Owens. You're an outsider at Haklo. Your impressions will be fresh."

Nela realized that she was being treated as an equal although she should always remember that Katie Dugan was a woman who could play many roles. "How can I help?"

"Francis Garth. Cole Hamilton. Peter Owens. Think sex."

Nela got it at once. There is office decorum and there is the rest of life, from an encounter on a beach to a glance across a crowded room. Men are men and women are women and there are glances and smiles and eye contact that say more than words ever could. Not that the lines often didn't blur. Hollis Blair could no more be around a woman without sending out a primal signal than he could forego using his diffident charm in any setting.

Katie nudged. "You're sitting in a bar and Francis Garth's on the next stool."

Removing the men from Haklo, placing them in a dusky, crowded bar with music and movement and the splash of whisky over ice cubes, she saw them without the veneer of work. "Francis Garth."

Nela's tone reflected her shift in perception. "Magnetic. Powerful. Definitely a man who notices women." She felt a flicker of surprise as she continued. "Cole Hamilton may have the aura of a kindly older man, but he's very aware of women." As Steve had observed, Cole Hamilton was old, but he wasn't dead. "Peter Owens has that tweedy, professorial aura, but he's very masculine. Any one of them could be sexually on the prowl."

M im looked up from the page layout on her monitor, gray eyes inquiring. She was to Steve unchanged and unchanging, a rock in his life, her short-cut white hair making her thin, intelligent face look young and vibrant. She had the air of a sprinter ready for the gun, poised, ready to go. She never wasted words, suffered fools impatiently, incompetence never.

Steve propped against the edge of her desk. "You know everybody in town." He grinned. "If I were a cub, you'd snap, 'Don't tell me something I already know.'"

She raised an eyebrow, waited.

"I want the backstairs gossip on Francis Garth, Cole Hamilton, Peter Owens. Bed playmates. If any." There was no playfulness in his voice. The request was serious.

Mim was always self-possessed. The only indication of surprise was a brief flicker in her eyes. Then, she gave an abrupt nod. She didn't take the time to say *not for publication*, to warn that she couldn't vouch for gossip, that of course she picked up scurrilous comments about Craddock movers and shakers that she never shared. She wasn't going to tell Steve something he already knew. "Francis reportedly has been sleeping with the mayor's wife, but lost out this summer to Mack Harris." Mack Harris was a tall, rangy rodeo champion who'd bought a ranch near Craddock. "Cole Hamilton spends a lot of time at the Cowboy Club and he likes 'em young." The Cowboy Club was a gentlemen's retreat with gambling, music, and dancing women dressed as briefly as Dallas Cowboys cheerleaders. "Denise Owens and the twins spent the summer at her parents' lake home in Minnesota. My granddaughter's on the same swim team as the Owens girls and there was a lot of surprise that they stayed away all summer. Press of 'work' kept Peter in Craddock."

With one ear cocked for the sound of Louise's brisk steps in the hall, Nela tidied and straightened the office, finally began to rearrange the contents of the center drawer in Chloe's desk. As she worked, she ignored the ringing of Louise's telephone. Trinkets and odds and ends brought her sister near, as if Chloe were smiling at her with laughing eyes: two ticket stubs from the Oklahoma City Civic Center production of *Peter Pan*, keepsake menus from a half-dozen Oklahoma City and Norman restaurants (on the menu from Legend's in Norman, Chloe had written in huge letters with a half-dozen exclamation points: *Better Than the Best!!!!!!*), a map of Turner Falls, a dog-eared copy of *Far Side* cartoons, jacks and a rubber ball in a plastic bag, a Rubik's cube, a deck of cards. The motley collection was typical of her quirky sister.

Finally, Nela picked up a much creased and folded sheet of ruled paper. She sensed something that was not meant for other eyes, not even those of a loving sister. She gently laid the folded strip in the back center of the drawer, returned each item. She had just closed the drawer when the staccato tap of heels sounded, coming fast, coming near. They stopped just short of Chloe's office. "Louise?" Blythe Webster's tone was sharp, just this side of angry. "Louise . . ." There was an exasperated sigh.

Nela knew that Blythe had realized Louise's office was empty. A flurry of steps and Blythe stood in Chloe's doorway. Blythe was trim in a soft gray cashmere sweater and black slacks. Impatience was evident in every line of her tense body. Her face was tight with irritation. "Where's Louise? I keep calling and I get her answering machine."

"I haven't seen her this morning." Nela glanced at the clock. Almost ten. She'd been at work for two hours. "She wasn't in her office when I arrived."

"Not here?" Blythe's voice was odd. "She's always here. She would have told me if she were going out."

"Her coat's in her office." Nela meant to be reassuring but realized that her voice held a question.

"Well." Blythe seemed at a loss, uncertain what to do. Then she looked relieved. She pulled a cell phone from a pocket, touched a number.

In only an instant, there was a faint musical ring, a ghostly far-away repetition of the first few bars of "Oklahoma."

Nela pushed up from her desk. Blythe was right behind her. The musical ring continued twice again, louder now as they reached Louise's desk. Nela pulled out the bottom-right drawer. The last ring was ending. A black leather shoulder bag nestled in the drawer.

"Well, she's here if her purse is here." Blythe sounded relieved. "She's somewhere in the building. Find her for me." She swung on her heel and surged out of the office.

Nela was glad to have a task. The directive hadn't been delivered with grace or charm, but if you ran the ship, you could navigate any damn way you pleased. Anyway, she had her orders, she'd carry them out.

S teve wasn't a lazy reporter. He had one more call to make. In fact, it took five calls to track down Anne Nesbitt. The connection crackled.

". . . almost time for the next presentation. I'm at an elementary school in Bartlesville. It's such fun. I have a slide show of our dinosaur exhibits. Kids love it." She sounded sunny and happy. "How can I help you?"

"This is Steve Flynn, *The Craddock Clarion*. The police haven't given up on the arson of your car."

A pause. "Oh"—a small sigh—"I appreciate the police continuing to try but I think it had to be some kind of nut. Not anybody I knew. Like"—she paused—"how do they put it when the criminal is a stranger? A casual crime. That's what happened."

Steve picked his words. "There have been other problems since you left Haklo. It's important, in fact it may be a matter of life and death, to know if the destruction of your car is linked to later vandalism. I want to ask a serious question. Was a male staffer at Haklo hitting on you? If so, did you rebuff him?"

She didn't rush to answer. "Men are"—now it was she who spoke with care—"often very nice to me. Some men always see women in a certain way. Hollis Blair was very friendly, but he was never over the line. Hollis"—there was good humor in her tone—"is a guy who automatically sends out signals to women. The other men were interested, but I made it clear that I'm in a committed relationship. I've been fortunate in both school and jobs that I've dealt with nice men who recognize boundaries. No one bothered me at Haklo."

Steve ended the call with a feeling of bewilderment. He'd been so certain . . .

Rosalind waggled a hand in greeting. She was speaking brightly into the phone. ". . . some unexpected repairs have to be made and the foundation won't be available for tours this Saturday. If you would like to reschedule, please call." She gave the number. "We're very sorry for the cancellation. Again, this is Rosalind McNeill at Haklo Foundation." She hung up and heaved a sigh. "The T is definitely out of sorts. But I kind of get her point. She cancelled the Saturday tours. She said there's not a good feeling here." Rosalind's round face suddenly looked half scared, half uneasy. "She's got that right. Anyway"—she managed a smile almost as bright as her usual—"I have the mail tray ready." She nodded at the blue plastic tray on the counter.

Nela started to explain she was looking for Louise, then realized she would be visiting each office with the mail and she could combine the tasks. She would, however, change her route and end up at Blythe's office. Hopefully, she would be able to report Louise's whereabouts when she delivered Blythe's mail. And, in fact, her answer might be right here at hand. Rosalind knew who came and who went.

"Is Louise in Hollis's office?" Louise handled correspondence and projects for both the director and the trustee.

"The director isn't here this morning. He called in and said he would be in around noon." Rosalind's face took on a conspiratorial glow. "Abby called in, too. She said she had an appointment and would come in around noon." Rosalind raised both eyebrows.

Nela had not paid particular attention, but remembered that

Abby's office had been dark. Nela had assumed Abby was upstairs in the artifact room. She didn't care about the twin absences of Hollis and Abby. "I guess Louise is upstairs." She gestured toward the broad steps of the curving twin stairways to the second floor. "What time did she go up?"

Rosalind was too good-natured to be offended by Nela's lack of interest in the activities of the director and assistant curator. Her smile was cheerful. "I've been here since eight. I haven't seen Louise this morning. She must have taken the back stairs."

Nela received the same answer everywhere she delivered mail. No one had seen Louise. Nela deposited mail in the in-box on Grace Webster's desk. There was no jacket on her coat tree, no evidence she had been to Haklo this morning. Nela very much doubted that Grace had bothered to inform Rosalind of her presence or absence.

There was no one left to ask.

As she stepped out of Grace's office, the plastic tray held only the mail for Louise and for the trustee. Nela headed for the back stairs that led down to the first floor of the west wing. She would leave Louise's mail, and if Louise had since returned to her office, all would be well.

Light spilled into the hallway from the open door to the artifact room. Abby had called in, said she wasn't coming until late morning. There was no reason for the light to be on if Abby wasn't working. Possibly Louise was there.

Nela walked faster. She reached the doorway and stopped. She glanced across the room. Her breath caught in her throat as she stared at death.

Louise's body lay facedown in a crumpled heap near the back table where Abby cataloged and mounted Indian war clubs. Yesterday Louise's pink blouse had been soft and pretty with the gray wool suit. Harsh light from overhead fluorescent panels threw splotched dark stains on the back of Louise's gray suit into stark relief.

—18—

Muttered voices and heavy footsteps sounded from the far end of the hallway near the staff entrance and the back stairway to the second floor. Nela assumed more police were arriving as well as the medical examiner and a forensic unit and all the various people involved in a homicide investigation. This time there was no question as to the cause of death. Homicide by person or persons unknown. Louise Spear had walked into the artifact room sometime late yesterday afternoon and someone, someone she knew, someone with a key to Haklo, struck her down, crushing the back of her head.

Nela sat numbly at Chloe's desk and waited. Dugan had taken only a moment to talk to Nela—how did she find the body?—then directed Nela and the other shaken and shocked Haklo staff members, who'd gathered in the upper-west hallway, to remain in their offices until further notice. Rosalind, eyes red-rimmed, brought lunch, ham sandwiches, chips, coffee. Nela forced herself to eat. The day was going to be long and hard. She needed energy to recall and tell Katie Dugan what she knew. Louise Spear had been worried and upset yesterday, but it had never occurred to Nela that Louise was in danger. Her distress had seemed natural, the care of a woman who had served Haklo for so many years. If only she had asked Louise what troubled her . . . *If only* . . .

Nela was painfully aware of the spread of light through the connecting doorway. This morning she'd assumed that any moment Louise would return to her office.

More steps, these coming from the other direction. "Yeah, yeah, yeah, I'm not going to talk to her. I'm on my way upstairs, but I want to see her, Mokie."

Nela came to her feet. Steve was coming down the hall.

"Katie'll have my head on a platter if any of the witnesses talk to anybody." Mokie's gravelly voice was steely.

Nela realized with a chill that there must be officers stationed in every hall to prevent conversation and ensure staff members stayed sequestered.

"That includes you, Steve." It was an order.

"Not to worry." Steve's voice was nearer, loud, determined. He came through the open door in a rush.

She moved to meet him.

He reached her, gripped her shoulders. His broad freckled face was grim, but his blue eyes looked deep into hers, saying, *It's bad, I'm here, I'll help.*

She drew strength from his reassuring gaze and from his touch, the warmth and certainty of his hands.

"I know it's rotten." His voice held a recognition of the grisly scene she'd found and taut anger at the death of a woman who had been good and kind and generous.

"I kept hunting for her." Nela hated thinking how long Louise's body had lain there. "And all the while—"

Mokie stood in the doorway. "Save it for Dugan." Mokie's voice was gruff.

Nela glanced at Mokie, nodded. "Right." She looked back at Steve.

He tightened his grip on her shoulders. "I've got to cover the story. I'll see you tonight. I'll bring dinner."

The afternoon dragged, one slow hour after another. Nothing to do. No one to talk to. Only the sounds of people coming and going. She tried not to remember what she had seen, tried to figure who might have committed murder, knew the list was long. All the staff members had been present late yesterday afternoon. Erik Judd had been in the library. Any of them could have killed Louise.

It was a quarter to five when footsteps came near, purposeful, quick steps. Detective Dugan came through the open door, followed by Mokie Morrison. He was much taller, but Dugan carried with her an air of command.

Dugan flicked a thumb at Mokie. He settled in a chair a little to one side, pulled out a small recorder, turned it on. "Office of Nela Farley, temporary assistant to murder victim. Time: four forty-six p.m. Investigating officers Detective Flynn, Detective Mokie Morrison. Investigation into homicide of Louise Spear."

Dugan didn't draw up a second chair. She stood in front of Chloe's desk, arms folded, and stared down at Nela. Although her white blouse, gray cardigan, and gray wool skirt would have been proper attire in any office, she looked every inch a cop, eyes sharp and questioning, face hard. "When did you last see Louise Spear?"

"Just before I left yesterday. A few minutes before five." When had Louise died? Why had she gone upstairs to the artifact room? That was where Abby worked. Once again, always, there was a link to Abby.

"Where did you see her?"

Nela gestured toward the connecting doorway. "In her office. I stood in the doorway, said good night."

"Did you talk to her?"

"Not then. I talked to her earlier in the day. She was very upset after the necklace was found in Abby's office. When I came back from lunch, she was sitting in her office and she looked dreadful. She wasn't doing any work. And later, I talked to everyone, asking about Marian Grant's last day—"

"We'll get to that in a minute." Dugan was impatient. "Tell me about Louise Spear."

Nela's eyes narrowed as she tried to remember Louise's words. "Louise said she didn't see Marian in the afternoon, that the last time she saw her, Marian seemed fine. Then Louise started talking about the necklace. Louise said that things sometimes weren't what they seemed to be, but we couldn't get away from the fact that the police found the necklace in Abby's office. It was all a little confused. She said either Abby put it in the cabinet or someone put it there to get Abby in trouble. And then she said"—Nela hesitated because the words seemed so damning now—"that 'she shouldn't have been there. But I saw her.'"

Dugan's expression was thoughtful. "'She shouldn't have been there. But I saw her.'"

* * *

When Nela opened the apartment door, Steve wished he could wipe away the pain and distress in her face. She carried too many burdens. He wanted to see her smile. He wanted her eyes to light up with happiness. He wanted her to know laughter and care-free days. And nights. Preferably with him. He held up a carryout bag. "Greek food. And"—he paused for emphasis, waggling a red can of coffee mixed with chicory—"I brought the Flynn special, coffee that will stiffen your spine."

Nela had already set the table.

He put the coffee on to brew while she emptied the sacks. "Dinner first, then I'll bring you up to date. But nothing about Haklo while we eat."

They feasted on chicken kabobs and Greek salad, finishing with baklava and steaming mugs of chicory coffee. "Can't end a meal at the Flynn house in the winter without coffee that barks." He looked toward Jugs, in his usual place at the end of the table. "Sorry for the language."

Resisting a second piece of baklava, Steve raised his mug in a salute to Jugs. "I don't usually like to share a girl with another guy, but I'll make an exception for you, buddy."

Jugs looked regal, front paws outstretched.

"Jugs is a gentleman." Nela smiled. "He has definite ideas on the proper place for a cat during meals, but he minds his manners."

Soon enough the dishes were done and they were in the living room.

Jugs settled between them on the sofa.

Nela smoothed Jugs's bristly coat, welcomed the warmth. "Tell me, Steve." The brightness from their cheerful interlude fled her eyes.

He didn't have to look at notes. He'd covered the investigation all through the afternoon, written the lead story with five minutes to spare on deadline. "You are the last person to admit seeing Louise, so she was alive at a few minutes before five. Her death occurred sometime between five and nine p.m. They can figure that from the state of rigor mortis. The autopsy will likely be more definitive. Katie thinks she was killed shortly after five p.m. For some reason, she went to the artifact room. There's no indication from the position of the body that she fought her attacker. Instead, she was apparently struck from behind, a blow that crushed the base of her skull. She fell and was hit at least three more times. Death from massive trauma. The weapon was a Plains Indian war club, a rounded polished ball of stone fastened by a strip of leather to a handle. The stone has a circumference of seven inches. The handle is eighteen inches long, partially wrapped in hide. On the length of the handle, there are several prints belonging to Abby Andrews along with some unidentified prints. Katie doubts the murderer was thoughtful enough to leave prints, and likely the unidentified prints belong to a previous collector or shop owner."

"Abby was cataloging the clubs. Of course her prints are on them." Nela had a quick picture of Abby yesterday as Nela crossed the room.

Steve shrugged. "Yeah. A point in her favor. Or a point against her. Everybody knew she was handling the war clubs. If she killed Louise, she didn't have to worry about gloves. Like you said, her prints are all over the clubs. Some of the prints are smudged either by Abby or by gloves worn by the murderer. If somebody else hefted the weapon, they must have worn gloves. But why not? If it was after five o'clock, maybe the murderer was already in a coat, ready to leave. Louise wouldn't be surprised at gloves in this weather."

"I don't see why Louise went to the artifact room."

"That's easy, whether the killer's Abby or someone else." Steve felt confident. "Abby could ask Louise to come up, say she needed to check out something with her. If it's someone else, it's even easier. Abby had the tail pinned on her a half-dozen times Wednesday. The murderer says, 'Louise, I may have found something in the artifact room that implicates Abby but I don't want to take it to the police unless you agree.'"

"Why did the murderer leave on the light?" Nela shivered. "That bothers me. I keep thinking about the light on all night and Louise lying there dead."

Steve didn't believe the light mattered one way or the other. "Maybe the idea was that the light would attract attention and Louise would be found sooner rather than later."

"She would have been found early today by Abby, except Abby and Hollis were gone this morning. I don't think Grace ever came in today, although she wouldn't pay any attention if she had."

"Why do you say that?"

Nela gave him a quirked smile. He noticed for the first time that she had a hint of a dimple in her right cheek. "Grace wouldn't consider it necessary to personally check on anything. She and Blythe are accustomed to having others take care of details for them. When Blythe came here Friday night, she hadn't given a thought to who would take care of Jugs. She'd assumed it was taken care of. Minions can always be dispatched."

"You aren't a big fan of the Webster sisters?"

Nela considered the question. "Neither for nor against. As

Fitzgerald said, 'the rich are different.' But"—and she looked a little shamefaced—"to be fair—"

Steve was touched by her rush to be generous. She had a kind heart. And that, he realized with an odd sense of sadness, was nothing he would ever have said about Gail.

"—Blythe is doing her best to find out what happened, even though I don't think either she or Grace were fond of Marian. Too much history there because of their father and mother. As for Grace"—and now she again felt the prickle of unease that she'd experienced when she spoke with Grace Webster about Marian's last day—"I don't know if she was warning me or threatening me when we talked about the necklace and she said that 'sometimes it's safer not to know.'"

"It could have been either?"

Once again Nela gave a question grave consideration. "It could have been either."

"We have to look at everything again." He hated the sense of uncertainty that enveloped him, but they had to face facts. "I was positive the car fire meant a lot, that one of the men was hot for Anne Nesbitt, that she'd brushed him off. I talked to her. If one of them was interested, she didn't pick up on it. I think she was telling me the truth. She would have known, right?" He wondered if she knew how he felt, sitting so near her.

Nela looked at him. Her eyes widened, then her gaze slipped away. Her voice was soft when she answered. "She would know."

He felt a quickening of his breath and then her eyes moved to the photograph of the dark-haired man in the latticed frame with its carefully worked border of red, white, and blue ribbons. Steve willed his voice to be businesslike. "So, scratch the idea that one of the men was getting back at her. That means we still have to figure out whether the vandalism started with the car fire or whether the fire gave someone a clever way of setting up camouflage to steal a necklace or whether the necklace was just one more way of attacking Haklo and making life miserable for the director and the trustee." His lips compressed for a moment. "It's like trying to catch minnows with your bare hands, too many of them and too slippery and fast."

Nela smoothed Jugs's fur.

Steve gazed at her long fingers, a lovely hand, smooth, graceful, gentle.

She look at him with quick intelligence. "If the objective was to steal the necklace, would there have been so much destruction? The Indian baskets were slashed. A crystal statuette was thrown at a mirror in Marian's apartment. The mess in her office was more than just the aftermath of a search. I think"—she spoke slowly—"someone is frighteningly angry."

"And scared." He tried to sort out his confusion. "Scared as hell, now. That's why Marian and Louise died. I don't think there was ever a plan to murder anyone. It was a campaign to cause trouble. Maybe Abby Andrews really did see a way to snatch a quarter million dollars worth of jewelry. If so, her heroine-tied-to-the-tracks posture is an act. But there are other reasons Haklo could be the target. Blythe decided to get really involved at Haklo this summer. Grace not only resents her sister's status as sole trustee, she's mad because Blythe squashed support for her lover's art exhibition. Erik Judd lost his job and Robbie Powell's been furious ever since. Cole's miserable about being pushed out as a vice president. Francis's budget has been whacked. Peter may be looking at the end of in-house publications if Blythe decides to use a local agency and that might ease him out of his job. Or maybe my first instinct was right and Anne Nesbitt's wrong. Maybe one of the overtures at the workplace wasn't gracefully deflected and somebody was infuriated by Hollis's usual approach to a good-looking woman."

Nela looked discouraged. "What troubles me is that when I think of everyone at Haklo, I see nice faces."

"I do, too. We have to hope Katie gets a break somewhere. She's smart. If anyone can ever figure out the truth, it will be Katie. She'll put on pressure. Somebody will crack. The murderer has to be in a panic now. Everything's spiraled out of control." He reached out, gently touched her shoulder. "Tomorrow will be better." He gathered up his papers. He wished he believed his words.

He stood and Nela came to her feet.

He looked down at her. She seemed small and vulnerable to him. He wished he could take her in his arms, reassure her, lift her face . . . "Yeah. Well. I better let you get some rest." He needed to leave before he said things he knew she didn't want to hear from him now. The best he could manage sounded lame and awkward. "We'll get through this."

Jugs twined around his ankles. He looked down, managed a grin. "Hey, Jugs, you'll look after the lady, right? Promise?"

"I'll count on Jugs." She managed a smile, said swiftly, "We'll talk tomorrow."

As the door closed behind him, he carried with him a memory of her smile.

As Nela picked up the coffee mugs, she heard a clatter behind her. She knew the sound now, Jugs pushing through the cat flap. She turned and glimpsed the end of a black tail as the flap dropped. It would be interesting to know what Jugs did when he was outside, what he saw, the thoughts in his mind. Was he watching Steve climb into his car and leave? Or was he immersed in stalking a mouse? Were mice frisking about on cold January nights? Surely a sensible mouse was ensconced behind a wall or nestled in a corner of the garage.

She knew Jugs's evening pattern now. He would return in a little while. She would be glad of his company tonight. They'd already established a routine, Jugs padding into the guest bedroom just before she shut and locked the door.

Nela rinsed out the mugs and the coffeepot. The apartment seemed empty without Steve. He brought strength and calmness and she wished that he were still here.

A knock sounded at the front door.

Nela dried her hands and stepped out into the living room. Had he left something behind? But the coffee table by the sofa was clear. As she walked toward the door, she felt eager. Perhaps he had something more to say. Perhaps they could talk for a while yet and she could feel safe and content. He hadn't left anything behind, except a vivid memory of his presence. She smiled. Not a coat certainly. She would have to encourage him to wear a coat.

She had left the porch light on for him to see his way to his car. She opened the door and felt an instant of déjà vu. Blythe Webster had worn her elegant mink coat over pajamas on Friday night. She again wore her mink, but tonight the coat was open to reveal a black sweater and slacks and ankle-high black leather boots, not pajamas and sneakers.

She appeared haggard, worried. "I couldn't relax and I decided to walk on the terrace. I saw Steve Flynn come down the stairs. I suppose he wanted more information about Louise since your office was next to hers. Anyway, I thought maybe he'd told you more about what's happened. I can wait and see what's in the paper in the morning, but I'm so upset about Louise. Do you mind telling me what he said?"

Nela understood. When something horrible happens, facts don't ease the pain, but there is a desperate hunger to know what there is to know.

Blythe's tone was almost beseeching. "If it isn't too late . . ."

Blythe's unexpected diffidence surprised Nela. Here was a woman who was accustomed always to having her way, accustomed to ordering, not asking.

"Of course." Nela held the door wide. "Please come in." She stood aside for Blythe to enter, then closed the door and led the way to the living room. Nela sank into the easy chair.

Blythe sat on the edge of the sofa, facing Nela. Behind her stretched a shining expanse of flooring. The bookcase next to the front door was bare tonight. Nela never saw it without remembering Marian's Coach bag and the secret it had held.

Light from a lamp beside the sofa emphasized Blythe's haggard appearance. One eyelid flickered. Lines were grooved deep beside her lips. Perched there, she looked small in the long luxurious coat.

Nela abhorred fur coats, sad that small living creatures were killed when cloth would serve as well. But tonight she found the huddled figure on the sofa pitiable. Blythe looked as if she would never be warm.

"I'm afraid none of us know very much." Nela marshaled her thoughts, made an effort to repeat all that Steve had said.

Blythe hunched in the big coat, absorbing every word. Her features remained tight and stiff. She looked much older than her late thirties.

A clatter.

Blythe's eyes flared. She jerked to look behind her. "Oh, it's the cat."

Jugs stood just inside the front door, the pupils of his eyes huge from his foray into darkness. He sat down just past the bookcase.

Nela smiled. "It's too cold out tonight even for Jugs."

Blythe let out a sigh. Her tense posture relaxed as she once again faced Nela.

Nela knew nothing she could share would ease the core of Blythe's distress, but she laid out the possibilities, one by one. ". . . and everything may hinge on why Anne Nesbitt's car was set on fire." Nela leaned forward. "Perhaps you can help. You were there every day. You know these men. Did one of them make a play for Anne Nesbitt?"

Not a muscle moved in Blythe's face. "Anne Nesbitt." Blythe's tone was cold.

Jugs paced silently across the floor, stood a few feet behind the sofa. He looked at Nela with his huge green eyes. ". . . *angry . . . angry . . . danger . . .*"

Nela stared at Jugs.

Anger.

Abruptly, Nela felt the presence of anger, hot as flickering flame. When she mentioned Anne Nesbitt . . .

Bill once told her that you could never fool a cat. A cat always knew exactly what someone thought and felt. There might be a smile, a face ostensibly expressing sympathy or welcome, but a cat knew the truth. A cat knew if there was sadness or heartbreak or fear or horror or love or hatred.

Or anger.

Slowly Nela turned her gaze to Blythe.

The older woman's posture hadn't changed, but naked now, unmistakable in that hard tight face, were eyes that glittered with fury.

Nela's recoil was instinctive. She reached to push up from the chair.

"Don't move." Blythe's right hand darted into the capacious pocket of the fur coat. In an instant, she held a black pistol aimed at Nela.

Nela sat rigid in the pretty chintz-covered chair, her hand gripping the arm. Was the feel of chintz beneath her fingers the last sensation she would ever know? Nela's chest ached. The hole in the barrel of the big gun seemed to expand. The gun never wavered in the grip of the small hand with brightly painted, perfect nails.

Nela looked into the eyes of death. "You hated Anne Nesbitt. Because of Hollis."

Blythe went to Kansas City and met Hollis, a handsome, lanky man who made women feel admired, attractive, desirable. It was in his nature. The woman across from her responded, but she didn't see that the admiring glances, the soft touch of a hand were meaningless. She'd once lost love, her father buying off a man she thought cared for her. She was lonely, hungry for a man. Marian Grant and Louise Spear saw the danger. Hollis's easy charm was automatic, any woman, anytime. Blythe thought he was hers for the taking and Hollis turned interested eyes on Anne Nesbitt.

Blythe's lips quivered. "We danced at the hotel. I thought . . . Oh, it doesn't matter what I thought. He was a lie. He made a fool of me. I brought Hollis here. I made him the director, introduced him to everyone, bought him a car, and then he went after that sluttish girl, had the nerve to tell me how beautiful she was. I thought when she left . . . but that's when I realized he'd been involved all along with Abby. She's a simpering, stupid, irritating fool. A nobody. I could have fired her, but I knew a better way." There was a flicker of malicious delight across her face. "No one ever suspected me." She was pleased with herself.

Nela's thoughts whirled. She was cornered. There was no one to help her, no one to save her. But she would fight. At the end, she would lunge to her feet, slam the coffee table hard against Blythe's legs, jump to one side. That's when the gun would roar. Perhaps if she kept Blythe talking long enough, she could take her by surprise. She'd keep her talking . . . "You're very clever, Blythe. You planned everything well. You must have felt confident that Abby would be blamed for the vandalism, but Marian saw you put the necklace in her office."

"Marian threatened me." Blythe's voice trembled with outrage. "She said I had to 'find' the necklace, say it had never been stolen. She said I had to step away from Haklo, leave the running of it to Hollis, move to the house in La Jolla."

A clatter at the door.

Blythe heard the sound behind her. This time she didn't look around. "I always hated Marian. She stole Dad from Mother. I had to be nice to her, but I hated her. She thought I would do whatever she asked. She said she had hidden the necklace."

This time it was not Jugs entering through the cat flap. Jugs crouched a few feet behind the sofa, tail flicking. His head turned to watch the figure coming inside.

Nela forced herself to look at Blythe, not at the figure that stepped inside, face somber. But there might not be hope there for Nela, either. "You took Abby's skateboard and put it on Marian's steps. You knew when she jogged and you were there to get the skateboard after she fell."

Blythe looked satisfied for an instant, then anger again distorted her features. "Marian told me the necklace was in a safe place. I was wild all week. I was afraid to go in the apartment during the daytime. There's always someone around, the housekeeper or one of the maids. I couldn't take a chance someone would see me. They knew I didn't like Marian. I hadn't been to Marian's apartment in years. At night your stupid sister was here and then I thought I had my chance Friday night. I had to find the necklace. No one told me you were in Marian's apartment."

How ironic that Blythe had desperately searched the apartment and Marian's office only to find the necklace, courtesy of Nela, lying a few days later in the center of her desk.

Near the front door, Grace Webster listened, too, her rounded face drawn and sad.

"I found the necklace in Marian's purse." Nela nodded toward the bookcase by the door, felt a lurch inside, prayed that Blythe didn't turn around.

Blythe's gaze never wavered, nor the gun in her hand. Another spasm of anger twisted her face. "Her purse?" There was a sudden blinking of Blythe's eyes. "Oh. A safe place. I thought she meant she'd hidden it away. I should have taken her purse but I didn't know anyone was here and I couldn't afford to be seen. I thought about taking the purse as I ran across the room. If only I had."

Grace Webster, slim and athletic in a rose turtleneck and gray slacks, walked nearer on the thick soles of running shoes.

Nela continued with only a flicker of a glance at Grace. "I put the necklace on your desk Monday night. You found it there Tuesday morning and thought you had another chance to destroy Abby, but Louise saw you, didn't she?" Now Louise's troubled words were clear. *She shouldn't have been there. But I saw her . . .* Louise wouldn't

290

have been surprised if Abby had come down to her office from upstairs, but the trustee didn't visit the offices of employees. Not usually. Not except the day Blythe came because she knew Louise lay dead upstairs and she wanted her found. Staff came to the trustee's office. Blythe shouldn't have been there . . . but she was.

Blythe sagged inside the big fur coat. Tears trickled down her cheeks. "Louise came to my office Wednesday and said she was glad I'd asked you to find out more about Marian's last day. Then she asked if I'd seen anything when I came to Abby's office. I couldn't have her tell anyone I'd gone to Abby's office. I told her I'd been worried and had dropped by to talk to Abby but she wasn't there. I told Louise I'd see if Abby would meet with us upstairs a few minutes after five. Just before five, I slipped upstairs and put one of the clubs just inside the door. I left the light on. I waited until I thought everyone had left. I put on my coat and gloves and stopped at Louise's office and said we could run upstairs and talk to Abby. We went inside and I said that Abby must have just stepped out and we'd wait for her. Louise walked over to look at the exhibit of clubs. I came up behind her . . ."

Grace Webster briefly closed her eyes, opened them. She looked at the woman huddled on the couch, the woman who was her sister. There were memories in Grace's haunted gaze, perhaps of an older sister pushing her on a swing, of family dinners, of sunny days and laughter, of a special link between an older and younger sister that quarrels might fray but never quite destroy.

Grace came around the end of the sofa. Her eyes dropped to the gun, rose to her sister's face. "You didn't know what you were doing, did you, Blythe?"

Nela looked into Grace's stricken blue eyes, saw a warning, a command.

291

"Gracie." Blythe still aimed the gun at Nela, but she looked up at her sister in dismay. "Gracie, why are you here? You have to go away. I can't let her tell the police."

"Everything's all right, Blythe. There won't be anything for her to tell."

Nela felt a rush of terror.

"You won't remember anything about your conversation with Nela. We'll go home now and call Dr. Wallis. You've simply been confused. Sometimes you get confused." Grace spoke with emphasis. She stared into her sister's eyes. Slowly she edged between Nela and the pistol in Blythe's hand.

Nela understood. Grace was telling her sister that she could pretend confusion, perhaps mental illness.

"Dr. Wallis will explain to the police that you are so upset you didn't know what you were saying." Grace was soothing, calm. "Everything will work out. Come home now."

Blythe shook her head. "Oh, no. I have to make sure she never tells anyone."

"Hush now. Don't talk anymore. I'll take care of everything."

Blythe bent to look beyond Grace at Nela. "She'll tell the police."

"That's all right. People can say anything, but there's no proof." Grace's voice was reassuring. "People don't know about your blackouts—"

Nela saw the surprise in Blythe's face and knew there were no blackouts.

"—and how sometimes you do things and don't even remember."

Nela watched the sisters. Blythe didn't have blackouts. But Grace was trying to save both Nela and her sister. The Webster money would probably protect Blythe from the death penalty, but no matter what happened, Blythe was burdened by guilt, would always be burdened.

Grace held out her hand. "I'll take the gun now."

"Why are you here?" Blythe was querulous.

"I saw you leave the house. When you didn't come back, I thought I'd better see. I couldn't find you anywhere, but your car was in the garage. I looked everywhere and finally I knew there was only one more place you could be. Now"—she was firm—"give me the gun. I'll put it back in the safe."

Slowly Blythe handed the gun to Grace.

"Thank you. The safe's a better place for it, don't you think?"

Grace held the gun in one hand, gripped Blythe's elbow with the other. It seemed to take forever for them to cross the space between the sofa and the door, Blythe talking faster and faster, words spewing, "Louise would have told someone . . . I had to keep her from talking . . . I didn't have any choice . . . Gracie, you see that I didn't have any—"

The front door closed.

Shaking, Nela came to her feet, struggling to breathe. She ran to the door, shoved the wedge into place, then raced across the room to the telephone. She yanked up the receiver, punched 911. "Help, please come. Blythe Webster has a gun. Her sister took the gun, but please come. One Willow Lane, behind the Webster mansion. Blythe Webster killed Marian Grant and Louise Spear. Please hurry. Get Detective Dugan. Grace Webster took the gun—"

Muffled by distance, Nela heard shouts. She strained to listen over the calming voice on the telephone. "Detective Dugan is off duty. Please explain . . ."

Jugs stopped a few feet from the door, shoulders hunched, ears

293

flicked forward. His acute hearing picked up movement and sound long before anyone in the apartment would know someone was coming up the stairs.

Nela now heard thudding on the steps.

The doorknob rattled. "Open up." Blythe's shout was angry.

Nela gripped the phone. "Hurry, please hurry." Where was Grace? Why had Blythe returned?

"Ma'am, remain calm. A car is en route. The car will be there quickly. If you can—"

Nela broke in. "There's a murderer trying to get inside."

Blythe's voice was hoarse and desperate. "Let me in. I have to come in. This place belongs to me. Open the door." The pounding on the door was loud, sounded like the hard butt of a gun against wood. Had Blythe managed to wrest the gun away from Grace?

"Blythe, stop." Grace's voice rose above the banging on the door.

The pounding stopped. "Go away, Grace. I can't talk to you now. You mustn't interfere. I have to be safe. Don't you see? Go away."

A shot and a panel of the door splintered.

Nela ducked down behind the desk.

Sirens wailed.

Nela's head swung back and forth. She needed a weapon. Her only chance was to find something to use as a club. When Blythe shot away the doorknob, Nela would strike. Stumbling to her feet, she ran to the small table beside the sofa, grabbed the brass table lamp, yanking its cord from the socket.

She was midway to the door when a deep voice shouted, the sound magnified by a megaphone, "Police. Drop that weapon. Police."

Nela stopped and listened.

"Drop that gun."

A final shot exploded.

—19—

The wind ruffled Steve's hair, tugged at his old gray sweatshirt. The day was beautiful, the temperature nudging sixty. "We'll stop in Norman, have lunch. There's a great new Mexican restaurant downtown. We'll have plenty of time to meet Chloe and Leland's plane."

Nela liked the way Steve sounded, as if they were going to a fun place and there would be fun things to do. Each day that passed eased some of the horror of the night that Blythe held a gun and planned for Nela to die. Grace had done her best, but Blythe was wily. She'd grabbed the gun from Grace, struck her sister and stunned her, then whirled to run back to the garage apartment stairs.

When the police came, when voices shouted out of the night and lights flooded the stairway, Blythe had lifted the gun to her own head. When they gathered around her on the concrete patch below, her body lay quite near where Marian Grant had been found.

Nela pushed away the memories. She didn't have to think about Blythe now or about Haklo and its future or whether Chloe would want to return there to work. She did have to make plans, for her and for Jugs. Ever since that dreadful night when she'd called Steve, she and Jugs had stayed at Mim Barlow's house. But Nela had to decide soon where to go, what to do.

On the highway, Steve turned those bright blue eyes on her. "You won't go back to California."

Was he asking? Or telling?

Or hoping?